SCHAUM'S OUTLINE OF

THEORY AND PROBLEMS

of

PROGRAMMING
WITH
FORTRAN 90

●

WILLIAM E. MAYO

Associate Professor
Department of Mechanics and Materials Science
Rutgers University

MARTIN CWIAKALA

Gemco

SCHAUM'S OUTLINE SERIES

The McGRAW-HILL Companies

New York   St. Louis   San Francisco   Auckland   Bogotá   Caracas
Lisbon   London   Madrid   Mexico City   Milan   Montreal
New Delhi   San Juan   Singapore   Sydney   Tokyo   Toronto

AßF9407

WILLIAM E. MAYO is an Associate Professor in the Department of Mechanics and Materials Science at Rutgers University. He received his Ph.D. from Rutgers (1982) and has been a member of the Rutgers faculty since then. He served as a postdoctoral fellow at Bell Laboratories (1982-83) where he worked on semiconductor lasers. His primary interests are in computer simulation of materials-related processes such as solid state diffusion and deformation processing. Dr. Mayo is the author of several books and has published over 50 papers in refereed journals and conference proceedings.

MARTIN CWIAKALA received his Ph.D. from Rutgers University in 1988. After graduation, he taught courses in CAD/CAM and Computational Methods for Mechanical Engineers at Rutgers. During this period, Dr. Cwiakala also served as a CAD consultant. This included educational seminars, software development, teaching computer aided design, and beta testing of CAD commercial software packages. Dr. Cwiakala joined Gemco (General Machine Company of New Jersey) as a project engineer and quality control manager. His areas of expertise include developing CAD tools, software to create standard process and instrumentation diagrams (P&ID), automatic generation of main assembly drawings, and an automated proposal generation system.

Portions of this book previously appeared in Schaum's Outline of Theory and Problems of Programming with Fortran 77/William E. Mayo and Martin Cwiakala/ISBN 0-07-041155-7

 This book is printed on recycled paper containing 10% postconsumer waste.

Schaum's Outline of Theory and Problems of

PROGRAMMING WITH FORTRAN 90

1 2 3 4 5 6 7 8 9 10 11 12 13 14 15 16 17 18 19 20 PRS PRS 9 8 7 6 5

ISBN 0-07-041156-5

Sponsoring Editor: John Aliano
Editing Supervisor: Patty Andrews
Production Supervisor: Cindy Regan

Library of Congress Cataloging-in-Publication Data

Mayo, William E.
    Schaum's outline of theory and problems of programming with
  Fortran 90/William E. Mayo and Martin Cwiakala.
        p. cm. —— (Schaum's outline series)
    Includes index.
    ISBN 0-07-041156-5
    1. FORTRAN 90 (Computer program language) I. Cwiakala, Martin.
II. Title.
QA76.73.F25M3947   1995
005. 13'3——dc20   95-15657
                                                              CIP

Preface

About This Book

This Outline is a concise introduction to Fortran 90, which is the latest version of the popular computing language. We have attempted to include many of the new features which we think will be of use to you. Since there is no substitute for experience in writing and running programs, we have included many complete programs that demonstrate the important points of Fortran. There are problems here that will challenge anyone, even experienced Fortran programmers. Yet, there are a large number of problems that even a beginning programmer can handle. Our objective therefore, in putting this Outline together, is to make anyone, from novice through expert, a better programmer.

Within this Outline, each chapter contains a number of worked examples that demonstrate the key points. These are reinforced by additional solved and supplementary problems appearing at the end of the chapter. Where appropriate, we have included algorithms and flowcharts with each of the worked examples. Most of the solved and supplementary problems, however, contain only the final program. It is left to you to develop the algorithm/flowchart and match your solution to the program that we give.

At the end of each chapter, we present a section on debugging techniques. This is something that is usually minimized in many textbooks, and we feel very strongly that this is a serious oversight. Therefore, we stress throughout this Outline how to detect and remove bugs. More importantly, we present advice along the way that will help make your programs "bug proof," so that you won't have to spend so much time later in removing bugs.

A History of Fortran

Fortran (Formula Translation) is the oldest, but still one of the most widely used, computer programming languages in science and engineering. Its continued success is due not only to its power and versatility in dealing with computationally intensive problems, but also to the availability of a wide range of specialized mathematical and statistical library programs.

Introduced by IBM in April, 1957, Fortran has gone through a number of revisions, with Fortran IV being the first standardized version issued in 1966 by the American Standards Association (ASA). From the beginning, the emphasis of the language was its ease of use and fast execution speed, which greatly contributed to its widespread success. When numerical computations were required, Fortran was often the programming language of choice. Other languages have come and gone, but Fortran has remained one of the most widely used languages, especially for engineers and scientists.

In 1977, the American National Standards Institute (ANSI) issued Fortran 77 as the new standard. It included many new, important features such as structured programming, improved character handling, and new control structures. In 1980, ANSI Fortran 77 was accepted as the international standard.

Since the adoption of the 1977 standard, many advances in programming languages have occurred, and as a result, many Fortran vendors have added *extensions* to the standard. These extensions added capabilities not found in the standard. But, while the vendor extensions were useful and important, they also contributed to problems with program portability. Fortran programs that contained such extensions would not always run on every computer without program modifications. Such changes were necessitated by the different implementations. Each vendor had its own set of extensions and set of syntax rules.

In the 1980s, a new committee was formed by ANSI and ISO (International Standards Organization) to begin work on updating Fortran. The result of their labors is the new standard Fortran 90. It represents a major advance in the language and codifies many of the extensions that had become commonplace among the compiler vendors. Among the new features included in the new standard are:

- Complete compatibility with the Fortran 77 standard, thus guaranteeing compatibility with programs written in the old standard.
- New control structures such as CASE, a DO construct with EXIT and CYCLE options, and a WHILE construct.
- Simplified array processing where an array is now treated as an object; also, subarray formation and manipulation with simplified assignment statements.
- Dynamic arrays permitted.
- Ability to create pointers and other dynamic data structures.
- Creation of user-defined data types, user-defined operators, and operator overloads.
- Expansion of data structures to allow the programmer to mix numeric and nonnumeric data within the same structure.
- Expansion of procedures to allow recursion, and to provide interface blocks that allow the compiler to check the validity of argument types.
- Modules as a new way to declare global data.

In addition to adding all these important new features (and several of lesser importance), the new standard also has identified several features for deprecation. These are features from the older Fortran standards that are considered obsolete, and *may* therefore be removed in future standards. In effect, programmers are being warned to avoid these features, lest they risk obsolescence.

We have made a deliberate attempt to avoid a comparison between Fortran 77 and Fortran 90 in this Outline, since this inevitably invites confusion. The new standard is significantly different from the older standard in many important ways and comparisons are difficult. Therefore, we treat Fortran 90 as almost a new language, and we do not use Fortran 77 as a crutch.

Acknowledgments

We would like to express our thanks to Daniel Handal, who ran the programs listed in this Outline and checked them for bugs; to Martin Cunningham, who proofread the text, and to Ira Kleinberg who prepared the Index. May they all live long and prosper.

William E. Mayo
Martin Cwiakala

Dedicated to the memory of
Steven B. Shapiro

WEM

CONTENTS

Chapter 1

Algorithm Development and Program Design

1.1 INTRODUCTION

Writing a computer program to solve a problem is a multistep process consisting of at least the four major elements shown in Fig. 1-1. Note that only one portion of this process (coding) focuses on the use of a specific programming language. The other three steps relate to the development of a *problem-solving approach*. Students often incorrectly assume that once they master a programming language they can solve almost any problem. This could not be further from the truth. In fact, most experienced programmers spend up to 90% of their time working on the logic of their programs, not on the coding. Therefore, it is crucial that you understand this four-step program development process and develop good problem-solving skills before attempting to write any programs.

The first stage of developing a program is the most crucial. If you *define the problem* carefully, you will find that the remainder of the process will be greatly simplified. Conversely, if you fail to define the problem adequately, you will usually have great difficulties at later stages.

The second step in the program development process is the *generation of the algorithm*. An algorithm is a map or an outline to a problem solution. This outline shows the precise order in which the program will execute individual functions to arrive at the solution. As we will see very shortly, all problem solutions, no matter how complex, can be reduced to combinations of only three basic building blocks. How we use these basic building blocks to arrive at a problem solution

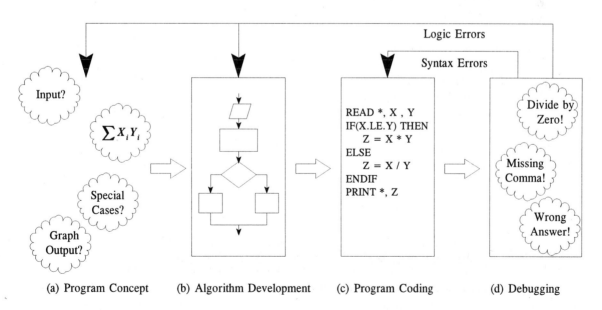

   (a) Program Concept   (b) Algorithm Development   (c) Program Coding   (d) Debugging

Fig. 1-1 Stages of program development

1

will be discussed in great depth in later sections of this chapter. It should be emphasized here that the algorithm is *language independent*. This means that it does not depend on the details of the language. For example, a Fortran programmer can use an algorithm developed by a Pascal programmer though the two programmers do not speak each other's language. Thus, the process of developing algorithms can be taught even before we begin a discussion of Fortran.

The third step in the program development process is the *coding* or conversion of the algorithm into the desired programming language. The algorithm allows the programmer to visualize the path to a solution, but it is too imprecise to run intact on a computer. Accordingly, we need to convert the algorithm into a more structured device, *the source code* or *program*. The program will follow specific rules required by the specific language. Every programming language has its own set of rigid and somewhat artificial rules, called *syntax*. Nonetheless, you will find these rules easy to master, and subsequently the coding process will be almost automatic.

The final step in the programming process is *debugging*. Most programs contain *bugs* that can range from simple mistakes in the language usage (syntax errors) up to complex flaws in the algorithm (logic errors). Removing syntax errors from your programs is usually very simple since the computer will give you *diagnostic messages* highlighting the problem. Logic errors, on the other hand, are much more difficult to remove since the computer will give you no clues. After all, the computer is simply executing your instructions. The computer cannot know what the answer is supposed to be and so you should not expect it to help you find the error. Consequently, removal of logic errors is an *art* and you must develop techniques to correct these problems.

This chapter will focus on the first two steps in the program development process: defining the problem and writing the algorithm. How to convert the algorithm into a program and how to debug it will be the subject of Chapters 2 through 10.

1.2 BASIC PROGRAMMING TOOLS

You will find that you will need only three basic building blocks to develop a solution to a problem. These building blocks are independent of the language and can be used to develop a conceptual plan to tackle a problem. The three basic building blocks are:

- *Sequential executions*, where instructions are performed one after the other;
- *Branching operations*, where a decision is made to perform one block of instructions or another; and
- *Looping operations*, where a block of instructions is repeated.

Each of these basic blocks may have several slightly different variations, but they are still recognizable. For example, the branching operation usually chooses between two alternative blocks of instructions. But there are other forms of the branching operation that choose between three or more choices. Yet they are all branching operations.

Figure 1-2 illustrates the three basic building blocks, along with their corresponding *flowchart symbols*, which are standardized figures used to show specific programming instructions. By combining these symbols you can generate a map of the algorithm, which makes it much easier to visualize the solution to the problem. Just think of the flowchart as a road map.

The arrows in the list of flowchart symbols are examples of unconditional transfer. No testing is performed – instead, the control of the logic simply follows the arrows to the next instruction for execution. The parallelogram symbol is used to represent either input or output of data. You

Block	Function	Flowchart Symbol

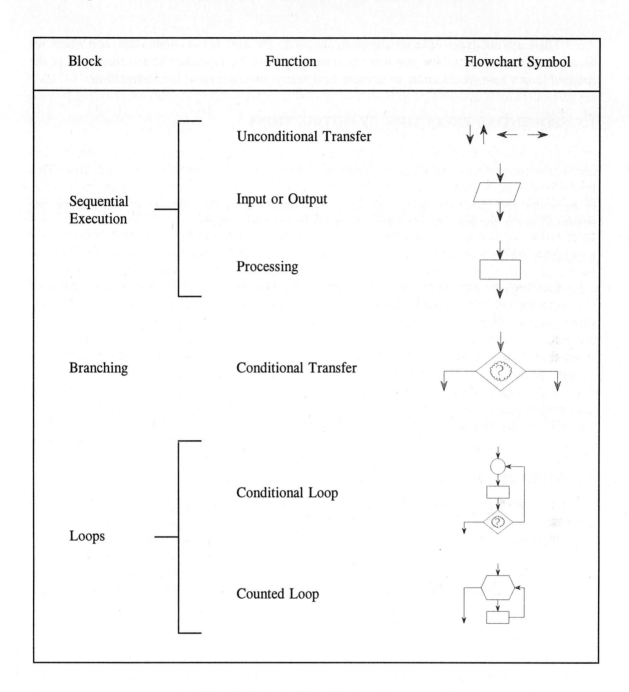

Fig. 1-2 Basic building blocks of programming

can usually tell which function is intended by its context. Input is usually (but not always) used at the beginning of the program, while output is usually done at the end. So although the same symbol is shared by two different functions, there is usually no ambiguity. The final symbol in the sequential category is the rectangle to represent simple processing such as mathematical operations.

The branching operations contain only a single flowchart symbol (diamond shaped) in which a question is posed, and, depending on the output, control goes in one direction or the other.

There are two types of loops shown in Fig. 1–2. The first is the *conditional* loop where we do not know in advance how many times something is to be repeated. The second type is the *counted* loop where we do know in advance how many times to repeat the instructions.

1.3 SEQUENTIAL EXECUTION OF INSTRUCTIONS

Sequential instructions are executed one after the other. The computer begins with the first instruction and performs the indicated operation, then moves to the next instruction and so on. This kind of sequence is seen often in engineering and science, where the computer evaluates a series of equations and uses these results in subsequent equations. Unless the series of equations are evaluated in the correct order, the correct answer cannot be obtained.

EXAMPLE 1.1

Construct an algorithm and a flowchart to compute the weight w of a hollow sphere of diameter d, wall thickness t, and density Δ, using the following equations:

$$r_o = \frac{d}{2} \qquad\qquad r_i = \frac{d}{2} - t$$

$$v = \frac{4}{3}\pi(r_o^3 - r_i^3) \qquad w = \Delta v$$

We start with the calculation of the outside and inside radii (r_o and r_i), based on the values of the diameter d and thickness t. From these, we next calculate the volume v of the hollow sphere. Finally, we calculate the weight, which is just the volume times the density, or Δv. Here are the algorithm and flowchart to perform these instructions:

Algorithm

Compute inner and outer radii by

$$r_o = \frac{d}{2} \qquad r_i = \frac{d}{2} - t$$

Compute volume of sphere by

$$v = \frac{4}{3}\pi(r_o^3 - r_i^3)$$

Compute weight of sphere by

$$w = \Delta v$$

Flowchart

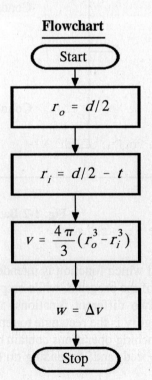

Note that the order in which the computations are performed is important. If the radii r_o and r_i are not calculated first, then it is impossible to calculate correctly the volume and the weight. Notice also that the values of d, t, and Δ have never been entered, nor is the value of w printed out once the computations are complete. We will present this in the next example. Instead, focus on the sequence in which the four instructions above are done.

When we wrote the algorithm, we did not need to follow any rigid rules about how to write it. Instead, we used *pseudocode*, which is a simple list of instructions to follow to solve the problem. You may think of it as a recipe. When you write pseudocode, you may use any English-like form with which you feel comfortable. That way, it will be intuitive and relatively easy to construct. One word of caution though. Sloppy use of pseudocode may lead to algorithms that cannot be converted easily into full programs.

Unlike pseudocode, the flowchart is more formal and requires correct use of the symbols. Therefore, flowcharts may be slightly more difficult to construct. The advantage, however, is that flowcharts force you to use symbols that exist as commands in the computer language. Therefore, they are easier to turn into source code than pseudocode.

The symbols that appear at the beginning and end of the flowchart indicate starting or end points. You may include these in your flowcharts to make it more convenient for other readers. One final point about this flowchart is that you can combine all the computations into one process box if you prefer. You may find this more convenient.

EXAMPLE 1.2

Rewrite Example 1.1 to allow for input of the values of d, t, and Δ. Also, allow for output of the values of v and w.

Algorithm

Enter values for d, t and Δ
Compute inner and outer radii by

$$r_o = \frac{d}{2} \qquad r_i = \frac{d}{2} - t$$

Compute volume of sphere by

$$v = \frac{4}{3} \pi \left(r_o^3 - r_i^3 \right)$$

Compute weight of sphere by

$$w = \Delta v$$

Print out values of v and w

Flowchart

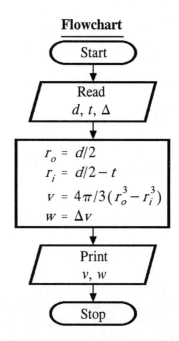

We have combined all the computations into <u>one</u> process box to simplify the flowchart. Also, we have used the same flowchart symbol (the parallelogram) for both input and output (I/O).

Since both the input and output functions use the same flowchart symbol, we usually add the *Read* or *Print* instruction to avoid any confusion.

The last sequential command is the *Unconditional Transfer*. In spite of its formidable name, this command is one of the simplest. It merely transfers control between points in a program. As we will see shortly, this command is implemented by the GO TO statement, which more clearly suggests its function. You may use this command to repeat a series of other instructions, for example, or to jump over another set of instructions.

EXAMPLE 1.3

Rewrite Example 1.1 and Example 1.2 to allow for repeated calculation of the weight of a hollow sphere of diameter d, wall thickness t, and density Δ. This time, however, allow for input of different values of d, t, and Δ before each calculation of w and v.

Algorithm

Enter values for d, t and Δ
Compute inner and outer radii by

$$r_o = \frac{d}{2} \qquad r_i = \frac{d}{2} - t$$

Compute volume of sphere by

$$v = \frac{4}{3} \pi \left(r_o^3 - r_i^3 \right)$$

Compute weight of sphere by

$$w = \Delta v$$

Print out values of v and w
Go back to beginning

Flowchart

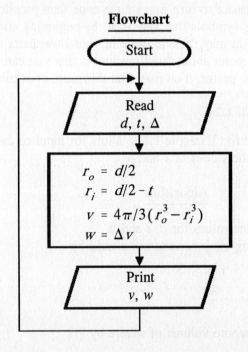

In this example we read in a new set of values for d, t, and Δ before each calculation. After the computer reads in these values, the new values of v and w will be calculated and printed. We have, in effect, created a *loop*. The series of instructions to calculate v and w are reused over and over again, each time with a different set of input data. A very important point to notice, however, is that we have set up an *infinite loop*. There is no way to stop the repeated calculations except to pull the plug on the computer! Therefore, using the unconditional transfer (or GO TO) to construct a loop is generally <u>not</u> a good idea. In almost all cases where an unconditional loop seems useful, one of the other control structures (loops or branches) can be substituted, and in fact is preferred. We will discuss these control structures in more detail in the next section.

1.4 BRANCHING OPERATIONS

With sequential instructions, the computer executes the instructions one after another. Note that there is no possibility of skipping over one instruction with only sequential execution. Many times though, there is a need to allow *branching*. A branch is a point in a program where the computer will make a decision about which set of instructions to execute next. A simple analogy is a fork in a road. At the fork, a question is posed, and depending on the answer to that question we will go to either the right or to the left. Of course, the question must be formulated such that it has a simple answer that will allow us to make the proper decision.

In programming, we also have "forks" that allow us to decide which way to proceed. In Fortran, these branches allow a choice between two alternatives. The questions that we use to make the decision about which branch to take must be set up so that the answers can only be *yes* or *no*. This is sometimes a restrictive requirement, but you will soon see the logic behind it.

The flowchart symbol for branching graphically summarizes its operation. It consists of a diamond in which a question is asked. The question must be set up so that the only possible outcomes are *yes* or *no*. Then, depending on the answer, control flows in one direction or the other:

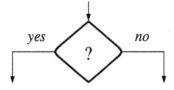

EXAMPLE 1.4

Construct an algorithm and flowchart to read two numbers and determine if they are equal.

Algorithm	Flowchart

Enter values of x and y
Is x equal to y?
   If yes, print "Equal"
   If no, print "Not equal"
End Branch

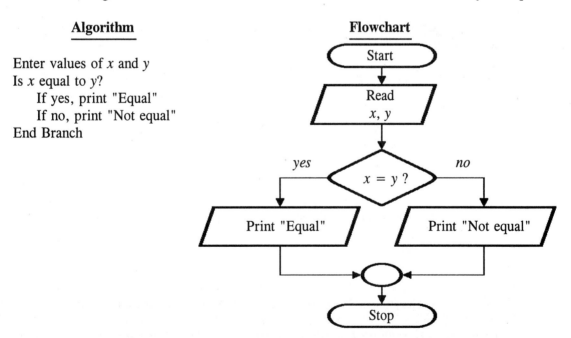

In this example, we have introduced a new flowchart symbol (the ellipse) to rejoin the two legs of the branch after their respective instructions are performed.

Note how we use the conditional transfer. If x equals y, then the block of instructions to the left is executed. In this case, there is only one instruction — a print statement saying "Equals." If, however, y were not equal to x, then the answer to the question would have been false, and the instruction to the right would be executed. Note that only <u>one</u> block of instructions is executed, not both! After one block or the other executes, the two paths merge (at the ellipse) and control transfers to the next sequential instruction.

The instructions within the branch can be of any complexity. For example, we could have another branch inside one of the blocks since we are not limited to just one instruction.

EXAMPLE 1.5

Construct an algorithm and flowchart to determine if a point (x, y) lies within a circle of radius r centered at the origin. Use the condition that if $(x^2 + y^2)^{1/2} < r$, then the point is within the circle. If the point lies within the circle, print out a message and the distance z of that point from the center of the circle.

Algorithm   **Flowchart**

Read in r and (x, y)
Is $(x^2 + y^2)^{1/2} < r$?
  If yes, then
    print "Inside"
    compute $z = (x^2 + y^2)^{1/2}$
    print z
  If no, then
    print "Outside"
End Branch

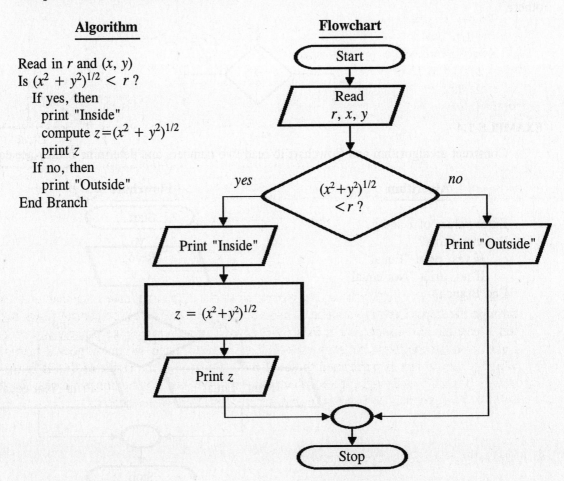

When the outcome of the test is yes, we execute the three instructions on the left side — print the message "inside," compute z, and print the value of z. But only one instruction is executed when the test is false — print the message "outside."

1.5 NESTING OF BRANCHING OPERATIONS

In the previous examples of branching only two alternatives were possible, but there are many times when we need to choose between more than two alternatives. One solution to this dilemma is to *nest* (or embed) one transfer operation within another.

EXAMPLE 1.6

Construct an algorithm and flowchart to see if a number *n* is negative, positive, or zero.

Algorithm

Read in *n*
Is $n < 0$?
  If yes, *n* is negative
    print "Negative"
  If no, is $n = 0$?
    If yes, *n* is zero
      print "Zero"
    If no, *n* is positive
      print "Positive"
    End Branch
End Branch

Flowchart

The easiest way to follow how this algorithm works is to substitute a number and trace through the steps. Let's try a value of $n=-5$. The first test is true, so control flows to the left where the next instruction is Print "Negative." This completes the process and control transfers to the end. Now, let's try $n=+5$. The first test is false, so control goes to the right, where a second test is performed to see if $n=0$. Of course, the result of this is false, so control transfers to the right again, where the Print "Positive" instruction is located. Try the value of $n=0$ yourself to make sure that you understand how this process works.

1.6 THE SELECT CASE STRUCTURE

A simpler way to handle multiple alternative problems is the *Select Case Structure*. It is not available on some Fortran 77 compilers, but it is now part of the Fortran 90 standard.

The following diagram illustrates how the select case structure works. Several alternatives are offered, but only one can be executed — the one selected inside the diamond. After this set of

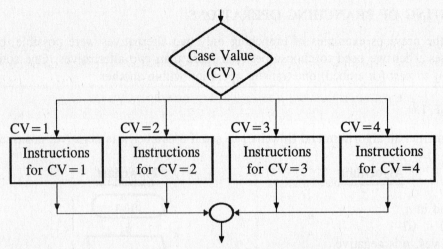

instructions executes, control transfers to the end of the structure. You may have as many alternatives as you wish (only 4 are shown in this example though). The computer decides which set of instructions to execute by examining the case value (CV). If CV=1, for example, the instructions listed under CV=1 will execute, and so on for the other possible values of CV.

EXAMPLE 1.7

Write an algorithm and flowchart to calculate the value of a based on the equations:

$$a = y \cdot z \quad \text{(when } x = 1\text{)} \qquad a = 3 / z \quad \text{(when } x = 3\text{)}$$
$$a = 5 \cdot y / z \quad \text{(when } x = 5\text{)}$$

Algorithm	**Flowchart**

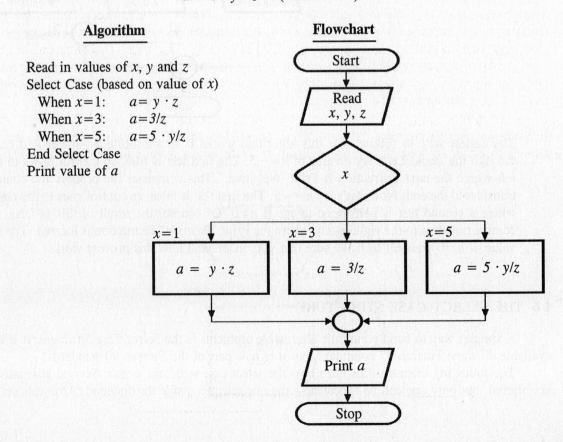

Algorithm:

Read in values of x, y and z
Select Case (based on value of x)
   When $x=1$: $a = y \cdot z$
   When $x=3$: $a = 3/z$
   When $x=5$: $a = 5 \cdot y/z$
End Select Case
Print value of a

1.7 LOOPS

Loops are the third major type of control structure that we need to examine. There are two different types of loops, the *counted* loop and the *conditional* loop. As the names imply, a counted loop repeats a predetermined number of times while a conditional loop repeats until a condition is satisfied. The block diagrams below schematically show how these work:

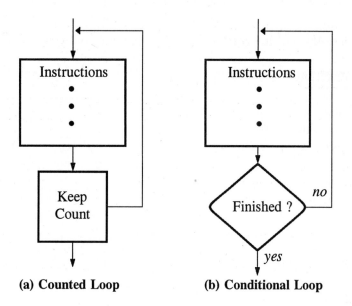

(a) Counted Loop   (b) Conditional Loop

The differences between these two structures are important. In the *counted loop*, a counter keeps track of the loop executions. Once the counter reaches a predetermined number, the loop terminates. The important point is that the limit for the number of loop executions is set <u>before</u> the loop begins and cannot be changed while the loop is running. The *conditional loop*, on the other hand, has no predetermined stopping point. Rather, each time through the loop the program performs a test to determine when to stop. Also, the value(s) being used for the test can change (and in fact *must change*) while the loop executes.

The *counted loop* is the most widely used loop in computer programming. This type of loop executes for a predetermined number of iterations, and the variables controlling the loop cannot be altered once the loop begins to execute. Below is the flowchart symbol for this type of loop:

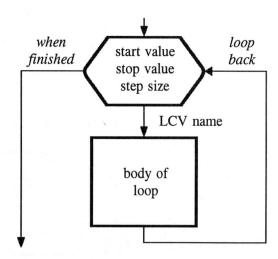

The hexagonal shape is the flowchart symbol for a counted loop. Inside the hexagon are the start and stop values for the *loop control variable (LCV)* that the computer uses to control the loop. Also included is a step size from which the computer will determine how many times to execute the loop. Inside the loop is the *body*, which can consist of any number of instructions. When the loop finishes, control transfers to the first statement outside the loop.

EXAMPLE 1.8

Write an algorithm and flowchart to print out the numbers from 1 to 100 and their squares.

Algorithm   **Flowchart**

Loop (LCV start = 1; stop = 100; step = 1)
    Print LCV value and LCV^2
End Loop

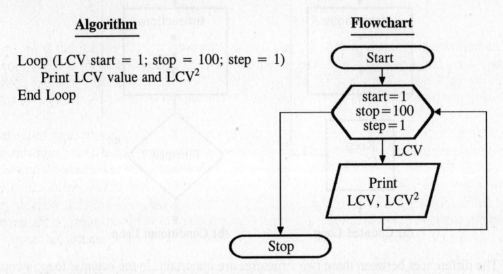

In this example, the computer will begin with LCV=1, and then print out the value of the LCV (1) and its square (1). Since the loop is not yet finished, the loop will cycle with a new value of LCV = 2. This second value of the LCV is determined from the previous value (1) plus the step size (also 1). So, in this example, the LCV will take on values 1, 2, 3, . . . , 100. Only when the LCV exceeds 100 will the loop stop.

EXAMPLE 1.9

Modify Example 1.8 to print out a list of only the even numbers and their squares.

Algorithm   **Flowchart**

Loop (LCV start = 2; stop = 100; step = 2)
    Print LCV value and LCV^2
End Loop

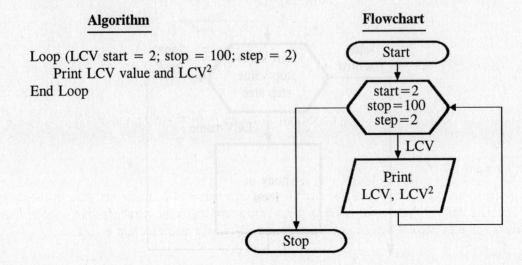

In this case, we want the LCV to have the values 2, 4, 6, . . ., 100. So, we will modify the previous algorithm to start at a value of 2 and to have a step size of 2. This will give the desired sequence of LCV = 2, 4, 6,. . ., 100. When we start the loop, the LCV has an initial value of LCV=2, and its square, of course, is 4. The next value of the LCV is determined by adding the step size of 2 to the old value of the LCV. Thus, the new value is 4, and its square is 16. If you examine this example carefully, you will note that the number of loop iterations is given by:

$$Number\ of\ iterations = \frac{stop\ value\ -\ start\ value}{step\ size} + 1$$

This housekeeping detail is done for you by the computer. All you need to do is set up the start, stop, and step size values. One important point to understand about counted loops is that the LCV is under the control of the computer. You may *look* at its value and *use* it in calculations as we did in these two examples. But, you are not allowed to *change* its value.

One of the keys to using counted loops is that you <u>must</u> know in advance how many times the loop will execute. But many times this information is not available. Yet the problem may demand a loop. So, how can we handle this situation? The solution is the *conditional loop*, where the machine will check every time through the loop to see if the loop should repeat. In such a situation, there must be one or more variables to control the loop. In addition, this variable <u>must</u> change within the loop. This is the key difference between the two types of loops. In the counted loop, the programmer cannot change the control variable, but in the conditional loop, the programmer *must* change the control variable.

The most common type of conditional loop is termed the *while loop*. In this loop, a set of instructions is repeated while some condition is true. When this condition becomes false, the loop terminates. There is no specific flowchart symbol for the while loop. Instead, we will reuse the conditional flowchart symbol. In this use of the diamond, though, we will return to a point <u>before</u> the diamond:

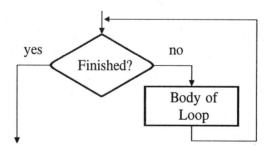

As with counted loops, the body of a conditional loop may contain any number of instructions.

EXAMPLE 1.10

Construct an algorithm and a flowchart to read in a series of numbers and keep track of the running total and the number of data items. Stop reading in the numbers when one of them has a value of zero. Then compute the average of all the numbers and report it.

Since we do not know how many times to repeat the process, the best way to deal with this is to use a conditional loop. We will do the following when the number is nonzero:

- Read in a number and add it to the total
- Add one to the number of items.

Once the critical value (zero) is entered, we can then compute the average:

- Stop the loop
- Divide the total by the quantity (number of items − 1)
- Report the average.

When we are finished, we will have read in one data item too many (the zero). That's why we have to subtract 1 from the number of data items before computing the average.

Algorithm

Set SUM=0, COUNT=1
Read in the first number, X
Add that number to SUM
Conditional Loop: (While X ≠ 0)
   Read in next value of X
   Add X to SUM
   Add 1 to COUNT
End Loop
AVG = SUM/(COUNT−1)
Print value of AVG and (COUNT−1)

Flowchart

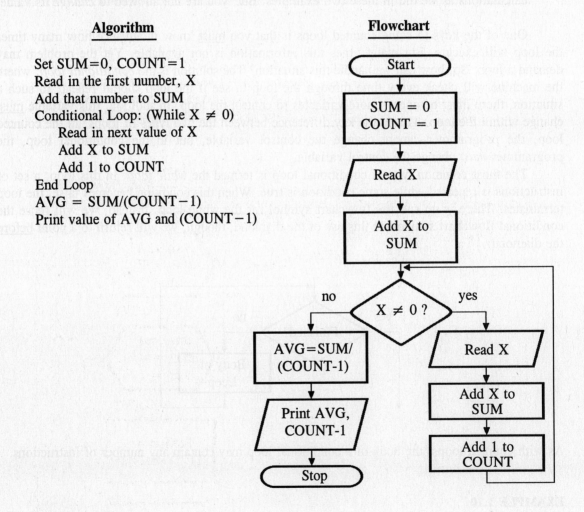

1.8 NESTED LOOPS

In Section 1.5, we showed you how to nest control structures. This can be done also with loops. You can place a counted loop within another counted loop, a conditional loop within another conditional loop, or a combination of different loops within each other.

EXAMPLE 1.11

Construct an algorithm and flowchart to create a 10 by 10 multiplication table such as $1 \times 1 = 1$, $1 \times 2 = 2$, and so forth. This problem is best solved by nesting two counted loops. One loop determines the value of the first number (LCV1), while the second loop cycles the second number (LCV2) from one to ten. When loops are *nested* like this, the loop control variable for the inner loop will change more rapidly than the loop control variable for the outer loop.

Value of LCV1 in Outer Loop	Value of LCV2 in Inner Loop	Product (LCV1 × LCV2)
1	1	1
1	2	2
1	3	3
:	:	:
10	9	90
10	10	100

Algorithm

Loop (LCV1 start = 1; stop = 10; step = 1)
   Loop (LCV2 start = 1; stop = 10; step =1)
      Product = LCV1×LCV2
      Print LCV1, LCV2, and Product
   End Loop
End Loop

Flowchart

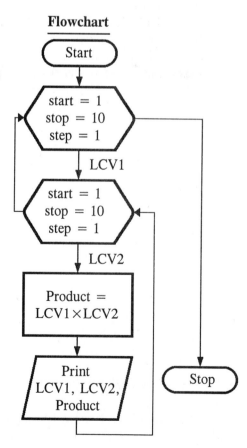

EXAMPLE 1.12

Construct an algorithm and a flowchart that accomplishes the following:

1. Reads in a series of _whole_ numbers (nonzero values), one at a time.
2. Determines how many digits are in each number.
3. Terminates the process when any of the numbers entered is less than zero.

First, let's consider how we determine the number of digits in a whole number. One way to do this is to continually divide the number by 10 until the number is less than or equal to 1 and keep track of the number of divisions. Note that we do not know in advance how many such divisions we need. So this will require a conditional loop. As an example, consider the number 123. Here is how the process proceeds:

Step	Number	Number of Divisions	Comments
1	123	0	_Starting value_
2	12.3	1	_First division_
3	1.23	2	_Second division_
4	0.123	3	_Stop, since number is less than 1_

Notice that the number of divisions (3 in this example) is the same as the number of digits in the starting number (123).

Once the analysis of the first number is completed, we will need to go back and get the next number and repeat the process. Note that this is a conditional loop, since we do not know how many numbers to analyze. For example, suppose we had the sequence of numbers 123, 17, and -10 to analyze. This is how the program should execute:

Step	Number	Number of Divisions	Comments
1	123	0	_Get the first number_
2	12.3	1	_Divide by 10 and continue_
3	1.23	2	_Divide by 10 and continue_
4	0.123	3	_Finished with first number_
5	17	0	_Get the second number_
6	1.7	1	_Divide by 10 and continue_
7	0.17	2	_Finished with second number_
8	-10	0	_Get third number_
9			_Stop since number less than zero_

Algorithm	**Flowchart**

Initialize *n* to zero
Read in a number *n*
Conditional Loop: (While *n* ≥ 0)
    Conditional Loop: (While *n* ≥ 1)
        Divide *n* by 10
        Add 1 to *dig* (# of digits)
    End Loop
    Print value of *dig*
    Read in next value of *n*
    Set *dig* to zero
End Loop

As in the example above, it is very crucial that the following three steps are taken in order to properly control the operation of a conditional loop.

- First, *initialize* the control variable to give it a starting value.
- Next, use this control variable to *test* whether to stop the loop or to continue.
- Finally, *increment* the control variable and give it its next value.

1.9 PROCEDURES

An important element in all programming languages is the ability to break a single large program down into several smaller ones. By doing so, what may have started as a seemingly intractable problem becomes a solvable one. Thus, breaking the problem down into several smaller components (sometimes called *modules* or *procedures*) allows you to focus on a smaller, more manageable part that attempts to perform only a single well defined task. By tackling one subproblem at a time, you can focus all your attention on that one problem. Also, the programming modules that you create can be reused. You may reuse them in the same program (with a different set of data for instance), or you may use the modules in another program.

The modularization process uses the following symbol:

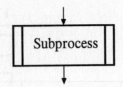

The *subprocess* refers to another set of instructions that describe the details. This is often called an *offpage* process, since it can be placed on another piece of paper. The main idea that you need to grasp here is that you don't want to be bogged down in details. You simply want to focus on the big picture and leave the details for later.

EXAMPLE 1.13

Construct an algorithm and a flowchart to evaluate the first ten terms of the infinite series:

$$a = \frac{1}{1!} + \frac{1}{2!} + \frac{1}{3!} + \cdots$$

where $n!$ is the factorial of n given by $(n)(n-1) \ldots (2)(1)$. To evaluate this, we will use a loop where we compute the terms one at a time. Since we know that we want ten terms, this loop will be a <u>counted</u> loop. It is convenient to use the LCV from this loop by noting that:

$$Value\ of\ individual\ term = \frac{1}{LCV!}$$

The first time through the loop, LCV = 1, and the first term is 1/1!. The second time through the loop, LCV = 2, and the value of the term is 1/2!; and so forth for LCV = 3 to 10.

Now, let's begin to work on the module to compute the factorial. All we have to do is take the value of the LCV and set up a counted loop (with a new LCV2 as its control variable which goes from 1 to LCV). Inside the body of this loop, we will multiply together all the values from 1 to LCV. As an example of how this works, let's assume LCV = 3. This value is transferred to the module for computing the factorial, which then computes the product of all integers from 1 to LCV or 1 to 3. The value of the factorial is $1 \times 2 \times 3 = 6$. In a similar manner, any other value of LCV can be used to compute $1 \times 2 \ldots \times LCV$.

Algorithm

Main Program:

```
Initialize TOTAL to 0
Loop (LCV = 1 to 10, step = 1)
     TERM = 1 / LCV!
     add TERM value to TOTAL
End Loop
Print TOTAL
```

Module for Factorial:

```
FACT = 1
Loop (LCV2 = 1 to LCV,  step = 1)
     FACT = FACT × LCV2
End Loop
```

Flowchart

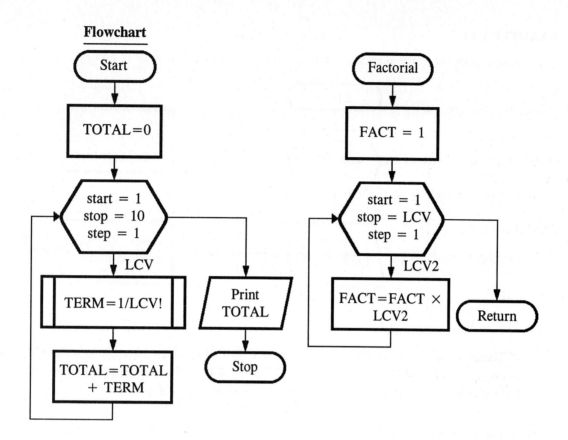

We use the Return statement to terminate the module for the factorial, just as we used the Stop statement to terminate the main part of the flowchart that requested the factorial calculation. Once the module to compute the factorial is set up, we can use it as many times as needed without having to rewrite the code. In this example, we will use the module ten times, but each time we will send down a different value for which the factorial is to be computed. For example, when LCV=1 in the main part of the flowchart, the value of 1 is transferred to the module, where 1! is computed. The next time though, LCV=2 and so 2! is computed.

1.10 COMMENTS

There are many times when you want to add comments to your flowcharts to make it easier for others to understand what you are doing. This is done with a special flowchart symbol:

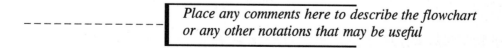

Comments improve the readability of your flowcharts and programs. You will find comments especially useful during debugging by reminding you what you were thinking when you first constructed the solution.

EXAMPLE 1.14

Add comments to the flowchart in EXAMPLE 1.9 to explain what is going on at each step.

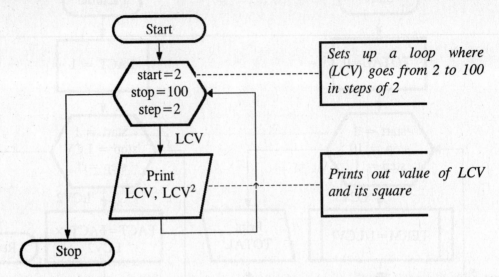

Sets up a loop where (LCV) goes from 2 to 100 in steps of 2

Prints out value of LCV and its square

There are no rules for comment statements. Just place them liberally wherever it makes sense to improve the clarity of your flowcharts. Later on, when you go to convert the flowchart into a program, you should also place them in the program.

1.11 DEBUGGING TIPS

Debugging is the process of removing errors from your program. Bugs fall into two general categories — *syntax* and *logic* errors. *Syntax* errors are mistakes in following the grammar of the computer language. These types of errors are easy to correct, and we will discuss them in the following chapters. *Logic* errors, on the other hand, are defects in the design of the algorithm. For example, you might have given the computer the wrong instructions, or you may have had a loop execute too many times. In any case, the machine will carry out the instructions in the exact sequence that you told it. As far as the machine is concerned, there was no error!

Logic errors are most easily corrected at the algorithm/flowchart level by a process known as *tracing* where you can see where your logic deviates from what it is supposed to be. Then it should be a relatively simple matter to correct the logic. Tracing is done by making a list of each variable and keeping track of how each one changes as you step through the algorithm. You can also trace the program, but it is preferable to do it at the logic forming stage.

EXAMPLE 1.15

The following flowchart is supposed to approximate the sum of the first 100 terms of the infinite series:

$$b = 1 + \frac{1}{2} + \frac{1}{4} + \frac{1}{8} + \cdots$$

However, there is an error in the algorithm constructed to evaluate this series.

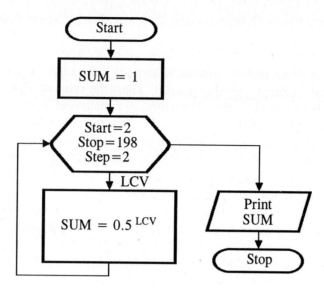

To find and correct the logic error, we must trace through the flowchart by hand. The flowchart is supposed to calculate one series term at a time and add it to the running total (SUM). Let's follow the variables as we step through the program:

Step	LCV	Sum	Comments
1	–	1.0	*Initialization before loop*
2	2	0.25	*Sum = $(0.5)^2$*
3	4	0.0625	*Sum = $(0.5)^4$*

The error has already occurred since the sum after two terms should be 1.5 instead of the 0.25 indicated in the table, so there is no need to go further. Instead, it is time to find out what went wrong. We do this by listing what the values *should* have been:

Step	LCV	Sum	Comments
1	–	1.0	*Initialization before loop*
2	1	1.5	*Sum = $1.0 + (0.5)^1$*
3	2	1.75	*Sum = $1.0 + (0.5)^1 + (0.5)^2$*
4	3	1.875	*Sum = $1.0 + (0.5)^1 + (0.5)^2 + (0.5)^3$*

There are two problems with the proposed flowchart. See if you can find them before reading any further.

- Once a value of any individual term is calculated, it should be added to the approximation previously obtained. Thus, the value of SUM should increase after each term is calculated. Therefore, the statement inside the loop should read $SUM = SUM + 0.5^{LCV}$, where 0.5^{LCV} is the value for the current term that is added to the old value of SUM to get the new value.
- The mathematical expression for the individual term is correct (0.5^{LCV}), but the limits on the loop are incorrect. Instead of having LCV values of 2, 4, 6, . . . , 198, they should be 1, 2, 3, . . . , 99.

In summary, the flowchart will be correct when the following changes are made:

- $SUM = 0.5^{LCV}$ should change to $SUM = SUM + 0.5^{LCV}$.
- LCV limits (start=2, stop=198, step=2) changes to
  LCV limits (start=1, stop=99, step=1).

After implementing these changes, this is what the corrected flowchart will look like:

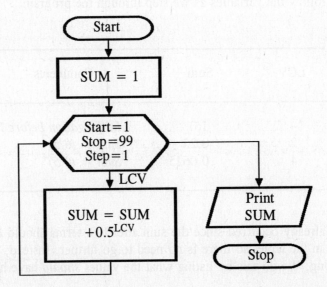

After you have made the changes in the program logic it is important for you to trace through the new algorithm or flowchart to make sure that it now provides the correct answers. One final word about tracing is that only rarely do you need to trace through the program completely. Usually, only a few data points need to be evaluated before you see what the problem is. That is what we did here. After only a few passes through the loop we were able to find the deviation between the expected results and the actual results. Finally, note that you need to have some idea of the intermediate results before you can begin to find logic errors. In this example for instance, we knew what the value of each term in the series had to be. This made it possible to locate the error.

Solved Problems

1.1 Construct an algorithm and a flowchart to read in three values and assign them to the variables x, y, and z.

Algorithm

Read in x, y, and z

Flowchart

1.2 Modify Solved Problem 1.1 to print a *prompt* message to remind you which variables to enter. (A *prompt* is a message that contains instructions about what to do next.)

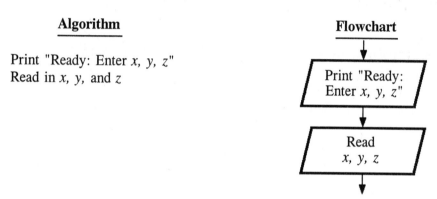

Algorithm

Print "Ready: Enter x, y, z"
Read in x, y, and z

Flowchart

1.3 Construct an algorithm and a flowchart to read in x, y, and z and then compute the value of

$$u = x^{y^z}$$

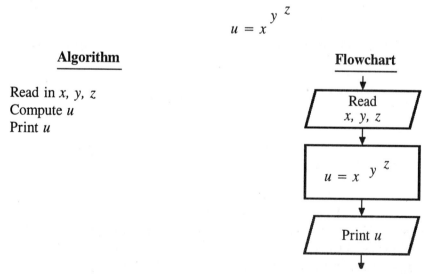

Algorithm

Read in x, y, z
Compute u
Print u

Flowchart

1.4 Construct an algorithm and a flowchart to determine if an integer n is odd or even. (Hint: integer division produces no remainder. Thus $5/2 = 2$, if both 5 and 2 are integers.)

Algorithm   **Flowchart**

Is $n/2*2 = n$?
    If yes, Print "n is even"
    If no, Print "n is odd"
End Branch

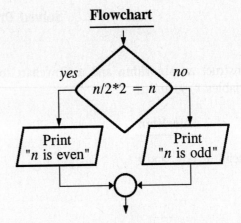

1.5   Construct an algorithm and a flowchart to determine if three whole numbers are all even.

Algorithm   **Flowchart**

Read i, j, and k
Is $i/2*2=i$ and $j/2*2=j$
and $k/2*2=k$ simultaneously?
    If yes, Print "All are even"
    If no, Print "Some are odd"
End Branch

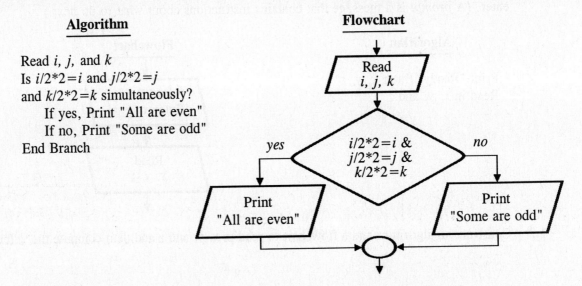

1.6   Construct an algorithm and a flowchart to calculate the roots of the quadratic equation:

$$a x^2 + b x + c = 0$$

Recall that this equation has *three* possible types of solutions that depend on the value of the *discriminant* (d) defined by $d = b^2 - 4ac$. When $d > 0$, there are two real roots (x_1 and x_2). When $d = 0$, there is only one real root (x_1). And when $d < 0$, there are two roots, but they are imaginary with a Real part (r), and Imaginary parts (i_1 and i_2). (Assume $a \neq 0$.)

Algorithm

Read a, b, c
Calculate $d = b^2 - 4ac$
Is $d \geq 0$?
    If yes, then
        Is $d > 0$?
            If yes, then

(*Algorithm continues on next page*)

$$\text{Print } x_1 = (-b + \sqrt{d})/(2a)$$
$$\text{Print } x_2 = (-b - \sqrt{d})/(2a)$$
If no, then
$$\text{Print } x = -b/(2a)$$
End Branch
If no, then
$$\text{Print } r = -b/(2a)$$
$$\text{Print } i_1 = + \sqrt{|d|}/(2a)$$
$$\text{Print } i_2 = - \sqrt{|d|}/(2a)$$
End Branch

Flowchart

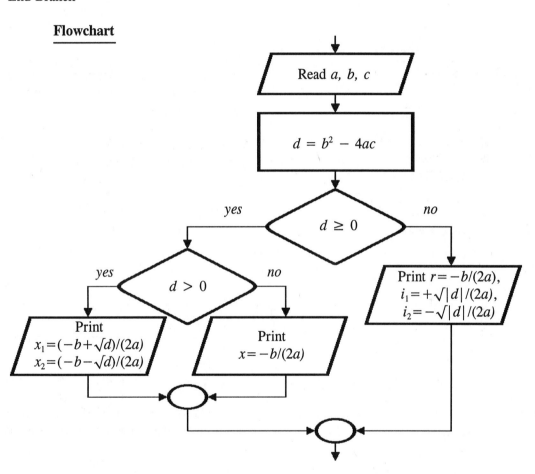

1.7 When we write a program, we often have the program ask questions which are answered "yes" or "no." People have a tendency, however, to answer the questions with things like yes, YES, y, Y, true, or True. A good program should consider how people are likely to answer such a question. Construct an algorithm and flowchart to read in an answer and print out one of three answers — "True," "False," or "Reenter," assuming that yes, YES, y, Y, true, True, t, and T are valid equivalents to "True," and that no, No, n, N, false, False, f, and F are equivalent to "False." Any other answer would result in the "Reenter" message. (Hint: Although you could use several nested branching operations, it is better to use the select case structure.)

Algorithm

Read ANS
Case Select based on ANS
    If ANS= t, true, T, TRUE, True
        y, yes, Y, Yes, or YES, then Print "True"
    If ANS= f, false, F, FALSE, False
        n, no, N, No, or NO, then Print "False"
    All other cases, Print "Reenter"
End Case Select

Flowchart

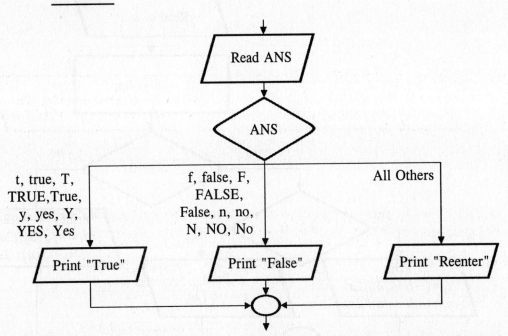

1.8 Construct an algorithm and flowchart to solve the quadratic equation using the Select Case structure. Refer to Solved Problem 1.6 for details about the three categories of possible roots for $a \neq 0$.

Algorithm

Read $a,\ b,\ c$
Calculate $d = b^2 - 4ac$
Case Select based on d
    If $d > 0$, then
        Print $x_1 = (-b + \sqrt{d})/(2a)$
        Print $x_2 = (-b - \sqrt{d})/(2a)$
    If $d = 0$, then
        Print $x = -b/(2a)$
    If $d < 0$, then

(*Algorithm continues on next page*)

$$\text{Print } r \ = -b/(2a)$$
$$\text{Print } i_1 \ = + \ \sqrt{|d|}/(2a)$$
$$\text{Print } i_2 \ = -\sqrt{|d|}/(2a)$$
End Case Select

Flowchart

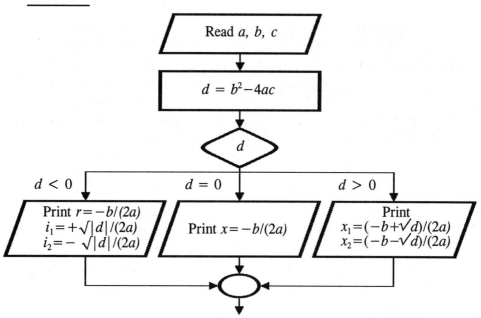

1.9 Construct an algorithm and flowchart to read in two integers i and j and find the sum of all integers between them.

Algorithm

Read i, j
$sum = 0$
Loop (LCV $= i+1$ to $j-1$, step $= 1$)
    $sum = sum + \text{LCV}$
End Loop
Print SUM

Flowchart

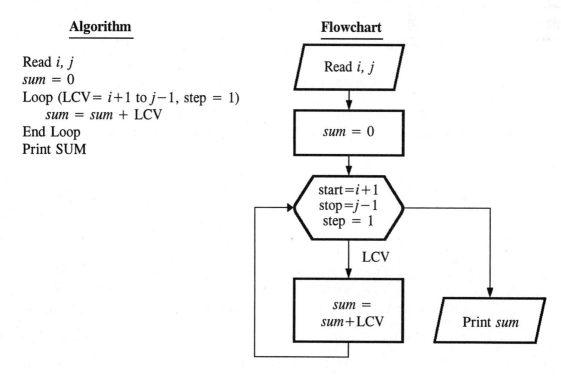

1.10 Construct an algorithm and a flowchart to calculate the values of y for values of $x = 1.0$ to 10.0 in increments of 0.01. The equation for y is given by:

$$y = \frac{1}{x} - 4.3 \log(x) + x^4$$

Algorithm	**Flowchart**

Loop (LCV = 1.0 to 10.0, step = 0.01)

$\quad y = \dfrac{1}{LCV} - 4.3 \log(LCV) + LCV^4$

$\quad$ Print y

End Loop

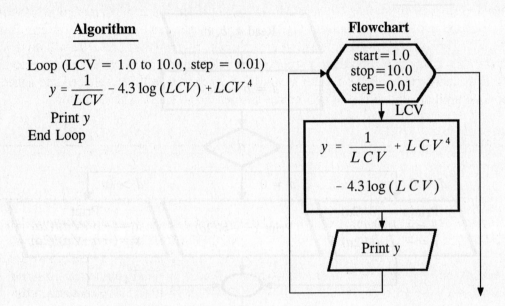

1.11 Construct an algorithm and a flowchart to read in values for a, b, and c and then print their sum. Stop this procedure if <u>any</u> value of a, b, and c is negative.

Algorithm	**Flowchart**

Conditional Loop: (While a, and b, and $c \geq 0$)

$\quad$ Read a, b, c

$\quad$ sum $= a+b+c$

$\quad$ Print sum

End Loop

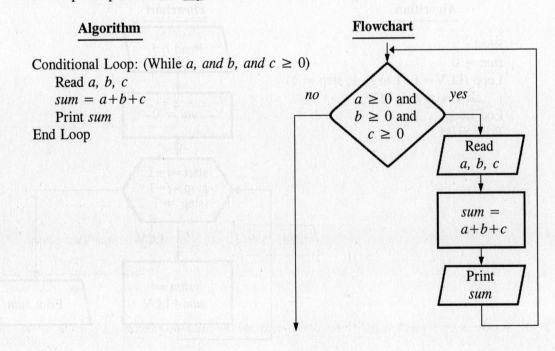

1.12 Construct an algorithm and a flowchart to compute an approximation to the series:

$$\frac{1}{1^3} + \frac{1}{2^3} + \frac{1}{3^3} + \frac{1}{4^3} + \cdots$$

This series continues indefinitely and it is impossible to add up an infinite number of terms. Yet we can *estimate* the series value by carrying out the computation until a term in the series adds a negligible amount to the total sum of all the previous terms. We will do this by performing the computation until any term falls below a critical value (δ) that you read in. As an example, if we read in a value of $\delta=0.005$, each term will be evaluated and added to the total until any individual term becomes smaller than 0.005 as shown below.

Term	Sum	Comments
$1/1^3$ (1.0)	1.0	*Term (1.000) > δ (0.005), so continue series*
$1/2^3$ (0.125)	1.125	*Term (0.125) > δ (0.005), so continue series*
$1/3^3$ (0.037)	1.162	*Term (0.037) > δ (0.005), so continue series*
$1/4^3$ (0.016)	1.178	*Term (0.016) > δ (0.005), so continue series*
$1/5^3$ (0.008)	1.186	*Term (0.008) > δ (0.005), so continue series*
$1/6^3$ (0.0046)	1.191	*Term (0.0046) < δ (0.005), so stop*

Algorithm

Read δ
term = 1
sum = 1
count = 2
Loop: (While *term* $\geq$ δ)
    term = 1/*count*^{3}
    sum = *sum* + *term*
    count = *count* + 1
End Loop
Print *sum*

Flowchart

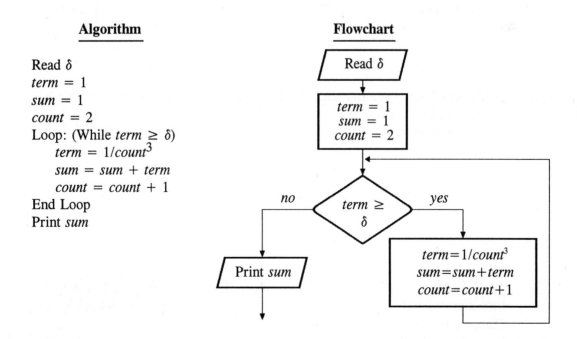

1.13 Construct an algorithm and flowchart to evaluate the following series for $n=3$ to $n=10$. For each value of n, evaluate n terms in the series. For example, if $n=4$ we will evaluate four terms in the series.

$$1 + \frac{1}{1^n} + \frac{1}{2^n} + \frac{1}{3^n} + \cdots$$

We will use the control variable (LCV1) from the first loop to set the upper limit on the second loop. For example, if LCV1 = 4, the inner loop will execute from LCV2 = 1 to 4.

Algorithm   **Flowchart**

```
Loop (start = 3, stop = 10)
    sum = 1
    Loop (start = 1, stop = LCV1)
        sum = sum + 1/LCV2 LCV1
    End Loop
    Print sum
End Loop
```

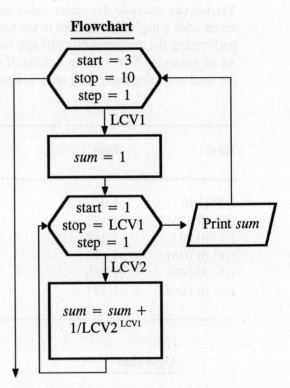

1.14 The number of combinations c into which you can organize a class of n students into groups of i and $n-i$ is computed with the formula shown below. Construct an algorithm and a flowchart to determine c for values of i and n. Use a module to compute the factorial.

$$c = \frac{n!}{i!(n-i)!}$$

Algorithm

Main Program:

Read, n, i
Compute $n!$
Compute $i!$
Compute $(n-i)!$
Compute $c = n!/(i!(n-i)!)$
Print c

Module for Factorial:

```
factorial = 1
Loop (LCV = 2 to VAL, step = 1)
    factorial = factorial × LCV
End Loop
```

Flowchart

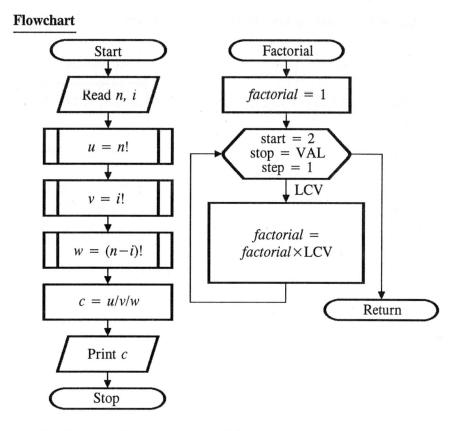

1.15 Construct an algorithm and flowchart of a module that switches two numbers a and b.

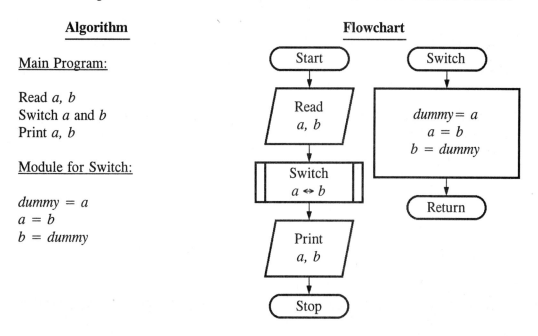

Note the three statements in the module to switch two numbers. The only way to switch two numbers is to use a *dummy* variable to temporarily store one of the values.

1.16 Trace through the following flowchart (or algorithm) and predict the output.

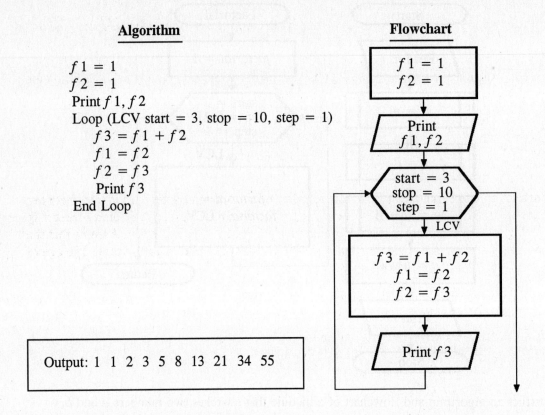

Algorithm

$f1 = 1$
$f2 = 1$
Print $f1, f2$
Loop (LCV start = 3, stop = 10, step = 1)
    $f3 = f1 + f2$
    $f1 = f2$
    $f2 = f3$
    Print $f3$
End Loop

Output: 1 1 2 3 5 8 13 21 34 55

Flowchart

$f1 = 1$
$f2 = 1$

Print $f1, f2$

start = 3
stop = 10
step = 1
LCV

$f3 = f1 + f2$
$f1 = f2$
$f2 = f3$

Print $f3$

1.17 The following algorithm and flowchart are flawed. They are supposed to evaluate $n!$, where $n! = (1)(2)(3) \ldots (n-2)(n-1)(n)$. Trace through the algorithm or flowchart to find the error(s).

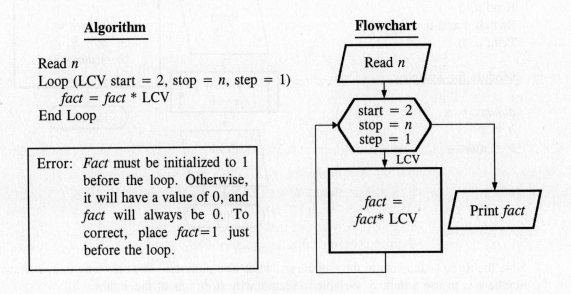

Algorithm

Read n
Loop (LCV start = 2, stop = n, step = 1)
    $fact = fact * LCV$
End Loop

Error: *Fact* must be initialized to 1 before the loop. Otherwise, it will have a value of 0, and *fact* will always be 0. To correct, place *fact*=1 just before the loop.

Flowchart

Read n

start = 2
stop = n
step = 1
LCV

$fact = fact* LCV$

Print *fact*

Supplementary Problems

1.18 Construct an algorithm and a flowchart to output the values of three variables, x, y, and z.

1.19 Construct an algorithm and a flowchart to show that for $a = 2.13$ and $b = 1.3$, the following trigonometric identity holds for the tangent function, tan (x).

$$\tan(a + b) = \frac{\tan(a) + \tan(b)}{1 - \tan(a)\tan(b)}$$

1.20 Construct an algorithm and a flowchart to calculate the apparent difference in ages between twins separated at birth. One is kept on earth while the other one is placed on a rocket ship traveling to the nearest star, Alpha Centauri, which is 4.8 light years away. Assume that the ship travels at 0.96 times the speed of light and that the trip takes 5 earth years. The age of the twin (to an earth observer) is given by

$$t_m = t_s[1 - (\frac{v}{c})^2]^{1/2}$$

where t_m = elapsed time measured on the moving object
t_s = elapsed time measured on the earth
v = velocity of the rocket
c = speed of light.

1.21 Construct an algorithm and a flowchart to calculate the current I in a diode (an electrical device), at any applied voltage V if the diode characteristics are given by

$$I = I_0(e^{kV} - 1) \qquad for\ V \geq V_R$$
$$I = -I_0(e^{-kV} - 1) \qquad for\ V < V_R$$

where I_0, V_R, and k are constants.

1.22 Construct an algorithm and a flowchart to read in three integers and determine if all are odd or all are even.

1.23 Construct an algorithm and a flowchart to issue grades to students. Use the following criteria:

if score is between 90 and 100, then grade = A
if score is between 80 and 89, then grade = B
if score is between 70 and 79, then grade = C
if score is between 60 and 69, then grade = D
if score is below 60, then grade = F.

1.24 Construct an algorithm and a flowchart to determine if a number read in is positive, negative or zero. Use a select case structure to make the decisions.

1.25 Construct an algorithm and a flowchart to read in two integers and find the sum of all *odd* numbers between these two. Include in the sum both numbers if they are odd.

1.26 Construct an algorithm and a flowchart to compute the terms in the following series:

$$1 \quad 1 \quad 2 \quad 3 \quad 5 \quad 8 \quad 13 \quad 21 \quad 34 \quad 55 \quad 89 \quad 144 \quad 233 \quad \ldots$$

The first two numbers are 1 and 1. All the other terms are determined by adding the previous two terms. Calculate n terms of this series, where n is read into the program.

1.27 Construct an algorithm and a flowchart to read in a number x and repeatedly divide it by 2 until the result is smaller than 0.001. Print out how many divisions it took.

1.28 Construct an algorithm and a flowchart to calculate the terms in this series:

$$a = 2\left[1 - \frac{1}{2} + \frac{1}{3} - \frac{1}{4} + \frac{1}{5} - \cdots\right]$$

Calculate the series until any one term is less than 0.1% of the value of the sum of the previous terms. Note that the sign of each term alternates.

1.29 Construct an algorithm and a flowchart to calculate the value of a, where

$$a = \frac{x - y}{x^y} - \frac{y - x}{y^x}$$

for values of $x = 1, 2, 3, \ldots, 10$ and for values of $y = 0.1, 0.2, 0.3, \ldots, 1.0$.

1.30 Construct an algorithm and a flowchart for a main program to receive two numbers and a module to determine which number is greater.

1.31 Construct an algorithm and a flowchart for a module to approximate the sine of x given by:

$$\sin(x) = x - \frac{x^3}{3!} + \frac{x^5}{5!} - \frac{x^7}{7!} + \cdots$$

Then use this module to test the identity $[\sin(3a) = 3\sin(a) - 4\sin^3(a)]$ for $a = 1, 2, \ldots, 5$.

Answers to Selected Supplementary Problems

1.18 Print out X, Y, Z

1.19 Read A, B
RTSIDE$=$[tan(A)+tan(B)]/[1−tan(A)tan(B)]
LFTSIDE$=$tan(A+B)
Print RTSIDE, LFTSIDE

1.20 Read RATIO, TS
TM$=$TS$[1-(\text{RATIO})^2]^{1/2}$
DIFFERENCE$=$TS−TM
Print DIFFERENCE

(Comment: The variable RATIO is the fraction of the speed of light that the rocket is traveling. In this case, RATIO=0.96.)

1.21 Read K, V, I0, VR
Is V $\geq$ VR?
   If yes, then I$=$I0(e^{KV} − 1)
   If no, then I$=$−I0(e^{-KV} − 1)
End Branch

1.22 Read I, J, K
Is I/2*2$=$I and J/2*2$=$J and K/2*2$=$K?
   If yes, Print "All are even"
Is I/2*2$\neq$I and J/2*2$\neq$J and K/2*2$\neq$K?
   If yes, print "All are odd"

1.23 Read SCORE
Is SCORE $\geq$ 90 and SCORE $\leq$ 100?
   If yes, GRADE = "A"
Is SCORE $\geq$ 80 and SCORE $\leq$ 89?
   If yes, GRADE = "B"
Is SCORE $\geq$ 70 and SCORE $\leq$ 79?
   If yes, GRADE = "C"
Is SCORE $\geq$ 60 and SCORE $\leq$ 69?
   If yes, GRADE = "D"
Is SCORE $<$ 60? − if yes, GRADE = "F"

1.24 Read X
Select Case (based on X)
   X$<$0: Print "X is negative"
   X$=$0: Print "X is zero"
   X$>$0: Print "X is positive"
End Select Case

1.25 Read I, J
SUM = 0
Loop (LCV start = I, stop = J, step = 1)
   Is (LCV/2)*2 = LCV?
    If yes, then skip
    If no, then SUM = SUM + LCV
   End Branch
End Loop

*(Comment: The statement LCV*2/2 = LCV checks to see if LCV is even. If it is, then we skip that value of LCV, and go on to the next one.)*

1.26 Read N
   F1 = 1

1.27 Read X
   NUM = 0

```
F2 = 1
Print F1, F2
Loop (start = 3, stop = N, step = 1)
    F3 = F1 + F2
    F1 = F2
    F2 = F3
    Print F3
End Loop
```

```
Conditional Loop: (While X ≥ 0.001)
    X = X/2
    NUM = NUM + 1
End Loop
Print NUM
```

1.28
```
I = 2
SIGN = +1
TERM = 2
SUM = 2
Loop: (While |TERM|/|SUM| ≥ 0.001)
    SIGN = − SIGN
    TERM = 2(SIGN/I)
    SUM = SUM + TERM
    I = I + 1
End Loop
Print SUM
```

[Comment: We need to independently calculate the sign (+ or −) and the magnitude for each term in the series. We then estimate the importance of the term by its   ratio |TERM|/|SUM|.   If   the contribution is negligible, then we stop calculating other terms.]

1.29
```
Loop (LCV1 start=1 to 10, step=1)
    Loop (LCV2 start=0.1 to 1.0, step=0.1)
```
$$A = \frac{LCV1 - LCV2}{LCV1^{LCV2}} - \frac{LCV2 - LCV1}{LCV2^{LCV1}}$$
```
    Print A
    End Loop
End Loop
```

1.30 <u>Main Program:</u>

```
Read A, B
C = MAX( A, B)
Print C
```

<u>Module for MAX:</u>

```
Is A > B?
    If yes, MAX = A
    If no, MAX = B
End Branch
```

1.31 <u>Main Program:</u>

```
Loop (LCV start = 1 to 5, step = 1)
Read A
U = sin(A)
V = [sin(A)]³
RTSIDE = 3U − 4V
LFTSIDE = sin(3A)
Is (|LFTSIDE−RTSIDE| < 0.01)?
    If yes, then print "identity valid"
    If no, then print "identity invalid"
End Branch
End Loop
```

Module for SIN(X) Approximation:

SUM = X
TERM = X
SIGN = +1
I = 3
Loop: (While |TERM|/|SUM| $\geq$ 0.0001)
    SIGN = $-$ SIGN
    TERM = SIGN*X^I/I!
    SUM = SUM + TERM
    I = I + 2
End Loop

Module for Factorial of I:

FACT = 1
Loop (LCV start = 2, stop = I, step =1)
    FACT = FACT * LCV
End Loop

Chapter 2

Getting Started

2.1 INTRODUCTION

In the last chapter, we presented the basic building blocks required for programming. So now it is time to introduce the specific details needed to construct simple Fortran programs using some of these basic ideas. To allow you to write your first program, we need to discuss four items:

- How a program is organized
- The different types of data, constants, and variables
- The assignment statement as a means of calculating and storing data
- Simple input and output

We will also review selected library functions for performing common mathematical operations and debugging tips. When you complete this chapter, you should be able to write a simple program consisting of input, sequential calculations, and output to a terminal screen.

2.2 PROGRAM ORGANIZATION

As we will soon see, a line in a program may contain items other than the programming instruction itself. These may include a *comment indicator* (indicating that what follows is for documentation purposes only), *continuation mark* (indicating that what follows is a continuation of the previous line), and *statement labels* (indicating a reference point within the program). The rules for program structure in Fortran 90 are:

- Statements can begin at any column, but they usually begin in column 1.
- Statement labels are placed at the beginning of a line and must be, at most, a 5-digit integer number.
- Comments are indicated by the "!" mark at the beginning of a line. A comment may also be placed after the program statement.
- Continuation of a line on the next line is indicated by placing an ampersand (&) at the end of the line to be continued.

In addition to these rules, every program must terminate with an END statement. If there are several program segments (called *subprograms* or *modules*), each of them must also terminate with an END statement that is used to mark the physical end of each module. Without the END statement, we would have no way of knowing where one module ends and the next one begins.

EXAMPLE 2.1

The following program computes the area of a right triangle after reading in the height and base into the variables H and B respectively. Note that we place comment statements liberally throughout the program to indicate the purpose of the various sections. Usually we start very long comments in column 1, while shorter comments are sometimes more conveniently placed at the end of a line. The choice is yours.

```
Column→ 10        20        30        40        50
        |         |         |         |         |
_____

! This example Fortran 90 Program calculates the area
! of a right triangle.
!
PRINT *, 'ENTER HEIGHT: '            ! Print message to screen
READ *, H                            ! Read value for H
PRINT *, 'ENTER BASE: '              ! Print message to screen
READ *, B                            ! Read value for B
A = 0.5 * H * B                      ! Calculate the area
! The following demonstrates the use of a continuation line.
!
PRINT *, &                           ! Print Area = value
'AREA = ', A                         ! to the CRT screen
!
! The above two lines are the same as PRINT *, 'AREA = ', A
!
END                                  ! Terminate the program
```

The line at the beginning of the program shows the column positions for the program and is not included in the program itself. It is shown only as a guide.

Optionally, a program may start with the PROGRAM *name* statement and end with END PROGRAM *name* statement. The sole purpose of this name is to make it easier for you to recognize the program at a later date.

EXAMPLE 2.2

```
PROGRAM AreaofCircle
!
! This example calculates the area of a circle.
!
PRINT *, 'Enter Circle Radius'
READ *, R
A = 3.1416 * R * R
PRINT *, 'Area of circle is ', A
!
END PROGRAM AreaofCircle
```

Note in both this example and in the previous one that we have terminated the programs with the END statement. This statement is required by the compiler and without it an error message will result.

2.3 INTRINSIC DATA TYPES AND INTEGER CONSTANTS

Fortran 90 contains six *intrinsic* data types that are built into the language. These are divided into two categories: *numerical* and *nonnumerical*. Numerical types are *integer, real, double precision*, and *complex*. Nonnumerical types are *character* and *logical*. In this chapter, we are mostly concerned with numerical types.

Integer Constants

Integer values are those that represent whole numbers. The range of values that can be represented on a computer depends specifically on the computer. However, a typical range is from $-2^{32-1} - 1$ to $+2^{32-1} - 1$ (−2,147,483,647 to 2,147,483,647) for a 32-bit computer.

EXAMPLE 2.3

The following illustrate correct and incorrect examples of integer constants:

Valid Examples	Invalid Examples	Comment
−999		*Negative sign required*
+10		*Plus sign optional*
10		*Can be written without plus sign*
	111 111 111	*Spaces not allowed*
	111,111,111	*No commas*
	174.00	*No decimal points in integer numbers*
	−7 1/2	*No fractions*

Fortran 90 also introduces the concept of KIND, which adds great flexibility to data types. We stated above that the range of an integer constant was −2,147,483,647 to 2,147,483,647 for a 32-bit computer. But in Fortran 90, you may use data types that require more or less storage space. For each of the intrinsic data types, the compiler will support a number of KINDs, indicated by an underscore (_) followed by a positive integer. This positive integer does not give any information about the memory allocation needed. Instead, the number is merely a choice from a menu listing a number of options that are computer and compiler dependent. For example, on several 32-bit computers Integer_1 represents an integer with range from −127 to 127, while Integer_2 represents an integer with a range of −32,767 to 32,767, and Integer_4 has the range -2,147,483,647 to 2,147,483,647.

EXAMPLE 2.4

Suppose your compiler is set up so that INTEGER (KIND=4) specifies an integer with range −2,147,483,647 to 2,147,483,647. This is how you would represent the integer value 1,234,567,890:

$$1234567890\_4$$

Note: Entering 1234567890 without the _4 would result as an error on some machines due to insufficient memory.

Sometimes, you may not know in advance what KIND is supported on your computer. Fortunately, there is an intrinsic (built-in) function that you can use to force the machine to select the appropriate KIND for the number of digits needed for your program. This function will return a KIND number that is based on the number of digits required.

EXAMPLE 2.5

To enter a 6-digit integer number into a program without necessarily knowing the appropriate KIND, use the SELECTED_INT_KIND function.

```
SELECTED_INT_KIND(7)          !(memory for a 6 digit integer is reserved)
SELECTED_INT_KIND(2)          !(memory for a 1 digit integer is reserved)
```

A function works much like a function key on a calculation. By calling a function and providing it data (arguments between the sets of parentheses), a desired value is returned. In the cases above, we send the values (7) or (2) to the function called SELECTED_INT_KIND to have the computer automatically determine which KIND will best fulfill our needs for a 7-digit or a 2-digit integer. In the first case, the machine would have selected Integer_4 and in the second case, it would have selected Integer_1.

Real and Double Precision Constants

The second type of numerical constant is called *real*. Real numbers are stored in the computer as two components: a mantissa ranging between 0.1 and 1.0 and an exponent that indicates the appropriate power of 10. Real constants are those that we think of as fractional numbers which may be positive or negative and *always* have a decimal point. We will use real constants primarily for arithmetic operations, while integers will be used primarily for counting. One of the distinguishing features that separates real and integer constants is the fact that real numbers are usually stored *inaccurately* in the computer while integers are stored accurately. This is due to the way that the numbers are stored internally in the computer. For real numbers, the inaccuracy occurs in approximately the seventh significant digit, although this may vary somewhat.

EXAMPLE 2.6

The following examples illustrate valid and invalid uses of real constants:

Valid Examples	Invalid Examples	Comment
−21.4		*Negative sign required*
+132.7		*Plus sign optional*
0.0000034		*Small numbers permitted*
	123 456.0	*Spaces not allowed*
	$ 1.23	*Only numbers permitted (no $)*
	0	*Requires a decimal point; otherwise this is an integer*
	123,456.00	*No commas*

Real constants can also use *scientific notation*, which is a useful method for denoting large or small numbers. Scientific notation relies on the use of a mantissa containing a decimal or integer value and an exponent that is a power of 10 and given by <mantissa> × 10 $^{<exponent>}$. The limit of accuracy of real constants is approximately seven digits with a magnitude from 10^{-38} to 10^{+38}.

EXAMPLE 2.7

The following examples show the use of real constants using scientific notation:

Valid Examples	Invalid Examples	Comment
0.6023E24		*Avogadro's number (6.023×10^{23})*
−0.123E24		*Negative mantissa permitted*
1.23E−24		*Negative exponent permitted*
0.0E0		*Zero!*
1E2		*Decimal point not required*
	0.1E−12.5	*Exponent must be integer*
	0.1E−123	*Value too small on most computers*
	0.1E+123	*Value too large on most computers*

If a number needs more than 7 digits of accuracy or needs exponent values outside the range of ±38, you use a *double precision* constant. Double precision is simple to use. Instead of using E for the exponent, double precision simply substitutes the letter D.

EXAMPLE 2.8

The following examples illustrate double precision constants using scientific notation:

Valid Examples	Invalid Examples	Comment
0.0D0		*Double precision form of zero*
0.23D−94		*Double precision will give greater range*
	0.123456789E23	*Not double precision! Extra digits ignored*

A word of caution: double precision numbers require two to ten times the computational time compared to single precision real numbers. Therefore, you should be careful to use double precision only when absolutely required.

As with the case for integers, the concept of KIND is also present for real numbers. Using the KIND parameter, numbers can be allocated sufficient memory in a much more controlled way.

EXAMPLE 2.9

If REAL (KIND=8) specifies a real number with range 10^{-308} to 10^{308} with 15 digits of accuracy, then this is how to enter such numbers:

```
1.23456789E98_8         ! 15 digit accuracy with a range of E−308 to E308
0.00000123456789_8      ! No lost digits
5.456E100               ! Error, 10^100 is too large for default KIND
```

Like the INTEGER (KIND=), the REAL (KIND=) parameters are processor and compiler dependent. So be sure to check your manual or ask your system operator which KINDs are supported. If this information is not readily available, then you can use the intrinsic function SELECTED_REAL_KIND to select the KIND that is most appropriate to match the accuracy and range that you desire.

EXAMPLE 2.10

If you don't know what KINDs are supported on your system, here are examples of how to get the computer itself to find the KIND that will give you the desired accuracy and range:

```
SELECTED_REAL_KIND(9,99)    ! 9 Digit accuracy with
                            ! E−99 to E+99 range
SELECTED_REAL_KIND(6,10)    ! 6 Digit accuracy with
                            ! E−10 to E+10 range
```

Complex Constants

Engineers and scientists often need to use complex numbers such as $4+3i$ (where $i^2 = -1$), which contain both real and imaginary parts. Since computers cannot work with imaginary numbers, we use a convention where a complex constant is represented by two components.

Algebraic representation: real part + i (imaginary part)

Fortran representation: (Real part, Imaginary part)

The first number represents the real part of the complex number, and the second number represents the imaginary part. These numbers may have either integer or real values. The following example summarizes these rules.

EXAMPLE 2.11

Here are some examples of commonly encountered complex constants:

Valid Examples	Invalid Examples	Comment
(1.23, −3.45)		*Either component may be negative*
(+1.23, 0.0)		*Positive sign is optional*
(1.23E−2, 3.45)		*Exponential format is permitted*
(1.23D−74, 3.45)		*Lower precision number is converted to*
		match higher precision number
(1.2_8, 3.45_8)		*KIND parameters may be present*
	(1)	*Must include both numbers, even if one is zero*

Character Constants

There are occasions when we need to work with nonnumerical data, which cannot be handled with the data types just discussed. Examples would be names and addresses. Accordingly, we will use a different type of constant, the *character* constant. A character constant is any set of the allowed symbols defined below and enclosed in either apostrophes (') or quote marks (").

Letters of the alphabet (upper or lower case)
Numbers 0 through 9
Special characters + − ( ) . , * / = ' $; " % : < > ? ! &
Blank space
Underscore _

Even though you can create symbols such as ☺ on your computer, Fortran will not accept them.

EXAMPLE 2.12

Here are some commonly encountered examples of character constants:

Valid Examples	Invalid Examples	Comment
"I'm OK"		*Can use apostrophe inside the quote marks*
'and he said, "Yes, I can" '		*Can use quote marks inside apostrophes*
"she said, ""That's right""""		*Use two sets of quote marks to include a quotation in the character constant*
	'I ♥ NY'	*Illegal character (♥)*
	Helen	*Missing apostrophes or quote marks*

As with integer and real constants, provision for different KINDs of character constants are also supported. Fortran 90 requires the presence of a character set such as the one previously described (called the *default* set), but it also allows for additional sets. The only condition on any additional character set is that it must include a blank space. Unlike the integer and real KINDs though, the KIND parameter must *precede* the character constant.

EXAMPLE 2.13

If CHARACTER (KIND=2) represents Greek letters and CHARACTER (KIND=3) represents special mathematical symbols, then the following would be valid examples assuming that no other character kinds have been declared:

Valid Examples	Invalid Examples	Comment
2_"Θηεσιλονικι"		*Acceptable to represent Greek letters*
3_"∑∇∞∴ ∮ ∃"		*Acceptable to represent math symbols*
	4_"ᴂœʄʤʞʦʃʧ"	*Character KIND=4 was not defined*

One final point about character data is not to confuse the character constant '1234' with its numerical counterpart 1234. While it is possible to perform mathematical operations with numerical constants, you cannot do the same thing with character constants. For example, you can add 123 to 456 (numerical constants), but you cannot write '123' + '456', since these are character constants.

Logical Constants

The final intrinsic data type is the *logical* constant, which can take on only two values. Thus the rules are very simple since the only allowed values of logical constants are .TRUE. and .FALSE. (note the use of the periods). The role of the logical constant will be made more apparent in the following chapters when we discuss control structures.

EXAMPLE 2.14

Here are some examples of common uses of logical constants:

Valid Examples	Invalid Examples	Comment
.True.		*Mixed case is acceptable*
.False.	FALSE	*Requires periods (.FALSE.)*
	.T.	*Must spell out complete word*

The KIND parameter is also supported for logical constants under Fortran 90. One use of the KIND parameter is for storing logical data in a more compact form. The default logical KIND may store its data in a way to maintain compatibility with earlier versions of Fortran. But other KINDs of logical data may use the minimum amount of storage space (called *bits*). Note that the KIND parameter is processor dependent, so you will need to check your operating manual to find what KINDs are supported.

EXAMPLE 2.15

Assume that (KIND=4) represents the *default* form of logical data. The default form is the one that is in effect unless you explicitly change it. Now assume that there is another non-default type (KIND=1) that results in more efficient memory storage. Then the following examples would be correct.

Valid Examples	Invalid Examples	Comment
.True._4		*Same as entering .True.*
.False._1		*Memory efficient storage of logical value*
	.True._3	*KIND=3 not defined*

2.4 VARIABLES AND SIMPLE INPUT/OUTPUT

Variables are names that we use to identify various quantities whose values can change during execution of a program. Thus they provide a means to manipulate data. But we may also use variables to introduce data into your program and print out results that are generated. The following example is a program that requests the user to enter the radius of a circle and returns its circumference and area.

EXAMPLE 2.16

Below is a simple program to compute the area and circumference of a circle of radius r. In the program, the variables used are PI, AREA, CIRCUM, and R. Note that we try to choose variable names that indicate their function in the program and sometimes refer to the variables as *mnemonic* names.

```
PROGRAM AreaofCircle
! The following statements request the user to type in
! a value of the radius
PRINT *, 'Enter circle radius'
READ *, R
! Once the radius is read in, the area is calculated
PI = 3.1416
AREA = PI * R * R
CIRCUM = 2 * PI * R
! The value of the area is now printed out
PRINT *, 'Area of circle is ', AREA
PRINT *, 'Circumference of circle is ', CIRCUM
END
```

When we execute this program, the following sequence of events will occur:

Printed on Screen	Comments
Enter circle radius	*(Printed by computer — line #4)*
5.0	*(Value typed in by user —line #5)*
Area of circle is 78.5400	*(Printed by computer — line #11)*
Circumference of circle is 31.4160	*(Printed by computer — line #12)*

The value of R was entered into the program with a READ statement and PI was given a value by using a real constant. AREA and CIRCUM were calculated by using simple mathematical expressions. Finally, the calculated values of AREA and CIRCUM were displayed at the terminal screen by using the two PRINT statements in lines 11 and 12.

When you give variables their names, try to choose names that describe their function within the program. The rules for defining Fortran 90 variable names are as follows:

- 1 to 31 characters long.
- Only letters (A - Z), numbers (0 - 9) and underscore (_) are allowed.
- First character must be a letter.
- Upper/lower-case are equivalent.
- Blank spaces are *not* allowed, unlike earlier versions of Fortran.

EXAMPLE 2.17

Here are some common forms of variable names:

Valid Examples	Invalid Examples	Comment
X		OK, but not very illustrative
TAXDUE		Better, since it describes its function
TEMP1		OK to mix letters and numbers
AmtDue		OK to mix upper and lower case letters
Amountdueme		OK, but hard to read
Amount_due_me		Underscores improves readability
Amt_Due	Amt Due	Blank spaces are not allowed
	$OWED	Illegal character ($)
	2BEE	Must start with a letter

Implicit Data Typing

In the previous sections, we discussed the six basic data types, but we did not discuss how to define variables. With constants, it was obvious what data type each constant was. For example, if a number had a decimal point it was real, and if it had no decimal point it was treated as an integer, and so forth. But with variables we must develop another way. With Fortran, we have two options, *implicit* or *explicit* typing.

The variables in Example 2.16 were *implicitly* defined, which means that each was assigned to a data type based on the <u>first letter</u> of the variable name and the following rules:

Variable names that begin with the letters A—H or O—Z are <u>real</u>.
Variable names that begin with the letters I—N are <u>integer</u>.

EXAMPLE 2.18

Here are some examples of implicit typing:

Variable	Type	Variable	Type
R	Real	CIRCUM	Real
PI	Real	LENGTH	Integer
AREA	Real	ICOUNT	Integer

Explicit Data Typing

Implicit typing rules make it easy to determine whether variables will be real or integer. But these rules do not apply to complex, character or logical variables. To use these types, you must use *explicit* typing rules. Explicit typing is simply the procedure of specifying how to treat each variable. These rules are also used if you want to override the implicit typing for integers and reals.

To declare a variable to be a specific type, enter the type followed by a list of the variables to be so treated, with each variable separated by a comma. This *declaration statement* <u>must</u> come before any executable statement (i.e., one where some sort of processing takes place). There may be several declaration statements at the beginning of the program, and their form is:

$$\text{TYPE} :: \textit{variable1, variable2, } \ldots$$

EXAMPLE 2.19

Here are some examples of explicit typing:

Declaration Statement	Result
REAL :: X, Y, Z	*Declares X, Y, and Z as real variables*
REAL :: LENGTH	*Defines LENGTH as a real variable*
INTEGER :: COUNT	*Defines COUNT as an integer variable*
COMPLEX :: PHASE	*Defines PHASE as a complex variable*
LOGICAL :: YESNO	*Defines YESNO as a logical variable*
DOUBLE PRECISION :: X	*Defines X as a double precision variable*

EXAMPLE 2.20

The following is similar to Example 2.16, except that the variables are now explicitly declared:

```
PROGRAM AreaofCircle
! The following requests the user to type in a value
! of the radius and store it in the variable R
REAL :: R, PI, AREA, CIRCUM
PRINT *, 'Enter circle radius'
READ *, R
! Once the radius is read in, the area is calculated
PI = 3.1416
AREA = PI * R * R
CIRCUM = 2 * PI * R
! The value of the area is now printed out
PRINT *, 'Area of circle is ', AREA
PRINT *, 'Circumference of circle is ', CIRCUM
END
```

When we want to declare a variable as a character variable, we need to specify the length of the variable in addition to its type. This is done with the following command:

CHARACTER (LEN=*length*) :: *variable1, variable2, . . . , variablen*

EXAMPLE 2.21

Here are some examples of declaration of character variables:

Declaration Statement	Result
CHARACTER (LEN=20) :: GRADE	*Defines GRADE as character of length 20*
CHARACTER :: GRADE*20, NAME*10	*Alternate way of defining GRADE with length 20 and NAME with length 10*

Recall that Fortran 90 supports various KINDs of data types. We can also include this statement in the declaration statement by adding the KIND statement after the data type.

EXAMPLE 2.22

Here are some examples of explicit typing in Fortran 90 where we identify the KIND parameter for each:

Declaration Statement	Result
REAL (KIND=4) :: X, Y	*X and Y are real variables of KIND=4*
INTEGER (1) :: AMTDUE	*Short form to indicate KIND=1*
CHARACTER (KIND=1) :: N	*If LEN is omitted, its assumed value is 1; thus, N is of KIND=1 and LEN=1*
CHARACTER (LEN=20, KIND=1) :: X	*X is a character variable of length 20 and KIND=1*
CHARACTER (20, 1) :: X	*Short form where LEN comes first, KIND second; therefore, this is the same as the previous example*
CHARACTER (20) :: X	*If KIND is omitted, then the machine assumes a default type; for characters, this is KIND=1*

EXAMPLE 2.23

You may also use the function SELECTED_INT_KIND and SELECTED_REAL_KIND with the declaration statements to force the computer to select the appropriate KIND for the desired accuracy and magnitude. For example, the declaration statement

```
INTEGER (KIND = SELECTED_INT_KIND(9)) :: B
```

will determine the KIND that will best allow the variable B to be stored with 9 significant digits. In a similar way, we can set up real variables to fit into one of the KINDs set up by the compiler that you are using. With real variables however, we must worry about both the *precision* and *range*. The precision is the number of significant digits to be saved, while the range is the magnitude of the number. Thus, for real variables we can use the following type of declaration statement:

```
REAL (KIND = SELECTED_REAL_KIND(9, 123)) :: C
```

The first number (9) inside the inner set of parentheses indicates that 9 digits of accuracy are desired, while the second number (123) indicates that the variable C may be as large as 10^{+123} or as small as 10^{-123}.

Named Constants

Named constants provide a safeguard against accidentally overwriting a value. For example, the variable C might be used to store the value of the speed of light in a vacuum (a constant). While modifying your program, you might forget that C has been defined to store this constant and you might assign a new value to C. To prevent this from happening, named constants or PARAMETERs are used. Named constants can never appear on the left-hand side of an assignment statement such as C=2. Doing so will result in a syntax error.

EXAMPLE 2.24

The following program segment assigns values to the variables C and PI that cannot be changed accidentally:

```
REAL ::  C, PI
PARAMETER ( C = 3.0E8, PI = 3.1416 )
```

While Fortran 90 supports the PARAMETER statement, a more concise means of declaring named constants is offered. This method combines both the declaration and the PARAMETER statements. Here is the same program segment, but now we combine both statements to coincide with the simplified Fortran 90 declaration statement:

```
REAL, PARAMETER :: C = 3.0E8, PI = 3.1416
```

Simple Input and Output

Most programs require the user to enter data into the program, and once calculations have been performed, the results must be sent to some sort of display device such as a CRT screen. These two functions are known as *input* and *output*, or collectively as I/O. We have already seen examples of I/O in Example 2.20. For the purpose of this section, only free formatted output (also called list directed) will be presented, and we will assume that all I/O will be at the terminal screen.

To input a value to a variable, we use the READ statement with the general form:

READ *, *variable1, variable2, . . .*

To display the value of a variable or variables on the terminal screen, we use the PRINT statement, whose general form is:

PRINT *, *variable1, variable2, . . .*

Character constants can be included in the output list of the PRINT command by placing the string to be printed inside apostrophes.

EXAMPLE 2.25

The following example reads in a person's name and age in years. It then converts the age from years into months:

```
PROGRAM Ageinmonths
! The declaration statement must come first
CHARACTER (LEN=10) :: NAME
REAL :: AGEYRS, AGEMTH
! Here is where we input the person's name and age
PRINT *, 'Enter your name and your age in years'
READ *, NAME, AGEYRS
! Now we convert the age from years into months
AGEMTH = AGEYRS * 12
! Print out the results
PRINT *, NAME, ' is approximately ', AGEMTH, ' months old'
END
```

This is how the input and output would appear on the CRT screen:

Enter your name and your age in years	*(Prompt from line #6)*
'Martin C.', 32	*(Entered by user; note apostrophes)*
Martin C. is approximately 384.000 months old	*(Printed by computer from line #11)*

When the data are entered, commas must be used to separate them and any character data must be enclosed inside apostrophes. Thus, the character data (MartinC.) was entered as 'MartinC.' and was separated from the numeric data by a comma.

Note that in the output produced by the computer, any unused characters in NAME are given blank spaces. For example, when the name was entered, it contained only 9 characters. So, when the computer prints out the name, there is an extra space that has not been filled. In such cases, the computer will pad the variable with blank spaces.

2.5 ASSIGNMENT STATEMENTS, EXPRESSIONS, AND HIERARCHY OF OPERATIONS

The *assignment statement* is the primary means of storing data in variables. We have seen a number of simple examples of assignment statements in the "AreaofCircle" program (Example 2.2) and the "Ageinmonths" program (Example 2.25). As the name assignment statement implies, we are telling the computer to assign a value to a given variable. The way to visualize this is as follows:

Target ◄ Value from an expression

The interpretation of this statement is "The target receives a value obtained from the expression." The way this is implemented in Fortran is:

Variable = Value from an expression

The expression on the right-hand side (RHS) of the equal sign can be one of several types as discussed below.

EXAMPLE 2.26

In the table below are several examples of assignment statements involving constants, variables, and mathematical operators:

Expression	Type of Expression
PAY = 5.12	*Constant assigned to the variable pay*
TAXES = CALC	*The value of the variable CALC assigned to TAXES*
PAY = GROSS – NET + 5.00	*Value of the numerical expression assigned to PAY*
X = SQRT(Y)	*Function used to evaluate the square root of Y ($\sqrt{Y}$)*

In each of these examples, something happens on the right-hand side to determine what value goes to the left-hand side. This is an important difference between an algebraic equation and an assignment statement. You must keep in mind that assignment statements are not equations to be solved. Instead, the right-hand side is evaluated first and the answer is then assigned to the variable on the left-hand side.

EXAMPLE 2.27

In a conventional algebraic equation such as:

$$x = 1 - x$$

we could solve for x very easily and obtain:

$$x = 1/2$$

But, the same line (X = 1.0 − X) in a Fortran program has a very different meaning. It is not an equation to be solved. Rather, it is an expression to be evaluated followed by an assignment of the result to a specific variable. For example, consider the following lines of code and try to predict the final value of X:

```
X = 1.0
X = 1.0 - X
PRINT *, X
```

When the first command (X=1.0) executes, the real variable X receives a value 1.0. When the second line (X=1.0 − X) executes, the expression evaluates as 1.0 − (1.0), since the old value of X is retrieved and substituted into the expression. The result, which is 0.0, is placed into the variable X, which now has the value 0.0. This process of following the logic of a program is known as *tracing*. It is a useful device, especially when you are attempting to debug a program. To aid in tracing a program, you should create a table of all the variables in the program. Whenever a variable is assigned a value, this value is entered into the table. Also, whenever a value is required, the last value entered into the table is used.

EXAMPLE 2.28

Trace through the following program segment and predict its output:

```
X = 1.0
Y = 2.0
Z = 3.0
X = -X
PRINT *, 'Value of X is: ', X
Y = Y - 1.0
PRINT *, 'Value of Y is: ', Y
Z = Z + X
Z = Z + X - Y
PRINT *, 'Value of Z is: ', Z
```

The variable table would look like this after performing the trace:

X:	1.000000	− 1.000000	
Y:	2.000000	1.000000	
Z:	3.000000	2.000000	0.000000

Note that the values of X and Y were changed once during the program after the initial assignment, but that Z changed value twice. So after execution, here is the final output where real values are printed with seven significant digits:

```
Value of X is:    -1.00000
Value of Y is:     1.00000
Value of Z is:     0.00000
```

Lines 1, 2, and 3 are constant assignment statements. They initialize the variables X, Y, and Z to the values 1.0, 2.0, and 3.0, respectively. Line 4 tells the computer to take the current value of X (which is 1.0) and change its sign. The value is placed back into X. X is now -1.0. Line 6 states to take the current value of Y and subtract 1.0 from it, or $2.0 - 1.0 = 1.0$. That value is placed back into Y. Y is now 1.0. Line 8 states to take Z + X and place that value back into Z, or $3.0 + (-1.0) = 2.0$. Z is now 2.0. Line 9 states to calculate Z + X − Y and place the result back into Z, or $2.0 + (-1.0) - 1.0 = 0$. Finally, Z is assigned the value 0.0. Note that during these evaluations the right-hand side is processed first, and then the answer is placed into the variable on the left-hand side.

Expressions and Hierarchy of Operations

All of the examples of expressions have been simple ones. They've consisted simply of multiplication, addition, or subtraction. There are only five basic arithmetic operations possible with Fortran. They are addition, subtraction, multiplication, division, and exponentiation, as presented in the following table:

Priority	Algebraic Symbol	Fortran Symbol	Meaning
1	(.....)	(.....)	Parentheses
2	A^b	**	Exponentiation
3	×	*	Multiplication
3	÷	/	Division
4	+	+	Addition
4	−	−	Subtraction

When you create mathematical expressions, it must be entered on a single line. While algebra permits the use of multiple line expressions, Fortran requires you to place the expression on a single line. Thus for example, to write the expression (x divided by y) in Fortran, we would write X/Y.

For all of the operators with equivalent position within the hierarchy (except **), evaluation is from left to right. For example 8.0/2.0*4.0 gives 16.0, since the division is done first and then the multiplication. For exponentiation however, the direction is from right to left. Thus, 2**3**4 is evaluated as 2**(3**4) or 2**81.

EXAMPLE 2.29

Here is how you might write a mathematical expression in algebra:

$$y = \frac{a + 2b + c}{d}$$

but in Fortran, this is how we would write the same expression:

$$Y = (A+2.0*B+C)/D$$

There are several key points that you should notice in this simple example:

- *Implied* operations are not allowed in Fortran. In algebra, we know that 2B means 2 multiplied by B. But, in Fortran, you must explicitly write out the implied multiplication as 2.0*B.
- Everything is written on one line. In algebra, the numerator is written above the denominator, as a fraction. But in Fortran, we place the numerator and the denominator on the same line and separate them with a slash (/) to indicate division.

In algebra it is understood that you perform the multiplication (2B) before any addition. Thus, in the expression A + 2B + C, 2B is evaluated first and then added to A and C since mathematical operations have a well-defined hierarchy. This is true also for Fortran as summarized in the preceding table.

EXAMPLE 2.30

Based on the hierarchy of mathematical operations, evaluate the following expression:

$$9.2 - (2.0**3 - 14.0 / 7.0) + 14.0 * 0.1$$

1. First priority is ( ), so evaluate the expression inside the parentheses (2.0**3 − 14.0 / 7.0)
2. Next in the hierarchy is exponentiation. Thus, the expression inside the ( ) is evaluated by performing the exponentiation first, which gives (8.0 − 14.0 / 7.0).
3. The next priority is the division, resulting in (8.0 − 2.0).
4. Finally, perform the subtraction (6.0).
5. Return to the original expression where the expression becomes 9.2 − 6.0 + 14.0 * 0.1.
6. Next is multiplication and the expression becomes 9.2 − 6.0 + 1.4.
7. Finally, addition and subtraction have the same priority. Therefore, they are evaluated left to right, which gives 3.2 + 1.4 = 4.6.

EXAMPLE 2.31

When two exponentiation operations appear together, they are evaluated right to left:

$$2**3**2 \quad\longrightarrow\quad 2**9 \quad\longrightarrow\quad 512$$

EXAMPLE 2.32

For the examples below, we supply the answer. Trace through each and make sure you get the same result:

Expression	Value	Comments
2.0 − 4.0 − 2.0	− 4.0	*Left to right*
2.0 − (4.0 − 2.0)	0.0	*Evaluate expression within ( ) first*
2.0 + 4.0 * 2.0	10.0	*Multiplication first*
2.0 / 4.0 / 2.0	0.25	*Left to right*
2.0 ** 4.0 * 2.0	32.0	*Exponentiation first*
2.0 ** (4.0 * 2.0)	256.0	*Expression within ( ) first*

In the preceding examples, we have been careful to make all the constants and variables real. This was done because there are special rules that govern integer arithmetic. Also, when you try to mix real and integer data types, complications may arise as illustrated in the following section.

2.6 INTEGER AND MIXED-MODE ARITHMETIC

When performing arithmetic with real numbers, the results match what you would normally expect. However, when performing calculations with integers or a mixture of integers and real numbers, different results may be obtained.

The two operations that are affected by data type are division and exponentiation. Division of two integers results in an integer value. This value is equal to the real number result with the decimal portion deleted.

EXAMPLE 2.33

The result can be very different if we do mathematics with real numbers and integers. Note in the following example that the integer division produces an unexpected result:

Using reals: 3.0 / 2.0 = 1.5   *(Note that 3.0 and 2.0 are real as is 1.5)*
Using integers: 3 / 2   = 1   *(Not 1.5! Note that 3 and 2 are integers as is 1)*

In the second example above, both 3 and 2 were integers because we did not use decimal points. Therefore, when the computer does the division, it will give an integer result. This is obtained by *truncating* any noninteger remainder.

You must be careful when using integer arithmetic, since unintended results can creep into your program. So be careful! But sometimes this effect is desired, as shown in the next example.

EXAMPLE 2.34

The following program makes change in terms of dollars, quarters, dimes, nickels, and pennies by making use of integer division:

```
INTEGER :: CENTS, DOLLAR, QUARTR, NICKEL, DIME, PENNY
PRINT *, ' Enter value in cents '
READ *, CENTS
!
!     Whole dollar part is the integer division of CENTS by 100
!
DOLLAR = CENTS / 100
!
!     What is left is the remaining change in CENTS
!
CENTS = CENTS - DOLLAR * 100
!
!     Repeat this process for QUARTR, DIME, NICKEL and PENNY
!
QUARTR = CENTS / 25
CENTS = CENTS - QUARTR * 25
DIME = CENTS / 10
CENTS = CENTS - DIME * 10
NICKEL = CENTS / 5
PENNY = CENTS - NICKEL * 5
!
! Print out the results
!
PRINT *, 'Dollars: ', DOLLAR
PRINT *, 'Quarters: ', QUARTR
PRINT *, 'Dimes: ', DIME
PRINT *, 'Nickels: ', NICKEL
PRINT *, 'Pennies: ',PENNY
END
```

Sample Output (input value = 78 cents)	
Dollars:	0
Quarters:	3
Dimes:	0
Nickels:	0
Pennies:	3

We took advantage of integer arithmetic in this example to give us the desired results. For example, if the change to be returned were 78 cents, the division of 78 by 25 (the amount in a quarter) would return exactly 3 (not 3 plus a remainder). Thus, the program would say to return 3 quarters. In a similar way, the number of dimes, nickels, and pennies are determined.

The second area where the results will depend on whether you use reals or integers is exponentiation. Under certain circumstances, an error will occur depending on the choice of variable type. This is because the method of performing the calculation is different depending on whether the exponent is integer or real.

In the case where the exponent is an integer, the value is determined by successive multiplications. But when the exponent is a real number, Fortran will use logarithms to calculate the desired value. This may cause the computer to take the logarithm of a negative number, which produces an error.

EXAMPLE 2.35

Try to use integer values for exponents. Otherwise, Fortran will use logarithmic functions to calculate the result.

2**6 is calculated as 2*2*2*2*2*2 = 64

but

2**6.0 is calculated as $Log^{-1}(6*Log(2))$ = 64.0

The result is the same, but there *may* be a problem, as shown below:

(−2)**3 is calculated as −2*−2*−2 = −8

but

(−2)**3.0 is calculated as $Log^{-1}(3.0*Log(-2))$ =　　　E R R O R o n s o m e compilers since log of a negative number is not defined.

In situations where integer and real numbers are mixed during division, the integer value is converted to a real number and the result is the expected value. These rules for integer and mixed-type division are applied on an operator by operator basis.

EXAMPLE 2.36

Evaluate the following mixed-mode arithmetic expression:

J = 2.3 * (3 / 2) − 5

First evaluate 3 / 2:

3 / 2 = 1　　　　　　　　*(Fraction is truncated because both numbers are integers)*

Next perform multiplication. An integer times a real yields a real number.

J = 2.3*(1) − 5 = 2.3 − 5.0 = − 2.7

Finally perform the subtraction. A real minus an integer yields a real.

J = −2.7 = −2　　　　*(Fraction is truncated because J is an integer)*

There may also be a problem if data of different KINDs are mixed together. In Fortran 90 the rules for real and integer mathematics are the same as those just described. However, the computer will also convert the result to the most accurate number of the different KINDs used.

EXAMPLE 2.37

Assume that REAL (KIND=1) is standard precision, REAL (KIND=2) is double precision, INTEGER (KIND=1) is standard integer, and INTEGER (KIND=2) is an extended or long integer. Then the following results will occur when we mix different KINDs:

Expression	Result	Comments
10_1*20_2	200_2	*Convert to most precise integer*
10_2*3.0_1	30.0_1	*Integer times a real results in a real*
2.0_2*3.0*1	6.0_2	*Convert to most precise real*

2.7 SELECTED LIBRARY FUNCTIONS

Fortran functions behave like the definitions for mathematical functions such as square root, sine, and so forth. You use a function by placing its name (followed by a list of its arguments inside parentheses) in an expression. You must take great care to match the type, number and order of arguments required for the function. The table below summarizes the most common mathematical functions that you are likely to use.

Name	Description	Arguments	Result	Example
ABS(X)	absolute value	integer	integer	J = ABS(−51)
		real	real	X = ABS(−17.3)
		double	double	Z = ABS(−0.1D04)
ACOS(X)	arccosine	real	real (rad)	X = ACOS(0.5)
		double	double (rad)	Z = ACOS(0.5D0)
ASIN(X)	arcsine	real	real (rad)	X = ASIN(0.5)
		double	double (rad)	Z = ASIN(0.5D0)
ATAN(X)	arctangent	real	real (rad)	X = ATAN(1.0)
		double	double (rad)	Z = ATAN(1.0D0)

(Table continues on next page)

Name	Description	Arguments	Result	Example	
COS(X)	cosine	real (rad)	real	X	= COS(1.04712)
		double	double	Z	= COS(1.04712D0)
COSH(X)	hyperbolic cosine	real	real	Y	= COSH(2.000)
DBLE(X)	converts to double	integer	double	Z	= DBLE(3)
		real	double	Z	= DBLE(3.0)
DPROD(X,Y)	double precision product of X and Y	real	real	A	= DPROD(2.0, 3.0)
EXP(X)	exponential, e^x	real	real	X	= EXP(1.0)
		double	double	Z	= EXP(1.0D0)
INT(X)	truncates to integer	real	integer	J	= INT(3.9999)
		double	integer	J	= INT(0.3999D01)
FLOAT(I)	converts to real	integer	real	X	= FLOAT(4)
		double	real	X	= FLOAT(0.4D01)
LOG(X)	natural logarithm	real	real	X	= LOG(2.71828)
		double	double	Z	= LOG(0.2718D01)
LOG10(X)	logarithm base 10	real	real	X	= LOG10(10.0)
		double	double	Z	= LOG10(0.1D0)
MAX(...)	returns largest value	integer	integer	I	= MAX(5,1,6,2)
		real	real	X	= MAX(0.2,5.6)
		double	double	Z	= MAX(1D0,3D3)
MIN(...)	returns smallest value	integer	integer	I	= MIN(4,3,−4)
		real	real	X	= MIN(0.2,5.6)
		double	double	Z	= MIN(1D0,3D3)
MOD(I,J)	remainder of I/J	integer	integer	J	= MOD(29,4)
NINT(X)	round to nearest integer	real	integer	J	= NINT(3.99)
		double	integer	J	= NINT(0.6D01)
SIN(X)	sine	real (rad)	real	X	= SIN(0.5202)

(*Table continues on next page*)

Name	Description	Arguments	Result	Example
SINH(X)	hyperbolic sine	real	real	Y = SINH(2.0)
SQRT(X)	square root	real double	real double	X = SQRT(17.6) Z = SQRT(0.17D2)
TAN(X)	tangent	real (rad) double	real double	X = TAN(0.785) Z = TAN(0.785D0)
TANH(X)	hyperbolic tangent	real	real	Y = TANH(2.0)

Be careful when using the trigonometric functions, since they require angles measured in radians (rad), not degrees. Similarly, the inverse trigonometric functions will report the results in radians.

EXAMPLE 2.38

The following program reads in two points (x_1, y_1) and (x_2, y_2) and calculates the distance between them with the formula $d = \sqrt{(x_1 - x_2)^2 + (y_1 - y_2)^2}$.

```
!Distance Between Two Points (X1,Y1) and (X2,Y2)
!
PRINT *, 'Enter X,Y location for first point'
READ *, X1, Y1
PRINT *, 'Enter X,Y location for second point'
READ *, X2, Y2
DIST = SQRT ( ( X2 - X1 ) ** 2 + ( Y2 - Y1 ) ** 2 )
PRINT *, 'Distance between the points is ', DIST
END
```

Once the values have been entered, they are used in the equation to determine the distance d. Note that we have used the Fortran function SQRT to perform this calculation. This is how the program input and output would look on the CRT screen:

Enter X,Y location for first point	*(Prompt for first data point)*
1.0, 3.0	*(First data point entered by user)*
Enter X,Y location for second point	*(Prompt for second data point)*
4.0, 5.0	*(Second data point entered by user)*
Distance between the points is 3.60555	*(Result printed by computer)*

It is permissible to place a call to one function within a call to another. In fact, many times common sense and defensive programming practices will require it. For example, if you are going to take the square root of a number, you may have to make sure that the number is positive before you can attempt the square root. Otherwise, you may be asking the computer to perform an illegal operation.

EXAMPLE 2.39

Here is the program of Example 2.38 that has been modified to take the absolute value of a number before attempting to take the square root of a number:

```
! Distance Between Two Points (X1,Y1) and (X2,Y2)
!
PRINT *, 'Enter X,Y location for first point'
READ *, X1, Y1
PRINT *, 'Enter X,Y location for second point'
READ *, X2, Y2
DIST=SQRT(ABS((X2-X1)**2 + (Y2-Y1)**2))
PRINT *, 'Distance between the points is ', DIST
END
```

In this situation, it made no difference that we added the ABS function, since the argument $(x_1-x_2)^2+(y_1-y_2)^2$ is positive (or zero). But there are occasions when this might be needed.

The second type of Fortran 90 intrinsic functions that you will find useful are those that are able to work with the KIND parameter. Of course, the functions listed above are still valid, but some of them have options to take into account the fact that Fortran 90 now supports KIND.

In the table below are listed functions that support the KIND option. The arguments to the functions will be written as (X, K), where X is the number passed to the function and K is its KIND. The exception to this convention is the DBLE function, where KIND usually is not used. Several of the following examples were shown before, but we now repeat them to demonstrate how to use them with the KIND option:

Name	Description	Arguments	Result	Example
CHAR(I,K)	returns character in position I of the ASCII sequence	integer	character	A =CHAR(36)
CMPLX(X,Y,K)	converts (X,Y) to complex type	real, kind	complex	X =CMPLX(3.0, 4.0, 4)
DBLE(X)	converts to double precision	integer real complex	double double double	X =DBLE(3) Y =DBLE(3.0_4) U =DBLE((3.041, 4.0_4))

(Table continues on next page)

Name	Description	Arguments	Result	Example
INT(X,K)	converts to integer	real	integer	J = INT(3.9999)
		real, kind	integer	J = INT(3.99,2)
		double	integer	J = INT(0.399D1)
		complex	integer	J = INT((3.0_4,4.0))
NINT(X, K)	round to nearest integer	real	integer	J = NINT(3.9999)
		real, kind	integer	J = NINT(3.9999, 4)
				J = NINT(3.9999_4)
REAL(I, K)	convert to real	integer	real	X =REAL(3)
		integer	real, kind	X =REAL(3, 4)
		complex	real, kind	X =REAL((3.,4.), 4)

EXAMPLE 2.40

The following program reads in two real values and converts them into a complex number where X is the real part and Y is the imaginary part:

```
! Program to create a complex number from the real
! part X and the imaginary part Y
COMPLEX :: Z
PRINT *, 'Enter Real part of complex number'
READ *, X
PRINT *, 'Enter Imaginary part of complex number'
READ *, Y
Z = CMPLX ( X, Y )
PRINT *, Z
END
```

The next group of Fortran 90 functions are those that operate on simple data types. These generally are simple mathematical functions or *inquiry* functions. Inquiry functions are those that return useful information about a number, such as its KIND (for all data types) or its length (for nonnumeric data). Generally, these functions will only accept arguments that are simple data structures, such as variables that contain a single number. Data that include a group of numbers (called arrays) will be considered separately.

Name	Description	Arguments	Result	Example
AIMAG(Z)	returns imaginary part of a complex	complex, kind	real, kind	X = AIMAG((3.0, 4.0))

Name	Description	Arguments	Result	Example
AINT(X, K)	truncates to a whole number	real, kind	real, kind	X = AINT(3.999) X = AINT(3.999_4)
ANINT(X, K)	rounds to nearest whole number	real, kind	real, kind	X = ANINT(3.999) X = ANINT(3.499_4)
KIND(X)	indicates KIND value for X	any	integer	I = KIND(1.0_4)
LEN(C)	indicates length of a character string	character	integer	I = LEN('abcde')

EXAMPLE 2.41

The following program reads in a real value and rounds it to the nearest whole number and prints the result.

```
! We first read in the value into the variable INPUT
REAL :: INPUT, NEAREST_WHOLE_NUMBER
PRINT*, 'Enter an integer value:'
READ*, INPUT
! Now we use the ANINT function to round off the number
NEAREST_WHOLE_NUMBER = ANINT(INPUT)
PRINT*, 'The nearest whole number is:', NEAREST_WHOLE_NUMBER
END
```

The third group of useful intrinsic functions are those that operate on arrays. Arrays, as we will learn in a later chapter, are a more complex form of data, in which a large group of numbers are stored as part of a single variable. You may have already had experience with arrays in the form of vectors and matrices. Recall, for example, that a force vector F in physics has three components representing the force quantities along each axis. Yet, you refer to the group of three components by a single variable name F. In a similar way, a matrix is a common way to represent a two-dimensional table of data. Other common forms of arrays that you are likely to encounter are lists and tables of data. In effect, arrays provide a simplified method of manipulating large groups of data with only a few programming instructions.

If you are not familiar with these concepts, skip over this section until we have discussed the concept of arrays. You can come back to this section later.

In the table below, only a few of the more common array intrinsic functions are presented and no values are given due to space limitations. These will be covered in some detail in the examples and exercises in later chapters of this book.

Name	Description	Arguments	Result	Example
DOT_PRODUCT(X, Y)				
	dot product of X and Y	real, kind integer, kind complex, kind	real, kind integer, kind complex, kind	A = DOT_PRODUCT(X,Y)
MATMUL(X, Y)	multiplies matrices	real, kind integer, kind complex, kind	real, kind integer, kind complex, kind	A = MATMUL(X, Y)
MAXLOC(X)	locates position of maximum value of an array	real, kind integer, kind complex, kind	integer integer integer	I = MAXLOC(X)
MAXVAL(X)	returns largest value in an array	real, kind integer, kind complex, kind	real, kind integer, kind complex, kind	A = MAXVAL(X)
MINLOC(X)	returns position of minimum value in an array	real, kind integer, kind complex, kind	integer integer integer	I = MINLOC(X)
MINVAL(X)	returns smallest value in an array	real, kind integer, kind complex, kind	real, kind integer, kind complex, kind	A = MINVAL(X)
SUM(X)	sums elements of an array	real, kind integer, kind complex, kind	real, kind integer, kind complex, kind	A = SUM(X)
TRANSPOSE(X)	transposes an array	real, kind integer, kind complex, kind	real, kind integer, kind complex, kind	Y = TRANSPOSE(X)

EXAMPLE 2.42

If the vector A = [1.0, 2.0, 3.0] and the vector B = [2.0, 4.0, 6.0], then the following program segment determines the *dot product* of A and B. The dot product is the sum of the products of the components of the two vectors = 1.0*2.0 + 2.0*4.0 + 3.0*6.0 = 28.0. We omit the code necessary to declare the arrays A and B:

```
        :
X = DOT_PRODUCT ( A, B )
PRINT *, X
        :
```

EXAMPLE 2.43

Assume that the matrices A and B given below are already stored in a program. This is how we would multiply the two matrices and generate the transpose of each:

$$A = \begin{bmatrix} 1.0 & 2.0 & 3.0 \\ 4.0 & 5.0 & 6.0 \end{bmatrix} \quad Transpose(A) = \begin{bmatrix} 1.0 & 4.0 \\ 2.0 & 5.0 \\ 3.0 & 6.0 \end{bmatrix}$$

$$B = \begin{bmatrix} 1.0 & 2.0 \\ 3.0 & 4.0 \\ 5.0 & 6.0 \end{bmatrix} \quad Transpose(B) = \begin{bmatrix} 1.0 & 3.0 & 5.0 \\ 2.0 & 4.0 & 6.0 \end{bmatrix}$$

$$Product(AB) = \begin{bmatrix} 22.0 & 49.0 \\ 28.0 & 64.0 \end{bmatrix}$$

The program segment to accomplish these operations is as follows:

```
        :
D = TRANSPOSE ( A )      ! Transpose of A put into D
E = TRANSPOSE ( B )      ! Transpose of B put into E
F = MATMUL ( A, B )      ! A and B multiplied together with result
        :                ! put into F
```

Once this program segment is executed, D will be an array containing the transpose(A), E will be an array containing transpose(B), and the array F will contain the product of A times B.

The fourth and final group of Fortran 90 procedures that you may find of use are called subroutines. These are used differently from the functions discussed so far, and we will have more to say about this in a later chapter. There are two such subroutines that you may find useful at this point. Others are available but you will use these subroutines only infrequently.

Name	Description	Result	Example
RANDOM_NUMBER(X)	returns a random number (0.0≤X<0)	Real	CALL RANDOM_NUMBER(X)
RANDOM_SEED	initializes random number generator		CALL RANDOM_SEED

Subroutines are used in a different way from the functions described before. As you will see in the example below, we use a CALL statement to summon the subroutine to perform the desired function. There will be much more said about CALL statements and subroutines in later chapters.

EXAMPLE 2.44

This code will cause the random number generator to be initialized (or restarted if it has already been started). Once the generator is initialized, the program then makes a call to the subroutine. The value that is returned will be a positive number less than 1.0:

```
    ⋮
    CALL RANDOM_SEED            !Initializes generator
    CALL RANDOM_NUMBER ( X )    !Put random number (<1.0) into X
    PRINT *, X                  !Print out the result
    ⋮
```

If you wanted to produce random numbers outside the range 0.0 to 1.0, you could still use the RANDOM_NUMBER subroutine by multiplying the result by the desired range. For example, if you wanted the random number to be between 0.0 and 100.0, all you need to is multiply the result X from the subroutine by 100.0. In the example given, the PRINT statement would look like this:

```
    ⋮
    PRINT *, 100.0*X            !Prints out value between 0.0 and 100.0
    ⋮
```

2.8 DEBUGGING TIPS

Debugging is the process of removing errors from your program. For the types of programs presented in this chapter, two error types are most likely to occur: improper use of integer/mixed-mode arithmetic and simple typographical errors.

You may also have programs that contain *run-time* and *logic* errors. Run-time errors are those that occur while the program is running, and can usually be traced to illegal mathematical operations such as the logarithm of a negative number. Logic errors are those where the program executes to completion, but gives you the wrong answer. You simply gave the computer a wrong series of instructions to execute. Both of these types of errors are best solved by tracing.

Typographical errors (typos) occur when you accidentally mistype the name of a variable or command. Since Fortran utilizes implicit typing, new variables can be created when you make a simple typo error. You can detect such mistakes by:

- Including the statement IMPLICIT NONE at the beginning of your program to turn off the usual rules for implicit data typing.
- Declaring all the variables that you intend to use in the program by explicit typing.

By disabling the implicit typing feature, variables that are not declared will result in a syntax error. This is one way of locating variables created by "typos."

EXAMPLE 2.45

Here is an example of how to use the IMPLICIT NONE statement to help locate typographical errors. Note that if we turn off the implicit typing feature by using the IMPLICIT NONE statement, we will then have to declare _every_ variable with the explicit typing.

```
! The IMPLICIT NONE statement is placed first in the program.
! We must then explicitly name all the variables in type
! declaration statements
IMPLICIT NONE
REAL :: X1, Y1, X2, Y2, LENGTH
READ *, X1, Y1, X2, Y2
LENGHT=SQRT((X2-X1)**2 + (Y2-Y1)**2)
PRINT *, 'Length is ', LENGTH
END
```

On line 7 LENGTH is misspelt as LENGHT. Because implicit typing is turned off, the compiler will generate an error due to an undeclared variable. If the IMPLICIT NONE statement is omitted, the computer would accept both spellings as different variables and will report no error.

Errors due to mixed-mode arithmetic can often be located by adding PRINT statements before and after each expression. Before an expression, print out the variables being used in the calculation. After an expression, print the result. Trace the program and see if the values being printed out at each step of the program agree with what you expect.

EXAMPLE 2.46

This program always returns the result "Length is 1.000000," no matter what values are entered. Find the error.

```
IMPLICIT NONE
REAL :: X1, Y1, X2, Y2, LENGTH
READ *, X1, Y1, X2, Y2
PRINT *, X2, X1, Y2, Y1                    ! Added print statement
LENGTH=((X2-X1)**2 + (Y2-Y1)**2)**(1/2)
PRINT *, 'Length is ', LENGTH              ! Added print statement
END
```

We have added PRINT statements _before_ and _after_ the calculation of LENGTH. The computer will always report "LENGTH=1.000000," but when you trace through by hand you should get a different result. By adding the PRINT statements, we find that the program line that calculates LENGTH is in error. The problem is the improper use of integer arithmetic in the exponentiation (** (1/2)). Because 1/2 involves integer division, the result is 0. This problem can be fixed by simply adding decimal points, producing (**(1./2.)).

Solved Problems

2.1   The following illustrate literal constants. Some are valid, while other are invalid. Where appropriate, indicate the default data type (Real, Integer, etc).

a)	1.00	*(Real)*
b)	123	*(Integer)*
c)	+8	*(Integer)*
d)	13 7/8	*(Invalid: Fraction is not allowed)*
e)	$78.24	*(Invalid: $ is not allowed)*
f)	−0.123E7.1	*(Invalid: Exponent must be an integer)*
g)	'She''s happy'	*(Character – She's happy)*
h)	(1.2, 3.4)	*(Complex)*
i)	1,234	*(Invalid: commas are not allowed.)*
j)	.False	*(Invalid: must have trailing "." to be logical)*
k)	"Again"	*(Character)*
l)	'abcde'_2	*(Invalid: KIND must precede string)*
m)	1_2	*(Integer (KIND=2))*

2.2   Here are examples of valid and invalid variables. Provide reasons for any invalid examples.

a)	X	*(Valid)*
b)	Height	*(Valid)*
c)	R P M	*(Invalid: Spaces not allowed)*
d)	1station	*(Invalid: 1st character must be a letter)*
e)	.TEST	*(Invalid: "." not allowed)*

2.3   Using implicit data typing, determine the data type of each of the following variables.

a)	X	*(Real)*
b)	Volume	*(Real — note that lower case letters are OK)*
c)	KOUNT	*(Integer)*
d)	nDia	*(Integer — mixing cases OK)*

2.4   Using explicit data typing, determine the data type of each of the following variables.

a)	REAL :: X, Y, Z	*(Valid, defines three real variables)*
b)	INTEGER :: COUNT	*(Valid, defines one integer variable)*
c)	CHARACTER :: NAME*20	*(Valid, defines one 20–character variable)*
d)	LOGICAL :: OK	*(Valid, defines one logical variable)*
e)	DOUBLE PRECISION :: VOL	*(Valid, defines one double precision variable)*

2.5　Which of the following assignment statements are valid?

　　a)　X = 3.1416*R^2　　　　　　　　(Invalid — "^" is not a valid operator)
　　b)　X1 = 3.0*Area　　　　　　　　(Valid)
　　c)　X = SQRT(ABS(X1−X2)**2)　　(Valid — OK to embed functions)
　　d)　SQRT((X1−X2)**2) = Y　　　　(Invalid — variable must be on left side)

2.6　The following examples illustrate the hierarchy of operations. The results of each operation are assigned 1st, 2nd, 3rd, etc. Those results are then used in the subsequent operations:

　　a)　ROOT = (A + 2 * B + C) / D
　　　　→ 1st　= 2 * B
　　　　→ 2nd　= A + 1st
　　　　→ 3rd　= 2nd + C
　　　　→ 4th　= 3rd / D
　　b)　X1 = (−B + (B * B − 4 * A * C) ** 0.5) / (2 * A)
　　　　→ 1st　= B * B
　　　　→ 2nd　= 4 * A
　　　　→ 3rd　= 2nd * C
　　　　→ 4th　= 1st - 3rd
　　　　→ 5th　= 4th ** 0.5
　　　　→ 6th　= −B + 5th
　　　　→ 7th　= 2 * A
　　　　→ 8th　= 6th / 7th
　　c)　A = 0.5 * B * H + H ** 2
　　　　→ 1st　= H ** 2
　　　　→ 2nd　= 0.5 * B
　　　　→ 3rd　= 2nd * H
　　　　→ 4th　= 3rd + 1st
　　d)　R = SQRT (3 * T ** 2 + (M * G) ** 2)
　　　　→ 1st　= M * G
　　　　→ 2nd　= T ** 2
　　　　→ 3rd　= 1st ** 2
　　　　→ 4th　= 3 * 2nd
　　　　→ 5th　= 4th + 3rd
　　　　→ 6th　= SQRT (5th)

2.7　The following examples illustrate how to evaluate expressions with mixed-mode arithmetic.

　　a)　10 * 3.0 + 10 / 3
　　　　→ 1st　= 10 * 3.0　= 30.0000　　(Integer times a real yields a real)
　　　　→ 2nd　= 10 / 3　　= 3　　　　(Since both numbers are integers, the
　　　　　　　　　　　　　　　　　　　　result is an integer or 3 by truncation)
　　　　→ 3rd　= 30.0 + 3　= 33.0000　　(Real plus an integer yields a real)

b)   4 ** (1 / 2.)
     → 1st   = 1 / 2.   = 0.50000   (*Result remains real*)
     → 2nd   = 4 ** 0.5 = 2.00000   (*Result is real since types are mixed*)

c)   (−5) ** 3.
     → ERROR   (*Raising to a real power is the same as*
                                                log⁻¹(3*log(−5)); it is not possible to take
                                                the log of a negative number, so an error
                                                occurs)

d)   10 − 10 / 3 * 3
     → 1st   = 10 / 3   = 3   (*Simple division of two integers*)
     → 2nd   = 1st * 3   = 9   (*No mixed mode*)
     → 3rd   = 10 − 2nd = 1   (*No mixed mode*)

2.8   The following examples illustrate the process of tracing a program.

a)   Assume an input of 100.0, 45.0

```
REAL, PARAMETER :: PI = 3.1416
PRINT *, 'Enter Velocity (ft/sec) and Elevation (deg)'
READ *, V, THETA
THETA = THETA * PI / 180.0
VX = V * COS ( THETA )
VY = V * SIN ( THETA )
PRINT *, 'X-component of velocity is ', VX ,' ft/sec'
PRINT *, 'Y-component of velocity is ', VY ,' ft/sec'
END
```

TRACE TABLE: OUTPUT:

V: 100.000   X-component of velocity is 70.7110 ft/sec
THETA: 45.0000, 0.785400   Y-component of velocity is 70.7110 ft/sec
VX: 70.7110
VY: 70.7110

b)   Assume an input of 10.0, 20.0, 30.0

```
REAL :: N1, N2, N3, X
READ *, N1, N2, N3
X = 0.0
X = X + N1
X = X + N2
X = X + N3
PRINT *, 'Value of X is: ', X
END
```

TRACE TABLE: OUTPUT:

X	0.00000, 10.00000, 30.00000, 60.00000	Value of X is 60.000
N1	10.0000	
N2	20.0000	
N3	30.0000	

c) Assume an input of 12.5

```
INTEGER :: FEET, INCHES
PRINT *, 'Enter distance in feet'
READ *, DIST
FEET = DIST
INCHES = ( DIST - FEET ) * 12 + 0.5
PRINT *, 'Distance is ', FEET, 'feet and ', INCHES, ' inches'
END
```

TRACE TABLE: OUTPUT:

DIST: 12.5000   Distance is 12 feet and 6 inches
FEET: 12
INCHES: 6

2.9 Convert the following mathematical expressions into Fortran code (assume all variables are real):

a) $2\,a\,b$ $\rightarrow$ 2.0 * A * B
b) $(a+3b)c$ $\rightarrow$ (A + 3.0 * B) * C
c) $(a+3b)(c+d)$ $\rightarrow$ (A + 3.0 * B) * (C + D)
d) $a^2 - 3ab + 4b^2$ $\rightarrow$ A ** 2 − 3.0 * A * B + 4.0 * B ** 2
e) $\dfrac{a-b}{c+4d}$ $\rightarrow$ (A − B) / (C + 4.0 * D)
f) $\dfrac{(a-b)^2}{(c+4d)^3}$ $\rightarrow$ (A − B) ** 2 / (C + 4.0 * D) ** 3

2.10 Convert the following mathematical expressions into valid Fortran code:

a) $|ab|$ $\rightarrow$ ABS (A * B)
b) $\sin^{-1}(3\pi x)$ $\rightarrow$ ASIN (3.0 * 3.14159 * X)
c) $\sqrt{|ab|}$ $\rightarrow$ SQRT (ABS (A * B))
d) $e^{|2a|}\tan(b)$ $\rightarrow$ EXP (ABS (2.0 * A)) * TAN (B)
e) $(e^{|2a|})^3$ $\rightarrow$ EXP (ABS (2.0 * A)) ** 3

Supplementary Problems

2.11 Which of the following are valid and invalid examples of literal constants? For the invalid examples provide the reasons why they are invalid. For the valid example indicate the constant type.

a) 3.1415927 b) −987 c) +9. d) 123 456 789

e) 1E10 f) 0D0 g) 'This is a test' h) 'he said, "hi"'

i) "She's happy" j) (1, 3) k) (7.8,9D4) l) 2_'abc'

m) .TRUE. n) .True._1

2.12 For each variable name indicate whether the variable name is valid or invalid.

a) Amt Due b) Amt_Due c) TotalVolume d) TIME

e) Circumference

2.13 Indicate the implicit data type based on the variable name.

a) LENGTH b) COUNT c) JOINT d) VOL

e) Imax

2.14 Indicate whether the following declaration statements are valid. For invalid declaration statements describe why they are invalid.

a) REAL :: X Y Z b) CHARACTER :: NAME

c) CHARACTER*20 :: FIRST d) CHARACTER(10) :: A, B (KIND=1)

e) LOGICAL (KIND=1) :: YESNO f) REAL(KIND=SELECTED_REAL_KIND(9,99))X

2.15 Indicate which of the following are valid assignment statements. For those statements that are invalid, provide the reason.

a) Y + 2 = X b) Dist := Y2 − Y1 c) NUM = NUM + 1

2.16 Illustrate the operator hierarchy by listing the results of each operation. The results of each operation are to be indicated as 1st, 2nd, 3rd, etc.

a) Dist = SQRT((X1 − X2) ** 2 + (Y1 − Y2) ** 2)

b) A = X ** Y ** Z + 10

c) D = 1 / (4 * N) * (M * G + T * (D + H) / B)

d) P = 2 * F * E / (C * (1 − A / B))

2.17 Evaluate the following arithmetic expressions.

   a) 4 ** (1 / 2)
   b) (−5) ** 3
   c) 10 / (1.0 * 3) − 10 / 3
   d) AREA = 1 / 2 * B * H

2.18 Trace the following programs and predict their output.

   a) Assume 1.0, 2.0, 3.0 for the 1st input request and 4.0, 5.0, 6.0 for the second request.

```
READ *, X1, Y1, Z1
READ *, X2, Y2, Z2
X3 = X1 + X2
Y3 = Y1 + Y2
Z3 = Z1 + Z2
PRINT *, 'Sum of two vectors is ', X3, Y3, Z3
END
```

   b) Assume an input of 1.0, 1.0, 1.0, 2.0, 3.0, 4.0

```
PRINT *, 'Enter two 3 component vectors'
READ *, X1, Y1, Z1, X2, Y2, Z2
ANS = 0
ANS = X1 * X2 + ANS
ANS = Y1 * Y2 + ANS
ANS = Z1 * Z2 + ANS
PRINT *, 'The answer is ', ANS
END
```

   c) Assume an input of 1.0, 1.0, 1.0, 2.0, 3.0, 4.0

```
READ *, X1, Y1, Z1, X2, Y2, Z2
X3 = Y1 * Z2 - Y2 * Z1
Y3 = Z1 * X2 - Z2 * X1
Z3 = X1 * Y2 - X2 * Y1
PRINT *, 'The Answer is ', X3, Y3, Z3
END
```

   d) Assume an input of 0.0, 0.0, 0.0, 100.0, 50.0, 25.0

```
PRINT *, 'Enter Position 1 (x,y,z) and Position 2 (x,y,z):'
READ *, X1, Y1, Z1, X2, Y2, Z2
DIST = SQRT((X1-X2)**2 + (Y1-Y2)**2 + (Z1-Z2)**2)
XM = ( X1 + X2 ) / 2.0
YM = ( Y1 + Y2 ) / 2.0
ZM = ( Z1 + Z2 ) / 2.0
PRINT *, 'Distance between points ', DIST
PRINT *, 'Midpoint location ', XM, YM, ZM
END
```

2.19 Create a program to solve each of the following problems.

a) There are 5280 feet in a mile. Write a program to read in a distance in miles and return the equivalent number of feet.

b) There are 25.4 millimeters/inch. Write a program that reads in a distance given in feet and inches and converts the distance to millimeters.

c) The equation to convert degrees F to degrees C is C=5/9*(F−32). Write a program to request temperature in degrees C and return the temperature in degrees F.

d) There are 4 quarts to a gallon, 2 pints to a quart, and 16 fluid ounces to a pint. Write a program which will read in a decimal value for gallons and return gallons, quarts, pints and ounces. For example 5.5 gallons is 5 gallons 2 quarts, 0 pints and 0 ounces. HINT: refer to the make change example (Example 2.34) in this chapter.

2.20 Convert the following mathematical expressions into valid Fortran code. Do not use any of the library functions.

a) $\dfrac{a}{b} - \dfrac{c}{d}$　　　　b) $\dfrac{a}{b-c}$　　　　c) $\dfrac{m_0}{[1-(v/c)^2]^{1/2}}$

d) $\dfrac{a}{bc}$　　　　e) $\sqrt{\sqrt{\dfrac{a-b}{c+4d}}}$

2.21 Convert the following mathematical expressions into valid Fortran code:

a) $e^b \tan^3(a)$　　　　b) $\dfrac{a^{c-1}}{\ln(b)}$　　　　c) $\tan^{-1}\sqrt{\sin^2|a|}$

Answers to Selected Supplementary Problems

2.11 a) Real b) Integer
　　　c) Real d) Invalid – blank spaces not permitted
　　　e) Real f) Double precision
　　　g) Character h) Character
　　　i) Character j) Valid
　　　k) Valid – Components need not match in precision
　　　l) Character of KIND=2 m) Logical
　　　n) Logical constant of KIND=1

2.12 a) Invalid – no spaces allowed b) Valid – underscore (_) allowed
　　　c) Valid d) Valid
　　　e) Valid – up to 31 characters allowed

2.13 a) Integer b) Real
c) Integer d) Real
e) Integer

2.14 a) Invalid – no spaces allowed b) Valid (assumes LEN=1)
c) Valid (LEN=20) d) Invalid – KIND parameter in wrong place
e) Valid f) Invalid – left out ::

2.15 a) Invalid: target must be a variable b) Invalid: Assignment operator is "="
c) Valid

2.16 a) 1st=X1 − X2; 2nd=Y1 − Y2; 3rd=1st ** 2; 4th=2nd ** 2; 5th=3rd + 4th;
6th=SQRT(5th).
b) 1st=Y ** Z; 2nd=X ** 1st; 3rd=2nd + 10.
c) 1st=4 * N; 2nd=D + H; 3rd=M * G; 4th=T * 1st; 5th=4th / B; 6th=3rd + 5th;
7th=1 / 2nd; 8th=7th * 6th.
d) 1st=A / B; 2nd=1 − 1st; 3rd=C * 2nd; 4th=2 * F; 5th=4th * E; 6th=5th / 3rd.

2.17 a) 1st=1 / 2 = 0 since both are integers.
2nd=4 ** 0 = 1 since integer raised to integer is an integer.
b) 1st=(−5) ** 3 = −125 integer exponentiation evaluated by repeated multiplication
(−5)*(−5)*(−5).
c) 1st=1.0 * 3 = 3.0 mixed multiplication converted to real numbers.
2nd=10 / 1st = 3.33333... integer value of 10 converted to real 10.0.
3rd=10 / 3 = 3 integer result due to both numbers being integers.
4th=2nd - 3rd = 3.33333 − 3 = 0.33333.
d) 1st=1 / 2 = 0 integer division will result in any remainder being dropped.
All remaining operations will result in a zero result.

2.18 a) X1: 1.00000 Y1: 2.00000 Z1: 3.00000 X2: 4.00000
Y2: 5.00000 Z2: 6.00000 X3: 5.00000 Y3: 7.00000
Z3: 9.00000
Output: Sum of two vectors is 5.00000 7.00000 9.00000
b) X1: 1.00000 Y1: 1.00000 Z1: 1.00000 X2: 2.00000
Y2: 3.00000 Z2: 4.00000
Output: The answer is 9.00000
c) X1: 1.00000 Y1: 1.00000 Z1: 1.00000 X2: 2.00000
Y2: 3.00000 Z2: 4.00000
X3: (1.00000*4.00000−3.00000*1.00000)=1.00000
Y3: (1.00000*2.00000−4.00000*1.00000)=−2.00000
Z3: (1.00000*3.00000−2.00000*1.00000)=1.00000
Output: The Answer is 1.00000 −2.00000 1.00000

d) X1: 0.00000   Y1: 0.00000   Z1: 0.00000   X2: 100.000
    Y2: 50.0000   Z2: 25.0000   XM: 50.0000   YM: 25.0000
    ZM: 12.5000   DIST: 114.564
    Output: Distance between points 114.564; Midpoint location 50.0000 25.0000 12.5000

2.20 a) A/B−C/D   b) A/(B−C)
c) M0/(1.0−(V/C)**2)**0.5   d) A/(B*C) *or* A/B/C
e) ((A−B)/(C+4.0*D))**0.25

2.21 a) EXP(B)*TAN(A)**3   b) (A**(C−1)/LOG(B))
c) ATAN(SQRT(SIN(ABS(A))**2))

Chapter 3

Input and Output

3.1 LIST-DIRECTED INPUT AND OUTPUT

The easiest way to input or output data from a program is via the so-called *list-directed* statements. In these types of statements we are not concerned about the appearance of the data, but rather about *what* we input or output. The general form of the list-directed input statement is:

READ *, *variable1, variable2, . . .*

and for output, the corresponding statement is:

PRINT *, *variable1, variable2, . . .*

The star (*) which appears in each of these statements indicates that we are using *free format*. Free format means that the computer will use a set of predetermined instructions to read or print data. For example, the machine will figure out how many decimal places to print, how many blank spaces to leave between each number, and so forth. Your only concern is to provide the proper information about what to print out or read in. In the next sections, we will replace the star with a series of specific instructions that will give us some control over the appearance of the data.

The list that follows the star in the READ or PRINT statements is called the *I/O list* and indicates what variables are to be used for either input or output. It also contains additional information that we will discuss shortly. In the case of such *list-directed I/O*, the computer will control all aspects of the output appearance.

EXAMPLE 3.1

To illustrate how list-directed I/O works, consider the following statement:

```
READ *, X, Y, Z
```

This will cause the first three numbers that you type in to be assigned to the corresponding variables. A typical input by you might look like this:

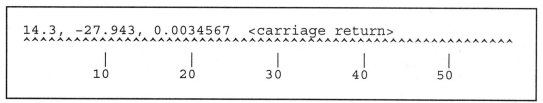

Reading the three data values is equivalent to the three assignment statements:

```
X = 14.3
Y = -27.943
Z = 0.0034567
```

In the example just described, we have shown what an input line might look like. For convenience, we have numbered all the columns, since spacing will be of great concern to us. In practice, this column spacing is not present on the CRT screen, but we have shown it for convenience. Note that each number is separated by a comma (technically known as a *delimiter*). Also note that the line is completed with the <carriage return> (or <CR> for short). No data values are entered until you press the carriage return key.

One advantage of the READ statement over the equivalent assignment statements is that you do not need to rewrite the program to enter a different set of data. All you need to rerun the program with different data is merely enter the new data with the same READ statement.

EXAMPLE 3.2

The PRINT command shown below will send the value of each variable to the CRT screen. For example, if we enter the data values given above, we can print them out using the following program segment:

```
READ *, X, Y, Z
PRINT *, X, Y, Z
```

The computer will print out the same values that you typed in:

```
14.3, -27.943, 0.0034567  <CR>                    (what you type in)
14.30000  -27.94300  0.003456700  (printout on CRT screen)
^^^^^^^^^^^^^^^^^^^^^^^^^^^^^^^^^^^^^^^^^^^^^^^^^^^^^^^^^^^^^^^^^
        |              |              |              |              |
        10             20             30             40             50
```

There are a few things to note in this example. First, the computer will use its own rules about printing out the results. These will vary from one compiler to another. The real numbers, for example, were printed here in decimal notation, but with another compiler they might be printed in scientific (exponential) notation. The second point to note is that the numbers were printed out with seven significant digits, even though none of the numbers that we typed in had this many digits of accuracy. This occurs because the computer internally stores real numbers with seven or eight digits of accuracy. Thus, the output will contain all seven digits even if the numbers were not entered this way.

The PRINT statement can also contain character strings in the output list. If you enclose a string inside apostrophes, the string will be printed out as written. Finally, you may include mathematical expressions in the list of items to be printed.

EXAMPLE 3.3

Here is an example of enhancing a PRINT statement with strings to describe the output data:

```
X = 2.4
PRINT *,'X = ', X,'X ** 2 = ', X*X
```

This will produce the following output on the screen:

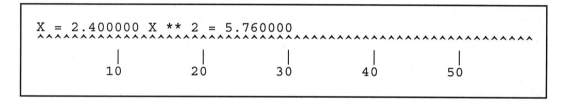

Once again seven digits of accuracy appear in the output. Note that the only time spaces appear in any formatted output is when we have included them <u>inside</u> the apostrophes.

With these simple tools, you can produce an organized printout of your data. However, since you are restricted by the internal rules of the compiler, you have little flexibility in the output appearance. Despite this, free formatting and list-directed I/O are useful for getting quick answers. To improve the appearance of the output, you will need formatted I/O.

3.2 THE FORMAT STATEMENT

Formatting provides a degree of control over the appearance of output that the simple list-directed commands do not. With formatting, you can make the output more attractive and more readable.

Formatting instructions can be used only with an input or output commands, which we often call an *I/O FORMAT pair*. Without the matching input or output commands, the FORMAT statement is useless. In general, the input pair will have the following structure:

> READ *sl* , *variable1* , *variable2* , . . .
> *sl*   FORMAT (*list of instructions*)

In a similar way, the output pair will look like this:

> PRINT *sl* , *variable1* , *variable2* , . . .
> *sl*   FORMAT (*list of instructions*)

The difference between the simple list-directed I/O and the formatted I/O is that the "*" has been replaced with a label number, which points to a FORMAT statement. The statement label (*sl*) in front of the FORMAT statement must go in columns one to six, and the statement itself begins after the label.

For output, the list of instructions that follows the FORMAT statement is composed of a carriage control character (output only) and a list of *edit descriptors*. The carriage control character resets a printer (if used), and the edit descriptor specifies the output instructions for each output item. Among the things that we can specify are

- Type of variable and number of significant digits
- Column in which to start printing
- Floating point or exponential form (real numbers only)
- Number of blank spaces and blank lines
- Any text to be included

There are specific rules for controlling each of these functions. Note that when you give up free formatting and take control yourself, there are a number of things that you will have to handle yourself. The computer will no longer do these things for you.

The general form of a FORMAT statement is

sl   FORMAT (*CCC, specifier1, specifier2, . . . , specifierN*)

where   sl   = statement label (integer up to five digits).
         CCC   = carriage control character.
         specifier   = instruction for individual variable.

The carriage control character CCC is always the first item inside the parentheses and is only present when formatting <u>output</u>. Its purpose is to reset a printer by moving the printing head to column 1. Sometimes you will not need the CCC (for example, with some compilers when you are printing to a CRT screen), in which case it can be omitted.

There are four different CCC characters to handle the printer reset:

Character	Description of Function
' '	Single vertical spacing
'0'	Double vertical spacing
'1'	New page
'+'	No advance; reset to beginning of <u>current</u> line

The most common carriage control character is the one for single spacing (' '), while the last CCC ('+') is used rarely for printing special characters by overstriking (e.g., you can create the $\neq$ character by printing '/' over '='). Do not forget to include the carriage control character in your output FORMAT statements when sending output to a printer. Failure to do so may cause a "runaway printer." Ask your instructor for local rules for any required CCC characters.

3.3 EDIT DESCRIPTORS

Edit descriptors provide detailed information on how data values are to be printed or read. For now, we will deal only with output, since formatted input is rarely used. Input can be handled in a similar way, and we will delay any discussion of formatted input until the exercise section.

Format specifiers fall into two main categories. The first category contains the rules for controlling numerical and character data, while the second controls spacing functions. Summarized below are the edit descriptors used for printing numerical and alphanumerical data.

Category	Descriptor	Function	Form	Example
Numerical data	I	Integer	Iw	I5
	F	Real	F$w.d$	F6.2
	E	Real (exponential)	E$w.d$	E12.4
	D	Double precision	D$w.d$	D20.8
	G	Real (general): switches between F and E format	G$w.d$	G8.2
Character data	A	Character variable	Aw	A20
	' '	Character strings	'xxx'	'Example'

When we wish to print out data, whether real, integer, or double precision, we usually have two primary concerns. These are the total number of spaces and the total number of significant digits to be displayed. The general form of a data edit descriptor is

$$\text{TYPE } width \ (.decimals)$$

where TYPE   = a letter (I, F, E, G, D, or A) indicating the data type to be printed.
      width   = total width of space desired.
      decimals = total number of decimal places (not used for integers or characters).

The second set of format specifiers are those which control the physical layout, such as spacing (both vertical and horizontal), tab stops, and alignment in column format. These are summarized in the following table:

Category	Descriptor	Function	Form	Example
Spacing	X	Skip r spaces	rX	5X
	T	Tab to column c	Tc	T20
	TR	Tab right s spaces	TRs	TR3
	TL	Tab left s spaces	TLs	TL5
	/	New line	/	/
Repeat	r( )	Reuse specifiers in ( )	r( )	2(F6.2,I3)

In these tables, the symbols have the following meanings:

c = column number.
s = number of spaces to move (left or right).
r = repeat factor, which is optional.

One of the key things to note when using formatted output is that the edit descriptor must match the type of data that you are printing. For example, if you are printing a real number, you can use only the F$w.d$, E$w.d$, or G$w.d$ descriptors. Similarly, you may use only the Iw descriptors for printing integers.

Edit Descriptor for Integer Values

When we print out integers, our only concern is that we leave enough space in the printed line for all the digits and the sign. We do not need to worry about the number of decimal places since integers can only be whole numbers. Therefore, the form of the specifier becomes:

$$I\,w$$

where I indicates an integer number and w indicates the total amount of reserved space.

EXAMPLE 3.4

To illustrate the use of the Iw edit descriptor, consider the following example:

```
       ICOUNT = 237
       JCOUNT = -14
       PRINT 33, ICOUNT, JCOUNT
33     FORMAT(' ', I6, I9)
```

In this example, the first descriptor inside the FORMAT statement is the CCC giving the command to start a new line. In the I/O list, the variable ICOUNT is the first variable and therefore will be printed with the first edit descriptor inside the FORMAT statement, which is I6. The second variable in the list, JCOUNT, will be printed with the second descriptor, I9. Thus, the output page will look like this:

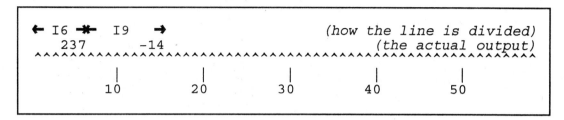

The descriptor I6 tells the computer to reserve six spaces for the numerical value of ICOUNT. Similarly, the descriptor I9 reserves 9 spaces for JCOUNT. When the computer fills in these reserved spaces with the numerical values, the values are *right-justified*. This means that the printer places them as far to the right as possible within the field reserved for the number. If the number is smaller than the space reserved for it, the printer will leave extra blank spaces. If however, the number is too large for the reserved space, the printer fills the field with asterisks (*) as in the next example.

EXAMPLE 3.5

In this example the edit descriptor does not allow sufficient space to print out the data:

```
        ICOUNT = 12345
        JCOUNT = -98765
        PRINT 98, ICOUNT, JCOUNT
98      FORMAT(' ', I5, I5)
```

This will result in the following output:

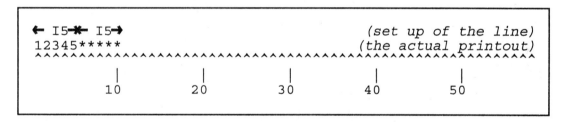

This may appear to be a strange result until you realize that a minus sign takes up one column in the output line. Thus, the variable JCOUNT, which is equal to -98765, requires 6 columns for printing. However, the FORMAT descriptor I5 allots only 5 columns, resulting in an overflow condition to occur. In such a case, you must enlarge the field width. In this example, we would increase the edit descriptor to at least I6.

Edit Descriptors for Real Values

When we wish to print out real data, we need to worry about both the total number of spaces (w) and the number of decimal places (d). Thus, when we use the form Fw.d, w must be at least three larger than d to allow for the decimal point, the leading negative sign (for negative numbers), and a leading zero (for numbers less than 1.0).

EXAMPLE 3.6

Here is an example of how to use the F edit descriptor:

```
          DIST  = 12.345
          TIME  = 0.00345
          VELOC = DIST/TIME
          PRINT 5, DIST, TIME, VELOC
   5      FORMAT(' ', F7.2, F9.6, F10.1)
```

will produce the following output:

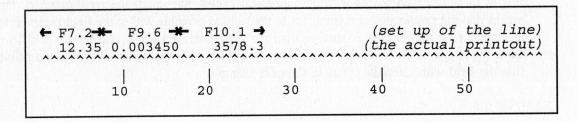

If you study the output for a moment, you will see that the computer has rounded off the value for DIST to fit into the allotted space. The same thing has happened to VELOC (which should be 3578.2608), which retains only 1 decimal place. The variable TIME, on the other hand, has had a trailing zero added to it before printing to fill out the allotted space.

We can also express real numbers in scientific notation as we discussed in Chapter 2. The general form for printing a real number in this exponential format is:

$$E\ w.d$$

where E = indicates exponential format (mantissa $\times 10^n$).
      w = total width of field reserved for number.
      d = desired number of decimal places for mantissa.

As with the F format, the E format has a special rule about how many additional spaces must be reserved. Besides the number of significant digits of the mantissa, the E format requires a total of 7 additional spaces. Thus, the rule for the E$w.d$ format is:

$$w \geq d + 7$$

EXAMPLE 3.7

To demonstrate the exponential format, let's revise Example 3.6 to use the E format:

```
          DIST  = 12.345
          TIME  = 0.00345
          VELOC = DIST/TIME
          PRINT 5, DIST, TIME, VELOC
   5      FORMAT(' ', E12.4, E14.6, F10.1)
```

This will produce the following output:

```
←    E12.4   ⁕      E14.6   ⁕  F10.1 →          (set up of line)
  0.1235E+02  0.345000E-02     3578.3   (the actual output)
^^^^^^^^^^^^^^^^^^^^^^^^^^^^^^^^^^^^^^^^^^^^^^^^^^^^^^^^^^^^^^^^^
       |          |          |          |          |
      10         20         30         40         50
```

Numbers will be rounded or zeros will be added if required to fit into a field. Also, numerical data will be *right justified* within the field so that any unused spaces in front of the number will be blank. Finally, note that the + sign for the mantissa or the exponent may or may not be printed, depending on the compiler. If either the mantissa or exponent is negative, however, the printout will include the appropriate minus sign.

We print out double precision numbers with a format very similar to that for exponential notation:

$$D \ w.d$$

where D = indicates double precision format (e.g., 0.123D+003).
      w = total width of field reserved for number.
      d = desired number of decimal places for mantissa.

The difference between E and D formats is that the exponent for double precision can be larger than that for single precision. Therefore, you must allow for a three-digit exponent with the D format compared to two digits for E format. Thus, the rule for the D format becomes:

$$w \geq d + 8$$

Otherwise, the D format is identical to the E format.

EXAMPLE 3.8

To demonstrate the double precision format, let's revise Example 3.7 to use the D format:

```
       DOUBLE PRECISION :: DIST, TIME, VELOC
       DIST  = 12.345
       TIME  = 0.00345
       VELOC = DIST/TIME
       PRINT 5, DIST, TIME, VELOC
5      FORMAT(' ', D12.4, D11.3, D10.1)
```

will produce the following output:

```
←    D12.4   ⁕    D11.3   ⁕   D10.1 →          (set up of line)
  0.1235D+002 0.345D-002  0.4D+004       (the actual output)
^^^^^^^^^^^^^^^^^^^^^^^^^^^^^^^^^^^^^^^^^^^^^^^^^^^^^^^^^^^^^^^^
       |          |          |          |          |
      10         20         30         40         50
```

Another format used with real numbers is the *general purpose* format G with the form:

$$G\ w.d$$

where   G = indicates general purpose format.
         w = total width of field reserved for number.
         d = desired number of significant digits.

The G format combines both the floating point and exponential formats into a single instruction. With the G format, the computer selects the format automatically by using either a modified F descriptor or an E$w.d$ descriptor. The computer has a specific rule to decide which format to choose based on the value of the exponent of the number. If the exponent is between 0 and d, the computer uses the modified F format and prints the number with d <u>significant digits</u> followed by 4 additional blank spaces. Otherwise, the number will be printed with the E$w.d$ format.

EXAMPLE 3.9

To see how the G$w.d$ format works, examine the following examples:

Value	G Format	Output
0.010000	G11.3	~ ~0.100E−01
0.100000	G11.3	~ ~0.100~ ~ ~ ~
1.000000	G11.3	~ ~ ~1.00~ ~ ~ ~
10.00000	G11.3	~ ~ ~10.0~ ~ ~ ~
100.0000	G11.3	~ ~ ~100.~ ~ ~ ~ ~
1000.000	G11.3	~ ~0.100E+04

(Note: ~ = blank space)

In the first example, the number 0.01 (or 0.1×10^{-1}) has an exponent of -1. Since this lies outside the range of $0 \le$ exponent ≤ 3, the computer selects the E11.3 format. The next four examples have exponents between 0 and 3. Thus, the computer prints them with the modified F format. Notice that these four examples are printed with 3 significant digits, which in one case requires four digits. Finally, the last number (1000.0 or 0.1×10^4) places the exponent outside the range of 0 to 3. Thus, it reverts to the E format.

Edit Descriptors for Character Values

We format character variables in a way similar to that for integers; the only thing we need to worry about is the total number of spaces. The form of the alphanumeric edit descriptor is:

$$A\ w$$

where   A = indicates character format.

        w = total width of field reserved for character output.

Recall that characters can be of any length. This distinguishes them from numerical data, which have a constant length (7 significant digits for reals for instance). Thus, when we declared character variables in the previous chapter, we had to specify the anticipated length. In a similar way, we must tell the computer how many spaces to reserve for character data.

EXAMPLE 3.10

Consider the following simple example:

```
        CHARACTER :: NAME*20
        NAME = 'martin cwiakala'
        PRINT 19, NAME
19      FORMAT(' ', A20)
```

This produces the following output:

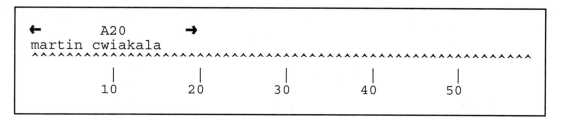

The only thing unusual about this line is that the character value is *left-justified* within its field, which means that the printer begins printing at the far left. Any extra spaces will appear after the printed value. By contrast, numerical data values are *right-justified*.

Character data are also different from numerical data in that it is not possible to overflow a field with characters. Recall that if the field is too small for numerical data, a string of asterisks appears. But if the field is too small for character data, the extra characters are truncated.

EXAMPLE 3.11

Here is what happens when the character data and the edit descriptor are mismatched:

Character Variable	Format	Output
BOSTON RED SOX	A1	B
BOSTON RED SOX	A10	BOSTON RED
BOSTON RED SOX	A20	BOSTON RED SOX ~ ~ ~ ~ ~ ~
BOSTON RED SOX	A	BOSTON RED SOX

In the last example, we have used an *option* that is available in many versions of Fortran. The simple specifier A without any indication of the field width will automatically allocate just the right number of spaces for that variable. Note that there are no extra leading or trailing blank spaces in the last example given.

Character output varies from system to system. So be sure to check your local manuals to see how the computer reads and prints characters. Among the things to check are whether the *default* format specifier A is allowed and if your compiler distinguishes between upper and lower case. Also, check to see that character data are left justified.

Edit Descriptors for Strings and Control

In addition to the edit descriptors to control the appearance of the data, you may also include *strings* and *spacing control*. Strings are lines of text that you can add to improve the readability of the output. The spacing control allows you to spread out the data horizontally or vertically on one or several lines to improve the readability.

In previous examples, we saw that you can print out a character string by placing it inside apostrophes inside the PRINT statement:

```
PRINT *, 'PLEASE ENTER X , Y , Z :'
```

To get the same effect with a FORMAT statement, you may move the character string inside the parentheses as a descriptor.

EXAMPLE 3.12

Strings which are placed inside apostrophes in the FORMAT statement are printed intact:

```
        PRINT 21
21      FORMAT(' ', 'PLEASE ENTER X, Y, Z:')
```

This will result in the following output:

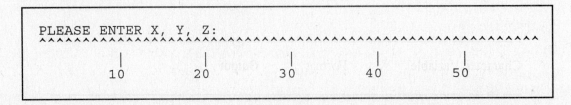

For this simple example, moving the string inside the FORMAT statement is no improvement over the list directed example. However, by combining strings with numerical data, we can improve comprehension.

```
            X = 12.34
            Y = -0.025
            PRINT 34, X, Y, X*Y
  34        FORMAT(' ','X = ',F7.2,' Y = ',F7.3, ' PROD = ',F10.5)
```

will produce the following output:

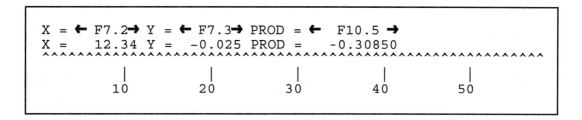

Let's examine the descriptors within the FORMAT statement a little more carefully. We reproduce each below with a brief explanation of its meaning:

' '	Carriage control character – begin new line
'X = '	Character string – print X =
F7.2	Floating point format – print out first number as XXXX.XX
' Y = '	Character string – print Y =
F7.3	Floating point format – print out second number as XXX.XXX
' PROD = '	Character string – print PROD =
F10.5	Floating point format – print out third number as XXXX.XXXXX

You should carefully match these descriptions with the printer output. Note that a blank space inside the apostrophes produces a blank space in the output. Thus, ' Y = ' produces [blank]Y [blank]=[blank] on the output line.

It is possible to leave spaces between various items that appear on the printed line. This is done with the *n*X edit descriptor, where *n* represents the number of spaces desired before the next item is printed.

EXAMPLE 3.13

The following example demonstrates how to control the number of digits printed and the spacing between two numbers. Also, we have included strings inside the FORMAT statement.

```
            X = 1.234567
            Y = 9.876543
            PRINT 10, X, Y
  10        FORMAT(' ','Value of X= ',F8.3,3X,'Value of Y= ',F5.1)
```

To better understand the format specifiers, we should interpret each one separately:

' '	The carriage control character – start a new line in column 1;
'Value...'	Character string – just print out what is inside the apostrophes;
F8.3	Descriptor for controlling the printout of the first variable, X. F8.3 specifies a total of 8 columns with 3 decimal places;
3X	Skip 3 spaces;
'Value...'	Another string – do as above;
F5.1	Descriptor for printing the value of the second variable Y in 5 columns and 1 decimal place.

When the above program segment is executed, this is what would appear on the screen:

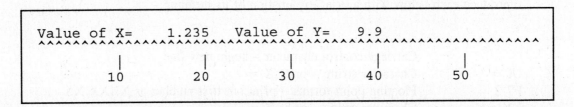

There are several additional format specifiers that are useful for spacing data output, aligning it into tables and improving the general appearance. Their only purpose is to determine the position for the next data value to be printed. There are three specifiers in this group:

Descriptor	General Form	Example	Function
X	nX	3X	Skip n spaces (3 spaces in the example)
/	/	/	Skip to next line
T	Tn	T32	Tab to column n (32 in this example) (Can move backward to column n)

These edit descriptors are different from the numeric descriptors since their only function is to control the positioning within a line.

EXAMPLE 3.14

The spacing edit descriptors are useful for improving the appearance of output as we show in the example below. Assume that BASE = 12.4, HEIGHT = 9.6 and VOL = 119.04.

```
          PRINT 9, BASE, HEIGHT, VOL
9         FORMAT(' ',5X,F9.3,/,3X,' X',T7,F9.3,/, &
          T6,'_____',/,T7,F9.3)
```

This will produce the following output:

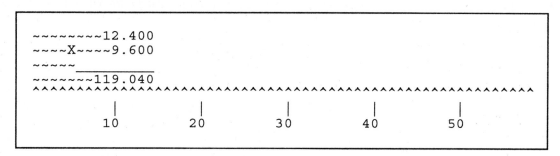

This may appear to be a complex example, but if you take the time to break down the descriptors one by one, you should be able to follow the process leading to the above printout. So follow the descriptions given below for each specifier:

' '	Carriage control character – begin new line　(line 1)
5X	Spacing command – skip 5 spaces on line 1 before printing the next data value.
F9.3	Floating point format – print out first number as XXXXX.XXX on the current line (1)
/	Spacing command – begin new line (line 2)
3X	Spacing command – skip 3 spaces on line 2 before printing the next data value.
' X'	Character string – print X preceded by a blank space (line 2)
T7	Spacing command – tab to column 7 (line 2)
F9.3	Floating point format – print out 2nd number as XXXXX.XXX on the current line (2)
/	Spacing command – begin new line (line 3)
T6	Spacing command – tab to column 6 (line 3)
'_____'	Character string – print _____ (line 3)
/	Spacing command – begin new line (line 4)
T7	Spacing command – tab to column 7 (line 4)
F9.3	Floating point format – print out 3rd number as XXXXX.XXX on the current line (4)

There are two additional forms of the T specifier that you may see occasionally. These forms tell the computer to move left or right a certain number of spaces from its current position. These instructions are:

TR*n*　(*move right n spaces from current position*)
TL*n*　(*move left n spaces from current position*)

Note that these two commands depend on the current position within a line, while the Tn command is independent of the line position. Be careful when using these commands since they can "overwrite" what has been printed before. Therefore, if you try to tab left on the CRT screen, anything which was previously written will be erased, and the new text will be written over the old text. Thus, on a CRT screen, the text seems to disappear. But on a hard-copy printer, the text will be underlined as intended. For this reason, you may wish to avoid the TR and TL edit descriptors.

There are many times when you need to reuse the same descriptor. A common situation is where all the data are of the same type and are to be printed out with the same format.

```
        PRINT 47, A, B, C, D, E, F, G, H
47      FORMAT(' ',F9.5,F9.5,F9.5,F9.5,F9.5,F9.5,F9.5,F9.5)
```

As you can see, all eight variables are to be printed with the same F9.5 format. Fortunately, Fortran offers a shortcut to avoid repetitious use of a descriptor. All you need to do is place the *repeat descriptor* in front of the edit descriptor to be repeated:

```
        PRINT 47, A, B, C, D, E, F, G, H
47      FORMAT(' ', 8F9.5)
```

This form of the repeat descriptor can be used with the I, F, E, D, G, and A formats. It cannot be used in this form with the / descriptor.

There is another form of the repeat descriptor where more complex combinations can be repeated. The repeat descriptor for complex instructions consists of an integer value representing the number of times something is to be repeated and a set of parentheses containing the repeat unit. Consider this example:

```
        PRINT 47, A, B, C, D, E
47      FORMAT(' ',F9.5,3X,F9.5,3X,F9.5,3X,F9.5,3X,F9.5)
```

Note that there is a unit consisting of (F9.5, 3X) which repeats 5 times. The idea introduced above (to place a repeat descriptor in front of the repeat unit) can also be used here. However, you must place the unit inside a set of inner parentheses:

```
        PRINT 47, A, B, C, D, E
47      FORMAT(' ', 5(F9.5, 3X))
```

There is a slight difference between these two format statements that you probably did not catch. Note that if you write out the unit (F9.5,3X) five times, the sequence will end in 3X. By comparison, the original format statement ended in F9.5. If you think about this, though, you will realize that the shortened form, 5(F9.5,3X), will leave 3 extra blank spaces at the end of the line. In many cases, this is not a problem and can be ignored. But if other things follow on the same line, then you must take these extra three spaces into account.

One exception to the above rules for the use of parentheses to specify a repeat descriptor is the '/' descriptor. The '/' mark indicates that you are finished with the current line and you want the next output value on the following line. If you wish to skip three lines however (the first terminates the current line), the following are equivalent:

$$/\,,\,/\,,\,/\,,\,/ \quad or \quad //// \quad or \quad 4(/)$$

EXAMPLE 3.15

Here are a few additional examples to show how the repeat descriptor works:

Original Format	Equivalent Format
F7.3, F7.3, F7.3	3F7.3
/ , / , / (*skip two lines*)	3(/) or ///
F7.3, I6, /, F7.3, I6, /	2(F7.3, I6, /)
F7.3, I6, 2X, I6, 2X, F7.3, I6, 2X, I6	2(F7.3, 2(I6, 2X))
F7.3, 2X, I6, F7.3, 2X, I6, F9.4, I4, F9.4, I4	2(F7.3, 2X, I6), 2(F9.4, I4)

Although FORMAT statements can be used with either READ or PRINT statements, they are usually used for controlling output. The reason is that if you use a FORMAT statement with a READ statement, the data must be entered exactly as spelled out in the FORMAT statement. If you type in too many or too few zeros or spaces, the data will be read incorrectly. Therefore, we recommend that you avoid formatted READ statements. The exception is when you want to read data from a data file, which we will discuss in Chapter 9. In some situations like this, you usually have no choice but to use a formatted READ statement. Remember, though, that when a FORMAT statement is used with a READ statement, there is no carriage control character. These are limited to output on a printer.

EXAMPLE 3.16

Examine the following program segment to see if you understand the appearance of the output (assume TEMP1 = 5.0, TEMP2 = 10.0, TEMP3 = 15.0, TEMP4 = 20.0, TEMP5 = 25.0, X1 = 12.400, X2 = 12.736, X3 = 13.055, X4 = 13.343, X5 = 13.587, EXPAN1 = 0.00, EXPAN2 = 2.710, EXPAN3 = 2.505, EXPAN4 = 2.206, EXPAN5 = 1.829):

```
        PRINT 23
        PRINT 19, TEMP1, X1 , EXPAN1
        PRINT 19, TEMP2, X2 , EXPAN2
        PRINT 19, TEMP3, X3 , EXPAN3
        PRINT 19, TEMP4, X4 , EXPAN4
        PRINT 19, TEMP5, X5 , EXPAN5
23      FORMAT(' ',T5,'TEMP (C)',T16,'LENGTH OF BAR (CM)', &
           T36,'EXPANSION (%)',TL44,9('_'),TR2,18('_'),  &
           TR2,13('_'))
19      FORMAT(' ', T5, F7.1, T15, F11.3, T35, F9.3)
```

Here's how each of the descriptors in the 23 FORMAT statement works:

' '	Carriage control character — begin new line (line 1)
T5	Spacing control — tab to column 5 (line 1)
'TEMP (C)'	Character string — print TEMP (C) (line 1)
T16	Spacing control — tab to column 16 (line 1)
'LENGTH ... '	Character string — print LENGTH OF BAR (CM) (line 1)
T36	Spacing command — tab to column 36 (line 1)
'EXPAN ...'	Character string — print EXPANSION (%) (line 1)
TL44	Spacing control — tab left 44 spaces (line 1)
9('_')	Repeat specifier — print character string "_" 9 times (line 1)
TR2	Spacing command — tab right 2 spaces (line 1)
18('_')	Repeat specifier — print character string "_" 18 times (line 1)
TR2	Spacing control — tab right 2 spaces (line 1)
13('_')	Repeat specifier — print character string "_" 13 times (line 1)

We will not discuss details of each of the specifiers within the 19 FORMAT statement since you should be able to do that for yourself by now. Here is what the printout looks like:

```
     TEMP  (C)    LENGTH OF BAR  (CM)     EXPANSION  (%)
        5.0          12.400                  0.000
       10.0          12.736                  2.710
       15.0          13.055                  2.505
       20.0          13.343                  2.206
       25.0          13.587                  1.829
   ^^^^^^^^^^^^^^^^^^^^^^^^^^^^^^^^^^^^^^^^^^^^^^^^^^^^^^^^^^^^^^

        |             |            |            |            |
        10            20           30           40           50
```

There are two things to note in this example. First, you may have a PRINT statement without an I/O list, such as PRINT 23. Second, you may refer to the same FORMAT statement as often as you need. Each time a PRINT statement references the FORMAT statement, the computer will simply reuse the edit descriptors from the beginning.

3.4 EMBEDDED FORMATTING

One of the key things that Fortran 90 attempts to do is to minimize or eliminate statement labels. This, of course, would include the statement labels associated with FORMAT statements. But in order to accomplish this goal, an alternative means for formatting is required. Actually, there are two methods:

- Method A: Include the format edit descriptors directly inside the I/O statements.
- Method B: Set a character variable equal to the set of edit descriptors, and use the character variable in the I/O statement.

The individual edit descriptors are the same as those that we have just finished describing. All that we are doing is to package the edit descriptors somewhat differently.

EXAMPLE 3.17

Here is an example of a PRINT/FORMAT pair with the method shown so far:

```
        PRINT 10 , I , A , B
   10   FORMAT(' ', I3, 2(F7.2, 1X))
```

In the first alternative method (method A), we move all the edit descriptors into the I/O statement. This will result in the following:

```
        PRINT "(' ', I3, 2(F7.2, 1X))", I , A , B
```

The two statements above are functionally equivalent. All that we have done is move the edit descriptors from inside the FORMAT statement to inside the I/O statement. Note however, that we have omitted any strings. If we wish to include strings, we will have to use a different method, as we will discuss shortly.

In the second alternative method, we set up a character variable with the edit descriptors and then refer to that variable in the I/O statement. This method has the advantage that we can reuse the formatting commands as many times as we wish, without having to rewrite them.

EXAMPLE 3.18

In alternative method B for writing edit descriptors, we set up a character variable such as FMT, which contains all the edit descriptors, and then refer to it in the I/O statement(s):

```
        CHARACTER (LEN=40) :: FMT
        FMT = "(' ', I3 , 2(F7.2, 1X))"
        PRINT FMT, I , A , B
```

In this example, we set up the variable FMT as a character variable that holds up to 40 characters. Recall that the quotation marks in the assignment statement are necessary to mark the beginning and end of the character string. In this case, the character string is now a series of edit descriptors.

Recall in our previous use of character variables that we assigned a value to the character variable by enclosing it inside apostrophes or quotation marks:

```
        NAME = ' JOE '         or          NAME = " JOE "
```

At this point, we can see that a problem lies ahead. What if we wanted to have a string (marked by '...') <u>within</u> the formatting commands? The computer may misinterpret the interior set of apostrophes as the end of the formatting instructions. So to avoid this problem, we will use quotes ("...") exclusively to mark the beginning and end of the set of instructions, and apostrophes will be used only for internal character strings.

EXAMPLE 3.19

Fortran 90 permits the use of the quote marks (") to mark the beginning and end of a character variable. Any internal character string is then placed inside apostrophes.

```
CHARACTER (LEN=50) :: FMT
FMT = "(' ','THE ', I3,' TH PAIR IS: ', 2(F7.2 ,1X))"
PRINT FMT,  I , A , B
```

will produce the following output for I = 5, A = 1.34567 and B = 9.87654:

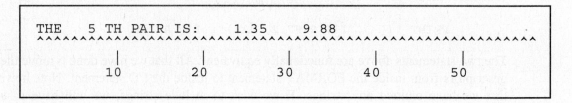

Note in this example that the carriage control character (' ') is included, along with other strings such as 'THE' and ' TH PAIR IS:'. But if we include these strings inside the format instructions stored in the character variable FMT, then we must define the entire variable with a set of quotes, "...".

Method B is the preferred method for using formatted I/O. The primary advantage over Method A is that you can reuse the format descriptors repeatedly without having to retype them and they may also include strings.

EXAMPLE 3.20

The following example uses edit descriptors with Method A:

```
PRINT "(' ','VALUE = ', F8.2)",  X
PRINT "(' ','VALUE = ', F8.2)",  Y
PRINT "(' ','VALUE = ', F8.2)",  Z
```

But a better way is to use Method B in which we use a character variable:

```
CHARACTER (LEN=35) :: FMT
FMT = "(' ','VALUE = ', F8.2 )"
PRINT FMT, X
PRINT FMT, Y
PRINT FMT, Z
```

There are a number of additional edit descriptors that you may find useful. Many of these are listed in the table below. This list is incomplete since we have chosen to leave out descriptors that are used with data types not discussed here.

Category	Descriptor	Function	Form	Example
Numerical Data	EN	Real - engineering notation	$rENw.d$	EN12.3
	ES	Real - scientific notation	$rESw.d$	ES12.3
Character Data	" "	Character string	"*string*"	"X= "
Control Function	SP	Print plus (+) sign	SP	SPF12.3
	SS	Do not print plus (+) sign	SS	SSF12.3
	P	Scale factor	kP	5PE13.6

EXAMPLE 3.21

Engineering notation of real numbers causes data to be printed in a format similar to the E edit descriptor. However in the engineering format EN$w.d$, the exponent will always be divisible by three to more closely resemble the metric system. Thus, the mantissa will not always be less than one, which was the case with the E$w.d$ format.

```
X = 12345.6789
Y = 98765.4321
PRINT "(' ',E14.4, EN14.4)", X , Y
```

will produce the following output:

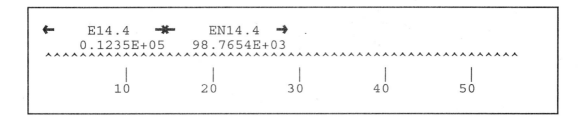

Notice that the mantissa is less than one, and the appropriate power of ten is chosen when we used the E14.4 format, . But when we use the EN14.4 format, the exponent is a multiple of three and the mantissa is adjusted accordingly.

EXAMPLE 3.22

Scientific notation of real numbers causes data to be printed in a format similar to the E edit descriptor. However, in the scientific format ES$w.d$, the mantissa will always be between 1.0 and 10.0. The exponent will then be adjusted accordingly.

```
X = 12345.6789
Y = 98765.4321
PRINT "(' ',E14.4, ES14.4)", X , Y
```

will produce the following output:

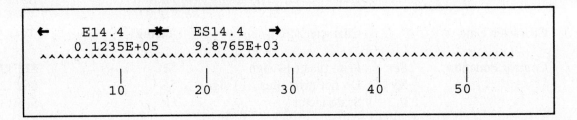

In summary, the Ew.d format produces a mantissa less than one, the EN*w.d* varies the mantissa so that the exponent is a multiple of three, and the ES*w.d* format adjusts the exponent so that the mantissa is always between one and ten. In most cases, the Ew.d format is all that you need. But you may find the EN and ES edit descriptors useful on occasion.

The *scale factor* format, *k*P, is frequently used with the E format to rescale the mantissa by *k* decimal places.

EXAMPLE 3.23

The scale factor *k*P will modify the output to rescale the numerical data by *k* decimal places.

```
X = 12345.6789
Y = 98765.4321
PRINT "(' ',E14.4, 2PE14.4)", X , Y
```

This will produce the following output:

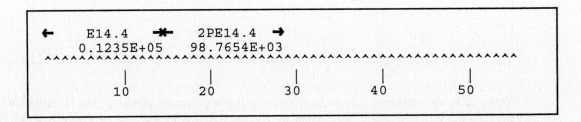

Ordinarily, the computer would print the value of Y (98765.4321) as 0.9877E+05 with the E14.4 format. But the scale factor (2P) in front of the E14.4 format causes the output to be shifted 2 decimal places to the left. Thus, the output is 98.7654E+03.

The *control functions*, SP and SS, are used to force or to suppress the printing of a leading "+" sign in front of a number. The SP edit descriptor forces the printing of the plus sign, while the SS descriptor deletes it. Once you issue the SP or SS command, though, it is in effect until it is countermanded by another command within the same format statement.

EXAMPLE 3.24

The control functions, SP and SS, force the printing of a "+" sign or suppress it, respectively. These commands only effect the *optional* plus signs in front of a number, and can be used with the I, F, E, EN, ES, D, and G edit descriptors. Plus signs in the exponent of a number are not affected however.

```
X = 12345.6789
Y = 98765.4321
PRINT "(' ',SP, E14.4, SS, 3PE14.4)", X , Y
```

will produce the following output:

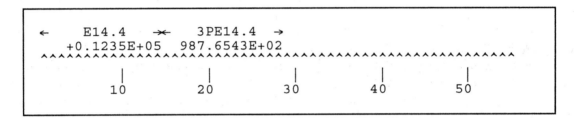

The first command inside the format specifier is SP. This will force printing of the leading plus sign in front of 0.1234E+05. If there were no other S_ type commands, the computer would continue to print any leading plus signs. But in this example, the next edit descriptor is the SS command, which stops printing of "+" signs. Thus, the next value has no plus sign. Note that the plus sign in the exponent is unaffected by either the SP or SS commands.

3.5 DEBUGGING TIPS

There are several types of problems that you are likely to encounter when you begin to use formatting. Some of these can be avoided by using good programming technique. Others can be solved by good debugging skills. For convenience, we will break this discussion into these two broad categories: good programming style and good debugging skills.

Programming style is often thought of as "defensive" programming. If you develop good basic skills, and pay attention to what is thought of as good style, then you will avoid many of the common programming errors and you will find your programs easier to debug. We present four guidelines at this point that will help you to improve your programming style:

- Use prompts to assure that you enter data in the correct sequence.
- Echo the entered data onto the screen to verify correct input.
- Do not insert formatting statements into your program until you have perfected the program logic.
- Avoid the use of the F format for real numbers in early versions of the program.

Prompts are short messages that your program prints on the CRT screen to remind you of the order in which to enter data. Without prompts, it is very easy to forget the sequence of the input data or when to enter the data. Also, it is a very good idea to have your program print out the input data as soon as it is read. This is called an *echo* and is an excellent way to detect errors early.

The third and fourth guidelines above suggest that you should use free formatted output and be slow to introduce FORMAT statements. First, make sure your program logic is correct before you add any FORMAT statements. Then, use only E-type edit descriptors for real data until you have a good idea of the approximate range of the output data. Only then should you add F edit descriptors.

EXAMPLE 3.25

Here is an example in which we use prompts and echoes to assist in entering data.

```
! Here is an example of a prompt to remind the user of
! the sequence of the input data.
PRINT *, 'ENTER HOURS, RATE, AND BONUS:'
READ * , HOURS, RATE, BONUS
! Here is an echo, where the values will be sent to the CRT
! screen so that you can check correct entry.
PRINT *, 'HOURS ENTERED = ', HOURS
PRINT *, 'RATE ENTERED = ', RATE
PRINT *, 'BONUS ENTERED = ', BONUS
```

will produce the following output (assuming HOURS = 123.45, RATE = 3.4567, and BONUS = 567.89):

```
ENTER HOURS, RATE, AND BONUS:        (Prompt from the program)
123.45, 3.4567, 567.89   <CR>        (Values that you type in)
HOURS ENTERED = 0.1234500E+03           (Echo from program)
RATE ENTERED = 0.3456700E+01            (Echo from program)
BONUS ENTERED = 0.5678900E+03           (Echo from program)
^^^^^^^^^^^^^^^^^^^^^^^^^^^^^^^^^^^^^^^^^^^^^^^^^^^^^^^^^^^^^^

        |           |           |           |           |
       10          20          30          40          50
```

Note in this example that we do not use any FORMAT statements. We will add them later to improve the appearance of the data. The first PRINT statement is the prompt. Its purpose is to remind us in what order we are to enter the data. Once we enter the data (on a single line, separated by commas or spaces), the program prints out the string "HOURS ENTERED = " followed by the value of HOURS that we entered. This is the echo portion of the input section. The only undesirable thing about this program segment is that the real data are printed in exponential format, which is somewhat difficult to read. But now that we know that the program logic works, we can modify the program segment to give a somewhat nicer output appearance:

```
! Here is an example of a prompt to remind the user of
! the sequence of the input data.
  PRINT *, 'ENTER HOURS, RATE, AND BONUS:'
  READ * , HOURS, RATE, BONUS
! Here is an echo, where the values will be sent to the CRT
! screen so that you can check correct entry.
  PRINT 5, HOURS, RATE, BONUS
5 FORMAT(' ','HOURS ENTERED = ', F10.5, /,' ', &
  'RATE ENTERED  = ', F10.5, /,' ', &
  'BONUS ENTERED = ', F10.5)
```

will produce the following output (assuming HOURS = 123.45, RATE = 3.4567, and
BONUS = 567.89):

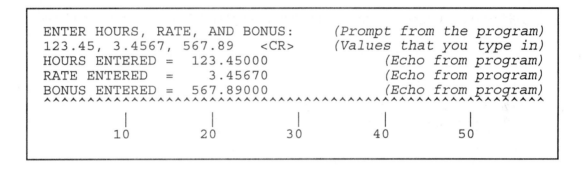

The bugs that you are mostly likely to encounter when using formatted I/O are the following:

- Overflow (data do not fit into the space allotted)
- Unbalanced parentheses
- Data type of the output variable and the edit descriptor do not match
  (Some compilers may permit a mismatch however.)

The first problem occurs during execution when you do not allow enough space to print the output data. For example, if you use an I5 edit descriptor to print out the value of J = 1234567, the computer will print ***** as the output line. Obviously, J is a seven-digit number and cannot fit into five columns. The solution is obvious: add additional digits to the edit descriptor, or in the case of real numbers, switch to the E edit descriptor.

The second error (unbalanced parentheses) occurs during compilation because FORMAT statements tend to contain several sets of parentheses, and it is very easy to have too few or too many. Remember, there must be an equal number of left and right parentheses. When this error occurs, simply count the number of left and right parentheses, and make sure they balance.

The third error (incompatible variable and edit descriptor) is the most frequent formatting bug. Recall that a real variable can only use the F, E, or G edit descriptor. If you accidentally forget and use another descriptor (I, for example), an error occurs during compilation. Make sure that the types of the variables and the edit descriptors match.

EXAMPLE 3.26

The following example contains several common formatting errors.

```
      X = 12.345
      Y = 98.765
      I = 123
      J = 987
      PRINT 5, X, Y, X*Y, I, J, I*J
    5 FORMAT(' ', 3(F7.3, 3X), /, 1X, 3(I3, 3X)))
```

will not compile, since there is an extra right parenthesis in the FORMAT statement. The compiler will detect this error and send you an appropriate error message. Once the extra parenthesis is removed, and the program is recompiled and executed, you should get the following output:

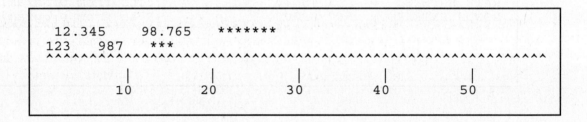

Notice that the product of X times Y (1219.2539) will not fit into the space allotted (F7.3), nor will the product of I times J (121401) fit into I3. So, the result is an overflow. To correct these problems, we should enlarge each of the output fields. In the corrected program below, we will use the E format for the product of the real numbers and expand I3 to something larger for the integer data.

```
      X = 12.345
      Y = 98.765
      I = 1234
      J = 9876
      PRINT 5, X, Y, X*Y, I, J, I*J
    5 FORMAT(' ', 2(F7.3, 3X), E15.5, /, 1X, 3(I10, 3X))
```

The output will now look like this:

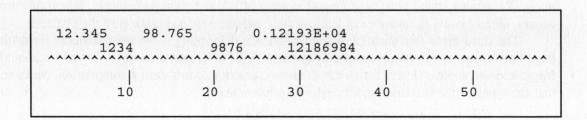

Solved Problems

Note: We assume that all output statements require a carriage control character. This is true when you are printing to a hard copy printer, but may not be required if printing to a CRT terminal. Therefore, you may have to modify the FORMAT statements accordingly.

3.1   Predict the output for the following program segments:

(a) I = 1234
     X = 12.34
     PRINT *, I, X

(b) I = 1234
     X = 12.34
     PRINT *, ' I = ', I, ' X = ', X

(c) I = 1234
     X = 12.34
     PRINT *, I
     PRINT *, X

(d) I = 1234
     X = 12.34
     PRINT *, ' I * I = ', I**2
     PRINT *, ' X * X = ', X**2

The results may be machine dependent because of the limit on storage of real and integer data, and because of the default rules on free formatted output. But assuming that reals are printed in exponential format with seven significant digits and integers with nine digits, and three blank spaces between data items, this is what the output should look like (note: ~ is a blank space):

(a) ~ ~ ~ ~ ~ 1234 ~ ~ ~ 0.1234000E+02
(b) ~ I ~ = ~ ~ ~ ~ ~ ~ 1234 ~ ~ ~ ~ X ~ = ~ 0.1234000E+02
(c) ~ ~ ~ ~ ~ 1234
     0.1234000E+02   *(Output on 2 lines.)*
(d) ~ I ~ * ~ I ~ = ~ ~ ~ 1522756
     ~ X ~ * ~ X ~ = ~ 0.1522756E+03 *(Output on 2 lines.)*

3.2   What would be the value of each variable after executing the following program segments?

(a) READ *, A, B, C   *(Input on one line: 12.34, 56.78, 98.76)*
(b) READ *, A, B, C   *(Input on three lines: 12.34, 56.78, 98.76)*
(c) READ *, I   *(Input: 1.5)*
(d) READ *, A   *(Input on line #1: 12.34, 56.78)*
     READ *, B, C   *(Input on line #2: 98.76, 54.32)*

(a) A = 12.3400, B = 56.7800, C = 98.7600
(b) Same as (a). It doesn't matter whether the data values are entered on the same or on different lines.
(c) I = 1, since I is an integer by default, the decimal part is dropped.
(d) A = 12.3400, B = 98.7600, C = 54.3200. The first READ statement needs only one value to complete its job, so the second number on the first line is never read. The second READ statement starts reading a new line.

3.3 If the real variable X has the value of 1234.567 and is printed with the statement PRINT 12, X, how would the output appear for each of the following FORMAT statements?

(a) 12   FORMAT(F12.4)   (b) 12   FORMAT(' ', F8.4)
(c) 12   FORMAT(' ', F12.4)   (d) 12   FORMAT('+', F12.4)
(e) 12   FORMAT(' ','X= ', F12.4)   (f) 12   FORMAT(' ','X= ', /, F12.4)

(a) ~~1234.5670   *(Since there was no carriage control character, the computer interpreted the first character (~) of the value to be used as the CCC. This is why there are only two blank spaces in front of the number.)*

(b) ********   *(If we insist on four decimal places, the number cannot fit into eight columns. Remember that the decimal point also takes up one column.)*

(c) ~~~1234.5670   *(Compare this to example (a), where we left out the carriage control character.)*

(d) ~~~1234.5670   *(Same as (c) except that this would be on current line, not on the next line.)*

(e) X=~~~~1234.5670   *(The blank space after the = sign in the string is also printed.)*

(f) X=~
~~~1234.5670   *(The CCC is needed for the second line.)*

3.4 If the real variable X has the value of −1234.567 and is printed with the statement PRINT 12, X, how would the output appear for each of the following FORMAT statements?

(a) 12   FORMAT(' ', E11.4)   (b) 12   FORMAT(' ', E8.4)
(c) 12   FORMAT(E11.4)   (d) 12   FORMAT('+', E11.4)
(e) 12   FORMAT(' ','X= ', E11.4)   (f) 12   FORMAT(' ','X= ', /, E11.4)
(g) 12   FORMAT(' ',ES11.4)   (h) 12   FORMAT(' ', EN11.4)

(a) −0.1235E+04   *(No extra blank spaces.)*

(b) no output   *(Would not compile since w is too small; must be at least 7 greater than d.)*

(c) 0.1235E+04   *(Since there was no carriage control character, the computer uses the first character (minus sign) as the CCC. Compare this to example (a).)*

(d) −0.1235E+04   *(The only difference between (c) and (d) is the line on which they appear. Example (c) appears on the next line, while (d) appears on the current line.)*

(e) X=~−0.1235E+04   *(The blank space after the = sign in the string is also printed.)*

(f) X=~
0.1235E+03   *(The CCC is needed for the second line.)*

(g) −1.2346E+03   *(In scientific notation, the mantissa is between 1 and 10.)*

(h) −1.2346E+03   *(In engineering notation, the exponent is a multiple of 3.)*

3.5 Assume that the real variable X has the value of -123.4567 and that it is printed with PRINT 12, X. How would the output appear for each of the following FORMAT statements?

(a) 12   FORMAT(G11.2)   (b) 12   FORMAT(G8.5)
(c) 12   FORMAT(' ', G14.5)   (d) 12   FORMAT(' ', G11.3)
(e) 12   FORMAT(' ','X= ', G8.3) (f) 12   FORMAT(' ','X= ', /, G11.2)

(a) ~ $-0.12E+03$ *(Since the exponent value (3) is greater than the d value (2) in Gw.d, the E format is used. Also, since there was no CCC, the computer interprets the first character (blank space) as the CCC.)*

(b) *******   *(The exponent value of 3 is now less than d in Gw.d, so the computer switches to the F format. But this does not leave room to print the answer, so we get an overflow.)*

(c) ~ ~ ~ -123.46 ~ ~ ~ ~   *(Since the exponent value of 3 is smaller than the d value of 5 specified in G14.5, the F format is used. For this example, the number is printed with 5 significant digits and four trailing blank spaces.)*

(d) ~ ~ $-123.$ ~ ~ ~ ~   *(The exponent (3) is equal to d in Gw.d, so we use the modified F format. This results in a number with 3 significant digits followed by 4 blank spaces.)*

(e) X= ~ ********   *(The minus sign occupies one column. Thus, the number cannot fit into the allotted 3 columns.)*

(f) X= ~
     ~ $-0.12E+03$ *(The CCC is needed for the second line.)*

3.6 If the real double precision variable X has the value of -12345.6789 and is printed with PRINT 12, X, how would the output appear for each of the following FORMAT statements?

(a) 12   FORMAT(D15.5)   (b) 12   FORMAT(' ', D15.5)
(c) 12   FORMAT(' ', D12.5)   (d) 12   FORMAT(' ', F11.3)
(e) 12   FORMAT(' ', G13.5)   (f) 12   FORMAT(' ', G15.3)

(a) ~ $-0.12346D+005$ *(Since there is no carriage control character, the computer interprets the first character (~) as the CCC.)*

(b) ~ ~ $-0.12346D+005$ *(The first blank space was interpreted in (a) as the CCC. But this has now been corrected.)*

(c) ***********   *(Not enough space reserved, so an overflow results.)*

(d) No output   *(Compilation error, since the variable is double precision and can only use D or G formats.)*

(e) ~ ~ $-12346.$ ~ ~ ~ ~   *(The exponent (5) is equal to d in Gw.d, so we use the F modified format with 5 significant digits.)*

(f) ~ ~ ~ ~ $-0.123D+005$ *(The exponent (5) is smaller than d in Gw.d, so we use the D format.)*

3.7 Assume that the integer variable I has the value of -123 and that it is printed out with PRINT 12, I. How would the output appear for each of the following FORMAT statements?

(a) 12 FORMAT(I3)   (b) 12 FORMAT(' ', I3)
(c) 12 FORMAT(' ', I5)   (d) 12 FORMAT(' ', 3X, F5.0)
(e) 12 FORMAT(' ','I= ', I5)   (f) 12 FORMAT(' ','I= ',/, I5)

(a) **   *(The minus sign takes up one column, so you need to allow for it. Also, the CCC was left out).*

(b) ***   *(Even after the CCC is included, we still need to enlarge the field to make room for the negative sign.)*

(c) ~ -123 *(Everything is OK now.)*

(d) no output   *(Error since I is an integer, but F is the edit descriptor for a real number, not an integer.)*

(e) I= ~ ~ -123 *(The blank space after the = sign in the string is also printed.)*

(f) I= ~
-123 *(The CCC is needed for the second line.)*

3.8 Assume that the character variable NAME has the value of "Joe Montana" and that it is printed out with PRINT 12, NAME. How would the output appear for each of the following FORMAT statements?

(a) 12 FORMAT(A1)   (b) 12 FORMAT(' ', A1)
(c) 12 FORMAT(' ', A12)   (d) 12 FORMAT(' ', A)

(a)   *(The line would be blank! Since we only allowed one column for the output, only the first letter (J) should be printed. But we also left out the carriage control character, so this would be used for the CCC instead.)*

(b) J   *(The problem from the previous example has been solved.)*

(c) Joe Montana ~   *(Characters are left justified, so the blank space comes at the end.)*

(d) Joe Montana   *(No extra blank space.)*

3.9 Assume that the real variables X and Y have the values 1.2345 and 9.8765, respectively, and that the integer variables I and J have the values 12345 and 98765, respectively. How would the output appear for each of the following PRINT/FORMAT pairs?

(a)   PRINT 12, X, Y, I, J
      12 FORMAT(F10.3, T15, F10.3, T29, I10, T43, I10)
(b)   PRINT 12, X, Y, I, J
      12 FORMAT(' ', F10.3, T15, F10.3, T29, I10, T43, I10)

(c)   PRINT 12, X, Y, I, J
     12   FORMAT(' ', 2(F10.3, 4X), 2(I10, 4X))
(d)   PRINT 12, X, Y, I, J
     12   FORMAT(' ',2(F10.3, 4X), //, 1X, 2(I10, 4X))

(a)   ~ ~ ~ ~ 1.235 ~ ~ ~ ~ ~ ~ ~ ~ ~ 9.877 ~ ~ ~ ~ ~ ~ ~ ~ ~ 12345 ~ ~ ~ ~ ~
      ~ ~ ~ ~ 98765   *(First blank space missing because CCC omitted. Output on 1 line.)*
(b)   ~ ~ ~ ~ ~ 1.235 ~ ~ ~ ~ ~ ~ ~ ~ ~ 9.877 ~ ~ ~ ~ ~ ~ ~ ~ ~ 12345 ~ ~ ~ ~
      ~ ~ ~ ~ ~ 98765   *(Slightly different from previous example since CCC now present.)*
(c)   ~ ~ ~ ~ ~ 1.235 ~ ~ ~ ~ ~ ~ ~ ~ ~ 9.877 ~ ~ ~ ~ ~ ~ ~ ~ ~ 12345 ~ ~ ~ ~ ~ ~
      ~ ~ ~ 98765   *(Last four blank spaces not shown. Output on 1 line.)*
(d)   ~ ~ ~ ~ ~ 1.235 ~ ~ ~ ~ ~ ~ ~ ~ ~ 9.877
                        (Blank line – the // descriptor double spaces.)
      ~ ~ ~ ~ ~ 12345 ~ ~ ~ ~ ~ ~ ~ ~ ~ 98765

3.10 Find the syntax errors, if any, in each of the following program segments. **Assume implicit** typing rules in effect for all variables.

(a)   PRINT I , J , K   (b)   READ *, 'ENTER THE VALUE OF X:',X
(c)   PRINT *, X , Y   (d)   PRINT *, "THE ANSWER IS:", X
(e)   PRINT 10, X   (f)   PRINT 20, X
     10   FORMAT(' ', I3)   20   FORMAT(' ','X= ')

(a) Comma and * missing   (b) No output permitted with a **READ statement**
(c) Correct   (d) Correct
(e) Integer descriptor for real variable (f) No edit descriptor for X

3.11 Trace through the following program segments and predict their output. **For problems with** formatted I/O, pay close attention to spacing.

(a)   X=1.5   (b)   X=123.4567
           Y=2.56   PRINT 10, X, X, X, X, X, X
           Z=100.01   10   FORMAT(' ', 2(F8.1,2(F8.2,2(F8.3))))
           PRINT 10, X, Y, Z, Y
           PRINT 10, Z * Y
     10   FORMAT(' ', 2(F6.1), 2F6.2)
(c)   X1=1.0   (d)   X1=1.0
           X2=2.0   X2=2.0
           X3=3.0   X3=3.0
           PRINT 100,X1,X2,X3,X3,X2,X1   PRINT 90, X1,X2,X3,X3,X2,X1,X2,X3,X1
    100   FORMAT(' ',10(1X,F6.2))   90   FORMAT(' ',3(1X,F6.2))

(a) ~ ~ ~ 1.5 ~ ~ ~ 2.6100.01 ~ ~ ~ 2.56
    ~ 256.0   *(Output on 2 lines.)*

(b) ~ ~123.5~ ~123.46~123.457~123.457~ ~123.46~123.457
(c) ~ ~ ~1.00~ ~ ~2.00~ ~ ~3.00~ ~ ~3.00~ ~ ~2.00~ ~ ~1.00
(d) ~ ~ ~1.00~ ~ ~2.00~ ~ ~3.00
    ~ ~3.00~ ~ ~2.00~ ~ ~1.00
    ~ ~2.00~ ~ ~3.00~ ~ ~1.00   *(Output on 3 lines.)*

3.12 Write a program which reads in a real number and prints out the whole number portion. For example, if your program reads in the real number 5.2, it would print out a value of 5 representing the whole number portion of the input. (Do not use any of the intrinsic functions.)

```
PRINT *, 'Enter a Real Number:'
READ *, X
I = X
PRINT 10, I
10  FORMAT(' ', 'Whole Portion of Number is:', I7)
END
```

3.13 Suppose there is a program which calculates the month, day and year (stored in MONTH, DAY, and YEAR) and also the time in hours, minutes, and seconds (stored in HOURS, MINUTE and SECOND). Write the Fortran code to output this information in military time (24-hour basis) following this example: *The date is 1/23/95, and the time is now 15:45:37 hours*. Assume that all variable types are integer. You do not need to print out any leading zero (such as 01/23/95).

```
INTEGER ::  DAY, YEAR, HOURS, SECOND
PRINT 10, MONTH, DAY, YEAR, HOURS, MINUTE, SECOND
10  FORMAT(' ', 'The Date is', I2,'/',I2,'/',I2,' and the time is now ',I2,':',I2,':',  &
        I2,' hours')
END
```

3.14 Write a program assigning I1=1, I2=2, I3=3, I4=4, I5=5, and I6=6. Have your program print these integers in the following ways:

(a) In a single row
(b) In two rows containing (I1, I2, I3) and (I4, I5, I6), using two PRINT statements but only one FORMAT statement
(c) In two rows, as above, but with only one PRINT statement

    I1=1
    I2=2
    I3=3
    I4=4
    I5=5

```
        I6=6
        PRINT *, 'Part a: Single row'
        PRINT 10, I1, I2, I3, I4, I5, I6
     10 FORMAT(' ', 6I2)
        PRINT *, ' Part b: 2 rows with 2 PRINT statements and 1 FORMAT statement'
        PRINT 20, I1, I2, I3
        PRINT 20, I4, I5, I6
     20 FORMAT(' ',3I2)
        PRINT *, ' Part c: 2 rows with 1 PRINT statement'
        PRINT 30, I1, I2, I3, I4, I5, I6
     30 FORMAT(' ', 3I2, /, 1X, 3I2)
        END
```

Supplementary Problems

Note: Assume implicit typing for all variables.

3.15 Predict the output for the following program segments. Assume that reals are printed in exponential format with seven significant digits and integers with nine digits, with three blank spaces between data items. Use the ' ~ ' symbol for blank spaces.

(a) I = −4567
    J = 123
    X = −0.001234567
    PRINT *, I, J, X

(b) I = −4567
    J = 123
    X = −0.001234567
    PRINT *, ' I = ', I, ' J = ', J, ' X = ', X

(c) I = −4567
    J = 123
    X = −0.001234567
    PRINT *, I, J
    PRINT *, X

(d) I = −4567
    J = 123
    X = −0.001234567
    PRINT *, ' I * J = ', I*J
    PRINT *, ' X * J = ', X*J

3.16 What would be the value of each variable after executing the following program segments?

(a) READ *, A, I, J   *(Input on one line: −0.1234, 12.0, 11.99)*
(b) READ *, A, I, J   *(Input on three lines: −0.1234, 12.0, 11.99)*
(c) READ *, X   *(Input: 1)*
(d) READ *, A   *(Input on one line: −0.1234, 12.34, 56.78)*
    READ *, B
    READ *, C

3.17 Assume that you enter the value of −0.00123456789 and assign it to the real variable X and then subsequently print it out with PRINT 13, X. How would the output appear for each of the following FORMAT statements?

(a) 13   FORMAT(F12.3)   (b) 13   FORMAT(F7.4)
(c) 13   FORMAT(' ', F12.3)   (d) 13   FORMAT(' ', F15.10)
(e) 13   FORMAT(' ','X= ', F9.5)   (f) 13   FORMAT(' ','X= ', /, F12.6)

3.18 Assume that you enter the value of -0.00123456789 and assign it to the real variable, X, and then subsequently print it out with PRINT 13, X. How would the output appear for each of the following FORMAT statements?

(a) 13   FORMAT(' ', E11.4)   (b) 13   FORMAT(' ', E11.2)
(c) 13   FORMAT(E11.4)   (d) 13   FORMAT(' ', E15.6)
(e) 13   FORMAT(' ', 'X= ', E11.4) (f) 13   FORMAT(' ', 'X= ', /, E11.4)

3.19 Assume that you enter the value of -1.23456789 and assign it to the real variable X and then subsequently print it out with PRINT 13, X. How would the output appear for each of the following FORMAT statements?

(a) 13   FORMAT(' ', G11.2)   (b) 13   FORMAT(G8.5)
(c) 13   FORMAT(' ', G14.5)   (d) 13   FORMAT(' ', G11.3)
(e) 13   FORMAT(' ','X= ', G11.3)   (f) 13   FORMAT(' ','X= ', G11.2)
(g) 13   FORMAT(' ', ES11.4)   (h) 13   FORMAT(' ', EN11.3)

3.20 Assume that you enter the value of -1.23456789 and assign it to the double precision variable X and then subsequently print it out with PRINT 13, X. How would the output appear for each of the following FORMAT statements?

(a) 13   FORMAT(D13.5)   (b) 13   FORMAT(' ', D13.5)
(c) 13   FORMAT(' ', D12.5)   (d) 13   FORMAT(' ', F11.3)
(e) 13   FORMAT(' ', G14.5)   (f) 13   FORMAT(' ', G11.1)

3.21 Assume the integer variable I has the value of 987654 and is printed out with PRINT 13, I. How would the output appear for each of the following FORMAT statements?

(a) 13   FORMAT(I6)   (b) 13   FORMAT(' ', I6)
(c) 13   FORMAT(' ', I9)   (d) 13   FORMAT(' ', 3X, G12.3)
(e) 13   FORMAT(' ','I= ', I6)   (f) 13   FORMAT(' ','I= ',/, I6)

3.22 Assume the character variable COURSE has the value of "Rocket Science 101" and is printed out with PRINT 12, COURSE. How would the output appear for each of the following FORMAT statements?

(a) 12   FORMAT(A18)   (b) 12   FORMAT(' ', A18)
(c) 12   FORMAT(' ','Course=',A15) (d) 12   FORMAT(' ','Course=', 5X, A)

3.23 Assume the real variables X and Y have the values of -0.12345 and -0.98765, respectively, and the integer variables, I and J, have the values 4567 and 890, respectively. How would the output appear for each of the following PRINT/FORMAT pairs?

(a)   PRINT 12, X, Y, I, J
    12   FORMAT(' ',F8.3, T13, F8.3, T25, I5, T34, I5)

(b)   PRINT 12, X, Y, I, J
    12   FORMAT(' ', 2(F8.3, 4X), 2(I5, 4X))

(c)   PRINT 10
    10   FORMAT(' ', T4, 'X', T16, 'Y', T27, 'I', T36,'J',//)
        PRINT 12, X, Y, I, J
    12   FORMAT(' ',2(F8.3, 4X), 2(I5, 4X))

3.24 Find the syntax errors, if any, in each of the following program segments. Assume implicit typing rules in effect for all variables.

(a)   PRINT 30, I , J , K , X
    30   FORMAT(4(I5,2X))

(b)   PRINT 40
    40   FORMAT('AMTDUE: ', AMTDUE)

(c)   PRINT 27, X , Y , Z ,
    27   FORMAT('+',3(F12.4),I4)

(d)   READ 41, U , V , W , I , J , K
    41   FORMAT(3(F12.4, I6))

(e)   PRINT 200, A , I , B , K
   200 FORMAT(F10.4, 3X, I4)

(f)   PRINT 19, X , Y , I , U , V
    19   FORMAT(' ',2E12.7,2(I7,1X,2D12.4))

(g)   READ 12, I , X , Z*Y
    12   FORMAT(' ',I4,4X,2F12.5)

3.25 Trace through the following program segments and predict their output.

(a)   X1=1.0
        X2=2.0
        X3=3.0
        PRINT 102,X1,X2,X3,X3,X2,X1
   102 FORMAT(' ',3(3(1X,F6.2),/,1X))
        END

(b)   X=1.2
        Y=1.3
        Z=1.4
        PRINT 10, X, Y, Z
    10   FORMAT(' ', 3(T10, F6.2, /))
        END

(c)   PRINT 2
        PRINT 3
    2   FORMAT(' ','O')
    3   FORMAT('+','/')
        END

(d)   X=100.2
        PRINT 10, X
    10   FORMAT(F6.2)
        END

3.26 Write a program which reads in a real number and prints out the fractional portion without using any of the intrinsic functions.

3.27 Write a program which will read in an angle measured in DEGREES, MINUTES, and

SECONDS and print it out in a decimal format as in the following example: *An angle of 22 degrees, 13 minutes, 47 seconds is equal to 22.3472 degrees.*

3.28   Write a program that will print out a table heading with "Student ID" starting in column 5, "Midterm Exam" in column 25, "Final Exam" in column 45, and "Grade" in column 65. On the next line, draw a line under all of the headings.

3.29   Write a program that reads in a real number and rounds it off to two decimal places. Use a prompt statement to assist the user.

Answers to Selected Supplementary Problems

3.15   (a) ~ ~ ~ ~ ~ −4567 ~ ~ ~ ~ ~ ~ 123 ~ ~ ~ −0.1234567E−02
     (b) ~I~ = ~ ~ ~ ~ ~ ~ −4567 ~ ~ ~ ~J~ = ~ ~ ~ ~ ~ ~ ~ 123 ~ ~ ~ ~
         X~ = ~ −0.1234567E−02   *(Output on 1 line.)*
     (c) ~ ~ ~ ~4567 ~ ~ ~ ~ ~ ~ 123
        −0.1234567E−02   *(Output on 2 lines.)*
     (d) ~I~ * ~J~ = ~ ~ ~ −561741
        ~X~ * ~J~ = ~ 0.1518517E+00   *(Output on 2 lines.)*

3.16   (a) A = −0.1234, I = 12, J = 11 (computer does not round off in this case).
     (b) Same as (a). It doesn't matter whether the data values are entered on the same or different lines.
     (c) X = 1.0 (computer adds decimal point).
     (d) A = −0.1234, B, and C are undefined. The first READ statement needs only one value to complete its job, so the second and third numbers on the first line are never read. Subsequent READ statements are still waiting for data. Therefore, the program will wait until you enter the requested data.

3.17   (a) ~ ~ ~ ~ ~ −0.001   *(Since there was no carriage control character, the computer interpreted the first character (~) as the CCC.)*
     (b) 0.0012   *(The leading negative sign was used for the carriage control since the CCC was left out. The character used as the CCC will reset the printer and start a new line.)*
     (c) ~ ~ ~ ~ ~ ~ −0.001   *(Compare this to example (a), where we left out the CCC.)*
     (d) ~ ~ −0.001234567x   *(Real numbers can store only 7 significant digits. So, if we request more in the printout, you can never be sure what the machine will print out. We highlight this by showing the last digit as x.)*
     (e) X= ~ ~ −0.00123   *(The last digit is rounded down.)*

(f) X=~
~ ~ −0.001235   *(In this case, the last digit is rounded up.)*

3.18 (a) −0.1236E−02   *(Note the rounding of the last significant digit.)*
(b) ~ ~ −0.12E−02   *(Similar to (a), except that the last digit is rounded down.)*
(c) 0.1236E−02   *(Compare this to example (a), where we included the carriage control character.)*
(d) ~ ~ −0.123457E−02   *(Note that the mantissa is rounded up.)*
(e) X=~ −0.1236E−02   *(The blank space after the = sign is also printed.)*
(f) X=~
0.1236E−02   *(The CCC is needed for the second line.)*

3.19 (a) ~ ~ ~ −1.2 ~ ~ ~ ~   *(Since the exponent in E format is one and is less than d(2) in Gw.d, the F format is used. The modified F format produces a number with 2 significant digits and 4 trailing blank spaces.)*
(b) *******   *(Since the exponent is less than d (2), the modified F format is used. Notice that the number cannot fit in this space, so an overflow condition results. Also, one of the blank spaces is used for carriage control, so only 7 stars are printed, not 8.)*
(c) ~ ~ ~ −1.2346 ~ ~ ~   *(Convert to modified F format with 5 significant digits.)*
(d) ~ ~ −1.23 ~ ~ ~ ~   *(Convert to modified F format with 3 significant digits.)*
(e) X=~ ~ ~ −1.23 ~ ~ ~ ~   *(Don't forget the blank space after =.)*
(f) X=~ ~ ~ ~ −1.2 ~ ~ ~ ~   *(Only 2 significant digits.)*
(g) −1.2346E+00   *(In scientific notation, the mantissa is between 1 and 10.)*
(h) ~ −1.235E+00   *(In engineering notation, the exponent is a multiple of 3.)*

3.20 (a) 0.12346D+001   *(Since there was no carriage control character, the first character (minus sign) is used as the CCC.)*
(b) −0.12346D+001   *(Carriage control problem now solved.)*
(c) ***********   *(Not enough space reserved, so an overflow results.)*
(d) No output   *(Compilation error, since the number is double precision and can only use D or G formats.)*
(e) ~ ~ ~ −1.2346 ~ ~ ~   *(Convert to modified F format with 5 significant digits.)*
(f) ~ ~ ~ ~ −1. ~ ~ ~ ~   *(Convert to modified F format with only 1 significant digit.)*

3.21 (a) 87654   *(Since the CCC was left out, the computer used the first digit for carriage control.)*
(b) 987654   *(CCC problems now solved.)*
(c) ~ ~ ~987654   *(Integers are right justified within output field.)*
(d) no output   *(Error since I is an integer and cannot use G format.)*

    (e) I = ~987654   *(The blank space after the = sign in the string is also printed.)*

    (f) I = ~
    87654   *(The CCC is needed for the second line.)*

3.22 (a) ocket Science 101   *(No CCC, so the first character is used.)*
     (b) Rocket Science 101   *(Problem from the previous example has been solved.)*
     (c) Course=Rocket ~ Science ~ *(No overflow condition with character data.)*
     (d) Course = ~ ~ ~ ~ ~ Rocket ~ Science ~ 101
                     (The A format allows just enough spaces.)

3.23 (a) ~ ~ −0.123 ~ ~ ~ ~ ~ −0.988 ~ ~ ~ ~ 4567 ~ ~ ~ ~ ~ 890
     (b) ~ ~ −0.123 ~ ~ ~ ~ ~ ~ −0.988 ~ ~ ~ ~ 4567 ~ ~ ~ ~ ~ ~ 890
     (c) ~ ~X ~ ~ ~ ~ ~ ~ ~ ~ ~ ~Y ~ ~ ~ ~ ~ ~ ~ ~ ~ ~I ~ ~ ~ ~ ~ ~ ~ ~ ~J
                     (this line is blank)
        ~ ~ −0.123 ~ ~ ~ ~ ~ −0.988 ~ ~ ~ ~ 4567 ~ ~ ~ ~ ~ 890

3.24 (a) X is real and cannot use I5 descriptor.
     (b) Variable to print out must be in PRINT statement, not in the FORMAT statement.
     (c) Extra comma at end of I/O list.
     (d) Should be 3F12.4,3I6.
     (e) Correct, since the FORMAT is reused.
     (f) E edit descriptors do not allow enough space. Use the edit descriptors as many times as needed (twice). U and V are not double precision.
     (g) Cannot do calculations in a READ statement.

3.25 (a) ~ ~ ~1.00 ~ ~ ~2.00 ~ ~ ~3.00
        ~ ~ ~3.00 ~ ~ ~2.00 ~ ~ ~1.00
     (b) ~ ~ ~ ~ ~ ~ ~ ~ ~ ~1.20
        ~ ~ ~ ~ ~ ~ ~ ~ ~ ~1.30
        ~ ~ ~ ~ ~ ~ ~ ~ ~ ~1.40
     (c) Ø   *(A slash (/) superimposed over the letter (O).)*
     (d) 00.20

3.26
```
      PRINT*, 'Enter a Real Number:'
      READ *, X
      I = X
      FRAC = X − I
      PRINT 10, FRAC
   10 FORMAT(' ', 'Fractional Part of Number is:', F10.4)
      END
```

3.27   INTEGER :: DEGREE, SECOND
             PRINT *, 'Enter degrees, minutes, and seconds:'
             READ *, DEGREE, MINUTE, SECOND
             DECIMAL=DEGREE+MINUTE/60.0+SECOND/3600.0
             PRINT 10, DEGREE, MINUTE, SECOND, DECIMAL
         10 FORMAT(' ','An angle of ',I3,' Degrees, ',I2,' Minutes, ',I2, &
                     ' Seconds is equal to ', F8.4,' degrees')
             END

3.28   PRINT 10
         10 FORMAT(' ', T5, 'Student ID', T25, 'Midterm Exam', &
                     T45, 'Final Exam', T65, 'Grade', &
                     /, T5, 10('_'), T25, 12('_'), T45, 10('_'), T65, 5('_'))

3.29   PRINT 10
         10 FORMAT(' ', 'Enter any real number with more than two decimal places')
             READ *, X
             PRINT 20, X, X
         20 FORMAT(' ', 'The original number:', F15.5, /, ' rounded to 2 decimal places:', F10.2)
             END

Chapter 4

Decision-Based Control Structures

4.1 OVERVIEW

So far you have learned to construct simple sequential Fortran programs with formatted input and output. While such programs are useful for straightforward tasks, there are a great many problems that require decision making. In this chapter we will discuss various kinds of *control* structures. These structures will allow you to select one set of instructions for execution from two or more groups of instructions. The topics to be covered in this chapter include:

- Unconditional transfer
- Conditional statements and constructs
- Special forms of the IF construct
- The SELECT CASE structure
- Debugging tips for branching and looping operations

Conditional and unconditional transfer statements provide fundamental instructions from which more complex control structures can be created. For example, suppose we would like to sum a list of 100 numbers. With what we know so far, we would have to write a program that uses 100 variables, adds them together, and then finally prints the result. This would be a tedious and long program to write. However, by using the statements provided in this chapter, such a problem can be solved with just a few lines. What's more, the program can be written to read in any arbitrary number of numbers. This is just one example of the power of control structures.

4.2 UNCONDITIONAL TRANSFER

The unconditional transfer statement, or GO TO statement, is the simplest transfer operation. It provides a means by which control transfers to another line in the program. The line to receive the control must be labeled using a statement label. The general form of the GO TO statement is:

GO TO *statement label (sl)*

The *statement label (sl)* is a positive integer value placed in columns 1 through 5 and indicates a specific line to which we can transfer.

The unconditional transfer is usually used for two purposes:

- Skip over a set of instructions
- Repeat a set of instructions.

118

At first glance, it may appear that the GO TO statement is all that we need to set up the two remaining building blocks of programming that we described in Chapter 1. But as we will see shortly, using the GO TO often gets programmers into trouble and can result in nearly unreadable code (sometimes jokingly called *spaghetti code*). There are better ways to implement the branching and looping operations without the use of the GO TO, but there are occasions when the GO TO is the simplest way to solve a logic problem. So we will review this simplest control structure first.

EXAMPLE 4.1

Here is a program that produces a list of the squares of positive integers

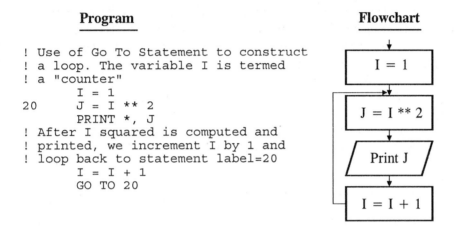

Program

```
! Use of Go To Statement to construct
! a loop. The variable I is termed
! a "counter"
        I = 1
20      J = I ** 2
        PRINT *, J
! After I squared is computed and
! printed, we increment I by 1 and
! loop back to statement label=20
        I = I + 1
        GO TO 20
```

Flowchart

When we first start this program, I has the value of 1. Its square is computed and printed, after which I increases by 1 and the whole process repeats. While this program works and produces the desired result, it is a very poor way to accomplish this task. Note for example, that the process presented is an *infinite loop*, and there is no way to get out.

The second way that we use the GO TO statement is to produce a branch, where we can jump over one set of instructions to perform another set.

EXAMPLE 4.2

In the example below, we use the GO TO statement to skip over a line within the program.

Program

```
! Demonstration of GO TO to skip
! over a set of instructions.
        X = X + 1
        GO TO 40
! The GO TO statement causes the
! next line to be skipped
30      X = X - 1
40      PRINT *, X
```

Flowchart

In this example, after executing X = X + 1, the program transfers to the line labeled 40 where the computer executes the PRINT statement. The only way of executing the statement labeled 30 would be for some other part of the program to issue a GO TO 30 command.

GO TO statements, FORMAT statements and other structures yet to be presented utilize statement labels. While there are few rules for statement labels, here are some suggestions that will help you make your program more understandable and easier to debug.

- Arrange statement labels in ascending order in your program. This will help you to locate the statement quickly when you are tracing through your program.
- Because programs are rarely correct the first time you write them, it is a good idea to increment your statement label by 10's, or even 100's. By initially assigning statement labels this way, you will be able to insert additional labels while maintaining the ascending order rule.

GO TO statements should be used sparingly and only when absolutely necessary since their excessive use can lead to programs which are more likely to contain logic errors and are hard to debug. We will show you alternate constructs that make use of the GO TO rare. Our purpose in showing the GO TO statement is to lay a foundation for the branch and loop discussed below.

4.3 CONDITIONAL STATEMENTS AND CONSTRUCTS

In this section we will present the IF statement and the IF construct. The difference between the IF statement and the construct is that the statement occupies only one line while the construct consists of a block of instructions over several lines. By using these commands it will be possible for you to construct conditional tests. Based on that test, you will be able to branch to other lines of code for other operations.

The IF statement provides a way to test a condition and execute a single command if the test condition is true. The general form is:

IF (*test condition*) *statement-to-execute-if-true*

The *test condition* is a comparison between two quantities (a variable with a constant for example). If the test condition is true, then the *statement-to-execute-if-true* is executed before control passes to the next line. If the test condition is false, however, control is immediately passed to the next line. Graphically, this is how the logic flows:

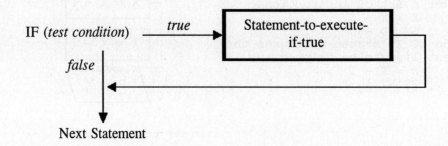

The test condition can be any expression that returns a logical value of *true* or *false*. For most applications, the test condition will be constructed of *relational operators* and *logical operators*. Relational operators are used to compare two numerical values and can return only one of two possible answers — *true* or *false*. The logical operators, on the other hand, are the operations to compare two truth values.

Relational Operators

Relational operators compare two quantities and return an answer of true or false. There are six relational operators available in Fortran, and they are listed in the table below:

Operator	Description	Example	Result
<	Less than (<)	1 < 2	True
< =	Less than or equal to ($\leq$)	3.14 < = 10.0	True
= =	Equal to (=)	0 = = 10	False
/=	Not equal to ($\neq$)	0 /= 10	True
>	Greater than (>)	1 > 2	False
> =	Greater than or equal to ($\geq$)	4 > = 3	True

When you use relational operators, you can compare a variable with a constant, a variable with another variable, a variable with an expression, and so forth. This comparison is done inside the parentheses following the IF key word.

EXAMPLE 4.3

Here are several examples of the use of relational operators:

Relational Operator	Description
IF (DENO = = 0) STOP	(Halt the program if the value of DENO = 0)
IF (TEMP < 0) PRINT *, TEMP	(If TEMP < 0 then print value of TEMP)
IF (X < = XMIN) XMIN = X	(If X ≤ XMIN, set value of XMIN to X)
IF (S > 1E6) S = 1E6	(Set S to 1×10^6 if S $> 1 \times 10^6$)
IF (A > = 0) GO TO 10	(Permissible to transfer to statement label 10)
IF (SQRT(X*Y) /= 4) X = Y	(You can use expressions for comparison)
IF (ABS(X) = = Y*Z) A=SQRT(X)	(You can compare an expression to an expression)
IF (I/2*2 = = I) PRINT *,'even'	(How to determine if an integer I is even or odd)

Logical Operators

In some instances you may wish to check more than one condition before carrying out an instruction. You can think of this as a compound test. For example, two things may need to be true simultaneously before a calculation can proceed. You are already familiar with this when you have a test like "Is x between 3.0 and 10.0?" expressed by:

$$3.0 < x < 10.0$$

This is equivalent to two individual relational comparisons:

Is $3.0 < x$ *and at the same time* is $x < 10.0$?

We treat this as two separate comparisons and connect them with a *logical operator*. Logical operators perform operations on truth values and return a truth value as their result. The following table lists some of the logical operators available in Fortran. Others will be presented later.

Operator	Description	Number of Arguments
.NOT.	Negation	1 argument
.AND.	Both simultaneously	2 arguments
.OR.	Either/or	2 arguments

These logical operators can only operate on logical expressions. The first (.NOT.) changes the logical value of its argument. Thus, if A is *true*, then (.NOT. A) is *false*. The other operators compare two logical values and return a single value based upon the two input values and the operator being used. The easiest way to summarize these is with the *truth tables* shown below:

.AND. Truth Table		
A	B	A .AND. B
T	T	T
T	F	F
F	T	F
F	F	F

.OR. Truth Table		
A	B	A .OR. B
T	T	T
T	F	T
F	T	T
F	F	F

.NOT. Truth Table	
A	.NOT. A
T	F
F	T

The .AND. operator is *true* only when <u>both</u> inputs are *true* while the .OR. operator is *true* when <u>either</u> input is *true*. Note carefully that these logical operators require two inputs. The .NOT. operator simply inverts the logical value of the expression that follows and requires only a single input value.

EXAMPLE 4.4

Construct a logical operator to see if a number x is within the range $1.0 < x < 10.0$. This test actually consists of two separate tests, both of which must be true simultaneously:

$$1.0 < x \quad and \quad x < 10.0$$

We construct the two tests and connect them with the .AND. logical operator:

```
READ *, X
IF(1.0<X .AND. X<10.0)PRINT *,X,'is between 1 and 10'
```

When you first look at this, you might have been tempted to write, as we do in mathematics:

$$1.0 < X < 10.0$$

But this is incorrect. The reason is that the operators can only compare data of the same type. They cannot compare *true* or *false* values with numerical data, for example. In our hypothetical solution, let's assume $X = 5.0$ and evaluate the tests from left to right:

$$1.0 < X < 10.0 \quad \rightarrow \quad 1.0 < 5.0 < 10.0 \quad \rightarrow \quad true < 10.0$$

An error occurs at this point since the $<$ operator attempts to compare two things that are incompatible (logical data with a real number in this instance).

In this last example, we combined relational operators ($<$) with logical operators (.AND.). But, you may also wish to write more complex test conditions that include mathematical operators. This may lead you to ask which operator would be performed first in such a complex test. Do we do the logical operators, the relational operators, or the mathematical operations first? The answers lie in the table below, which updates the hierarchical rules to include the two new operators:

Priority	Math Symbol	Fortran Symbol	Meaning
1	(...)	(...)	Parentheses
2	A^b	**	Exponentiation
3	$\times, \div$	*, /	Multiplication & division
4	$+, -$	$+, -$	Addition & subtraction
5	$=, \neq, <$	==, /=, <	Relational operators
	$\leq, >, \geq$	<=, >, >=	
6	$\overline{\times}$	.NOT.	Logical negation
7	$\odot$	.AND.	Logical AND
8	$\oplus$	.OR.	Logical OR

There are three new mathematical symbols in this table that you may not be familiar with. These are $\overline{X}$ (read as *bar x*) for logical negation, $\odot$ (read as *and*) for the logical AND function, and $\oplus$ (read as *or*) for the logical OR function. In this hierarchical list, the mathematical operators are performed first, the relational comparisons second, and the logical comparisons last. Thus, in a complex test, there is now an established order that you can use to decide which operations to perform first.

EXAMPLE 4.5

Evaluate the following expressions, assuming that X = 10.0, Y = −2.0, and Z = 5.0:

$$(X*Y < Z/X \text{ .OR. } X/Y > Z*X \text{ .AND. } Z*Y < X)$$

First, substitute values for X, Y, and Z, and perform the arithmetic operations:

$$(10.0*-2.0 < 5.0/10.0 \text{ .OR. } 10.0/-2.0 > 5.0*10.0 \text{ .AND. } 5.0*-2.0 < 10.0)$$

Next, perform the relational comparisons (<, >, <, from left to right):

$$(true \text{ .OR. } false \text{ .AND. } true)$$

From the hierarchy table, we see that .AND. takes precedence over .OR.. Thus, this reduces to

$$(true \text{ .OR. } false) \quad \rightarrow \quad (true)$$

4.4 THE BLOCK IF STRUCTURE

The IF statement that we discussed in the previous section is useful when you have only a single instruction to execute after the test condition is evaluated. But if you have more than a single instruction, you need a different structure. In Fortran, this is the *block IF* structure. As its name implies, it consists of blocks of instructions to execute. One block executes when the test condition is *true*, while a second block of instruction will execute when the test condition is *false*. The general form of the block IF construct is as follows:

```
IF (Test-Condition) THEN
        Block of statements if test-condition is true
ELSE
        Block of statements if test-condition is false
END IF
```

Nothing appears on the same line as the THEN, ELSE, or END IF key words. For convenience, we have indented the individual blocks to make it easier to visualize breaks in the control. But the indentation is not required. The individual blocks of statements can be as complex as you wish. They may be a single line or they may be hundreds of lines with complex structures.

EXAMPLE 4.6

The following segment checks to see if the number X you have entered is greater than or equal to zero. If it is not, the user is sent an error message and requested to reenter the data.

Program

```
! Use a prompt to request
! input for X
   10   PRINT *,'Enter Value:'
        READ *, X
! If X is negative, then
! print a message and go
! back to the input section.
! Otherwise, accept the
! value.
        IF(X < 0) THEN
            PRINT *,'Invalid'
            GO TO 10
        ELSE
            PRINT *,'Valid'
        END IF
```

Flowchart

In this example, the IF statement checks to see if the entered number is less than 0. If it is, then the test condition is *true* and the series of instructions between THEN and ELSE will be executed. In this case, the computer prints out the error message and returns to the input section. But if the number is greater than or equal to 0, the test condition is *false*, and control transfers to the block between the ELSE and the END IF statements. The only effect here is to produce the message "Valid." A key point is that no matter what the outcome of the test condition, only *one* block of instructions or the other is performed, not both!

When you write an IF-THEN-ELSE-END IF block, it is good programming practice to indent the block of instructions. All the key words (IF, ELSE, END IF) begin in the same column, while the instructions in each of the blocks are indented by an amount of your choosing. You will find this to be useful when you need to trace through your program while debugging. The indentations help you to visualize groups of instructions as blocks, and will become a valuable aid later on. We will also offer this same advice when we get to the other block structures.

There are times when it is advantageous to reverse the logic of the test condition. For example, if we set up the test to ask "Is x is equal to y?," it may be better to rephrase the question as "Is x not equal to y?" Of course, if we do this, we must reverse the block of instructions that accompany each of the answers (true or false).

EXAMPLE 4.7

The following program segment modifies Example 4.6 to reverse the logic.

Program   **Flowchart**

```
! Use a prompt to request
! input for X
   10   PRINT *,'Enter Value:'
        READ *, X
! The logic is reversed from the
! previous problem. The opposite
! of < is >=. We also need
! to switch the instructions to
! be executed for a true or
! false answer.
        IF(X >= 0) THEN
             PRINT *,'Valid'
        ELSE
             PRINT *,'Invalid'
             GO TO 10
        END IF
```

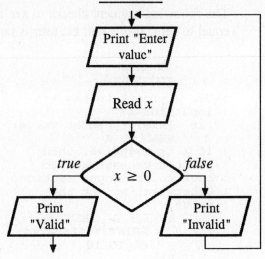

The program produces the same result as the segment in Example 4.6, but the route is somewhat different. When we reversed the logic, we also had to exchange the instructions to be executed when the decision is made. How you choose to write programs is a matter of personal style. Select the method that is most understandable to you.

When we discussed the block IF construct earlier, we introduced you to the concept of *program blocks*. Aside from the IF statement, many other Fortran commands also utilize program blocks. We will see them again when we discuss the Select Case structure and loops. Therefore, it is worthwhile to stop here and discuss briefly the rules for program blocks. These rules are:

- From inside the block, control can be transferred to a statement *outside* of the block.
- It is valid to transfer control from one statement of a block to another statement *within* the same block.
- You cannot transfer control from outside a block to *inside* a block except by way of the controlling structure.
- It is possible to nest constructs as long as the inner construct is completely within the outer block (no crossing of block boundaries is permitted).
- It is valid for a GO TO to send control to the closing statement of a construct.

We will demonstrate more fully what these rules mean in the next few examples.

EXAMPLE 4.8

The following example demonstrates that it is permissible to transfer *out* of a block IF construct. We will see shortly that the reverse operation (transferring *into* the body of a block) is never permitted.

Program	Flowchart

```
! The GO TO statement in
! this example transfers
! out of the block IF
        IF(D==0) THEN
            PRINT *,'D = 0'
            GO TO 10
        ELSE
            ANS = 1 / D
            PRINT *,ANS
        END IF
10      STOP
        END
```

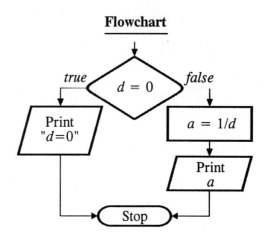

If the value of D is zero, the block IF prints out a statement that D=0 and transfers outside the block (to the STOP statement). But for any other value of D, the program proceeds to calculate the reciprocal of D and print it.

EXAMPLE 4.9

It is permissible to transfer control from one statement of a block to another statement *within* the same block.

Program	Flowchart

```
! The second IF statement
! will cause the program to
! jump to a position within
! the block IF
        IF(Y==1) THEN
            IF(X>0) GOTO 10
            X=-X
10          Y=Y+X
        ELSE
        END IF
```

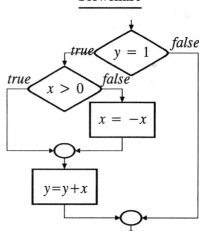

In this example, control jumps over the line X = −X when X is greater than 0. This is permitted since the jump is entirely within the block of instructions between the IF and ELSE statements. As long as the transfer begins and ends within the same block of the IF construct, it is permitted. Thus, if we wished, we could have transferred to a line before the IF (X > 0) statement and created a loop. The only restriction is that the line to which we are transferring must be situated within the block.

One final note about this and the previous examples: there are no instructions to be executed between the ELSE and the END IF statements. This is allowed, and in such cases the ELSE statement can be omitted without loss of clarity.

If jumping out of a block structure is allowed, how about jumping into the middle of a block? This <u>cannot</u> be allowed, since it would bypass the mechanism that controls a block of instructions.

EXAMPLE 4.10

In the following example, we show how you might attempt to transfer into the middle of a block. The Fortran compiler, however, will not allow you to do this.

```
        IF (X == 0) GO TO 20
        IF (Y == 0) THEN
20          X=X+1                    (This statement is inside the block IF construct)
        ELSE
        END IF
```

When the program attempts to jump to statement label 20, the statement that controls the branching operation (IF (Y == 0)) is completely bypassed and therefore cannot be allowed.

It is possible to place one block IF within another block IF, provided that they do not violate any of the previous rules. Not only is this structure acceptable, but it is often desirable, since it allows you to construct branching operations with more than two outcomes. In general, if you desire a structure with n outcomes, you will need $n-1$ nested block IF structures.

EXAMPLE 4.11

Here is a sample program to determine if a is positive, negative, or zero. Notice that this requires two nested block IFs, since there are three possible outcomes:

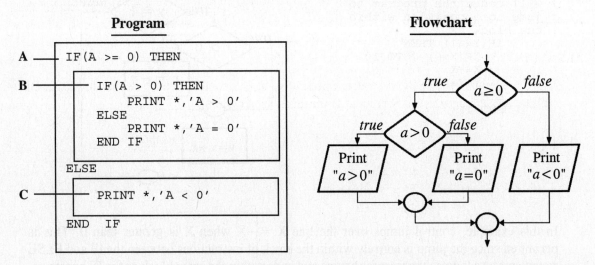

For clarity, we have drawn boxes around the different segments of the nested blocks. These will not appear when you create the program. Instead, we present them as a tool to recognize the concept of blocks. Note that block B is completely within the *true* section of the block IF represented by A. Similarly, block C is completely within the *false* block. As a result, the blocks are termed *properly nested*. If however, the blocks are not properly nested, the program will not compile.

Here is an example of invalid nesting:

EXAMPLE 4.12

Here is the same program as in Example 4.11, except that the blocks are improperly nested:

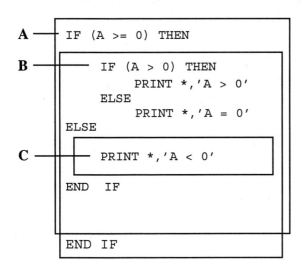

In this example, the *true* block, labeled B, overlaps the boundaries of block A. Thus, one of the components of the block IF actually extends outside the block that is supposed to contain it. This is not a legal structure, and the compiler will report a nesting error.

Block C is correctly nested, so there is no error for this part of the nested structure. One way to tell that the two structures are improperly nested is to look at one of the *key words* — ELSE. Notice that this structure has two consecutive ELSE statements. If the structures are properly nested, you will not have the situation where the same key word is repeated.

The final rule about block structures is that it is permissible to transfer to the end of the structure.

EXAMPLE 4.13

In this example, a GO TO statement inside a block IF structure is used to transfer to the end of the structure, which in this case is the END IF statement.

Program

```
! The GO TO 10 statement
! transfers control to the
! end of the block IF.
      IF(A > 10) THEN
         A = A + B
         Y = Y + 1
         IF(Y > 10)GOTO 10
         X = X - 1
      ELSE
         PRINT *, A, B
10    END IF
```

Flowchart

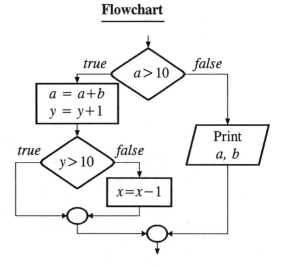

4.5 THE ELSE IF CONSTRUCT

The previous section introduced the IF construct and some of the rules for using it. In this section we will discuss a special form of the IF construct called the ELSE IF form. The ELSE IF construct is a nested block IF structure in which a block IF is placed inside the ELSE block of an outer block. By using the ELSE IF form, a *list* of conditions can be tested more concisely than with the block IF statements previously shown to you. The general form of the IF-THEN-ELSE-IF is:

```
IF (Test-Condition-1) THEN
        Block-1
ELSE IF (Test-Condition-2) THEN
        Block-2
        ⋮
ELSE IF (Test-Condition-N) THEN
        Block-N
ELSE
        Block-N+1
END IF
```

This is the only time that an instruction is allowed to be on the same line with the ELSE key word. If the first test condition is true, Block-1 executes. After completing the execution of Block-1, control then passes to the single END IF. If test condition 1 is false however, control passes to the next ELSE IF. If that test condition is true, then its block is executed and so on. This structure can have any number of ELSE IF blocks, so it offers the possibility of setting up a structure that has N+1 alternatives. Recall that the block IF structure can have only two alternatives. But by nesting these within each other, we can construct more complex structures, such as this multiple alternative form.

There are two ways of achieving the desired result. The first is to embed block IFs within each other. In this case, there will be an equal number of ELSE and END IF statements. The second way is to use the ELSE IF construct, where there will be only one END IF statement, and the construct will contain fewer lines. As you will see in the following example, the ELSE IF construct is usually easier to read than the equivalent nested IF-THEN-ELSE-END IF structures.

EXAMPLE 4.14

The following program reads in a temperature in degrees C and prints out an appropriate message using the following criteria:

Temperature ≤ 0 C	Print "It's below freezing"
0 C < Temperature ≤ 10 C	Print "It's cold out"
10 C < Temperature ≤ 20 C	Print "It's cool out"
20 C < Temperature ≤ 30 C	Print "It's warm"
Temperature > 30 C	Print "It's hot!"

First, we show the logic of the program with the nested block IF structure. Note that the structure is properly nested since none of the blocks crosses any other block.

To help you visualize the many blocks within this structure, we have indented each of them. Thus, the first nested block is indented by seven columns; the second nested block is indented 14 columns and so forth. We find that indentations that are multiples of seven are convenient since they correspond to one tab stop on many key boards. The choice of whether to tab or not and how much to tab are up to you. We highly recommend indentation of some sort, however, to help you avoid nesting errors.

Program with Nested IF Constructs:

```
PRINT *,'Enter the temperature in degrees C'
READ *,C
IF (C <= 0) THEN
      PRINT *,'It''s below freezing'
ELSE
      IF (C <= 10) THEN
            PRINT *,'It''s cold out'
      ELSE
            IF (C <= 20) THEN
                  PRINT *,'It''s cool out'
            ELSE
                  IF (C <= 30) THEN
                        PRINT *,'It''s warm'
                  ELSE
                        PRINT *,'It''s hot!'
                  END IF
            END IF
      END IF
END IF
```

Notice that the key words (IF−ELSE−END IF) line up and make it easy to see if each block IF structure has been properly constructed. Here now is the program with the ELSE IF construct:

Modified Program Using the ELSE IF Construct:

```
PRINT *, 'Enter the temperature in degrees C'
READ *, C
IF (C <= 0) THEN
      PRINT *, 'It''s below freezing'
ELSE IF (C <= 10) THEN
      PRINT *, 'It''s cold out'
ELSE IF (C <= 20) THEN
      PRINT *, 'It''s cool out'
ELSE IF (C <= 30) THEN
      PRINT *,'It''s warm'
ELSE
      PRINT *,'It''s hot!'
END IF
```

This is a more compact structure than the equivalent nested block IF structure shown in the first part of the example. Note that the ELSE IF option works by passing control to the END IF statement only when a *true* test condition is found.

The choice of which structure to use — the nested block IFs or the ELSE IF structure is up to you since they perform equivalent functions. Most programmers, however, tend to prefer the ELSE IF construct because it is generally easier to follow.

When constructing programs with a large number of nested IF constructs, it is convenient to have a means of labeling them. Fortunately, Fortran 90 now provides this feature. The following illustrates the general form of the IF Construct with the optional use of block names.

```
name:   IF (Test-Condition) THEN
              block-1
        ELSE name
              block-2
        END IF name
```

The use of the names, which are optional makes programs more readable by identifying the various portions of the construct. The *name* can be any valid Fortran variable name and must be the same in all the indicated spots. It has no function other than to label the various sections of the construct to make it easier to read.

The important advantage of named blocks comes when you begin to nest one construct within another one. In this case, you give each construct its own unique name to help you identify the various blocks. Finally, when you use names with nested block IFs, the names of the inner and outer block structures must be different.

EXAMPLE 4.15

Here is Example 4.14 with named nested block IF constructs:

```
Freeze:     IF (C <= 0) THEN
                  PRINT *,'It''s Below Freezing'
            ELSE Freeze
Cold:             IF (C <= 10) THEN
                        PRINT *,'It''s Cold out'
                  ELSE Cold
Cool:                   IF (C <= 20) THEN
                              PRINT *,'It''s Cool out'
                        ELSE Cool
Warm:                         IF (C <= 30) THEN
                                    PRINT *,'It''s Warm'
                              ELSE Warm
                                    PRINT *,'It''s Hot'
                              END IF Warm
                        END IF Cool
                  END IF Cold
            END IF Freeze
```

Notice at the end of this program how the END IF names are in the reverse order that their corresponding block-IFs were opened. For example, Cold was opened first, but closed last. Cool was opened second, and closed next to last, and so forth for all the other blocks. This is necessary for proper nesting of the blocks. By using the names it is easier to see that the structure is correct.

4.6 THE SELECT CASE STRUCTURE

The select case provides a means of selecting an action (which can be a block of statements) by comparing the value of an expression against a list of values. The general form of the select case construct is:

```
SELECT CASE (expression)
        CASE (selector list 1)
            block-1
        CASE (selector list 2)
            block-2
              ⋮

              ⋮
        CASE DEFAULT
            block-n
END SELECT
```

As with the previous block structures, there are key words to mark the beginning and end of the structure — the SELECT CASE and END SELECT statements, respectively. In between are a series of CASES, only one of which is executed based on the value of the expression in the SELECT CASE statement. The expression is a scalar (single-valued) expression which can have integer, character, or logical data type only. Once this expression is evaluated, its value is compared with the values contained in the *selector lists* until a match is found. The list of instructions that follow this CASE is then executed. If the expression in the CASE SELECT expression has no match among the various selector lists, then the instructions in the CASE DEFAULT are executed. The CASE DEFAULT statement is optional and may be listed anywhere within the construct.

The selector list for each of the CASES can be a single value, a list, or a range of values specified by low-value:high-value, or a list of values which include ranges. This will become more obvious in the following examples. Also, the selector lists must not overlap in values. This last requirement prevents any ambiguities regarding which set of instructions the program is to execute.

The type of the expression and selectors must match. Thus, if the expression is a character, a character string, or a range of character strings, then the selectors must also be character strings. Lengths of strings do not necessarily have to match. If the expression is of type integer or logical, then the selectors also be of the same type. Notice that the selectors cannot be real variables or real constants.

EXAMPLE 4.16

Here is a simple SELECT CASE example that will type out a message about which set of instructions has been selected by the user:

Program

```
! Demonstration of Select Case Structure. An integer
! is read into N. If the value read in is 1, 2, or 3
! a message such as "#2 Entered" is printed. But if any
! other number is read in, the message "Error" is printed.
PRINT *,'Select value 1-3'
READ *, N
SELECT CASE (N)
   CASE (1)
      PRINT *,'#1 Entered'
   CASE (2)
      PRINT *,'#2 Entered'
   CASE (3)
      PRINT *,'#3 Entered'
   CASE DEFAULT
      PRINT *,'Error'
END SELECT
```

Flowchart

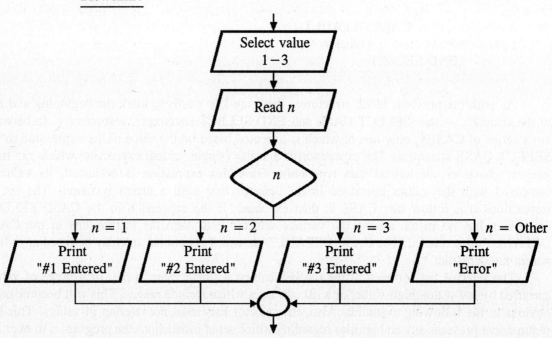

After the value of *n* is read in, the SELECT CASE structure examines its value, and decides which section to execute. If *n*=1, 2, or 3 for example, control transfers to the instructions inside the first, second, or third CASE, respectively. But if *n* is any other value, control transfers to the section labeled CASE DEFAULT where the computer will print out an error message.

The switching within this structure depends upon the value of the expression following the SELECT CASE command and the list of selectors that define each of the CASEs. Therefore, it is important that the expression and the corresponding selector list be as flexible as possible. In the example below, we illustrate the many ways that you can set up the selector lists.

EXAMPLE 4.17

Shown below are several examples of selector lists along with an interpretation of their meanings.

Selector	Description
CASE(1)	Single value (1)
CASE(1, 3, 5)	List of values (1, 3 or 5)
CASE(1:5)	The range of integer values 1,2,3,4 and 5
CASE(:0)	The range of integer values less than or equal to 0
CASE(1:)	The range of integer values greater than or equal to 1
CASE(1,10,100:)	List of integer values 1, 10, plus all values more than 100
CASE('A')	String with value 'A'
CASE('A':'H')	Range of characters A through H
CASE('BOB':'MARY')	Range of character strings that fall in the collating sequence between BOB and MARY
CASE(1,'a')	Invalid: selector must be of one type only
CASE(2.25)	Invalid: real values are not allowed

The value inside the parentheses of the above examples will be used by the computer to decide which block of instructions to execute. If, for example, we set up CASE(1, 3, 5), and the CASE SELECT expression evaluates to 1, 3, or 5, then the set of instructions that follow this CASE would be executed.

In addition to the rule about matching the expression and selector types, it is also necessary that selectors do not overlap in values.

EXAMPLE 4.18

Shown below are two examples of valid select case structures and one invalid example:

```
a)      SELECT CASE (N)          (Choice of CASE depends on value of N)
           CASE (:-1)
               NSIGN=-1          (Sets NSIGN to –1 for values of N less than 0)
           CASE (0)
               NSIGN=0           (Sets NSIGN to 0 for value of N equal to 0)
           CASE(1:)
               NSIGN=1           (Sets NSIGN to 1 for values of N greater than 0)
        END SELECT
```

```
(b)        SELECT CASE (N)           (Value of N used to select CASE)
               CASE (1,3,5)
                   X = -X            (If N=1, 3, or 5, change sign of X)
               CASE (2,4,6)
                   X = ABS(X)        (If N=2,4, or 6, replace X by its absolute value)
               CASE(:0)              (If N is 0 or negative, do nothing)
               CASE DEFAULT
                   X = X**2          (For any other value of N, replace X by its square)
           END SELECT
```

```
(c)        SELECT CASE(I)            (Invalid example because value of 7 used twice)
               CASE(1,3,5,7)         (One of the allowed values is 7)
                   RANGE=1
               CASE (7,9)            (Value of 7 used again, which is not allowed)
                   RANGE=2
           END SELECT                (Error detected at compilation time)
```

EXAMPLE 4.19

Let's now rewrite the weather report program in Example 4.14 using the select case construct.

```
! We can use the select case structure to give a rough
! weather report. First, we convert the temperature to
! an integer value with the NINT function. Then this value
! is used to select a range. For example, if IC=23, it
! would fall into the range for CASE(21:30), and the
! program would print the message "It's warm"
PRINT *,'Enter the temperature in degrees C'
READ *, C
IC = NINT( C )
SELECT CASE (IC)
    CASE( :0)
        PRINT *,'It''s below freezing'
    CASE(1:10)
        PRINT *,'It''s cold out'
    CASE (11:20)
        PRINT *,'It''s cool out'
    CASE (21:30)
        PRINT *,'It''s warm'
    CASE DEFAULT
        PRINT *,'It''s hot!'
END SELECT
```

Note that in order to use the CASE construct, we had to convert the temperature entered from a real to an integer value. The reason for this is that the CASE structure can operate only with integer, character, or logical data. Real, double precision, and complex data cannot be used. Thus, the results for this program may be slightly different from the previous example because of rounding of real values.

4.7 DEBUGGING TIPS

Debugging is something that no programmer can escape. Most inexperienced programmers start with the assumption that debugging is a *post mortem* event and begins only after the program crashes. An experienced programmer, however, knows that debugging starts when you are writing the program at the earliest stages. Good programming style pays handsome dividends when it comes time to debug. Thus, many of our debugging tips focus on style, so that we try to make our programs bug proof from the beginning.

Here are some things you can do to develop good style:

- *Assign Statement Labels in Ascending Order*
  By arranging statement labels in ascending order, the location of statement labels can be more easily seen. Incrementing statement labels by 10's or 100's will allow you to leave room for future modifications. Remember, programs rarely work correctly the first time. Be sure to prepare for future changes.

- *Indent Block Structures*
  Indenting of blocks within constructs such as the block IF and SELECT CASE structures makes it easier to find nesting errors.

- *Use Comment Statements Liberally*
  One of the most useful capabilities of any programming language is the ability to include comment statements. Use comment statements to describe the functionality of a program block. Think of your comment statements as a road map. When you return to your program, you will understand more easily the logic you were trying to implement when you worked on the program. Comments might include the objectives of the program, descriptions of all the variables used, and the logic.

- *Enter the Key Words of a Construct First*
  By completely writing the key words of the construct and then entering the blocks, you guarantee that all of the components will be in the correct location. By using this technique you can eliminate misplaced END IFs, ELSEs, and other construct pieces that are always so bothersome.

EXAMPLE 4.20

In the following example, we will construct a program to determine if 1) A > 0 and B ≤ 10, or 2) A > 0 and B > 10, or 3) A ≤ 0. Note that this will require nested block IF structures since there are three possible outcomes. We start with one block IF based on the IF (A > 0) construct, and put down only the skeleton consisting of the key words (IF-THEN-ELSE-END IF).

```
Step 1:        IF (A > 0) THEN
               ELSE
               END IF
```

Next, fill in the inner blocks, being sure to indent for clarity. In this case, however, one of the blocks contains another block IF construct. So we will follow our own advice and fill in only the skeleton of this inner construct by adding the key words IF-THE-ELSE-END IF in the appropriate locations:

Step 2:
```
IF (A > 0) THEN
    IF (B <= 10) THEN
    ELSE
    END IF
ELSE
    PRINT *, 'A <= 0'
END IF
```

Finally, fill in the blocks for the second, innermost IF construct. Once again, remember to indent the blocks you are adding so that they will be easy to identify at a later date:

Step 3:
```
IF (A > 0) THEN
    IF (B <= 10) THEN
        PRINT *, 'A > 0 and B <= 10'
    ELSE
        PRINT *, 'A > 0 and B > 10'
    END IF
ELSE
    PRINT *, 'A <= 0'
END IF
```

A convenient way to think of this process is to think of the constructs as the logic of the program and the blocks as the specific actions. By entering the constructs first, you lay out the logic first and then fill in the details of the action at a later time. Notice that by writing the program in this fashion, it is difficult for you to misplace an END IF or ELSE statement. While this will not make the program segment foolproof, it will greatly help to minimize the number the number of errors.

Even if you faithfully carry out all of the suggestions we have given you, you will still have bugs in your programs. Hopefully, they will be far fewer in number, and easier to find. So how do you locate the bugs? The first way to find them is to trace through your program as we discussed in Chapter 2. To review, tracing is the process of manually following the changes in a program. We will be doing the same thing here, but the tracing steps are somewhat more involved because of the control structures introduced so far (GO TO, Block IF, ELSE IF, and SELECT CASE constructs).

When tracing programs that contain constructs, you will have to determine which IF-THEN statement matches which END IF. The same is true for the SELECT CASE and END SELECT statements. If you had used indentations when you wrote the program, this would be a simple task. But if you did not use indentations when you wrote the program, the method presented in the following example can be used.

EXAMPLE 4.21

The following illustrates how to match the initiating and terminating statements for blocks:

```
        IF (A > 0) THEN
        IF (B <= 10) THEN
        PRINT *, 'A > 0 and B <=10'
        ELSE
        PRINT *,'A > 0 and B > 10'
        END IF
        SELECT CASE (N)
        CASE (:-1)
        NSIGN=-1
        CASE (0)
        NSIGN=0
        CASE(1:)
        NSIGN=1
        END SELECT
        IF (A+B<10) STOP
        ELSE
        PRINT *,'A <= 0'
        END  IF
```

First, connect terminating statements to initiating statements as we did in the example by starting at the top of the program and reading down until a terminating statement is encountered (END IF, or END SELECT). Draw a line from the terminating statement back to the closest initiating statement that is appropriate (IF-THEN or SELECT-CASE). Repeat until all terminating statements are matched. At this point, indent any line that is inside any of the connecting lines. Then locate the connecting intermediate and optional statements (shown below as dashed lines) from the intermediate statement out to the connecting lines. The first line encountered indicates the ownership of the intermediate statement.

```
        IF (A>0) THEN
            IF (B<=10) THEN
                PRINT *,'A > 0 and B <=10'
            ELSE
                PRINT *,'A > 0 and B > 10'
            END IF
            SELECT CASE (N)
                CASE (:-1)
                NSIGN=-1
                CASE (0)
                NSIGN=0
                CASE(1:)
                NSIGN=1
            END SELECT
            IF (A+B<10) STOP
        ELSE
            PRINT *,'A <= 0'
        END IF
```

The final step is to see if any of the block structures are improperly nested. You can easily see this by checking to see if any of the lines cross each other. Since no lines cross each other in the example above, the blocks are properly nested.

Tracing as a Debugging Tool

The process of manually tracing a program can be time consuming. However, by providing yourself with tools such as indentations of block structures and variable tables, you can trace even the most complex programs to find logic errors. To help guide you, we offer two more guidelines:

- *Document your trace.*
  Document your trace by writing out key components of the manual trace. If you are unable to complete the trace, this will help the next person who looks at it.

- *Use variable tables as outlined in Chapter 2.*

EXAMPLE 4.22

To aid in documenting a trace, it is recommended that you assign a number to each line of the program. This way, as you trace through the program, you can write down the lines of code your are evaluating. Also, identify each of the key words in block structures, and identify the nesting level if appropriate. For the following trace, assume A=5, B=1, and N=15:

Program Line		Identify Key Word and Level
001	IF (A > 0) THEN	*IFTHEN (level 1)*
002	IF (B < = 10) THEN	*IFTHEN (level 2)*
003	PRINT *, 'A > 0 and B < = 10'	
004	ELSE	*IFTHEN (level 2)*
005	PRINT *, 'A > 0 and B > 10'	
006	END IF	*IFTHEN (level 2)*
007	SELECT CASE (N)	*SELECT CASE (level 1)*
008	CASE (:-1)	*CASE (level 1)*
009	NSIGN=-1	
010	CASE (0)	*CASE (level 1)*
011	NSIGN=0	
012	CASE(1:)	*CASE (level 1)*
013	NSIGN=1	
014	END SELECT	*CASE (level 1)*
015	IF (A+B<10) STOP	
016	ELSE	*IFTHEN (level 1)*
017	PRINT *,'A < = 0'	
018	END IF	*IFTHEN (level 1)*

For the input data given, this is how the program would be executed:

Line 01 Is (5 > 0)? True, go to line 02 (the true-block of IFTHEN1.)
Line 02 Is (1 < = 10)? True, go to line 03 (the true-block of IFTHEN2.)
Line 03 Prints: A > 0 and B < = 10.
Line 04 Else of IFTHEN2, go to END IF of IFTHEN2.
Line 06 END IF of IFTHEN2.
Line 07 SELECT CASE (15), go to next line.
Line 08 CASE(:-1) 15 in range of negative integers? False, go to next CASE line 10.
Line 10 CASE(0) is 15 equal to 0? False, go to next CASE line 12.
Line 12 CASE(1:) 15 in the range of positive integers? True, go to next line (CASE block).
Line 13 NSIGN is set to 1, go to next line.
Line 14 END SELECT: end of structure, go to next line.
Line 15 Is (5+1<10)? True, so execute STOP statement. End of program.

And here is the output:

A > 0 and B < =10

Variable Table (assuming integer values):

A: 5
B: 1
N: 15
NSIGN: 1

Tracing is a tedious task. So, if you can get the computer to do some of the work for you, your job will be much easier. Most compilers have options, one of which is known as "list," which creates a file of your program with line numbers, tables of variables used, and any errors encountered by the compiler. When performing a trace, this is a convenient place to start.

In addition to containing line numbers and a listing of all errors, the file listing created by the debugger also creates a table listing each variable. This table can be used for the variable table during tracing. Another use for the variable table is to check the variable typing. Along with the list of variables will be a column indicating the type of variable. This is a way to check that all variables are declared as you would like them.

If the results of the program are incorrect, use PRINT statements to display the value of variables and the results of expressions. If your manual calculations of an expression do not agree with the computer-generated result, then check for mixed-mode arithmetic and proper hierarchy of operations. The following list summarizes these additional guidelines:

- *Use PRINT statements liberally to display values of variables and expressions.* Include PRINT statements in your program and have the computer do the tracing for you.

- *Validate your results using known solutions.* Try to test your program with data sets for which you already know the answer. This will improve the confidence in using the program with other data for which no solution is known.

Solved Problems

4.1 Locate errors in the following IF-THEN constructs:

```
(a)  IF(A > B) Print *,'A>B'  (b)  IF(A > 10)
     END IF                        X = 1
                                   END IF
(c)  IF(A == B) THEN X = 1   (d)  IF (A < 10 .AND. B) THEN
     ELSE X = 2                    PRINT *,'A is less than 10 and',B
                                   END IF
```

(a) No END IF allowed with one-line IF statement.
(b) THEN is missing.
(c) No statement can appear after the THEN or ELSE key words. Any desired statement must go on the next line. Also, the entire structure must be terminated by an END IF.
(d) Expression is incorrect. Rewrite as A < 10 .AND. A < B

4.2 Indicate which of the following logical expressions are valid. If the expression is invalid, explain why. For each of the following examples, assume *LOG1* is a logical variable. Assume default typing (Implicit) for all other variables.

(a) (A = B)   *(Invalid. Should be == instead of =)*
(b) (1 < X & X < 10)   *(Invalid. "&" is not a valid operator. Use .AND.)*
(c) (.NOT. (A>10 .AND. A<2)) *(Valid)*
(d) (SQRT(A) == LOG1)   *(Invalid. Cannot compare real and logical data.)*

4.3 Trace the following logical expressions illustrating the hierarchy of operations. Assume X = 10.0, Y = −2.0, and Z = 5.0 and underline the next operation to be performed.

(a) (X == Y .OR. X / Y + Z == 0.0 .OR. Y >= Z)
(b) (.NOT. (X == Y .OR. X * Y + Z == 0.0))
(c) (.NOT. (X > 10 .AND. Z < 2))
(d) (Y < Z .AND. X < Z)
(e) (.NOT. (Y < Z .AND. .NOT. X > Z))

(a) (10.0 == −2.0 .OR. <u>10.0/−2.0</u> +5.0 == 0.0 .OR. −2.0 >= 5.0)
    (10.0 == −2.0 .OR. <u>−5.0 + 5.0</u> == 0.0 .OR. −2.0 >= 5.0)
    (<u>10.0 == −2.0</u> .OR. <u>0.0 == 0.0</u> .OR. <u>−2.0 >= 5.0</u>)
    (*false* .OR. *true* .OR. *false*)
    (*true* .OR. *false*) → *true*
(b) (.NOT. (10.0 == −2.0 .OR. <u>10.0 * −2.0</u> + 5.0 == 0.0))
    (.NOT. (10.0 == −2.0 .OR. <u>−20.0 +5.0</u> == 0.0))
    (.NOT. (<u>10.0 == −2.0</u> .OR. −15.0 == 0.0))
    (.NOT. (*false* .OR. <u>−15.0 == 0.0</u>))

$\qquad$ (.NOT. (*false .OR. false*))
$\qquad$ (.NOT. (*false*)) → *true*
(c) (.NOT. (<u>10.0 > 10</u> .AND. 5.0 < 2))
$\qquad$ (.NOT. (*false* .AND. <u>5.0 < 2</u>))
$\qquad$ (.NOT. (*false .AND. false*))
$\qquad$ (.NOT. *false*) → *true*
(d) (<u>−2.0 < 5.0</u> .AND. 10.0 < 5.0)
$\qquad$ (*true* .AND. <u>10.0 < 5.0</u>)
$\qquad$ (*true .AND. false*) → *false*
(e) (.NOT. (<u>−2.0 < 5.0</u> .AND. .NOT. 10.0 > 5.0))
$\qquad$ (.NOT. (*true* .AND. .NOT. <u>10.0 > 5.0</u>))
$\qquad$ (.NOT. (*true* .AND. <u>.NOT. true</u>))
$\qquad$ (.NOT. (*true .AND. false*))
$\qquad$ (.NOT. *false*) → *true*

4.4   Which program segments have incorrect transfer instructions?

```
(a)  IF (X > 10) THEN   (b)   SELECT CASE (N)
         A = X**2 + 1            CASE (:-1)
         B = 10 + X                GO TO 30
         GO TO 10               CASE (0)
     ELSE                          IF(X<10) GOTO 20
         A = X + 1          20     Z=Z+1
10       C = 10                 CASE DEFAULT
     END IF                 30     Q = Q + Q**2
                              END SELECT
```

(a)   GO TO 10 is incorrect. Transfers control to a line inside the ELSE block.
(b)   GO TO 30 is incorrect since this statement label appears inside another block.

4.5   Which program segments are incorrect due to overlapping blocks?

```
(a)  IF ... THEN               (b)   SELECT CASE...
         IF ...THEN                     CASE...
             SELECT CASE ...              SELECT CASE...
                 CASE...                    CASE...
                     IF...                  CASE DEFAULT
                         IF...THEN          CASE...
                         ELSE               CASE...
                 CASE...                  END SELECT
             END SELECT            END SELECT
         ELSE
         END IF
     END IF
```

(a)   CASE and third IF-THEN structures cross.
(b)   CASE DEFAULT appears as an intermediate case to the second SELECT CASE. One END SELECT should come after the CASE DEFAULT block.

4.6   Determine which SELECT CASE constructs are valid or invalid. For invalid constructs indicate why. Assume default typing of the variables.

```
(a)  SELECT CASE (N)              (b)  SELECT CASE (X)
         CASE (:-1)                        CASE (1.0,3.0,5.0)
            NSIGN = -1                         PRINT *,'X was 1,3 or 5'
         CASE (-1)                         CASE DEFAULT
            NSIGN=0                            PRINT ,'X was NOT 1,3,5'
         CASE(1:)                      END SELECT
            NSIGN=1
     END SELECT
```

(a)   Invalid. Overlapping of CASE values in first and second cases.

(b)   Invalid: Case selector must be an integer, character, or logical value. X is real.

4.7   Predict the output for the program presented in Example 4.21 based on the input values given below. Be sure to use a trace table and to document your trace.

(a) $A = 2, N = -1,$ and $B = 5$ (b) $A = 0, N = 0,$ and $B = 15$

(a) Program Trace:

Line 01 (2 > 0):true, go to line 2
Line 02 (5 <=10):true, go to line 3
Line 03 PRINT A>0 and B <= 10, go to next line
Line 04 ELSE of IFTHEN2. Go to END IF for IFTHEN2
Line 06 END IF for IFTHEN2. Go to next line
Line 07 SELECT CASE (−1) go to first case
Line 08 CASE (:−1): true. Execute block for case
Line 09 NSIGN=−1. Last statement in block. Go to END SELECT
Line 14 END SELECT, go to next line
Line 15 is (2+5 < 10)? true. Execute STOP

Output:

A > 0 and B <= 10

Trace Table:

A:	2	B:	5
N:	−1	NSIGN:	−1

(b)   Program Trace:

Line 01 Is (0 > 0)? False. Go to ELSE block for IFTHEN1
Line 17 Print A <= 0 Last line of ELSE block. Go to END IF
Line 18 END IF

Output:

A <= 0

Trace Table:

| A: | 0 | B: | 15 |
| N: | 0 | NSIGN: | never assigned a value |

4.8 Write a program to read in values for *a*, *b*, and *c*, and print their sum. Repeat this procedure until all values of *a*, *b*, and *c* are negative.

```
10   PRINT *, 'Enter value of A, B, and C:'
     READ *, A, B, C
     IF( A .LT. 0 .AND. B < 0 .AND. C < 0) STOP
     SUM =A + B + C
     PRINT *, 'SUM = ', SUM
     GO TO 10
     END
```

4.9 Read in three integer values *i*, *j*, *k* and determine if *all* are odd or *all* are even.

```
! An integer I is even if I/2*2 = I. Recall that if we use
! the rules of integer division that any remainder is dropped.
! Thus, if I is odd, division by 2 will produce a remainder.
! The easiest way to do this is with the MOD function, where
! the function returns the remainder of integer division.
     READ *, I, J, K
     IF(MOD(I,2)==0 .AND. MOD(J,2)==0 .AND. MOD(K,2)==0) THEN
         PRINT *, 'ALL EVEN'
     ELSE
         IF(MOD(I,2)==1 .AND. MOD(J,2)==1 .AND. MOD(K,2)==1) THEN
             PRINT *, 'ALL ODD'
     ELSE
             PRINT *, 'MIXED'
     END IF
     END IF
```

4.10 Write a program to read in the radius *r* of a circle centered at the origin. Then read in coordinate pair (*x*, *y*) of a point and determine if that point lies within the circle.

```
     PRINT *, 'Enter R'
     READ *, R
     PRINT *, 'Enter X, Y'
     READ *, X, Y
     RXY = SQRT(X**2+Y**2)
     IF(RXY<R) THEN
         PRINT*, 'Inside Circle'
     ELSE
         PRINT*, 'Outside Circle'
     END IF
     END
```

4.11 When we write a program, we often have the program ask questions which are answered yes or no. People have a tendency, however, to answer with things like yes, YES, y, Y, true, TRUE and so forth. A good program should consider how people are likely to answer such a question. Write a program that will convert yes, YES, y, Y, true, TRUE, t, and T into TRUE. Similarly, your program should report FALSE for n, NO, N, no, false, f, FALSE or false. Can you think of any other possible responses that someone might use?

```
CHARACTER (LEN=5) :: ANS
PRINT *, 'Enter Answer'
READ *, ANS
SELECT CASE (ANS)
  CASE('t', 'T', 'y', 'Y', 'true', 'TRUE', 'yes', 'YES')
    PRINT *, 'TRUE'
  CASE('f', 'F', 'n', 'N', 'false', 'FALSE', 'no', 'NO')
    PRINT *, 'FALSE'
  CASE DEFAULT
    PRINT *, 'Answer not recognized'
END SELECT
```

(Also consider mixed capitalization such as Yes, True, No, etc.)

Supplementary Problems

4.12 Locate errors in the following IF-THEN constructs:

(a) ```
IF (A>=B) THEN Z=Y
END IF
```

(b) ```
REAL :: A,B,C
IF(A<B<C) THEN
PRINT *,' A < B < C'
END IF
```

(c) ```
IF (C<=0) THEN
   PRINT *,'freezing'
ELSE (C<=10)
   PRINT *,'cold'
ELSE (C<=20)
   PRINT *,'cool'
ELSE (C<=30)
   PRINT *,'nice'
ELSE
   PRINT *,'hot'
END IF
```

(d) ```
IF A>10 GO TO 100
```

(e) `IF (B .NOT. 10) PRINT *,'B is not equal to 10'`

4.13 Indicate which of the following logical expressions are valid. Assume *LOG1* and *LOG2* are logical variables. Assume default typing for all other variables.

(a) (A EQ B)

(b) (.NOT. LOG1)

(c) (LOG1 .AND. X + 1 > 10)

(d) ((.NOT. (X+B)) == 0.0)

(e) (.NOT. LOG2 .OR. .NOT. LOG1)

4.14 Trace through the following logical expressions step by step, illustrating the hierarchy of operations. For each problem assume that X = 10.0, Y = –2.0, and Z = 5.0:

    (a) (X /= Y .AND. Y /= Z .AND. X /= Z)
    (b) (X > =Z .AND. .NOT. ((Z*Y < =X) .OR. .NOT. (X==Y)))
    (c) (X*Y < Z / X .OR. X / Y > Z * X)
    (d) (.NOT. Y < Z .AND. X > Z)
    (e) (–INT(X / Y) == X / Y)

4.15 Which of these program segments has incorrect transfer operations?

```
(a)  IF(A+B>=2.34)GOTO 15     (b)  IF(X+Y>0)  THEN
     IF(X==10)  THEN               IF(X>0)GOTO 10
        Z=A+B+X                       Y=X+Y
15      DIST=10+Z             10 END IF
     END IF
```

4.16 Which of these program segments is incorrect due to overlapping blocks?

```
(a)  IF...THEN                (b)  IF...THEN
     ELSE                          ELSE IF...THEN
         IF...THEN                     IF...THEN
         ELSE                          ELSE IF...THEN
         END IF                        ELSE
         IF...THEN                         SELECT CASE
         ELSE IF...THEN                        CASE...
         ELSE                                      IF...
             SELECT CASE...            END SELECT
             CASE...                       CASE...
                 END IF                END SELECT
             CASE...                   ELSE IF...THEN
             CASE DEFAULT              ELSE
             END SELECT           END IF
     END IF
```

4.17 Determine which constructs are valid. Assume that STRING is a character variable.

```
(a)  SELECT CASE(STRING)      (b)  SELECT CASE(N/2)
        CASE("A":"H")                CASE (1)
          TEST=1                       PRINT *,'RANGE 1'
        CASE ("Y","Z")             CASE DEFAULT
          TEST=2                       PRINT *,'RANGE 2'
     END SELECT                    CASE (2)
                                     PRINT *,'RANGE 3'
                                  END SELECT
```

4.18 Predict the output for the program presented in Example 4.21 based on the input values given below. Be sure to use a trace table and to document your trace.

    (a) $A = 0$, $N = -1$, and $B = 15$ (b) $A = 2$, $N = 0$, and $B = 5$
    (c) $A = 0$, $N = 1$, and $B = 15$.

Answers to Selected Supplementary Problems

4.12 (a) Assignment statement Z=Y must go on the following line
    (b) Expression is invalid. Replace with A<B .AND. B<C
    (c) Missing IF and THEN statements on the ELSE lines
    (d) The ( ) is missing around the logical expression
    (e) NOT is a logical operator. A relational operator is needed to check a numerical value. The line should be IF (B /= 10)....

4.13 (a) Invalid: " EQ " should be "=="
    (b) Valid
    (c) Valid
    (d) Invalid: cannot use .NOT. operator on real numbers
    (e) Valid

4.14 (a) (10.0 /= −2.0 .AND. −2.0 /= 5.0 .AND. 10.0 /= 5.0)
        (*true* .AND. *true* .AND. *true*)
        (*true* .AND. *true*) → *true*
    (b) (10.0 >= 5.0 .AND. .NOT. ((5.0 * −2.0 <= 10.0) .OR. .NOT. (10.0 == −2.0)))
        (10.0 >= 5.0 .AND. .NOT. ((−10.0 <= 10.0) .OR. .NOT. (10.0 == −2.0)))
        (10.0 >= 5.0 .AND. .NOT. (*true* .OR. .NOT. (10.0 == −2.0)))
        (10.0 >= 5.0 .AND. .NOT. (*true* .OR. .NOT. *false*))
        (10.0 >= 5.0 .AND. .NOT. (*true* .OR. *true*))
        (10.0 >= 5.0 .AND. .NOT. *true*)
        (*false* .AND. .NOT. *true*)
        (*false* .AND. *false*) → *false*
    (c) (10.0*−2.0 < 5.0/10.0 .OR. 10.0/−2.0 > 5.0*10.0)
        (−20.0 < 5.0/10.0 .OR. 10.0/−2.0 > 5.0*10.0)
        (−20.0 < 0.5 .OR. 10.0/−2.0 > 5.0*10.0)
        (−20.0 < 0.5 .OR. −5.0 > 5.0*10.0)
        (−20.0 < 0.5 .OR. −5.0 > 50.0)
        (*true* .OR. −5.0 > 50.0)
        (*true* .OR. *false*) → *true*
    (d) (.NOT. −2.0 < 5.0 .AND. 10.0 > 5.0)
        (.NOT. *true* .AND. 10.0 > 5.0)
        (.NOT. *true* .AND. *true*)
        (*false* .AND. *true*) → *false*
    (e) (−INT(10.0/−2.0) == (10.0/−2.0))

$(-INT(-5.0) == -5)$
$(5 == \underline{10.0/-2.0})$
$(5 == \underline{-5.0}) \rightarrow false$ *(May not work since the real number (−5.0) may not be exactly equal to the integer (−5) because of roundoff errors)*

4.15   (a)   Invalid transfer from IF statement
         (b)   Branching to the END IF is acceptable

4.16   (a)   END IF of third IF-THEN crosses the SELECT CASE 1st block
         (b)   Invalid structure; one too many END SELECTs and too few END IFs

4.17   (a)   Program is valid
         (b)   Program is valid since CASE DEFAULT can be listed anywhere in the construct

4.18   (a)   <u>Program Trace:</u>
            Line 01 0>0: False. Go to ELSE block for IFTHEN1
            Line 17 Print 'A <= 0' Last line of ELSE block. Go to END IF
            Line 18 END IF

         <u>Output:</u>
            A <= 0

         <u>Trace Table:</u>

A:	0	B:	15
N:	−1	NSIGN:	never assigned a value

         (b)   <u>Program Trace:</u>
            Line 01 Is (2 > 0)? true, go to line 2
            Line 02 Is (5 <= 10)? true, go to line 3
            Line 03 PRINT "A>0 and B <= 10", go to next line
            Line 04 ELSE of IFTHEN2. Go to END IF for IFTHEN2
            Line 06 END IF for IFTHEN2. Go to next line
            Line 07 SELECT CASE (0) go to first CASE
            Line 08 Is 0 in the range of all negative integers? False. Go to next CASE
            Line 10 Is 0 equal to 0? True. Execute next line
            Line 11 NSIGN=0. Last statement of block. Go to END SELECT
            Line 14 END SELECT, go to next line
            Line 15 Is (2+5< 10)? True. Execute STOP
         <u>Output:</u>
            A > 0 and B <= 10

         <u>Trace Table:</u>

A:	2	B:	5
N:	0	NSIGN:	0

(c) <u>Program Trace:</u>
    Line 01 Is (0 > 0)? False. Go to ELSE block for IFTHEN1
    Line 17 Print 'A < = 0' Last line of ELSE block. Go to END IF
    Line 18 ENDIF

<u>Output:</u>
    A < = 0

<u>Trace Table:</u>

A:	0	B:	15
N:	1	NSIGN:	never assigned a value

Chapter 5

Loops

5.1 OVERVIEW

The third type of control structure is the *loop*. As we discussed in Chapter 1, there are two types of loops:

- The counted loop
- The conditional loop

The counted loop executes a predetermined number of times and the variables controlling the loop *cannot* be altered during the loop execution. The conditional loop, on the other hand, lacks a predetermined stopping point, and the variables controlling the loop *must* change inside the loop.

5.2 THE COUNTED LOOP

The counted loop is the most widely used loop among the high level languages (such as Fortran, C, Basic, and Pascal) used by engineers and scientists. As we discussed in Chapter 1, these loops have a very rigid structure. They execute for a predetermined number of iterations, and the variables controlling the loop *cannot* be altered once the loop begins. In Fortran, we call these *DO loops*, which have the following general structure (anything in brackets is optional):

> DO   *Loop Control Variable = start, stop [, step]*
> ⋮
> *[series of instructions]*
> ⋮
> END DO

The DO statement marks the beginning of the loop and contains all the information necessary to control the loop such as the *loop control variable* (LCV). The program assigns the starting value to this variable and after each cycle through the loop, the LCV increases by the *step* size. Before the loop can recycle, however, the computer checks to see if the new value of the LCV exceeds the *stop* value. If it does, then the loop stops and control passes to the next line after the END DO statement that marks the end of the loop.

The computer has complete control of the loop and handles all the tasks associated with it. These include:

- *Initialize* the LCV to the start value.
- *Increment* the LCV by the step value each time through the loop.
- *Test* the LCV to see if it exceeds the stop value.
- *Decide* when to terminate the loop.

After starting the loop, you don't need to do any of these things yourself. The computer does all this automatically. The only pitfall that you might encounter is if you attempt to modify the LCV inside the loop. The LCV belongs to the computer. You may use it for calculations, but you may not change it.

EXAMPLE 5.1

Here is an example of a DO loop:

Program   **Flowchart**

```
! The following loop will
! execute 10 times using
! I as the loop control
! variable. Note that we
! can look at the value of I
! inside or outside the loop.
DO   I = 1, 10, 1
    PRINT *, 2*I
END DO
PRINT *, I
```

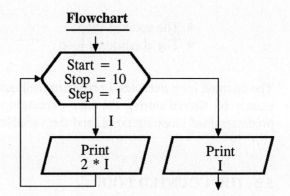

This is a simple loop, which will print out the even numbers from 2 to 20. An interesting point is that the LCV increments inside the loop until it *exceeds* the final value (10 in this example). Of course, the first integer number that exceeds 10 is the number 11. Therefore, the PRINT statement outside the DO loop will print the final value of I as 11.

Notice in the example above that we can *use* the LCV inside the loop, but we cannot *modify* it. Thus, we were allowed to use the LCV to perform the calculation 2*LCV and then print it. But notice that we ourselves did not change the value of the LCV; we merely used it in a computation. Instead, the program changed the value of I automatically during execution of the DO loop.

EXAMPLE 5.2

In the following program segment, we attempt to change the value of the LCV inside the loop. But since this is not allowed, we would receive a compilation error.

```
DO I = 1, 10, 1
    I = I + 1
END DO
```

Inside the loop body of this example, the program attempts to reset the value of the variable I, which is the loop control variable. So there is a conflict. The LCV is under the control of the computer, but the program is attempting to override this control. This kind of error is sometimes not so obvious as we will see in Chapter 7. So be careful when using the LCV inside a loop.

The *start*, *stop*, and *step* values need not always be constants as in the previous examples. In fact, it is common practice to use variables instead. This will allow you to set up your loops so that they are general purpose and do not need to be modified every time you run the program with a different set of input data.

EXAMPLE 5.3

The loop control variables (LCV) themselves can be either variables that are read in at execution time or the results of a computation. In this example, we will read in the variables i and j, and use these as the start and stop variables in the DO loop to compute all the even integers between (and including) $2i$ and $2j$.

Program   **Flowchart**

```
! We will read in I and J
! for use as the loop
! control variables.
PRINT *, 'ENTER I, J'
READ *, I, J
DO  L = I, J, 1
    PRINT *, 2*L
END DO
```

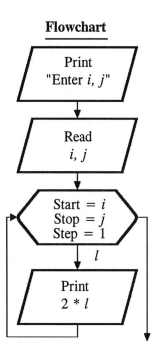

With this structure, we can enter values for i and j when we run the program (called execution time). For example, if we type in 1 and 10, we will simply obtain the results of Example 5.1. If we run the segment a second time and type in new values of 5 and 9, we will obtain a different set of output data: 10, 12, 14, 16, 18. These values correspond to 2×5, 2×6, 2×7, 2×8, and 2×9. In this example, we indicated a step size of 1. But this is redundant, since the computer assumes a step size of 1 if no step size is specified. Although it was not used in this example, you may also use a variable for the step size.

EXAMPLE 5.4

The step size of a DO loop may be a variable that is read in at execution time.

Program   **Flowchart**

```
! Here we read in two integers
! I and J, along with a step
! size K. We then print out
! all integers between I and
! J in steps of K.
PRINT *, 'ENTER I, J, K'
READ *, I, J, K
DO  L = I, J, K
    PRINT *, L
END DO
```

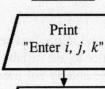

Sample output on CRT screen:

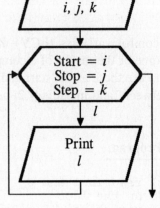

ENTER I, J, K	*(program prompt)*
3, 10, 3	*(values that you enter)*
3	*(output – first value of l)*
6	*(output – second value of l)*
9	*(output – third value of l)*

In the sample program output, we have entered 3, 10, and 3 for i, j, and k, respectively. The loop control variable l will take on values of 3, 6, and 9 inside the loop and these will be the values printed on the CRT screen. Outside the loop, the final value of l will be 12.

There are several rules and guidelines for setting up the loop and the loop control variables:

- The LCV should be an integer.
- The start, stop, and step size values used in the LCV can themselves be variables.
- The LCV cannot be changed inside the body of the loop.
- The step size can be omitted. If it is, the computer assumes a step size of 1.
- You may leave a loop body. But you may not enter a loop body from outside.

EXAMPLE 5.5

Here are some examples of the DO statements:

Correct	Potential Problems	Comments
DO I = 1, 10		*(Step is optional (assumed=1))*
DO I = J, 10		*(Mixing variables, constants OK)*
DO I = 10, 1, −1		*(Decreasing index OK)*
	DO I = 1.0, 5.0, 0.1	*(Mixed mode)*
	DO I = 1, 10, I	*(Subtle attempt to modify LCV)*
	DO I = 10, 1	*(Loop does not converge)*
	DO I = 1, 10, 0	*(Zero step size is not allowed)*

The compiler will probably report all seven examples above as correct. But when you attempt to run them, the last four may perform in unexpected ways:

- In example four (DO I=1.0, 5.0, 0.1) there is mixed mode. The LCV is an integer (I), while the start, stop, and step size are real. Therefore the computer will convert the real numbers to integer values, resulting in an equivalent statement of DO I = 1, 5, 0.0. Notice that the step size is reduced to 0.0 as a result of this conversion, causing an infinite loop to be created.

- In example five (DO I = 1, 10, I) there is a subtle attempt to change the LCV. Note that if the machine did as we directed, the step size (I) would be the same as the LCV. Therefore, it is not clear what will happen when this runs. On some compilers, a divide by zero error is reported.

- In example six (DO I = 10, 1), the body of the loop will never execute, but it will compile. If we had included a negative step size, the loop would execute. But because we left it out, the compiler assumes a step size of 1. Consequently, the LCV would start out with a value of 10, and increase by 1 every time through the loop. Consequently, it could never converge on the final value (1). In these situations the compiler recognizes the difficulty and simply skips over the loop body without ever executing a single iteration. In some older Fortran compilers (Fortran IV and earlier), a loop must always execute at least once. But in Fortran 90, loops can be skipped without ever executing.

- In the final example (DO I = 1, 10, 0) the 0 step size causes an infinite loop at execution time. The compiler will usually not recognize this problem in advance.

Named Loops

Sometimes, it is desirable to identify the boundaries of a loop. To do this, Fortran 90 allows *naming* of loops with the following format:

```
[name:]              DO     Loop Control Variable = start, stop [, step]
                              ⋮
                              ⋮
                     [series of instructions]
                              ⋮
                              ⋮
              END DO [name]
```

The *name* is optional, but if you use a name, the same name must appear in both positions (beginning and end of the loop). Also, the name must adhere to the usual conventions for variable names , that is, it must be 31 characters or less and must use only characters from the Fortran set.

EXAMPLE 5.6

Here is Example 5.1 to print out even integers between 2 and 20, but now rewritten to use a named loop:

```
DEMO:   DO I = 1, 10, 1
            PRINT *, 2 * I
        END DO DEMO
        PRINT *, I
```

Because we have named the loop, it is now clear where the loop begins and ends. In the case of a single loop, this naming convention is not very useful. Only when there are a number of loops will this device become important.

Nesting and the DO Loop

So far, the loops that we have shown contain only simple instructions within the body of the loop. But the body can have any desired complexity. For example, you can put other branching and looping instructions in the body. In fact, one of the most common structures in Fortran is to *nest* one loop inside another. You will see this frequently with array processing and I/O in Chapter 6. One thing that you must watch for when nesting a control structure inside a loop is the possibility that the boundaries of the two structures cross.

EXAMPLE 5.7

The Fibonacci series is a famous sequence that dates back to the thirteenth century and describes many phenomenon in nature. One use of the series is that the ratio of two consecutive terms (8/13, 21/13, 34/21, . . .) approaches the *golden ratio* (0.618). It has been observed that some of the most famous buildings, representing the finest examples of architecture (The Parthenon in Athens and The Lincoln Memorial in Washington), were built with a ratio of the building width to length with the golden ratio. The terms of this series are:

$$1, 1, 2, 3, 5, 8, 13, 21, 34, . . .$$

The first two terms in the series are 1 and 1, but every term after that is the sum of the two previous terms. For example, the next term in the series is 55 (21 + 34).

In this problem, we are going to calculate the series up to the *n*th term, where *n* is a number entered at execution time. In cases like this we have to be careful that the value of *n* is a valid number. Thus in the program below, we will first see if *n* is a number not less than 3 (with a block IF). If it is, then we will compute *n* terms in the series (with a loop). Note that we will nest the DO loop within the block IF structure. When nesting control structures like this, it is important to make sure that the boundaries of the different block structures do not cross. Note carefully in this example that the DO loop is completely inside the false branch of the IF-THEN-ELSE-END IF structure.

Program

```
! First we read in N
INTEGER :: FIB1, FIB2
PRINT *, 'Enter N:'
READ *, N
! Now check to see if N is not
! less than 3. If it is, then
! use the DO loop to compute
! N terms of the series.
IF(N<3) THEN
    PRINT *,'ERROR'
ELSE
    FIB1=1
    FIB2=1
    PRINT *, FIB1, FIB2
    DO  I=3,N
        NEW=FIB1+FIB2
        FIB1 = FIB2
        FIB2 = NEW
        PRINT *, NEW
    END DO
END IF
END
```

Flowchart

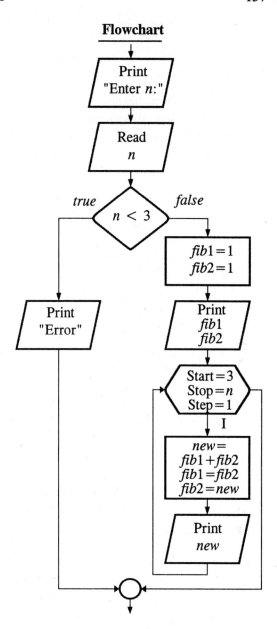

Notice in the flowchart that the DO loop is entirely within one branch of the block IF structure. If it had not been, an error would have been detected.

In this example we use the two variables $fib1$ and $fib2$ as the first two terms in the series and assign them initial values of 1 and 1. We check to see that the number entered is valid ($n \geq 3$). If it is, then we enter the loop to calculate the next term new by equating it to $fib1$ + $fib2$. Thus, the third term in the series becomes 2 (obtained from $1+1$). The next step is to update $fib1$ and $fib2$ by shifting $fib2$ to $fib1$ and new to $fib2$. As we generate each new number in the series, we will retain only the last two terms in the series. To illustrate how this program works, we show a trace of the program for $n=4$ and follow how each variable in the program changes:

Step	Instruction	FIB1	FIB2	NEW	I	Output
1	Print prompt					Enter N:
2	Read in value of 4					
3	Is N < 3? No, so transfer to false branch of block IF					
4	FIB1 = 1	1				
5	FIB2 = 1		1			
6	Print values of FIB1 and FIB2					1 1
7	Enter DO loop for I = 3 to 4					
8	Calculate NEW (I=3)			2	3	
9	Reassign FIB1	1				
10	Reassign FIB2		2			
11	Print value of NEW					2
12	Calculate NEW (I=4)			3	4	
13	Reassign FIB1	2				
14	Reassign FIB2		3			
15	Print value of NEW					3
16	Terminate loop					
17	Terminate program					

When nesting DO loops, the inner loop must lie completely within the outer loop. Also, the two loops must use different LCVs. The general form is as follows:

$$DO \quad LCV1 = start1, stop1 \ [, step1]$$
$$DO \quad LCV2 = start2, stop2 \ [, step2]$$
$$\vdots$$
$$END \ DO \ (Loop \ 2)$$
$$END \ DO \ (Loop \ 1)$$

Notice that the DO *LCV2* loop begins and ends completely within the DO *LCV1* loop, and that each loop has its own loop control variable. A common error that programmers make is to give the two LCVs the same name. For example, if the LCV in the outer loop is named I, the inner loop must have a different name, such as J. Otherwise the inner loop will be attempting to change the LCV of the outer loop. Finally, you may use the value of LCV1 as the start, stop, or step value in the inner loop. When the nested loops execute, the innermost loop will increment to completion before the LCV in the outer loop changes to its next value.

EXAMPLE 5.8

Here is an example of how to use nested loops to generate a simple multiplication table. At this point, we don't yet have the means to produce a nice square table. But at least this program will generate the values.

Program   **Flowchart**

```
PRINT *, 'Enter I, J:'
READ *, I , J
DO  OUTER = 1, I
    DO  INNER = 1, J
        PRINT *, OUTER*INNER
    END DO
END DO
```

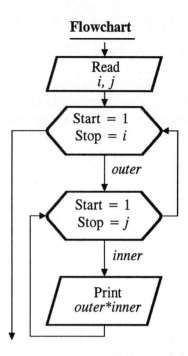

Suppose that we enter 2 for I and 3 for J. The nested loops tell us that the innermost loop will execute more rapidly than the outer loop. Thus for example, OUTER will be fixed at a value of 1 while INNER will cycle through the values 1, 2, and 3. Only then will OUTER move to the next value of 2. Here is a trace table for the variables:

OUTER	INNER	Output
1	1	1
1	2	2
1	3	3
2	1	2
2	2	4
2	3	6

Once the trace starts, the variable OUTER remains fixed while the variable INNER goes through its range. After the inner loop finishes, OUTER increases by one and then the inner loop begins all over again. Note that INNER will actually increment to a final value of 4, but the inner loop will not execute since this value exceeds the stated limit (3). In a similar way, OUTER will go to a value of 3. Thus, if the values of OUTER and INNER were printed outside the nested loops, their values would be 3 and 4, respectively. Be sure that you understand how these nested loops execute, since you will see them repeatedly when we get to arrays in Chapter 6.

5.3 THE CONDITIONAL LOOP

The *DO WHILE* structure is a form of a conditional loop, as we discussed in Chapter 1. The loop will execute indefinitely until the test condition based on the loop control variable(s) becomes *false*. Of course, to start the loop, the condition must initially be *true*. Obviously, the condition must somehow change from *true* to *false*. This is a stark difference from the DO loop, where the computer does not allow us to change the control variable(s). For the DO WHILE loop, the control variable(s) that is the basis of the test condition <u>must</u> change. Otherwise, we will be trapped in an infinite loop.

The general form of the DO WHILE construct is

> DO WHILE (*condition is true*)
> ⋮
> ⋮
> *[block of instructions]*
> ⋮
> ⋮
>
> END DO

When the loop is first entered, a test is performed where the only allowed outcomes are *true* and *false*. If the condition is *true*, the block of instructions is executed. But if the test condition is *false*, the loop terminates and control jumps to the statement after the end of the loop.

The test condition that controls the operation of the while loop is set up just like the test in the IF constructs, and is based on one or more control variables. One of the keys to the while construct is that one of the control variables must change within the body of the loop. Sometimes this is done with a READ statement. More often, it is done through reassignment of a variable with an assignment statement.

EXAMPLE 5.9

The DO WHILE loop should be used where we do not know in advance how often to execute the loop. A good example is a problem where we wish to read in some data but we do not know how many data items there will be. A common solution to this problem is to set up a loop to read in one data item at a time, and stop the loop if the data point has a specific value (a negative value for example).

To demonstrate how this works, let's assume that we are calculating the average weight of rabbits in a laboratory. Since rabbits multiply so fast, we never know in advance how many there will be. So we set up the loop to read in the weights, one at a time, until one of the weights is greater than 500 pounds. When this occurs, the loop will stop. We sometimes call this special value a *sentinel* value. The loop is set up so that we watch for this key value, which we have chosen so that it is not possible to be part of the data set. So when you enter this value, the program will recognize it as the signal to stop.

Program   **Flowchart**

```
! We use 500 as the sentinel
! value to control the loop
! to read in the weights.
TOT = 0.0
NUM = 0
WGT = 0.0
DO WHILE(WGT <= 500.0)
    PRINT *,'Enter Weight'
    READ *, WGT
    TOT = TOT + WGT
    NUM = NUM + 1
END DO
AVG = (TOT-WGT)/(NUM-1)
PRINT *,'Avg Wgt=', AVG
```

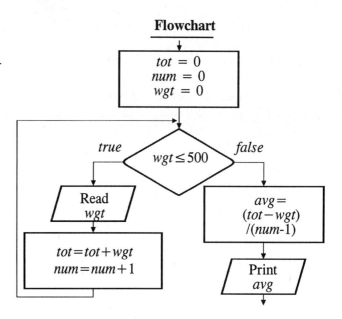

The variables TOT, NUM, and WGT represent the total weight of all the rabbits, the total number of rabbits, and their individual weights, respectively. When the loop begins, the computer checks to see if WGT is less than or equal to 500. The first time through, of course, WGT equals 0.0, so the loop proceeds. Inside the loop, we read in a weight, add it to the total, and increase the counter (NUM) by 1. The loop then repeats. Notice if the weight that we enter is greater than 500 the loop will stop, but not until after this very large value is added to the total. That is why we subtract this artificially high value after we leave the loop. Also, we need to subtract 1 from NUM to calculate the average weight (AVG).

Why did we set the sentinel value to 500? Actually, we could have chosen any value as long as it was unlikely that any genuine value would be as large as this. Since no rabbit weighs 500 pounds, this condition will always be *true* while we are entering realistic values. When we have entered all the data, we purposely type in a weight like 99999, and the loop will end. Since a weight of 99999 exceeds 500, the condition is now *false* and the loop will stop. There are other ways to do the same thing (one of which is known as a structured read loop), and we will explore some of these in future exercises and examples.

The EXIT and CYCLE Statements

Fortran 90 also offers a general purpose DO loop that can be used as either a counted or a conditional loop, with the following general form (anything in brackets is optional):

DO *[label]* *[loop control structure]*
        ⋮
    [IF (condition is true) EXIT]
        ⋮
    [IF (condition is true) CYCLE]
        ⋮
[label] END DO

If the loop control variable is included on the same line as the DO statement, the loop becomes a counted loop. But if the loop control variables are left out, the loop becomes a conditional one. In this case, however, there must be a means of stopping the loop. This is done with the two new commands: EXIT and CYCLE. As their names imply, the EXIT command inside the loop causes the loop to terminate, while the CYCLE command causes the loop to jump to the next LCV value. In effect, both commands are substitutes for the GO TO command. The EXIT command is equivalent to GO TO a point outside of the loop. Similarly, the CYCLE command is equivalent to GO TO the end of the loop.

EXAMPLE 5.10

Below is the rabbit weighing program rewritten to use the EXIT command as the means to terminate the loop.

```
TOT = 0.0
NUM = 0
DO
    PRINT *, 'Enter Weight (less than 500)'
    READ *, WGT
    IF (WGT > 500.0) EXIT
    TOT = TOT + WGT
    NUM = NUM + 1
END DO
AVG = TOT/NUM
PRINT *,'Avg Weight=', AVG
END
```

Compare this structure carefully with that shown in Example 5.9. In this version, the execution is much more natural. As soon as we read in a weight, we check to see if it exceeds the sentinel value. If it does, then we exit the loop and compute the average weight. Note that we don't have to make the corrections (TOT−WGT) and (NUM−1) that we had to make in the previous example.

The key point to note here is that we can conduct our test to see if the weight exceeds the sentinel value wherever we wish inside the loop. It's most natural to do this just after we read in the value as in this example. But with the DO WHILE structure, we had to wait until the next iteration of the loop to perform this check.

EXAMPLE 5.11

The program below shows how to use the CYCLE command. Once again, we will use the rabbit weighing problem. But here we will allow for a typographical error during the data entry. Experienced programmers will often think defensively when writing programs and often ask themselves "What can possibly go wrong?" In the rabbit weighing problem, one of the potential problems is that someone may accidentally type in a negative or zero weight. In the previous versions of this program, this value would be accepted. In this version however, we will print out an appropriate message, ignore the input, and give the person the opportunity to reenter the data.

```
            TOT = 0.0
            NUM = 0
            DO
                PRINT *, 'Enter Weight'
                READ *, WGT
                IF (WGT > 500.0) EXIT
                IF (WGT <= 0.0) THEN
                    PRINT *, 'Invalid Weight, Please Reenter'
                    CYCLE                        !The CYCLE statement is optional
                ELSE
                    TOT = TOT + WGT
                    NUM = NUM + 1
                END IF
            END DO
            AVG = TOT/NUM
            PRINT *,'Avg Weight=', AVG
            END
```

We have retained the EXIT command introduced in the last example, but added the additional IF-THEN-ELSE construct. If the weight is 0 or negative, the program prints out an error message and asks the user to reenter the data. Otherwise, we proceed with the calculations as before.

The CYCLE statement in this example was not needed since it duplicates the functions of the block IF statement. However, we have included it here to illustrate its use. Note that if there had been executable statements between the END IF and the END DO statements, then the CYCLE command would have been needed.

5.4 DEBUGGING TIPS

Previously, we gave you several suggestions to help locate syntax errors related to assignment statements and branching operations. These suggestions are equally valid for finding syntax errors for loops. So we won't repeat them here. Instead, we want to focus on locating logic and run time errors. These errors are typically more difficult to remove.

Before you try to trace through a loop, you may want to do a few preliminary things. One of the first things to do is to print out the program and *highlight* the loop bodies and the other control structures. A convenient method of doing this is by drawing boxes or lines around the body of each loop. (Of course, if you had indented while writing the program, this would have already been done.) By blocking out the control structures you will be able to locate errors such as missing key words and improper nesting. Also, it will be easier to spot errors in the program logic. Finally, by blocking out the loops, it will be easier to trace through the program.

EXAMPLE 5.12

The following program is an example of nested loops without any highlighting. Its purpose is to print out a table of lengths in feet and inches (up to 12 feet, 11 inches) together with the corresponding measure in total inches. As an example, it will print out messages such as "10 Feet and 4 Inches = 124 Inches".

In the following program, the outer loop will increment the number of feet to be converted, while the inner loop will increment the number of inches. Thus, the value of feet will be fixed, while the inches loop through the possible values of 1 to 11 for each iteration of the outer loop.

| **Program** | **Flowchart** |

```
INTEGER :: FT
DO   FT = 0, 12
    DO   IN = 0, 11
        INTOT = IN + FT*12
        PRINT 5, FT, IN, INTOT
    END DO
END DO
5   FORMAT(' ',I3,'Feet and', I3,&
        'Inches =', I5, 'Inches')
```

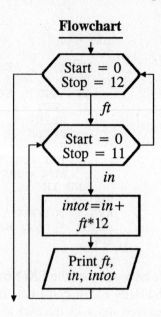

We show the same program below with the loop structures highlighted using both methods.

| **Blocked Out** | **Indented** |

```
INTEGER :: FT
DO   FT = 0, 12
DO   IN = 0, 11
INTOT = IN + FT * 12
PRINT 5, FT, IN, INTOT
END DO
END DO
5   FORMAT(...)
```

```
INTEGER :: FT
DO FT = 0, 12
    DO IN = 0, 11
        INTOT = IN + FT * 12
        PRINT 5, FT, IN, INTOT
    END DO
END DO
5   FORMAT(...)
```

The indentation method is strongly recommended because you can do it while first entering the program and is much clearer. Also, by indenting, you prepare for the likelihood of tracing.

The most important step in locating logic errors is to trace through the structures, since tracing will allow you to find where the program logic goes wrong. Tracing a DO loop takes a bit of patience since some of the variables change frequently. Because of the large number of changes within loops, trace tables are even more important than with other structures. Therefore, we recommend that the first step in performing a trace to detect faulty logic is to set up a complete trace table.

EXAMPLE 5.13

Let us now use some of these ideas to help debug a program containing a logic error. We designed this program to produce the following sequence of fractions:

$$\frac{2}{1} \quad \frac{3}{2} \quad \frac{5}{3} \quad \frac{8}{5} \quad \cdots$$

The numerator of each fraction is the sum of the numerator and denominator of the previous fraction, while the denominator of the new fraction is the numerator of the previous fraction. The program shown below is supposed to print out the first 40 terms of this sequence using real arithmetic. The output contains the term number (2.0/1.0 is term number 1 for example), with the numerator, denominator, and value of the fraction.

```
REAL :: NUM
INTEGER :: TERM
NUM = 2.0
DEN = 1.0
DO TERM = 1, 40
    VAL = NUM / DEN
    PRINT *,TERM,'# ',NUM,'/',DEN,' = ',VAL
    NUM = NUM + DEN
    DEN = NUM
END DO
END
```

When we execute the above program, the computer prints the following output on the CRT screen:

```
1#   2.00000/ 1.00000  =   2.00000
2#   3.00000/ 3.00000  =   1.00000
3#   6.00000/ 6.00000  =   1.00000
                 ⋮
```

As you can see from the output, the program is incorrect since the numerators and denominators are equal, except for the first term. The first debugging step is to perform a trace. Below is a listing of the variable table and the trace for the first few terms:

Variable Trace Table:

NUM	2.0, 3.0
DEN	1.0, 3.0
VAL	2.0
TERM	1, 2

Program Execution:

> NUM = 2.0
> DEN = 1.0
> Enter DO Loop, assign TERM=1
> Is TERM > 40? No, then execute loop
> VAL = NUM/DEN = 2.0
> PRINT TERM, NUM, DEN, VAL
> NUM=NUM+DEN=3.0
> DEN=NUM=3.0

We can carry out this trace further, but it is not necessary since the error has already occurred. After the first iteration through the loop, the expected values of each variable and the actual values already differ as summarized below:

Variable	Expected Value	Actual Value
NUM	3.0	3.0
DEN	2.0	3.0
VAL	1.5	1.0

We copied the expected values from the problem statement. For the second term (3/2) we expect the denominator to be 2.0 and the numerator to be 3.0. The program however, returns the values of 3.0 and 3.0. Clearly then, the problem lies with the variable DEN. The problem is that the statement that updated the numerator destroys the value of the previous numerator (which we need to define the new denominator). One method of solving this is to use additional variables to store the previous numerator and denominator. By using those values, we can then calculate the new numerator and denominator. The corrected program now includes the two new variables, PRENUM and PREDEN:

```
REAL :: NUM
INTEGER :: TERM
NUM = 2.0
DEN = 1.0
DO TERM = 1, 40
   VAL = NUM / DEN
   PRINT *,TERM,'# ',NUM,'/',DEN,' = ',VAL
   PRENUM = NUM
   PREDEN = DEN
   NUM = PRENUM + PREDEN
   DEN = PRENUM
END DO
END
```

Once we correct the logic error, the output is now correct:

```
1#    2.00000/ 1.00000              =     2.00000
2#    3.00000/ 2.00000              =     1.50000
3#    5.00000/ 3.00000              =     1.66667
            ⋮
40#   0.267914E+09/ 0.165580E+09 =     1.61803
```

As you can see from this output, the program is now working correctly. You will find that there is no substitute for tracing in removing logic errors. You must be willing to trace through the program by hand to detect logic problems.

Solved Problems

5.1   Locate syntax and run-time errors in each of the following loops:

```
(a)  DO I = 1, 5, I          (b)  DO , J = 1, K, L
(c)  DO I = K, L, M          (d)  DO J = 1, 9, 2
        DO I = L, M, K                J = J**2
           PRINT *, I, K, L, M        PRINT *, J
        END DO                     END DO
     END DO
(e)  DO J = 1, 3, 1          (f)  DO J = 1, 3, 1
        PRINT *, J                    DO K = 1, 4, 1
        DO K = 1, 3, 1                   L = K ** 2
           PRINT *, K                    PRINT *, L
        END DO                        END DO
     END DO                        J = L
                                   DO L = 1, 3, 1
                                      PRINT *, L
                                   END DO
(g)  DO J = 1, 10, 0.5       (h)  DO J = 1, 10
(i)  DO  I = 1, J            (j)  DO J = 2, 95
        DO J = I, 2*I              IF(MOD(J,25)==0) CYCLE
           PRINT *, I, J           PRINT*, MOD(J,25)
        END DO                  END DO
     END DO
```

(a) You cannot use I both as the step size and loop control variable.

(b) No error. The comma after DO is permitted.

(c) You cannot use I as the LCV for the inner loop since it is already being use as the loop control variable in the outer loop. This is detected as a syntax error by the compiler.

(d) Attempt to change LCV inside the loop.

(e) OK.

(f) One of the loops is not closed and there is an attempt to modify J inside the loop.

(g) The step size of 0.5 will be converted to zero, which is not allowed. A step size of zero would result in an infinite loop and produce a run-time error. Some compilers may report it as a syntax error.

(h) OK to omit step size (assumed value = 1).

(i) The inner loop may change the upper limit in the outer loop depending on how your compiler sets up the limits on the outer loop. Some compilers may not allow this.

(j) Correct.

5.2   Assuming that the variables X, I, and J have been declared as integers, convert the following structures into loops:

```
(a)  X = 1                   (b)  I = 1
10   IF (X <= 10) THEN       5    IF ( I <= 10) THEN
        Z = Z/C                      J = 1
        P = C ** 2           10       IF (J <= 10) THEN
```

```
        X = X + 1                      PRINT *, I, J
        GO TO 10                       J = J + 1
     ELSE                                GO TO 10
        PRINT *, P                    END IF
     END IF                           I = I + 1
                                      GO TO 5
                                    END IF
```

(a)
```
     DO I = 1, 10, 1
        Z = Z/C
        P = C ** 2
     END DO
     PRINT *, P
```

(b)
```
     DO I = 1, 10
        DO J = 1, 10
           PRINT *, I, J
        END DO
     END DO
```

5.3   Trace through the following program segments and predict the output:

(a)
```
     DO J = 1, 9, 2
        K = J ** 2
     END DO
     PRINT *, J
     END
```

(b)
```
     DO J = 1, 3
        IF (J <= 2) K = J**2
        IF (J > 2) K = J
        A = J**2 + K**2
        PRINT *, A
     END DO
     END
```

(c)
```
     INTEGER :: A, B, C
     DO A = 2, 8, 2
        DO B = A, 2
           DO C = 1, B, 2
              PRINT *, A, B, C
           END DO
        END DO
     END DO
     END
```

(d)
```
     L =0
     DO J = 1, 100, 50
        PRINT *, J
     END DO
     DO K = J, 100-J, -50
        L = L + J
     END DO
     PRINT *, L
     END
```

(a)   Trace Table:
       J: 1, 3, 5, 7, 9, 11
       K: 1, 9, 25, 49, 81

       Output:
       11

(b)   Trace Table:
       J: 1, 2, 3
       K: 1, 4, 3
       A: 2, 20, 18

       Output:
       2
       20
       18

(c)   Trace Table:
       A: 2, 4
       B: 2, 3, 4
       C: 1, 3

       Output:
        2   2   1

(d)   Trace Table:
       L: 0, 101, 202, 303
       J: 1, 51, 101
       K: 101, 51, 1, −49

       Output:
        1
       51
       303

5.4   Locate syntax errors in each of the following loops:

(a) `DO WHILE (X /> 0)`   (b) `DO WHILE (I <= 5)`
                                           `PRINT *, I`
                                       `END WHILE`

(c) `DO WHILE (X == 0)`   (d) `DO WHILE (X >= Y)`
       `DO WHILE (Y /= X)`   `IF(X > 0) THEN`
          `PRINT *, X, Y`   `PRINT *, X`
       `END DO`   `END DO`

(a) `/>` is not a valid relational operator.
(b) Terminating statement on most compilers is END DO, not END WHILE.
(c) Must have two terminating statements, one for each DO WHILE.
(d) Missing terminating statement for block-IF construct.

5.5   Trace through the following program segments and predict the output:

(a) `J = 1`   (b) `X = 1.0`
    `DO WHILE (J <= 100)`   `SUM = 0.0`
       `PRINT *, J`   `DO WHILE (X >= 0.01)`
       `J = J + 1`   `SUM = SUM + X`
    `END DO`   `X = X/10.0`
    `END`   `END DO`
                                      `PRINT *, SUM`
                                      `END`

(c) `X = 1.0`   (d) `TERM = 1.0`
    `Y = 1.0`   `ISIGN = +1`
    `SUM = 0.0`   `SUM = 0.0`
    `DO`   `X = 1.0`
       `IF(X <= 0.01) EXIT`   `DO`
       `X = X /10.0`   `ISIGN = -ISIGN`
       `Y = 2.0 * Y`   `X = X + 1.0`
       `IF(Y >= 4.0) CYCLE`   `TERM = ISIGN / X**2`
       `SUM = SUM + X * Y`   `IF(ABS(TERM)<0.05)EXIT`
       `PRINT *, X, Y, SUM`   `SUM = SUM + TERM`
    `END DO`   `PRINT *, SUM`
    `END`   `END DO`
                                      `END`

(a) Trace Table: (b) Trace Table:
        J: 1, 2, 3, 4, ..., 101   X: 1.0, 0.1, 0.01, 0.001
                                          SUM: 0.0, 1.0, 1.1, 1.11
     Output: Output:
        1   1.11000
        ⋮
        100
(c) Trace Table: (d) Trace Table:
        X: 1.0, 0.1, 0.01, 0.001   TERM: 1.0, -0.25, 0.111, -0.0625, 0.04
        Y: 1.0, 2.0, 4.0, 8.0   ISIGN: $+1$, -1, $+1$, -1, $+1$
        SUM: 0.0, 0.2   X: 1.0, 2.0, 3.0, 4.0, 5.0
                                          SUM: 0.0, -0.25, -0.1389, -0.20139

Output: Output:
    0.10000 2.00000 0.20000   −0.250000
                                        −0.138889
                                        −0.201389

5.6   The following suggestions are designed so that you can find out the limitations or extensions of your Fortran compiler. Run small programs to find out if the following suggestions work. You may need also to consult the documentation for your system.

    (a)   Some compilers will always execute a loop at least once, even if the structure of your loop tells it otherwise. Try the following:

```
DO I = 1, 0
    PRINT *, I
END DO
```

    (b)   See if your compiler supports the DO WHILE extension. Some compilers use the DO WHILE structure. Others may use the WHILE(..)DO structure. Try both:

```
DO WHILE (X <= 1.0)           WHILE(X <= 1.0) DO
    PRINT *, X                    PRINT *,X
    X = X + 1                     X = X + 1
END DO                        END WHILE
```

5.7   Write a program that prints out all even numbers including the end points between two positive values (i and j where $j > i$) that are read in at execution time.

```
PRINT *, 'Enter I and J:'
READ *, I, J
DO LCV = I, J
    IF(MOD(LCV,2) == 0) PRINT *, LCV
END DO
END
```

5.8   Write a program to read in a real value x and repeatedly divide it by 2 until $x < 0.001$. Print out the result after every five divisions, along with the total number of divisions.

```
! NUMBER_DIV is the number of divisions to reduce X to
! <0.001. Note that if NOSDIV is a multiple of 5,
! MOD(NOSDIV,5) will be 0 and the printing is skipped.
PRINT *, 'Enter value of X:'
READ *, X
NUMBER_DIV = 0
DO
    X = X/2.0
    NUMBER_DIV = NUMBER_DIV + 1
    IF(X < 0.001) EXIT
    IF(MOD(NUMBER_DIV,5) == 0) PRINT*, X, NUMBER_DIV
END DO
END
```

5.9　　Write a program to read in a series of numbers and find the largest and smallest. Stop reading data when a negative value is entered.

```
! We use the MIN and MAX functions to find the largest
! and smallest values. When a negative value of X is
! entered, the EXIT command terminates the loop.
READ *, X
XMIN = X
XMAX = X
DO
    PRINT *, 'Enter a value:'
    READ *, X
    IF(X < 0) EXIT
    XMIN = MIN(XMIN, X)
    XMAX = MAX(XMAX, X)
END DO
PRINT *, 'Min Value: ', XMIN
PRINT *, 'Max value: ', XMAX
END
```

5.10　　Write a program that prints the powers of 2 between 1 and 256.

```
DO I = 0, 8
    PRINT *, 2.0**I
END DO
END
```

5.11　　Write a program to find all integers that are divisible by three and lie between two integers that you enter at execution time.

```
! The program reads in the limits I and J and tests
! all integer values between them. By using the MOD
! function, the program determines if an integer
! value is evenly divisible by 3. Note that if a
! number is divisible by 3, the remainder is equal
! to 0.
PRINT *, 'Enter Limits'
READ *, I, J
DO N = I, J
    IF(MOD(N, 3) == 0) PRINT *, N, 'is divisible by 3'
END DO
END
```

5.12　　Write a program to compute the value of a given by the first ten terms of the following series:

$$a = 1 + \frac{1}{2} + \frac{1}{3} + \frac{1}{4} + \cdots$$

```
A = 0.0
DO I = 1, 10
    A = A + 1.0/I
END DO
PRINT *, 'A = ', A
END
```

5.13 Write a program to compute the value of *b* given by the series shown below. Continue computing the sum of the terms until the absolute value of any individual term falls below 0.01. By doing this, we evaluate the series for all terms that are significant. We will ignore any term whose value is so small that it has little effect on the series total.

Note in this series that the terms have an alternating sign. This is best handled by defining a variable SIGN whose initial value is set to 1.0. For each successive term in the series, we will multiply SIGN by -1.0, in effect, alternating the sign.

$$b = 1 - \frac{1}{2} + \frac{1}{3} - \frac{1}{4} + \cdots$$

```
! Program using DO/EXIT
! commands
TERM = 1.0
B = 1.0
SIGN = -1.0
I = 2
DO
   TERM = 1.0/I*SIGN
   IF(ABS(TERM) < 0.01)EXIT
   SIGN = -SIGN
   B = B + TERM
   I = I + 1
END DO
PRINT *, 'B = ', B
END
```

```
! Program using a DO
! WHILE loop
TERM = 1.0
B = 1.0
SIGN = -1.0
I = 2
DO WHILE (ABS(TERM) >= 0.01)
    TERM = 1.0/I*SIGN
    SIGN = -SIGN
    B = B + TERM
    I = I + 1
END DO
B = B - TERM
PRINT *, 'B = ', B
END
```

5.14 The factorial of a number (*n*!) is the product of all integers between 1 and *n*. Write a program to compute the factorial of an integer value entered at execution time.

```
PRINT *, 'Enter N:'
READ *, N
FACT = 1.0
DO I = 2, N
    FACT = FACT * I
END DO
PRINT *, N,'! =', FACT
END
```

5.15 Write a program to read in the radius r of a circle centered at the origin. Then read in the coordinate pairs (x, y) of a point and determine if that point lies within the circle. Use the condition that if

$$(x^2 + y^2)^{0.5} < r$$

then the point is inside the circle. Terminate the program the first time that $(x^2 + y^2)^{0.5} > 2r$.

```
PRINT *, 'Enter radius:'
READ *, R
DO
    PRINT *, 'Enter X, Y: '
    READ *, X, Y
    Z = SQRT(X**2 + Y**2)
    IF( Z > 2*R) EXIT
    IF( Z <= R) THEN
        PRINT*, 'Point is inside the circle'
    ELSE
        PRINT*, 'Point is outside the circle'
    END IF
END DO
END
```

5.16 The value of $e = 2.718282$ can be approximated by the infinite series:

$$e = \sum_{n=0}^{n=\infty} \left(\frac{1}{n!}\right) \approx \left(\frac{1}{0!}\right) + \left(\frac{1}{1!}\right) + \left(\frac{1}{2!}\right) + \left(\frac{1}{3!}\right) + \left(\frac{1}{4!}\right) + \cdots$$

The factorial function $n!$ is the product of integers from 2 to n and $0! = 1$ by definition. Write a program to approximate e for the first five terms in this series. Then modify it to compute the approximation for n terms in the series, where n is read in at execution time.

```
PRINT *, 'Enter Number of Terms:'
READ *, N
E = 0.0
DO I = 0, N-1
    FACT = 1.0
    DO II = 2, I
        FACT=FACT * II
    END DO
    E = E + 1.0/FACT
END DO
PRINT *, 'Approx = ', E
END
```

5.17 Write a program to determine if a number n is *prime*. A prime number is one which is divisible only by itself and 1. Use the following algorithm:

(a) Successively divide n by all integers lying between 2 and $n/2$.

(b) With each division, check for a remainder.

(c) If there is no remainder for a given division, then the number is not a prime, so stop.

(d) Print out a message in either case (prime or nonprime).

```
PRINT *, 'Enter Number: '
READ *, N
DO I = 2, N/2
   IF(MOD(N,I) == 0) THEN
       PRINT *, 'not prime'
       STOP
   END IF
END DO
PRINT *, 'prime'
END
```

5.18   Write a program to simulate a population explosion. Start out with a single bacteria cell that can produce an offspring by division every 4 hours. The new cell must incubate for 24 hours before it can divide. The parent cell meanwhile will continue to divide every 4 hours. Assume that any new cells will follow this same pattern. How many cells will you have in 1 day (24 hours), 1 week (168 hours), and 1 month (720 hours), if none of the new cells die?

```
! H24 is the number of cells that are 24 hours old or older.
! Similarly, H20 is the number of cells that are 20 hours
! old and so forth. Every four hours, we move the number
! stored in each variable to the next higher level. Thus,
! H16 receives the value from H12. The number of new cells
! created (NEWCEL) is the value stored in H24. Notice that
! we need to use real numbers because the values can become
! very large (E+19) in this example.
REAL NEWCEL
H24=1
PRINT *, 'Enter Number of Hours'
READ *, HOURS
DO I = 1, HOURS/4
    NEWCEL=H24
    H24=H24+H20
    H20=H16
    H16=H12
    H12=H8
    H8=H4
    H4=H0
    H0=NEWCEL
END DO
TOT=H0+H4+H8+H12+H16+H20+H24
PRINT *,'TIME = ', HOURS, ' Number of Cells = ', TOT
END
```

When the program is run with time of 24, 168, and 720 hours, the results will look like this:

Hours	Number of Cells
24.0	7.00000
168.0	24851.0
720.0	0.106770E+19

If we had not used real variables in this problem, we would have received very strange results. In fact, some of the numbers computed would have been negative, because of the way the computer handles integer overflow.

Supplementary Problems

5.19 Locate syntax and run-time errors in each of the following loops:

(a)
```
DO L = 1, M,
```

(b)
```
DO M = 1, I**2 + 1, -1
```

(c)
```
DO 10 J = 1, 9, 2
    K = J**2
    PRINT *, K
    J = J + 1
END DO
```

(d)
```
DO J = 1, 10.5, 0.5
    PRINT *, J
END DO
```

(e)
```
DO J = 1, 10
    PRINT *, J
    DO J = 1, 5
        PRINT *, J**2
    END DO
END DO
```

(f)
```
DO J = 1, 2
    DO K = 2, 5
        DO K = 1,3
            PRINT *, J, K
        END DO
    END DO
END DO
```

5.20 Convert the following structures into loops:

(a)
```
    I = 10
5   IF (I >= 1) THEN
        PRINT *, I
        I = I - 2
        GO TO 5
    END IF
```

(b)
```
    I = 1
5   IF (I <= 10) THEN
        J = I
10          IF (J <= 2*I) THEN
            PRINT *, J
            J = J + 2
            GO TO 10
        END IF
        PRINT *, I
        I = I + 2
        GO TO 5
    END IF
```

5.21   Trace through the following program segments and predict the output:

(a)
```
DO J = 1, 1
    DO K = 1, 2
        L = J + K
        PRINT *,'L=', L
    END DO
END DO
```

(b)
```
DO J = 1, 2
    DO K = J, 3
        L = J + K
        PRINT *, 'L=', L
    END DO
    M = J - K
    PRINT *, 'M=', M
END DO
PRINT*, J + K
```

(c)
```
DO J = 1, 2
    DO K = 1, 2
        DO L = 1, 2
            Z = J+K+L
        END DO
        L = J + K
        M = L**2
        PRINT *, Z, M
    END DO
END DO
```

(d)
```
DO I1 = 5, 17, 3
    I2 = I1 / 5
    DO I3 = 7, I2, 4
        IF(I1==I1/I3*I3)CYCLE
    END DO
    PRINT*, I1, I2, I3
END DO
```

5.22   Locate syntax and run-time errors in each of the following conditional loops:

(a)
```
DO WHILE(X>Y.OR.<Z)
    PRINT *, Y
END DO
```

(b)
```
DO WHILE (A * B < 0)
    DO I = 1, 10
        PRINT *, I/A*B
    END DO
END DO
```

(c)
```
DO WHILE(X*X > 0.0)
    READ *, X
    PRINT *, X, X*X
END DO
```

(d)
```
IF(X < A .AND. B > X)
    DO I = 1, 6
        DO WHILE (I>0)
            READ *, I
            X = I * X
        END DO
    END DO
END IF
```

5.23   Trace through the following program segments and predict the output:

(a)
```
X = 1.5
DO WHILE (X <= 5.0)
    PRINT *, X
    X = X * 1.5
END DO
```

(b)
```
X = 1.0
DO WHILE (X <= 100.0)
    PRINT *, X
    X = (X-1)**2 + 2.0
END DO
```

(c)
```
X = 2.0
Y = 1.0
SUM = 0.0
DO
    X = X * Y
    Y = X * Y
    IF(X > 5.0) EXIT
    IF(Y >= 4.0) CYCLE
```

(d)
```
TERM = 0.0
ISIGN = +1
X = 1.0
DO
    ISIGN = -ISIGN
    X = X + 1.0
    SUM = 2.0 * X**ISIGN
    TERM = 2**X*ISIGN
```

```
        SUM = SUM + X*Y              IF (X >= 5) EXIT
        PRINT *, X, Y, SUM          SUM = SUM + TERM
     END DO                         PRINT *, TERM, SUM
                                 END DO
```

5.24 The following suggestions are designed so that you can find out the limitations or extensions of your Fortran compiler. Run small programs to find out if the following suggestions work. You may need also to consult the documentation for your compiler.

(a) Most FORTRAN compilers will not allow you to transfer into the middle of a DO loop. Try the following code to see if your compiler catches this problem.

```
        READ *, N
        IF (N /= 0) GO TO 10
        DO  I = 1, 10
10          PRINT *, 'I = ', I
        END DO
```

(b) Using real values to control a DO loop is generally not a good idea because reals are stored imprecisely. Run both segments on your system and compare results.

```
    SUM = 0.0                      ISUM = 0
    DO X=0.0, 1.0, 0.000001        DO I = 1, 1000000
        SUM = SUM + X                  ISUM = ISUM + I
    END DO                         END DO
    PRINT *, SUM                   PRINT *, ISUM/1000000.0
```

5.25 Write a program segment that reads in two integer values (i and j where $i > j$) and prints out all integer values between them in reverse order. Do not include i and j in the output.

5.26 Write a program to read in a series of numbers and keep track of the running total and the number of data items. Stop collecting data when a negative sentinel value is entered. Then calculate the average and report it.

5.27 Write a program to read in a dollar amount and a monthly interest rate. Calculate the interest earned each month and the total amount on deposit. Terminate the program when the initial deposit has doubled.

5.28 Write a program to calculate the values of y, where y is given by:

$$y = 1/x - 4.3 \log(x) + x^4$$

for values of x between 0.01 and $+10.0$ in increments of 0.01. Since this will produce almost 1,000 values, provide statements to print out the values of x and y for every nth x value (for example, every 100'th value). The value of n is to be read in at execution time.

5.29 One difficulty with the approach of problem 5.16 (approximating the value of an infinite series like that for e) is that you never know how many terms to use for the approximation. One way that has proven to be very successful is to have the summation terminate when each new term adds little to the approximation. For example, the 13th term is 1/13! or 1.6059×10^{-10}, which is insignificant compared to the sum of the previous terms. Therefore, you should modify the program for problem 5.16 to allow for termination of the series when any term is less than a small quantity (which we will call delta or Δ), and which is read in at execution time.

5.30 One of the most famous series is that due to Fibonacci

$$1\ 1\ 2\ 3\ 5\ 8\ 13\ 21\ 34\ \ldots$$

This series is known to describe many naturally occurring phenomena. For example, the number of seeds in successive rows of sunflowers duplicate the series. It also describes a population explosion among rabbits. The first two numbers in the series are 1 and 1. All the additional terms of the series are the sum of the two previous terms. Thus, the ninth term (34) is the sum of the seventh and the eighth terms, or 13 + 21. Write a program to calculate the first *n* terms of the series.

5.31 A lot of people place much faith in the study of numbers. They believe that they can predict your future if they know one of your vital statistics such as your social security number. They base their method on reducing your number to a single digit number by adding all the digits together. For example, if your SS# is 123-45-6789, the sum of the digits is 45. Since this is still a two-digit number, the process needs to be repeated. The result (4 + 5) is 9. Write a program to carry out this unusual addition process for any general number such as a phone number or body weight.

Answers to Selected Supplementary Problems

5.19 (a) Extra comma at end of loop control variable.
(b) Loop does not converge. I**2 + 1 will always be a positive value.
(c) Attempt to change LCV inside the loop.
(d) Should not mix real and integer values inside the loop control statement. This will result in a step size of 0, which in turn causes an infinite loop at run time.
(e) Cannot use J as the LCV for the inner loop.
(f) Cannot use K as the LCV in the innermost loop.

5.20 (a)
```
DO I = 10, 1, -2
    PRINT *, I
END DO
```
(b)
```
DO  I = 1, 10, 2
    DO J = I, 2*I, 2
        PRINT *, J
```

```
                                    END DO
                                    PRINT *, I
                              END DO
```

5.21   (a)   Trace Table:
                        J: 1, 2
                        K: 1, 2, 3
                        L: 2, 3

                  Output:
                        L = 2
                        L = 3

(b)   Trace Table:
            J: 1, 2, 3
            K: 1, 2, 3, 4, 2, 3, 4
            L: 2, 3, 4, 4, 5
            M: −2, −1, −3

      Output:
            L = 2
            L = 3
            L = 4
            M = −3
            L = 4
            L = 5
            M = −2

(c)   Trace Table:
            J: 1, 2, 3
            K: 1, 2, 3, 1, 2, 3
            L: 1, 2, 3, 1, 2, 3,
                   1, 2, 3, 1, 2, 3
            Z: 3,4,4,5,4,5,5,6
            M: 4,9,9,16
      Output:
            4.00000   4
            5.00000   9
            5.00000   9
            6.00000   16

(d)   Trace Table:
            I: 5, 8, 11, 14, 17, 20
            I2:   1, 1, 2, 2, 3
            I3:   7, 7, 7, 7, 7

      Output:
            5   1   7
            8   1   7
            11   2   7
            14   2   7
            17   3   7

5.22   (a)   Improper compound conditional. Should be (X > Y .OR. X < Z).
          (b)   Infinite loop — no way for DO WHILE construct to stop.
          (c)   Infinite loop — X*X will never be negative. Therefore, the loop cannot stop.
          (d)   READ statement inside the DO WHILE loop attempts to change value of I. This is
                forbidden since I is the LCV for the counted loop. Also, THEN key word is missing.

5.23   (a)   Trace Table:
                        X: 1.5, 2.25, 3.375, 5.0625
                  Output:
                        1.500000
                        2.250000
                        3.375000

(b)   Trace Table:
            X: 1.0, 2.0, 3.0, 6.0, 27.0, 678.0
      Output:
            1.00000
            2.00000
            3.00000
            6.00000
            27.0000

(c)   Trace Table:
            X: 2.0, 2.0, 4.0, 32.0

(d)   Trace Table:
            TERM: 0.0, −4.0, 8.0, −16.0, 32.0

Y: 1.0, 2.0, 8.0, 256.0   ISIGN: +1, −1, +1, −1, +1
SUM: 0.0, 4.0, 36.0   X: 1.0, 2.0, 3.0, 4.0, 5.0
<u>Output:</u>   SUM: 1.,−3.,6.,14.,0.5,−15.5,10.
2.00000   2.00000   4.00000   <u>Output:</u>
                                                   −4.00000   −3.00000
                                                    8.00000   14.0000
                                                   −16.0000   −15.5000

5.25
```
PRINT *, 'Enter I and J:'
READ *, I, J
DO LCV = J-1, I+1, -1
    PRINT *, LCV
END DO
END
```

5.26
```
NOS = 0
SUM = 0.0
DO
    PRINT *, 'Enter a value:'
    READ *, X
    IF(X < 0) EXIT
    NOS = NOS + 1
    SUM = SUM + X
END DO
AVG = SUM/NOS
PRINT *, AVG
END
```

5.27
```
PRINT *, 'Enter amount and percentage rate:'
READ *, AMT, PERCENT
START = AMT
DO
    ADD = AMT * PERCENT
    PRINT *,'Interest:',ADD
    AMT = AMT + ADD
    PRINT *, 'Total: ', AMT
    IF(AMT > 2.0* START) EXIT
END DO
```

5.28
```
PRINT *, 'Printout Frequency?'
READ *, N
DO I = 1, 1000
    X = I/100.0
    Y = 1/X-4.3*LOG10(X)+X**4
    IF(MOD(I,N) == 0) THEN
        PRINT *, X, Y
    END IF
END DO
END
```

(Note: the LCV <u>should</u> be an integer. So we created I to control the loop and then we calculated X inside the loop to match the problem statement.)

5.29
```
        PRINT *, 'Enter DELTA:'
        READ *, DELTA
        SUM = 1.0
        TERM = 1.0
        I = 1
        DO
           FACT = 1.0
           DO II = 1, I
              FACT=FACT*II
           END DO
           TERM = 1/FACT
           IF(TERM <= DELTA) EXIT
           SUM = SUM + TERM
           I = I + 1
        END DO
        PRINT *, 'Approx = ', SUM
        END
```

5.30
```
        PRINT *, 'Number of terms?'
        READ *, N
        TERM1=1
        TERM2=1
        PRINT *, 'Term1:', TERM1
        PRINT *, 'Term2:', TERM2
        DO I = 3, N
           TERM = TERM1 + TERM2
           PRINT *,'Term',I,':',TERM
           TERM2 = TERM1
           TERM1 = TERM
        END DO
        END
```

5.31
```
        INTEGER :: SUM              ! You may omit the ::
        PRINT *,'Enter number(max 9 digits)'
        READ *, NUM
        DO
           SUM = 0
           DO
              SUM=SUM+MOD(NUM,10)
              NUM=NUM/10
              IF(NUM < 10) EXIT
           END DO
           SUM=SUM+NUM
           NUM=SUM
           IF(NUM < 10) EXIT
        END DO
        PRINT *,'Sum of Digits:',NUM
        END
```

Chapter 6

Subscripted Variables and Arrays

6.1 OVERVIEW

Arrays are a convenient way to work with large quantities of data. For example, by using arrays you can easily store 100 numbers with only a single variable. Without arrays, you would need 100 conventional single-valued variables to do the same thing.

Each array has an *index* that allows you to locate and manipulate the quantities stored in the array. We sometimes also call this index the *subscript*. The idea of the subscripted variable is a common one in mathematics. For example, if you have a series of numbers, $x_1, x_2, \ldots, x_n$, you can represent the average $\bar{x}$ by a mathematical shorthand.

$$\bar{x} = \frac{1}{n} \sum_{i=1}^{i=n} x_i = \frac{1}{n}(x_1 + x_2 + \cdots + x_n)$$

Here we represent the individual numbers as x_i, where i is the subscript that locates the desired number in the list. This x_1 represents the first number in the list, x_2 is the second number, and so on. The summation sign Σ indicates that we are to add together the specified numbers in the list. All we need do to manipulate these numbers is to specify their position (1, 2, 3, etc.) within that list. Thus, if we wanted to add together the third and fourth numbers in the list, we would write:

$$\text{total} = x_3 + x_4$$

As we will soon see, subscripted variables will greatly increase our ability to manipulate large quantities of data. The topics to be covered in this chapter include:

- The need for arrays
- Declarations and one-dimensional arrays
- Manipulation of arrays
- Higher-order arrays
- Input/output of arrays
- Debugging tips

6.2 THE NEED FOR ARRAYS

Scientists and engineers often work with large amounts of data. For example, we may run an experiment in which there are several thousand data points to process. Using only the techniques that we have presented so far, this would be a difficult task. To demonstrate this, let's focus on a simple task to write a program that reads in ten numbers and prints them out in reverse order. One possible solution is:

```
READ *, X1, X2, X3, X4, X5, X6, X7, X8, X9, X10
PRINT *, X10, X9, X8, X7, X6, X5, X4, X3, X2, X1
```

This program segment will work of course, but it's neither elegant nor very practical. If we want to do the same thing for 11 numbers, we would have to modify our program. So if we wanted to perform this task on 100 numbers, we would have a lot of work ahead of us.

Before we show you the structure of an array, you must understand the difference between the *single-valued variable* and the *subscripted variable*. The variables that you have studied so far are all *single-valued*. This means that they can take on only a single value:

```
X = 1.23456
```

In this simple assignment statement, the variable X has only a single value. When we wish to create a *subscripted variable*, we must add one additional piece of information —the *subscript*:

```
X(1) = 1.23456
X(2) = 9.87654
```

The number that appears within the parentheses is the *index* and indicates the position within the array X that contains all the data. Thus, the first number in the list is X(1) or 1.23456. In mathematics, we indicate this type of variable by using a subscript. In Fortran, however, the rule is that we must write the subscript inside a pair of parentheses. The quantity that goes inside the parenthesis can be a constant, a variable, or an expression. Thus, we could have:

```
X(1) = ......
X(J) = ......
X(2*K-1) = ......
```

The advantage of arrays is that the subscript can be a variable that can be controlled by the program. Since we have only a single index in these examples, we will refer to these arrays as *one-dimensional*.

EXAMPLE 6.1

The array subscript can be controlled by a DO loop. The most common way is to use the loop control variable (LCV) as the array subscript. In the following example, we will use I as the LCV, and then use it to store values in X(1), X(2), ..., X(10). The values will be I^2. Thus, X(1) will contain 1^2, X(2) will contain 2^2, and so forth, up to X(10) storing 10^2.

```
DO I = 1, 10
   X(I) = I**2
END DO
```

The variable I will change each time through the loop. Thus, when I=1, a value will be assigned to X(1). When I=2, a value will be assigned to X(2), and so forth.

The primary restriction on the subscript is that it must be an *integer* constant, variable, or expression. You may not use real values.

EXAMPLE 6.2

The subscript of an array may be an <u>integer</u> constant, variable, or expression. Shown below are some examples showing the allowed array subscripts:

Rule for Subscript	Correct Example	Incorrect Example
Constant	X (1)	X (1.2)
Variable	X (J)	X (Z)
Variable + constant	X (J+1)	X (J+1.0)
Constant × variable	X (2*J)	X (2.0*J)
Constant × variable ± constant	X (2*J−1)	X (2*J−4.0)
Function value	X (INT(SQRT(Z)))	X (SQRT(Y))

Older versions of Fortran had stringent rules about the subscript and you may run into these when maintaining programs written in the old standard. This should not cause problems however, since Fortran 90 will allow any subscript that was valid in the older versions.

6.3 THE DECLARATION STATEMENT

Before you can use arrays, you must first *declare* them. Declaration statements go at the beginning of the program before any executable statements and provide important information that allows the compiler to reserve enough space in memory for the arrays. The declaration is usually done with the *type declaration* statement, which also indicates the *size* or number of elements in each of the arrays. The general form is:

   type, DIMENSION (Lower limit : Upper limit) :: arrayname

where *type* indicates the type of the array (REAL, INTEGER, LOGICAL, etc.)
   arrayname is any valid Fortran variable name (X, TIME, etc.)
   Lower limit indicates the minimum value for the subscript
   Upper limit indicates the maximum value for the subscript
   DIMENSION indicates the number of subscripts.

The DIMENSION statement may be omitted, but the size of the array (namely, the lower and upper limits) must then be appended to the variable name. Also, if the lower limit on the array is omitted, a value of 1 is assumed. The "Lower limit : Upper limit" pair of numbers can be any integers (even negative) as long as the upper limit is larger than the lower limit. Usually, though, arrays will begin with a lower limit of 1. It makes sense to start your arrays this way, since the conventional way of thinking of a list is that it begins with the "first" item. If you set up arrays this way, you may omit the lower limit and specify only the upper limit without the colon. In some instances, however, it may make sense to start the array at a value other than a lower limit of 1.

Fixed-Size Arrays

A fixed size array is *static* – it does not change in size. An important point about declaring arrays is that you promise the compiler what the <u>maximum</u> array size will be. You are not required to use all this space. All that you are doing is telling the compiler to reserve sufficient space for the data. For example, if you create an array with 100 elements and use only 10 of those, there is no problem. The reverse situation (using more than you reserve) is not allowed.

EXAMPLE 6.3

In the following example, we modify the program segment in Example 6.2 to now declare the array before we begin to use it:

```
REAL, DIMENSION(10) :: X
DO I = 1, 10
    X(I) = I**2
END DO
```

Notice that the declaration statement (REAL, DIMENSION (10) :: X) establishes the array X with a <u>maximum</u> size of 10 elements. If we had attempted to store data in an array element outside this range, we would have received an *out-of-bounds* error.

There are also several additional ways to declare fixed-size arrays as illustrated in the following table:

Example	Comments
REAL, DIMENSION (1:10) :: X	*(X is a real array with 10 elements)*
REAL, DIMENSION (10) :: X	*(Same as previous example but lower limit is assumed to be 1)*
REAL X(10)	*(Same result as previous two examples)*
INTEGER, DIMENSION (1:10) :: A, B	*(A and B are both integer arrays with 10 elements each)*
REAL X(–5:10), Y(20)	*(Declares X and Y to be real with 16 and 20 elements, respectively)*
INTEGER AMT, M(10)	*(Can declare scalar variables and arrays in the same declaration statement)*

Variable-Sized Arrays

Fortran 90 has a feature known as an *Allocatable Array*, where the memory for the array is set aside only at execution time. This effectively allows you to read in or calculate the necessary size of the array, and then have the computer reserve memory for it.

To create an allocatable array, you must execute two steps:

- First, the array is declared with the ALLOCATABLE option. You do not set the size of the array at this point. You are merely setting it up so that it can be modified later.
- The ALLOCATE statement is then used to declare the actual size of the array.

After you are finished with the array, you can clear it and resize it for further use with the DEALLOCATE statement. These features are illustrated in the next two examples.

EXAMPLE 6.4

The following program segment allows you to read in the value of N, which is then used to size the one-dimensional array as X(N):

```
REAL, DIMENSION(:), ALLOCATABLE::X    ! Declare array to be allocatable
PRINT *,'Size of array?'
READ *, N                             ! Read in the array size
ALLOCATE (X(N))                       ! Allocate memory to the array
```

Notice that when an array is declared as allocatable we do not specify any upper or lower limits in the DIMENSION clause. But we need to add the ALLOCATABLE attribute to the declaration statement as shown in the first line. Then when the value of N is known through the READ statement, the array can be established with the ALLOCATE command.

In addition to the ALLOCATE command, the DEALLOCATE command can be used to release the memory assigned to the array. If the previous example were inside a loop to repeat the process, then DEALLOCATE X would allow the array X to be reallocated for subsequent executions.

EXAMPLE 6.5

This program segment sets up an array of size N, reads in the data, sums the squares of the array elements, and then deallocates the array so that we may reuse it for another data set of different size. In this example, we will perform this summation twice.

```
REAL, DIMENSION(:), ALLOCATABLE::X    ! Declare array to be allocatable
DO I=1, 2
    PRINT *,'Size of array?'          ! A prompt to enter array size
    READ *,N                          ! Read in the array size
    ALLOCATE (X(N))                   ! Allocate memory to the array
    SUM=0.0                           ! Initialize total before loop
DO J=1, N
    SUM=SUM+X(J)**2
END DO
```

```
    PRINT *, 'Sum of squares = ', SUM ! Print results when finished
    DEALLOCATE (X)                    ! Clean up when finished
END DO
```

In this example we have used the value of N to perform the summation of the squares of the elements of the array X, after which we release the array with the DEALLOCATE command to prepare the array X for the next data set.

6.4 MANIPULATING ARRAYS

One thing to keep in mind is that one-dimensional arrays are an efficient way to store and manipulate lists (and later, tables) of data. Quite often, these data will be systematically stored, retrieved, and processed. For example, when we enter data we usually intend to store the items in ascending order (1st, 2nd, etc.). Similarly, if we add all the data, we usually add them in a systematic way (1st + 2nd + 3rd etc.). Because of the organized way in which we handle the data, the process is an ideal candidate for control by loops. Therefore, you will find that arrays and loops are almost inseparable. Chances are that if you are using an array, you will be using loops.

EXAMPLE 6.6

Sigma notation (Σ) is used very frequently in engineering, science, and mathematics as a shorthand notation. So we will explore this subject in considerable detail in this and subsequent examples. Recall that sigma notation indicates the sum of the individual elements of the subscripted expression is to be computed. Here is a simple example:

$$a = \sum_{i=1}^{i=100} y_i$$

The Σ expression computes the sum of all the elements stored in the subscripted variable y and the statement stores the result in a. We add one element of the array at a time, and systematically change the subscript from $i=1$ to $i=100$. We implement this in Fortran with a DO loop (we leave out the input statements since we haven't discussed I/O of arrays yet):

Program

```
REAL, DIMENSION (100) :: Y
! We have left out the input
! statements that assign
! values to Y
A = 0.0
DO I = 1, 100
   A = A + Y(I)
END DO
```

Flowchart

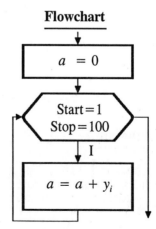

The DO loop takes each element of the array and adds it to the running total A. For example, when I=1, Y(I) or Y(1) is added, and when I=2, Y(2) is added, and so forth. An important thing to note is that the subscript of the array is also the loop control variable.

EXAMPLE 6.7

The following program reads in a list of numbers (up to 100) from the terminal, calculates the average, and prints a list of the individual deviations of each number from the average. The deviation is the difference between the number and the average.

   To solve this problem, we will use two arrays, X and DEV. The X array will store the numbers as we enter them. Once all the numbers are entered, we will be able to compute the average. Finally, we can then compute the deviations by subtracting the average value from each of the input numbers. Note that we have to save the entered numbers so that we can use them a second time for the computation of the deviations.

Algorithm	Flowchart

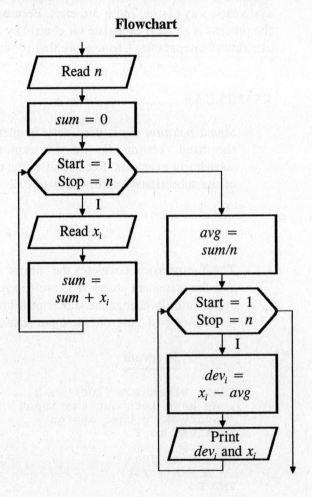

1. Read in number of data points, N
2. SUM = 0.0
3. Loop (1 to N)
   Read in a value and assign it to X(I)
   Add X(I) to SUM
4. Compute average (AVG = SUM/N)
5. Loop (1 to N)
   DEV(I) = X(I) − AVG
   Print X(I) and DEV(I)

Program

```
REAL, DIMENSION (100) :: X, DEV
! Enter the number of data items for the computation
PRINT *, 'Number of values (less than 100)?'
READ *, N
```

```
! We will read in one data value at a time and store it in X(I)
SUM = 0.0
DO I = 1, N
   READ *, X(I)
   SUM = SUM + X(I)
END DO
AVG = SUM/N
! Once the average has been computed, we can use it to
! calculate the deviations defined by X(I)-AVG:
PRINT *, 'Average = ', AVG
DO I = 1, N
   DEV(I) = X(I) - AVG
   PRINT *, 'NUMBER=', X(I), 'DEVIATION=', DEV(I)
END DO
END
```

Another area where one-dimensional arrays are useful is the processing of vectors. Vectors, as you may recall, are quantities that have both magnitude and direction. In the following examples, we store vectors by placing the vector components into individual array elements.

EXAMPLE 6.8

The *dot product z* of two vectors *a* and *b* is defined by:

$$z = \sum_{i=1}^{i=3} a_i b_i$$

The summation process can be done with a DO loop where we add the product of the appropriate components of each vector. For example, for the vectors $a = (1.2, 3.5, 4.1)$ and $b = (2.0, 5.1, -1.1)$, the dot product is $1.2 \times 2.0 + 3.5 \times 5.1 + 4.1 \times (-1.1) = 15.74$. The algorithm and flowchart for doing this is:

Algorithm	**Flowchart**

1. Z = 0.0
2. Loop (1 to 3)
    Read A(I) and B(I)
    Add A(I) × B(I) to Z
3. Print Z

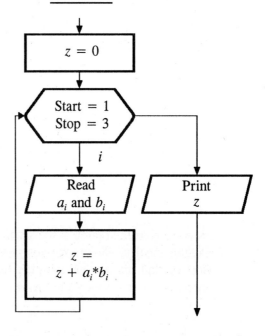

Program

```
! The two vectors A and B each contain 3 components. So
! we declare each to be a one-dimensional array with 3 elements.
REAL, DIMENSION(3) :: A, B
Z = 0.0
! Inside the following loop, we read in the components of each
! vector and perform the required summation of the products.
DO I = 1, 3
   READ *, A(I), B(I)
   Z = Z + A(I) * B(I)
END DO
PRINT *, 'Dot Product = ', Z
END
```

Another common application of one-dimensional arrays is to process a list of numbers, such as sorting in ascending order. We give here one example of such a sorting process.

EXAMPLE 6.9

A common application is to take a list of numbers and put them into ascending or descending order. For example, if you had a list such as 7, 3, 2, 6, 9, 0 and put it into ascending order, the list becomes 0, 2, 3, 6, 7, 9.

One of the simplest sorting methods is the *min–max* sort. It works by first searching all the elements in a list to locate the minimum value. This minimum value is then swapped with the value in the first position of the list. Since the first position within the list now has the smallest value, we do not need to consider it any longer. So we repeat the process, but now start at the second position in the list. Thus, the program searches element 2 through the end of the list for the smallest value and then swaps the value in the second position with the smallest value. This process is repeated until the entire list has been sorted.

To demonstrate how this works, consider the following list and watch how the numbers swap after each search:

Starting values

7	3	2	6	9	0

We assume that the minimum value is in the first position. But, as we search through the list, we find the smallest value is in the sixth position. So, we switch the first and sixth values:

Swap first and sixth values

0	3	2	6	9	7

Now we start the search at the second position (since we know that the first position already has the smallest value). We now assume that the minimum value is in the second position. But we find that the value in the third position is smallest (of the remaining items in the shortened list), so we swap the values in the second and third positions:

Swap second and third values

0	2	3	6	9	7

Now we start the search at the third position, assuming that its value is the smallest. This time the assumption is correct, so we do nothing:

Leave third value alone

0	2	3	6	9	7

Now we start the search at the fourth position, assuming that its value is the smallest. Once again, the assumption is correct, so we do nothing:

Leave fourth value alone

0	2	3	6	9	7

Next, we start at the fifth position, and we find that we must swap the fifth and sixth values:

Swap fifth and sixth values

0	2	3	6	7	9

Flowchart

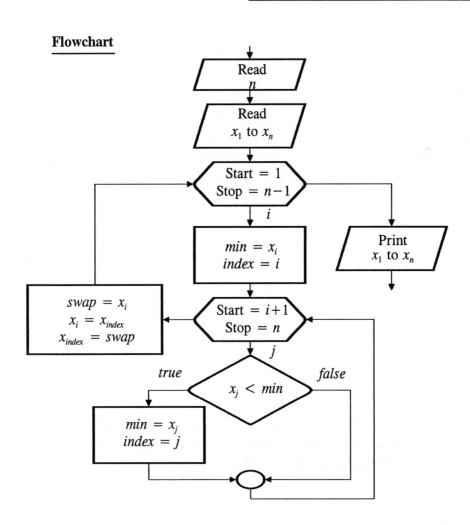

Program

```
REAL, DIMENSION (100) :: X
PRINT *, 'How many numbers?'
! Input N values into X(1) to X(N)
READ *, N
DO I = 1, N
   READ *, X(I)
END DO
! This loop continues until all the values are sorted
DO I = 1, N-1
    XMIN = X(I)
    INDEX = I
! This loop locates the position INDEX of the smallest value
   DO J = I+1, N
      IF (X(J) < XMIN) THEN
         XMIN = X(J)
         INDEX = J
     END IF
   END DO
! The following section swaps the value in X(I) and the
! smallest value located in X(INDEX)
   SWAP = X(I)
   X(I) = X(INDEX)
   X(INDEX) = SWAP
END DO
! Finally, after sorting the array, we print out the results
DO I = 1, N
   PRINT *, X(I)
END DO
```

For convenience, we have used a shorthand notation in the flowchart when we entered or printed the data. Instead of using a loop to enter all the values, we have condensed this block of instructions into a single read instruction, such as Read X_1 to X_N. As we will see shortly, Fortran has an instruction corresponding to this shorthand notation.

Another common application is the compiling of statistics from a list of data. For example, we may want to know how many students achieved scores of 90 to 100 on an examination.

EXAMPLE 6.10

A data set contains a list of integers ranging from 0 to 10 where the same number may be entered multiple times. The following program counts the number of occurrences for each value. We will create an array C(I) that increases by one each time a number is entered. Thus, C(0) represents the number of zeros, C(1) represents the number of ones, and so forth:

C(0)	C(1)	C(2)	C(3)	C(4)	C(5)	C(6)	C(7)	C(8)	C(9)	C(10)

When we read in a value, we will put that number into the appropriate bin. For example, if we read in the number 5, we would increase the count in C(5) by one:

C(0)	C(1)	C(2)	C(3)	C(4)	C(5)	C(6)	C(7)	C(8)	C(9)	C(10)
0	0	0	0	0	1	0	0	0	0	0

Flowchart

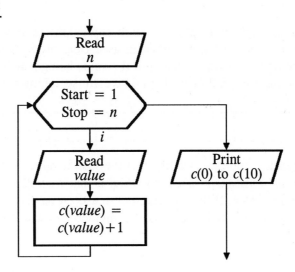

Program

```
! In this situation, it makes sense to declare the array to start at
! the zero position. Note also that VALUE must be declared as an
! integer since we will be using it later as a subscript to store a
! value in C(VALUE)
INTEGER C(0:10), VALUE
PRINT *, 'Number of values?'
READ *, N
! First, we initialize all elements of C to 0.
DO I = 0, 10
   C(I) = 0
END DO
! Read in a value and increment the appropriate list position.
DO I = 1, N
   READ *, VALUE
   C(VALUE) = C(VALUE) + 1
END DO
! Print out the results
DO I = 0, 10
   PRINT *, 'Number of', I, '''s:', C(I)
END DO
```

This example utilizes an array as a group of counters. Because the values read in were integers, it was possible to use these values to select the counter. COUNT(0) was used to keep track of the zeros, for example. By selecting the counter based on the value, the process was straightforward. Because this example included values starting at 0, this was a good opportunity to take advantage of the special index range feature for arrays. That is why the declaration statement [INTEGER C(0:10)] had the array start at element 0.

The previous examples were concerned with manipulation of lists. But, we can also use lists to look up data. For example, we may wish to find a certain number within a long list of values.

EXAMPLE 6.11

The following example illustrates a search algorithm for locating a value in a list. The program requires that the list be sorted in ascending order. The process to locate a given number will be to read down the list until the value being sought is located. As an example, assume that we have the following list and we are searching for a specific value of 19:

Search value = 19	-4	5	11	13	19	20	41	52

When the search is completed, we find that the search value (19) is in the fifth position. The reason that the list must be in ascending order is that we will stop the search once any value exceeds the search value. If the list were not in ascending order, then we would have to test every number before we could say that the number was not in the list.

Program   **Flowchart**

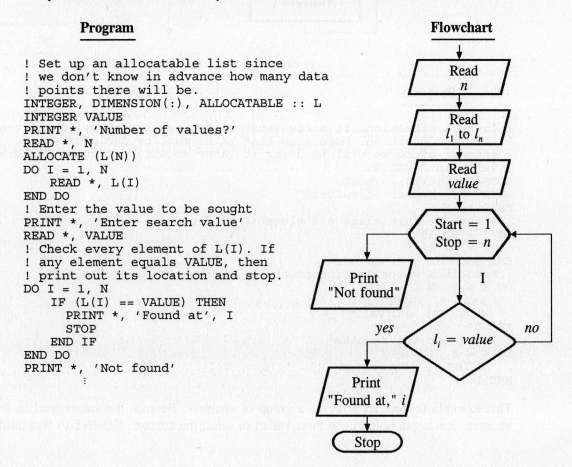

```
! Set up an allocatable list since
! we don't know in advance how many data
! points there will be.
INTEGER, DIMENSION(:), ALLOCATABLE :: L
INTEGER VALUE
PRINT *, 'Number of values?'
READ *, N
ALLOCATE (L(N))
DO I = 1, N
    READ *, L(I)
END DO
! Enter the value to be sought
PRINT *, 'Enter search value'
READ *, VALUE
! Check every element of L(I). If
! any element equals VALUE, then
! print out its location and stop.
DO I = 1, N
    IF (L(I) == VALUE) THEN
      PRINT *, 'Found at', I
      STOP
    END IF
END DO
PRINT *, 'Not found'
    ⋮
```

This process is not very efficient since we may have to search through every data point before finding the location of the desired value. In the case of a short list, this is not a serious drawback, but when the list is very long, the algorithm shown above is time consuming. A much more efficient method, known as the *binary* search, is outlined in the following example.

EXAMPLE 6.12

The *binary search* method works by bracketing a group of values within a list that is already in ascending order. By comparing the search value with the value in the <u>middle</u> of the list, it is possible to determine which half of the list contains the value. This process is then repeated on the narrowed portion of the list until the value is found or the range goes to 0.

To demonstrate how this method works, consider the following list already, which is in ascending order:

Starting values

2	9	11	23	49

We start by comparing the search value (*e.g.,* 23), with the value at the middle of the list:

Compare search value (23) with midpoint value

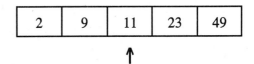

If the search value (23) is less than the value in this position, then the search value is in the lower half of the list; otherwise, it is in the upper half. In this case, the search value (23) is larger than the value in the middle (11), so the search will focus on the second half. We then repeat the process by dividing the remaining numbers into two halves:

Cut search area in half and repeat previous step

		11	23	49

↑

The value in the center of the reduced search area is now equal to the search value (23), so our search stops. The program will then print out that it found the value in the fourth position. If the search area ever goes to zero, then the search number is not in the list and the program will print out an appropriate message such as "number not found."

Notice that the field that we are searching is always being cut in half, thereby reducing the number of comparisons that we have to do. This greatly improves the overall efficiency of the search.

Flowchart

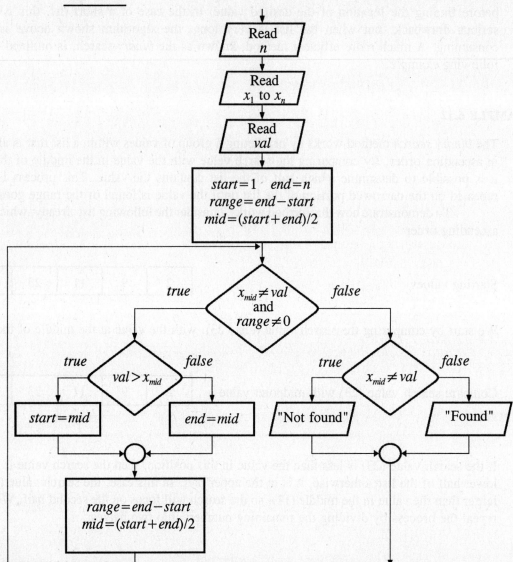

Program

```
INTEGER, DIMENSION (1:100) :: X
INTEGER :: RANGE, START, END_OF_RANGE
! The input section
PRINT *, 'Number of values?'
READ *, N
DO I = 1, N
   READ *, X(I)
END DO
! Enter the value to be sought
```

```
PRINT *, 'Enter value'
READ *, VAL
!
! Define the range and midpoint
!
START = 1
END_OF_RANGE = N
RANGE = END_OF_RANGE - START
MID = (START + END)/2
!
! As long as the value is not found, cut the range in half
! and check which half the value might be in.
!
DO WHILE (X(MID) /= VAL .AND. RANGE /= 0)
   IF (VAL > X(MID)) THEN
       START = MID
    ELSE
       END_OF_RANGE = MID
    END IF
    RANGE = END_OF_RANGE - START
    MID = (START + END)/2
END DO
!
! If the value being sought is not in the middle of the last
! range, then the value is not in the original list.
!
IF (X(MID) /= VAL) THEN
   PRINT *, VAL, 'not found'
ELSE
   PRINT *, 'Value at', MID
END IF
END
```

6.5 SIMPLIFIED ARRAY PROCESSING

Fortran 90 offers a variety of tools for processing arrays that can greatly simplify some of your programs. Some of the new features that we will discuss are:

- Array expressions, functions, and constructors
- WHERE statement and construct
- Array subobjects

These special features greatly enhance the ability to process arrays. As we will see shortly, the code needed to manipulate data can be greatly reduced, with a significant increase in ease of use.

Before we begin discussing some of the advanced array features in Fortran 90, we need to define some special terms dealing with the array declaration statement:

RANK: The dimension or number of subscripts of an array. For example, the array defined by REAL A(10) has rank 1, indicating a one-dimensional array.

EXTENT: The number of elements along a dimension of an array. For example:

```
REAL, DIMENSION(10) :: A        ! A has an extent of 10
REAL, DIMENSION(0:9) :: B       ! B also has an extent of 10
```

Fortran 90 supports *array expressions*. This means that an array can be present in an expression <u>without specifying its subscripts</u>. This greatly simplifies array processing.

EXAMPLE 6.13

For the following examples, assume that the arrays A, B, C, D, X, Y, and Z are declared as follows:

```
REAL, DIMENSION(10) :: A, B, X, Z
REAL, DIMENSION(5) :: C, D, Y
```

These arrays can be processed in either of two ways, as illustrated in the following table:

Simplified Method	Conventional Way	Comments
Z=A/B	DO I=1, 10 Z(I)=A(I)/B(I) END DO	*(Real array Z of extent (10) is computed where each element is Z(I)=A(I)/B(I))*
A=Z/10.0	DO I=1, 10 A(I)=Z(I)/10.0 END DO	*(Divides elements of Z by 10.0 and stores results in A)*
X=X+9.0	DO I=1, 10 X(I)=X(I)+9.0 END DO	*(Adds 9.0 to all elements of X)*
D=C+Y	DO I=1, 5 D(I)=C(I)+Y(I) END DO	*(Real array of extent (5) is computed with elements D(I)=C(I)+Y(I))*

The above operations can take place because the operators (/ and +) are *context sensitive*. This means that the operation taking place depends on the type of data the operator is working on. When the division operator divides an array by a scalar, for example, that scalar is applied to all elements of the array. When an operator works with two arrays, then the operations are performed on values in each array at the matching positions. For example, to create $Z(I)=A(I)/B(I)$, the computer will divide only elements in the same position within the two arrays, such as $Z(3)=A(3)/B(3)$ and so forth for all other values of I. The only limitation on this rule is that for an array operation to be valid, the arrays must be *conformable*.

CONFORMABLE: Two arrays are conformable when they have the same rank and extent in each dimension. However, a scalar is always conformable with any array.

This context-oriented concept extends to built-in functions. If a function is defined for a scalar, then it may also be applied to an array. The array that is returned will be the result of applying the function to each element of the array. Functions that require array arguments will return values that are dependent on their definition. The following is a partial list of functions that operate on arrays.

Function	Description
SUM(ARRAY)	*(Returns the scalar value of the sum of the elements of an integer, real, or complex array.)*
PRODUCT(ARRAY)	*(Returns the scalar value of the product of all the elements of an integer, real or complex array.)*
MAXVAL(ARRAY)	*(Returns the scalar value of the maximum value for the element of an integer or real array.)*
MINVAL(ARRAY)	*(Returns the scalar value of the minimum value for the element of an integer or real array.)*
MAXLOC(ARRAY)	*(Returns an integer array of rank 1 indicating the location where the maximum value was found.)*
MINLOC(ARRAY)	*(Returns an integer array of rank 1 indicating the location where the minimum value was found.)*
DOT_PRODUCT(A,B)	*(Returns the dot product scalar value of two real or integer vectors A and B, which must be the same size.)*

EXAMPLE 6.14

The following examples illustrate these various functions and expressions.

a)   Calculate the magnitude of a vector. Recall that the magnitude of a vector is the sum of the squares of the individual components.

```
REAL, DIMENSION(3) :: X        !X is a 1-D array with 3 elements
REAL MAG
PRINT *,'Enter the VECTOR'
DO I = 1, 3                     !Read in the vector components
   READ *, X(I)
END DO
```

```
MAG = SQRT(SUM(X**2))              !Add the squares of the elements
PRINT *,'Magnitude is', MAG
END
```

The key statement is SUM(X**2), where SUM determines the sum of all the elements of X times X. Once this value is obtained, its square root is taken and assigned to MAG.

b)   Calculate the DOT product between two vectors A and B

```
REAL, DIMENSION(3) :: A, B         !Declare the two vectors
PRINT *,'Enter Vector A'
DO I=1, 3                          !Read in components of A
    READ*, A(I)
END DO
PRINT *,'Enter Vector B'
DO I=1,3                           !Read in components of B
    READ*, B(I)
END DO
C=DOT_PRODUCT(A,B)                 !Take dot product of A & B
PRINT *,'Dot product=', C
END
```

The DOT_PRODUCT is given by $\sum A_i B_i$, where the corresponding elements of A and B are multiplied and the products are added.

In the last example, we used READ statements to initialize the value of the arrays. While this is the usual way of entering data, Fortran 90 offers an additional method of assigning values to an array. This mechanism is known as the *array constructor*. There are two general forms of the array constructor:

   (/*array-constructor-value-list*/)

and

   (/(*variable, variable=start, end, step*)/)

In the first definition, the slash marks (/ ... /) enclose a list of the desired values to be given to the array elements. In the second method, a variable will take on the values calculated from the start, stop, and step size values given, and this variable behaves just like the loop control variable used for loops and is sometimes called an *implied DO loop*.

EXAMPLE 6.15

The following table gives several examples of array constructors:

Constructor	Description/Resulting Value
K = (/1, 2, 3, 4, 5, 6/)	*(Loads values 1 through 6 into array K)*
L = (/(I, I = 1, 6)/)	*(Same as the above example using an implied DO loop)*
REAL, DIMENSION(10):: X=(/(I, I=1,10)/)	*(Constructors may be used in the declaration statement)*
Z = (/(SQRT(2.0*I), I=1,10)/)	*(You may use functions with the constructor)*

In the following example program, we use the array constructor to load the numbers 1, 2, and 3 into the array A, and the numbers 10, 9, and 8 into array B It then calculates the new array C where C(I) = (A(I) +2*I)/B(I).

```
! First, set up the A and B arrays with a declaration statement. The
! A array is initialized with an implied DO loop, while B is
! initialized by simple assignments. The two methods are
! interchangeable in this example.
        INTEGER, DIMENSION (3) :: A(/(I, I=1,3)/), B(/10, 9, 8/), C
! Now use the array constructor to set the elements of C
        C = (/((A(I) + 2*I)/B(I), I = 1, 3)/)
        ⋮
```

Up to now, we have seen that Fortran 90 has simplified array processing by providing a means of having array expressions, functions that return array values, and a simplified means of assigning values to an array. There are two additional ways to manipulate arrays - the WHERE statement and construct. Their purpose is to execute a statement on individual elements of an array based on a logical expression. The WHERE statement is a one-line statement with the form:

> WHERE (*logical-array-expression*) *statement*

while the WHERE structure can contain several lines and has an ELSEWHERE and END WHERE statements that behave like a block IF construct:

> WHERE (*logical-array-expression*)
>   *statements to execute if true*
> ELSEWHERE
>   *statements to execute if false*
> END WHERE

The logical array expression is identical to the logical comparison used in the block IF construct. For every value of the array where the condition is true, the statement that follows will execute.

For the false values of the logical expression, nothing is done. The difference between the block IF and the WHERE, however, is that WHERE operates on as many elements as needed, whereas the IF construct executes on only one item.

EXAMPLE 6.16

The following example uses two different methods to square all elements of the array that are positive.

<u>Block-IF Form</u>

```
REAL, DIMENSION (10) :: A
DO I=1, 10                         ! Enter the data
   READ *, A(I)
END DO
DO I=1, 10
   IF(A(I) > 0) A(I)=A(I)**2       ! Square only the terms
END DO                             ! that are positive
```

<u>Using WHERE statement:</u>

```
REAL, DIMENSION(10) :: A
DO I=1, 10
   READ *, A(I)
END DO
WHERE (A>0) A=A**2                 !Square only if positive
```

For each value of I, the operation defined by the expression (A=A**2) is evaluated and assigned to the corresponding element of the array only if A(I) is positive.

In the WHERE <u>statement</u> only one instruction can be executed if the logical array value is true. But, if there are a number of instructions to execute, then you must use the WHERE <u>structure</u>. The execution of this block structure is similar to the Block-IF structure. First, the logical expression is evaluated. If it is true, then the block of instructions in the true block executes. But, if the logical expression is false, then the second block of instructions execute. If the false block of instructions is empty, then the ELSEWHERE statement may be omitted.

EXAMPLE 6.17

A single line in a digital image is stored in an integer array of 100 elements. Each element stores a value ranging from 0 to 15. The value 0 represents black, 15 white, and the intermediate values are shades of gray. The following program creates a line of a black and white image that has higher contrast than the original image by assigning the value 0 to each element whose original value is less than 8, and a value of 15 to all elements whose values are greater than or equal to 8.

```
INTEGER, DIMENSION(100) :: IN, OUT    !Define original and new arrays
DO I=1, 100                           !Enter original gray scale values
    READ*, IN(I)
END DO
WHERE (IN<8)                          !Check each element of IN
    OUT_0                             !If < 8, set value of OUT to zero
ELSEWHERE
    OUT=15                            !Otherwise set value to 15
END WHERE
DO I=1, 100                           !Print out modified values
    PRINT *, OUT(I)
END DO
END
```

Note in this example that the array used in the logical comparison (IN) does not have to be the same as the array in the assignment statements (OUT). The only requirement is that they must match in rank. Furthermore, no more than one array can be operated on with the WHERE construct at the same time. If you want to modify a second array, you will need to set up a second WHERE structure.

You must take great care when working with <u>functions</u> inside the WHERE structure. If the function is a scalar function (works on only a single valued variable), then the operation will occur as expected. But if the function requires an array argument, the function will operate on <u>all</u> elements, not just the selected ones.

EXAMPLE 6.18

Below are examples of scalar and array functions used with the WHERE statement and construct:

Expression	Comments
WHERE (Z>0) Z = LOG(Z)	(Elements with values greater than 0 are replaced by the natural log of the original value. LOG is a scalar function operating on individual array elements)
WHERE (Z>0) A = SUM(LOG(Z))	(The SUM function returns the sum of all elements in an array. Since SUM operates on an entire array, the LOG operation will occur even on those values which are less than or equal to zero. The result is a math error)

The final topic that we will discuss in this section is the *array subobject*. This provides a means to access a <u>portion</u> of an array. For example, you may wish to find the maximum value of the elements. Array subobjects allow you to do this is a very concise fashion, by simply selecting the particular positions within the array that you wish to examine.

EXAMPLE 6.19

Here are examples of the process of selecting array subobjects. A subobject is a small section of the parent array chosen for processing. For these examples, assume that the array A has been declared by REAL, DIMENSION (10) :: A

Expression	Comments
A(1:10)	*(The entire array A)*
A(:)	*(The entire array A can also be designated this way)*
A(4:7)	*(Elements 4 through 7 of the array)*
A(:5)	*(If the first subscript is omitted, then the subobject will start at the beginning of the array. In this case, this is the same as A(1:5))*
A(4:)	*(If the second subscript is omitted, then the subobject will terminate at the end of the array. In this case, this is the same as A(4:10))*

EXAMPLE 6.20

One common problem with digital image processing is random noise caused by transmission interference. One way to reduce the noise is by a method known as "local averaging." Assume that a single line from a digital image is represented by a one-dimensional array with 100 elements. The values stored range from 0 to 15 (with 0 being black, 15 being white, and intermediate values being shades of gray). A new "averaged image" can be constructed by computing the average of the element values of the "nearest neighbors" of each element. Thus, if we wish to smooth the data point IMAGE(I), we will replace it by (IMAGE(I-1) + IMAGE(I) + IMAGE(I+1))/3. The first and last values will not be processed because they represent special cases where one of their nearest neighbors does not exist.

```
INTEGER, DIMENSION(100) :: IMAGE, NEW_IMAGE
DO I=1, 100                              ! Read in the original data
   READ *, IMAGE(I)
END DO
NEW_IMAGE = IMAGE                        ! Create a duplicate array
! Create a subarray centered around the point I and include the
! points I-1, I, and I+1 for averaging. Then copy the average into
! the NEW_IMAGE(I).
DO I = 2, 99
   NEW_IMAGE(I) = NINT(SUM(IMAGE(I-1 : I+1))/3.0)
END DO
DO I = 1, 100                            ! Print out the new image
   PRINT *, NEW_IMAGE(I)
END DO
END
```

The assignment statement inside the DO I=2, 99 loop deserves some discussion. First, note that IMAGE(I−1 : I+1) represents a sub-array surrounding IMAGE(I). The subarray includes IMAGE(I) plus the two nearest neighbors. The SUM function then adds all three elements of this subarray and divides by 3.0. This is nothing more than the average of the neighbors of the element IMAGE(I). Finally, the function NINT takes this average and returns the nearest integer value.

6.6 HIGHER-ORDER ARRAYS

In the previous section we illustrated several applications of one-dimensional arrays. You can think of the array dimension as the number of subscripts required to locate a value stored in the array. As an example, one-dimensional arrays represent lists of values. All we had to do to locate a desired value was to specify a single subscript. Two-dimensional arrays can be thought of as representing a table of information. To select a value from a table, we will need to specify the row and column. Consequently, two subscripts in the arrays will be required.

EXAMPLE 6.21

Consider the following list *A* and table *B*:

A
A(1) =4
A(2)=7
A(3)=18

B		
B(1,1)=3	B(1,2)=−2	B(1,3)=30
B(2,1)=47	B(2,2)=15	B(2,3)=0
B(3,1)=70	B(3,2)=−8	B(3,3)=39

Notice in the list (A), that we need only a single index to locate a value. Thus, A(2) has the value 7. A table, however, requires two subscripts to locate a value. The only question is which subscript (row or column) comes first? Fortran adopts the convention that the row will come first. Thus, B(2,3) has the value 0. Similarly, B(3,2) has the value −8. Note that B(3,2) is not equal to B(2,3). If we wanted to add the values in the second column, we could do this with B(1,2) + B(2,2) + B(3,2) = 5. As we did when processing one-dimensional arrays, we will use subscripts to process the data contained within a two-dimensional array. But this time, we will need two subscripts. Therefore, we will very often use a nested loop. One loop usually controls the row index, while the other loop controls the column index.

EXAMPLE 6.22

The table below shows the result of a survey of the computing experience levels of engineering students. The columns represent the different classes (freshman, sophomore, junior, and senior). The rows represent the experience levels (none, < 1 year, 1–2 years, 2–3 years, and more than 3 years).

	(Column 1) Freshman	(Column 2) Sophomore	(Column 3) Junior	(Column 4) Senior
(Row 1) None	13	5	2	1
(Row 2) < 1 year	27	30	20	18
(Row 3) 1–2 years	30	32	36	38
(Row 4) 2–3 years	16	19	22	25
(Row 5) >3 years	7	11	13	14

When the survey questionnaires are passed out, the student is requested to indicate his/her class and level of experience using these categories:

Class: 1) freshman   2) sophomore   3) junior   4) senior
Experience: 1) none   2) < 1 yr   3) 1–2 yrs   4) 2–3 yrs   5) >3 yrs

The data are entered as a pair of numbers such as 2, 3 (sophomore, 1–2 years experience). When these numbers are read in, our program will increment the appropriate cell by 1.

Flowchart

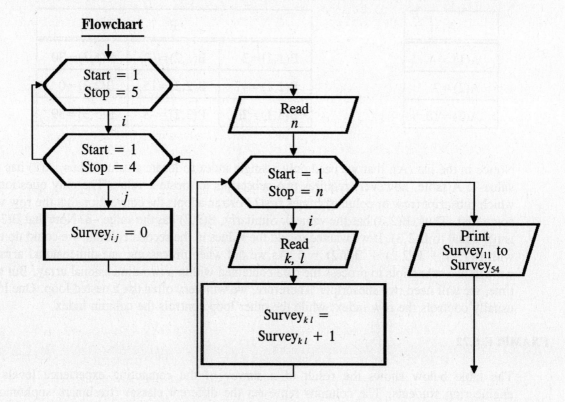

At the beginning of the flowchart is the initialization section that consists of nested loops setting all elements of the array to zero. It is a good idea to do this even if your compiler automatically initializes variables, including arrays, to zero.

In the next section of the flowchart is an input statement to read in the number of survey results. This value (n) is then used to control a counted loop, where a single pair of numbers (k, l) is read in indicating the year and experience level. This pair is then used to increment the appropriate counter by 1.

The final section of the flowchart is the output section, where the two-dimensional array Survey$_{11}$ to Survey$_{54}$ is sent to the CRT screen. This will actually be implemented with a loop, although we show it here as only a simple I/O instruction.

Program

```
! Declare SURVEY to be a two-dimensional 5 row, 4 column array
INTEGER  SURVEY(5,4)
CHARACTER (LEN=10), DIMENSION(5):: LABEL(/"None","<1 yr","1-2 yrs",&
                                        "2-3 yrs", ">3 yrs"/)
! Initialize the entire array to zero. You may also use SURVEY=0.
DO I = 1, 5
   DO J = 1, 4
      SURVEY(I,J) = 0
   END DO
END DO
PRINT *, 'Number of Responses?'
READ *, N
! As each response is read in, increment the appropriate
! position in the table.
DO I = 1, N
   PRINT *, 'Enter year and experience level'
   READ *, K, L
   SURVEY(K,L) = SURVEY(K,L) + 1
END DO
! Print out the survey results
PRINT *, 'Freshman   Sophomore   Junior    Senior'
DO I = 1, 5
   PRINT *,LABEL(I),SURVEY(I,1),SURVEY(I,2),SURVEY(I,3),SURVEY(I,4)
END DO
```

(More program to follow)

Once the above table has been generated with this program, we can begin to manipulate the data to answer such questions as "How many freshmen are nonprogrammers?" or "What percentage of the students are expert programmers (>3 years' experience)?" The following example illustrates how to manipulate values in the array to get such answers.

EXAMPLE 6.23

After a table of data has been created, we can compile statistics about the data by using some of the operations already discussed. This time, however, we need to worry about two indices. So very often we will need to have nested loops. To demonstrate this, we will construct program segments to answer the following questions based on the program in Example 6.22.

a)   <u>How many freshmen are nonprogrammers?</u> Freshmen nonprogrammers have year
      equal to 1 and experience level equal to 1. Thus, all we need do is look at
      SURVEY(1,1). We could do this with a simple PRINT statement such as:

```
PRINT *,'Freshmen nonprogrammers = ',SURVEY(1,1)
```

b)   <u>How many sophomores are programmers with 1 year or more of experience?</u>
      Sophomores with 1–2 years of experience, 2–3 years of experience, and more than
      3 years of experience would fall into this category. Thus, year is equal to 2, and
      experience levels of 3, 4, and 5 are needed to compute the total:

```
TOTAL = SURVEY(3,2) + SURVEY(4,2) + SURVEY(5,2)
```

      Notice that one of the indices remains fixed, while the other index cycles through
      a range of values (3, 4, 5 in this example). Thus, this problem is a candidate for
      a DO loop, where we will replace the first index (indicating the row) with a loop
      control variable:

```
TOTAL = 0
DO I = 3, 5
   TOTAL = TOTAL + SURVEY(I,2)
END DO
```

      In this example, the DO loop actually results in a lengthier program segment. Yet,
      it may be more desirable. What if the table had contained more than three entries?
      The DO loop approach would have been much easier to construct in this case.

c)   <u>How many total nonprogrammers were in the survey?</u> This would be the sum of
      nonprogramming freshmen, sophomores, juniors, and seniors:

```
SUM = SURVEY(1,1) + SURVEY(1,2) + SURVEY(1,3) + SURVEY(1,4)
```

      We can also compute this with a loop:

```
SUM = 0
DO J = 1, 4
   SUM = SUM + SURVEY(1,J)
END DO
```

d)   <u>How many students participated in the survey?</u> To determine this, we would add
      up all the values in the array. The most direct way to do this is with:

```
TOT = SURVEY(1,1)+SURVEY(1,2)+SURVEY(1,3)+SURVEY(1,4)+ &
      SURVEY(2,1)+SURVEY(2,2)+SURVEY(2,3)+SURVEY(2,4)+ &
      SURVEY(3,1)+SURVEY(3,2)+SURVEY(3,3)+SURVEY(3,4)+ &
      SURVEY(4,1)+SURVEY(4,2)+SURVEY(4,3)+SURVEY(4,4)+ &
      SURVEY(5,1)+SURVEY(5,2)+SURVEY(5,3)+SURVEY(5,4)
```

Clearly, this approach has gotten out of hand. So nested loops are better:

```
TOT = 0
DO I = 1, 5
    DO J = 1, 4
        TOT = TOT + SURVEY(I,J)
    END DO
END DO
```

Another common area where arrays are useful is the processing of matrices, such as multiplication of a matrix by a scalar, or addition or multiplication of two matrices. We will think of a matrix as a table in which we can locate a data item by referring to its row and column in the matrix, just as we did with tables of data.

EXAMPLE 6.24

The process of multiplying two arrays together can be expressed using sigma notation.

$$c_{ij} = \sum_k a_{ik} b_{kj}$$

This expression indicates how to calculate each entry in the product array c. Note that the number of columns in the a array must match the number of rows in the b array. The resulting array will have the same number of rows as a and the same number of columns as b. To illustrate how this summation works, let's compute the term c_{12}. This will require the summation of the individual products of $a_{1k}b_{k2}$. Assume for example, that we have the a matrix of size 3×2 and the b matrix of size 2×3, which when multiplied produce a c matrix with 3 rows and 3 columns:

$$a = \begin{bmatrix} 1 & 2 \\ 4 & 6 \\ 1 & 0 \end{bmatrix} \qquad b = \begin{bmatrix} 2 & 1 & 4 \\ 3 & 0 & 7 \end{bmatrix}$$

The desired term c_{12} would be $a_{11}b_{12} + a_{12}b_{22}$ or $(1)(1) + (2)(0) = 1$. In a similar way, we can generate all other elements in c, which will have 3 rows and 3 columns:

$$c = \begin{bmatrix} (1)(2) + (2)(3) & (1)(1) + (2)(0) & (1)(4) + (2)(7) \\ (4)(2) + (6)(3) & (4)(1) + (6)(0) & (4)(4) + (6)(7) \\ (1)(2) + (0)(3) & (1)(1) + (0)(0) & (1)(4) + (0)(7) \end{bmatrix}$$

Before you look at the flowchart and program, be sure you can follow how each of the elements of c is generated. See if you can duplicate the results given above.

Program   **Flowchart**

```
!  VARIABLE LISTING:
!    A,B  = Input Matrices
!    C    = Output Matrix
!    IMAX = Number of rows in A
!    JMAX = Number of columns in B
!    KMAX = Number of rows in B, and
!         = Number of columns in A
!-----------------------------------
REAL, ALLOCATABLE, DIMENSION (:,:):: A, B, C
PRINT *, "Number of rows and columns in A?"
READ *, IMAX, KMAX
PRINT *, "Number of columns in B?"
READ *, JMAX
PRINT *, "ENTER A AND B MATRICES:"
READ *, A, B
DO I = 1, IMAX
   DO J = 1, JMAX
      C(I,J) = 0.0
      DO K = 1, KMAX
         C(I,J)=C(I,J)+A(I,K)*B(K,J)
      END DO
   END DO
END DO
END
```

The innermost loop multiplies the ith row of a by the jth column of b. After summation of the products, the result is placed into c_{ij}. Note that each element of c had to initialized to 0.0.

We can also use *array expressions* with two-dimensional arrays, just as we did with one-dimensional arrays. One additional piece of information needed is how the second array subscript is to be handled.

EXAMPLE 6.25

For the following examples, assume that the arrays A, B, X, and Y are declared as follows:

```
REAL, DIMENSION(5,10)  :: A, B, X, Z
```

Simplified Method	Previous Method	Comments
Z = A/B	DO I = 1,5 DO J=1,10 Z(I,J)=A(I,J)/B(I,J) END DO END DO	*(Real Array Z of shape (5,10) with elements Z(I,J) = A(I,J)/B(I,J))*

(Table continued on next page)

Simplified Method	Previous Method	Comments
A−Z/10.0	DO I=1,5 　DO J=1,10 　　A(I,J)=Z(I,J)/10.0 　END DO END DO	*(Divides all 50 elements of Z by 10.0 and stores results in A)*
X=X+9.0	DO I=1,5 　DO J=1,10 　　X(I,J)=X(I,J)+9.0 　END DO END DO	*(Adds 9.0 to all 50 elements of X and puts the results back into X)*

There are also two new intrinsic functions that operate on two-dimensional arrays.

Function	Description
MATMUL(MATRIX_A, MATRIX_B)	*(Returns a matrix that contains the result of multiplying the two matrices together)*
RESHAPE(SOURCE, SHAPE)	*(Converts the matrix SOURCE into an array of shape given by the variable SHAPE)*

EXAMPLE 6.26

The following examples illustrate these various functions and expressions.

a) We will rewrite Example 6.24 to use the MATMUL function to multiply two matrices A and B together and store the result in matrix C. For simplicity, we assume all the matrices have 3 rows and 3 columns each.

```
REAL, DIMENSION (3,3) :: A, B, C
DO I=1, 3                              ! Read in the A and B
   DO J=1, 3                           ! matrices
      READ *, A(I, J), B(I,J)
   END DO
END DO
C=MATMUL(A, B)                         ! Multiply A and B
```

```
    DO I=1, 3                          ! Print out the product C
       DO J=1, 3
          PRINT *, C(I, J)
       END DO
    END DO
    END
```

b)   Use the RESHAPE function to convert an array of shape (6) to an array of shape
     (3,2). In other words, change the array from a one-dimensional array with 6
     elements to a two-dimensional array with 3 rows and 2 columns.

```
    REAL, DIMENSION(6)::IN          !The 1-D array to be reshaped
    REAL, DIMENSION(3,2)::OUT       !The 2-D array after reshaping
    INTEGER, DIMENSION(2)::SHAPE    !The desired SHAPE of OUT
    PRINT *, 'ENTER INPUT ARRAY:'   !Data for the IN array
    DO I=1,6
       READ *, IN(I)
    END DO
    SHAPE(1)=3                       !Data for SHAPE
    SHAPE(2)=2
    OUT=RESHAPE(IN,SHAPE)            !Convert IN to OUT
    DO I=1,3                         !Print out the new 2-D array
       DO J=1,2
          PRINT *, OUT(I,J)
       END DO
    END DO
    END
```

To demonstrate how this works, let's assume that IN has the values 1.0, 2.0, 3.0,
4.0, 5.0, 6.0. After execution of the program, the arrays will look like this:

IN:

1.0	2.0	3.0	4.0	5.0

OUT:

1.0	4.0
2.0	5.0
3.0	6.0

When the function RESHAPE is used, it converts the one-dimensional array into
the desired from given by the array SHAPE. Since SHAPE has values 3 and 2, the
array IN is rearranged so that the data stored in its elements are in the form of a
matrix with 3 rows and 2 columns. Thus, the OUT array was filled by columns.

6.7 INPUT AND OUTPUT OF ARRAYS

The simplest way to print arrays is to refer to each element individually, just as you would
with a single-valued variable (scalar). For example, if we wished to print out the first two elements
of the array X, we could do it with this command:

```
PRINT *,X(1), X(2)
```

While this is the simplest way, it is impractical if we wish to print out a long list of array elements. Instead, we more often use a loop with the input or output statement to simplify the process:

```
DO I = 1, 100
    PRINT *, A(I)
END DO
```

While this approach is more versatile, it does pose a problem. Whenever the computer executes a PRINT statement, a new line of output is created. The preceding code segment would generate 100 lines of output, for example! To solve this problem, we can use a special form of the DO loop known as the *implied DO loop*, whose use is limited to input/output statements and the DATA statement presented in the next section. The general form of an implied DO loop to print out arrays is as follows:

I/O Command (array(LCV), string, or numeric expression, LCV = Start, Stop, Step)

I/O Command refers to any input/output statement such as READ, PRINT, or WRITE. The LCV is the loop control variable, and start, stop, and step set up values for the loop control.

EXAMPLE 6.27

Listed below are examples of explicit forms of I/O and their equivalent implied DO loops:

Explicit Form	Implied Form	Comments
DO I=1, 10 READ *, A(I) END DO	READ *,(A(I),I=1, 10)	*(Reads 10 values into array A)*
DO I=1, 10 READ *, X(I), Y(I) END DO	READ *,(X(I),Y(I),I=1, 10)	*(Reads in 10 sets of data as (x_1, y_1), (x_2, y_2), etc.)*

DO I=1,20
    DO J=1,10
        READ*, Z(I,J)
    END DO
END DO
	READ *,((Z(I,J),J=1,10),I=1,20)	*(An implied DO loop within another implied DO loop is permitted)*

The implied DO loop prints out all of the array variables to a single line, unless formatting is used to control the output appearance. But with the READ statement, the computer will attempt to read in the values from the <u>current</u> line. If all of the required data are not present on a single line, then the next line of input is used. Thus, if an input statement for an array uses an implied DO loop to read in 100 values, those 100 values can appear on a single line or 100 lines with a single value per line, or some combination.

When printing output, however, you must be more careful since you typically want the data to have a style that is easily readable. So you must take care in using implied DO loops with output of arrays. Among the things you must consider are the number of data items per line and vertical alignment, in addition to conventional formatting requirements such as compatible edit descriptors.

EXAMPLE 6.28

For the following example, A is a one-dimensional integer array of 10 elements and B is a 3×3 two-dimensional integer array. The value assigned to each element is:

A | 4 | 2 | 6 | 7 | 0 | 3 | 9 | 1 | 5 | 8 |

B
1	2	3
4	5	6
7	8	9

Below are examples of how the output would appear for a variety of implied DO loops:

Program Segment	Output
a) PRINT *, A(1), A(2), A(3)	4 2 6
b) PRINT *, (A(I), I = 1, 3)	4 2 6
c) PRINT *, (A(I), I = 2, 8, 2)	2 7 3 1
d) PRINT *, ((B(I,J), I=1,3), J=1,3)	1 4 7 2 5 8 3 6 9
e) PRINT *, B	1 4 7 2 5 8 3 6 9
f) PRINT *, ((B(I,J), J=1,3), I=1,3)	1 2 3 4 5 6 7 8 9
g) DO I=1, 3	1 2 3
PRINT *, (B(I,J), J=1,3)	4 5 6
END DO	7 8 9
h) PRINT *, ('+', I=1,10)	+ + + + + + + + + +

Example (a) illustrates the method that we have been using up to this point to output array elements, whereas example (b) performs the same task using an implied DO loop. Note that even in this simple example of printing out only three array elements, the implied DO loop requires less typing. Of course, the savings are more significant when printing larger numbers of elements.

Example (c) illustrates how to use the loop control variable to print the even-numbered elements from element 2 to element 8. Example (d) illustrates how to print a two-dimensional array using nested implied DO loops. In this example the first subscript represents the most rapidly changing one. Thus, the first elements printed are B(1,1), B(2,1), and B(3,1). Only when I runs through all its values does the value of J change. Example (e) illustrates Fortran's default output of a two-dimensional array. In this case, the computer will print the array elements by columns, starting with column 1. These two examples (d and e) are equivalent, if the two-dimensional array is declared to be a 3 × 3 array. Example (f) illustrates the effect of making the second subscript change more rapidly than the first. The result is that the computer prints the array by rows. One problem with examples (d), (e), and (f) is that the computer prints all of the array elements on a single line. We solve this problem in example (g) where we combine an explicit DO loop with an implied one. Each time the computer encounters a PRINT statement, it starts a new output line.

The final example (h) illustrates that implied DO loops do not have to be used only with arrays. By placing a character constant ('+') within the implied DO loop, ten "+" characters were produced. This can be used as a way of creating special effects such as an underlined table heading.

EXAMPLE 6.29

The following program will print out a simple graph of a sine wave over a range of 0 to 2π.

```
DO I = 0, 20
    X = I*2*3.1416/20.
    Y = SIN(X)
    N = NINT(30+Y*30+1)
    PRINT *, ('*', J = 1, N)
END DO
END
```

The loop calculates the position of the curve at 21 different positions. Inside the loop, X will vary between 0 and 2π, and Y represents the value of sin(X) for each value. The purpose of N is to scale the sine wave so that it will fit conveniently on your screen. Note that the minimum and maximum values of Y are -1 and 1, respectively. Thus, N will be between 1 and 61. So in the next program line, when we use N to print out a string of stars on the screen, the stars will be between columns 1 and 61, which should easily fit on your screen. Run this program on your computer to see the effect.

6.8 FORMATTING OF ARRAY OUTPUT

Because of the large quantities of data that arrays can output, formatting requires careful planning and relies very heavily on the use of the repeat specifier. Recall that repeat specifiers (see page 94) allow you to repeat a section of formatting instructions without having to explicitly retype any of the descriptors.

EXAMPLE 6.30

In the following example, A is a one-dimensional real array of 10 elements and B is a 3×3 two-dimensional real array. The value assigned to each element is:

A | 4.0 | 2.0 | 6.0 | 7.0 | 0.0 | 3.0 | 9.0 | 1.0 | 5.0 | 8.0 |

B

1.0	2.0	3.0
4.0	5.0	6.0
7.0	8.0	9.0

Below are several examples of how the output would appear for a variety of formatted implied DO loops:

	Program Segment	Output

a)
```
      PRINT 10, (A(I), I = 1, 5)
   10 FORMAT (' ', 5(F4.1, 1X))
```
     4.0   2.0   6.0   7.0   0.0

b)
```
      PRINT 10, (A(I), I = 1, 5)
   10 FORMAT (' ', 20(F4.1, 1X))
```
     4.0   2.0   6.0   7.0   0.0

c)
```
      PRINT 10, (A(I), I = 1, 10)
   10 FORMAT (' ', 5(F4.1, 1X))
```
     4.0   2.0   6.0   7.0   0.0
     3.0   9.0   1.0   5.0   8.0

d)
```
      PRINT 10, ((B(I,J), J=1, 3), I=1, 3)
   10 FORMAT (' B:', 3(/, 1X, 3(F4.1, 1X)))
```
     B:
     1.0   2.0   3.0
     4.0   5.0   6.0
     7.0   8.0   9.0

e)
```
      PRINT 10, ((B(I,J), J=1, 3), I=1, 3)
   10 FORMAT (' ', 3(F4.1, 1X))
```
     1.0   2.0   3.0
     4.0   5.0   6.0
     7.0   8.0   9.0

f)
```
      N = 3
      DO I = 1, N
         PRINT 10, (B(I,J), J = 1, N)
   10    FORMAT (' ', 100(F4.1, 1X))
      END DO
```
     1.0   2.0   3.0
     4.0   5.0   6.0
     7.0   8.0   9.0

The first example is a straightforward use of the repeat specifier. In the FORMAT statement, 5(F4.1, 1X) repeats the descriptors "F4.1, 1X" five times. In effect, the FORMAT statement in example (a) is the same as FORMAT(' ', F4.1, 1X, F4.1, 1X, F4.1, 1X, F4.1, 1X, F4.1, 1X). Example (b) illustrates what happens if there are more edit descriptors than actually needed. The result is that the unused formatting is simply ignored. Example (c) illustrates the reverse problem — an insufficient number of edit descriptors. In this case, the output is printed until all the descriptors are used. Then the output continues on a new line and the format instructions are reused. For example (c), this results in printing two rows of five columns each, even though the array is one-dimensional.

Example (d) demonstrates the use of repeat specifiers and the end-of-line descriptor (/). When using the end-of-line descriptor to generate output on a new line, remember to include a carriage-control character. Most often, this is conveniently done with the 1X edit descriptor. Example (e) illustrates how to take advantage of the fact that when formatting runs out, the computer repeats the edit descriptors on a new line. This allows for a simple format statement to print out a two-dimensional array. The only drawback of this approach is that you must know the size in advance, and you cannot change it without changing your FORMAT statement. Example (f) illustrates a means around this by combining explicit and implicit DO loops.

6.9 THE PARAMETER AND DATA STATEMENTS

The PARAMETER statement is an easy way of creating *named constants*. Named constants have elements of both constants and variables. On the one hand they are constants whose value cannot change under any circumstances, and on the other hand they are given names like a variable. A good example would be PI. Once we assign a value to the named constant PI with the PARAMETER statement, its value cannot change. Any attempt to change a named constant results in an error during compilation.

One of the most common uses of the named constant is to declare arrays whose size is likely to change. The advantage of this approach is that you can make many changes throughout the program by making a single change in the named constant. The general form of the PARAMETER statement is:

PARAMETER (*variable1 = value, variable2 = value, . . .*)

Each named constant is given its value inside the parentheses following the PARAMETER key word. Once a name is specified here, it cannot be used as a conventional variable within the program, and its value <u>cannot</u> be reassigned by an assignment statement, function, or READ statement.

EXAMPLE 6.31

Here is an example of how to use a PARAMETER statement to declare several arrays simultaneously. First, suppose you write a program to process 100 data points with the following array declarations (without the PARAMETER):

```
REAL VOLTS(100), I(100), IMPED(100), RESIST(100)
INTEGER TIME(100), COUNTS(100), SIZE(100)
```

If you use this approach and now wish to change the program to allow for 1000 data points, you must change each array dimension from 100 to 1000. An easier way is to use the PARAMETER statement. When you first set up your program, you can define a named constant such as *N* below:

```
PARAMETER (N = 100)
REAL VOLTS(N), I(N), IMPED(N), RESIST(N)
INTEGER TIME(N), COUNTS(N), SIZE(N)
```

Now, when you want to increase the size of the arrays, you need only change a single PARAMETER statement. This method is especially useful for changing values scattered throughout your program. For example, you might have declaration statements for arrays and DO loop variables to process the data, and I/O statements with implied DO loops.

```
PARAMETER (N = 100)
REAL VOLTS(N), I(N), IMPED(N), RESIST(N)          ! Changes array size
INTEGER TIME(N), COUNTS(N), SIZE(N)
      ⋮
READ *, (VOLTS(K), K = 1, N)                       ! Changes loop limit
      ⋮
DO L = 1, N
      ⋮
END DO
      ⋮
PRINT *, (IMPED(M), M = 1, N)
END
```

Another useful structure is the DATA statement. It is used to assign <u>initial</u> values to a variable. Whereas the PARAMETER statement assigns <u>permanent</u> values, the DATA statement assigns <u>initial</u> values. DATA statements are most useful to replace READ statements at the beginning of a program; they save you the trouble of having to type in repetitive data every time you run a program. The general form of the DATA statement is:

DATA *variable1, variable2, . . . / value1, value2, . . . /*

The list of variables after the DATA statement can include either single-valued variables or arrays. Values to be assigned to these variables are contained within the slash (/) marks and will be assigned to the corresponding variable by virtue of the *position* within the list. The third value for example, will be assigned to the third variable, and so forth.

If arrays are specified within the DATA variable list, we may use an implied DO loop, just as we do with the output or input statements:

DATA *(array(subscript), subscript = start, stop, step) /value1, value2, . . ./*

The implied DO loop will specify the array elements to receive the values listed inside the slashes.

EXAMPLE 6.32

a) One common area where we use DATA statements is to assign initial values to a list of single-valued variables:

<u>Without DATA Statements:</u>

```
VOLTS = 5.3
RESIST = 1000.0
CAPICT = 0.000035
```

<u>With DATA Statements:</u>

```
DATA VOLTS, RESIST, CAPICT /5.3, 1000.0, 0.000035/
```

b) Quite often when we use DATA statements, several of the variables may receive the same value. In this case, we have a shorthand notation

<u>Long Way:</u>

```
DATA A, B, C, D, E, F /1.0, 1.0, 1.0, 1.0, 1.0, 1.0/
```

<u>Short Way:</u>

```
DATA A, B, C, D, E, F /6*1.0/
```

The star (*) here does not imply multiplication. Instead, it indicates that the number which follows is to be repeated the indicated number of times.

c) DATA statements are particularly useful when initializing arrays:

```
REAL A(100)
DATA (A(I), I = 1, 100) /50*0.0, 50*1.0/
```

These statements assign 0.0 to the first 50 elements of A, and 1.0 to the last 50 elements.

d) The implied DO loop may not be necessary if <u>all</u> elements are to be assigned. Here is a shorter way of writing example c):

```
REAL A(100)
DATA A /50*0.0,50*1.0/
```

If the array is two-dimensional, data will be assigned by <u>columns</u> if you use this form:

```
REAL B(3, 3)
DATA B /1.0, 2.0, 3.0, 4.0, 5.0, 6.0, 7.0, 8.0, 9.0/
```

This will result in the following assignments:

B:	1.0	4.0	7.0
	2.0	5.0	8.0
	3.0	6.0	9.0

e) If you wish to assign the data by rows instead of by columns, you must use the full implied DO loop:

```
REAL A(3, 3)
DATA ((A(I,J), J=1,3), I=1,3)/3*10.0, 6*100.0/
```

The first row are filled with 10.0's and the remaining two rows are filled with 100.0's. If the implied DO loops were not present, then this array would have been filled differently (the first column would have 10.0's and the remaining columns would have been 100.0's). The result of the example shown is given below. When in doubt about how the data will be assigned, use an implied DO loop.

A:	10.0	10.0	10.0
	100.0	100.0	100.0
	100.0	100.0	100.0

6.10 DEBUGGING TIPS

One of the topics presented in this section was the use of the PARAMETER statement when declaring an array. This statement is an ideal tool for debugging purposes where we would like to have the ability to rescale the program to something more manageable. After all, debugging a program with a 5 × 5 array is a much easier task than debugging a program with a 100 × 100 array. Here are a few suggestions about how to debug programs containing arrays:

SUGGESTION #1:   Whenever you declare an array, consider using a PARAMETER statement.

SUGGESTION #2:   When you are initially testing your program, use small arrays.

Tracing arrays can be very time consuming. With a single declaration statement it is easy to create thousands of storage locations with a single variable. By reducing the size of the problem to something manageable (suggestion #2), it is possible to perform a manual trace as described in earlier chapters. Finally, learn how your compiler deals with array errors. For example, what happens if you go beyond the limit of a subscript? Does your program stop, or do you get erroneous data? This type of error can be very difficult to find, particularly if you are not looking for it. To test what happens, write a small program (five lines or less) and deliberately make errors to go outside the bounds of the arrays that you have declared.

SUGGESTION #3:   Test your compiler to learn how it deals with array errors such as "subscript out of bounds" or a real value for a subscript.

Proper declaration of arrays is very important. If the array is improperly declared, errors will propagate through your program, producing dozens of error messages.

SUGGESTION #4:   If you encounter a large number of errors on every line where you use a particular array, then check your declaration statements.

Solved Problems

6.1   Locate the syntax or run-time errors in the following program segments:

```
(a)  INTEGER I              (b)  REAL A(1,10)
     REAL ARRAY(I)               DO I=1, 10
                                   A(I)=I**2
                                 END DO

(c)  INTEGER I(10)         (d)  REAL A[10]
     DO I=0, 9                   DO I=0, 9
       I(I+1)=I**2                 A(I+1)=I**2
     END DO                     END DO
(e)  REAL, DIMENSION(0:10)::A  (f)  REAL, DIMENSION(2,2)::A,B,C
     READ *,(A(I),I=1,100)          WHERE (A(I:J)+B(I:J)>0)
                                      C(I,J)=1
                                    END WHERE
```

(a) ARRAY(I) does not indicate the number of desired elements.
(b) A is a two-dimensional array, but inside the loop it is used as a one-dimensional array.
(c) I is being referred to both as an array and as a scalar (DO loop control variable).
(d) Declaration statement used square brackets instead of the required parentheses.
(e) Attempt to assign data to an array element that is out of bounds.
(f) Inside the WHERE statement, the conditional should read: (A+B>0) and the assignment statement inside the block should read C=1.

6.2   Write program segments to accomplish the following:

   (a) Add the third and fourth elements of the array X.
   (b) Determine the average of the 10 elements of an array Y.
   (c) If the 10 elements of the x, y, and z subscripted variables are defined by:

$$y_i = i + 3$$
$$x_i = i$$
$$z_i = x_i + y_i$$

determine the following:

$$a_i = [\sum_{j=1}^{10} (x_j)(y_j)(z_j)]^{0.5}$$

   (d) If the elements of the one-dimensional arrays X and Y are defined as X(I) = 3*I−15
        and Y(I) = 2*I+5, write a program segment to print the sum of X(I) + Y(I) for all
        values of I up to IMAX.

   (a) `SUM=X(3)+X(4)`

   (b)
```
SUM=0.0
DO I=1, 10
   SUM=SUM+Y(I)
END DO
AVG=SUM/10.0
```

   (c)
```
DO I=1, 10
   X(I)=I
   Y(I)=I+3
   Z(I)=X(I)+Y(I)
END DO
DO I=1, 10
   PROD=0.0
   DO J=1, 10
      PROD=PROD+X(J)*Y(J)*Z(J)
   END DO
   A(I)=SQRT(PROD)
END DO
```

   (d)
```
DO I=1, IMAX
   X(I)=3*I-15
   Y(I)=2*I+5
END DO
DO I=1, IMAX
   PRINT *, X(I)+Y(I)
END DO
```

6.3   Write program segments to accomplish the following. Assume all arrays are 10 × 10
            unless specified otherwise.

   (a) Set the corresponding elements of B(I, J) equal to C(I, J) if A(I, J)>0. Otherwise, set
        B(I,J) equal to 0.
   (b) Create a 4 × 5 array whose elements are computed by copying elements from every
        third row (first, fourth, etc.) and every second column (second, fourth, etc.) from a
        larger 10 × 10 array.
   (c) Declare an integer two-dimensional array with three rows and three columns. Then
        set all the values in the first column to 1, all the values in the second column to 2, and

all the values in the third column to 3.

(d)   Declare a real one-dimensional array with five elements and initialize the array to the values (1.0, 0.0, 1.0, 0.0, 1.0).

(a)   ```
      REAL, DIMENSION (10,10) :: A, B, C
      READ *, ((A(I,J), I=1,10), J=1,10)
      READ *, ((C(I,J), I=1,10), J=1,10)
      WHERE (A>0)
        B=C
      ELSEWHERE
        B=0.0
      END WHERE
      ```
(b)   ```
      REAL A(10,10), B(4,5)
      READ *, A
      B=A(1:10:3, 2:10:2)
      ```
(c)   ```
      INTEGER, DIMENSION(3,3) :: NUM
      NUM(1:3, 1) = 1
      NUM(1:3, 2) = 2
      NUM(1:3, 3) = 3
      ```
(d)   ```
      REAL, DIMENSION(5)  :: A=(/1.0, 0.0, 1.0, 0.0, 1.0/)
      ```

6.4   The standard deviation σ of a series of numbers is determined by the following:

$$\sigma = [\ \frac{1}{n-1} \sum_{i=1}^{i=n} (x_i - \bar{x})^2\ ]^{0.5}$$

where n = number of samples
        x_i = list of data values
        $\bar{x}$ = average of data items.

Write a program to read in a list of numbers (of unknown size) and calculate σ.

```
REAL, DIMENSION (:), ALLOCATABLE :: X
PRINT *, 'Number of Points?'
READ *, N
ALLOCATE (X(N))
READ *, X
XBAR=SUM(X)/N
STD=SQRT(SUM((X-XBAR)**2)/(N-1))
PRINT *, 'Std Deviation is', STD
END
```

6.5   Write separate programs to perform the following tasks on the array A(100, 100):

(a)   Sum any column.
(b)   Sum the entire two-dimensional array.
(c)   Find the minimum in the two-dimensional array.

(d) Subtract a scalar value (S) from all elements in a two-dimensional array.

(a)
```
REAL, DIMENSION (100, 100) :: A
PRINT *, 'Column Number?'
READ *, JCOL
TOT=SUM(A(:,JCOL))
PRINT *, 'Sum =', TOT
END
```

(b)
```
REAL, DIMENSION(100,100) :: A
ARRAY_SUM = SUM(A)
PRINT *, 'Sum =', ARRAY_SUM
END
```

(c)
```
REAL, DIMENSION(100,100) :: A
AMIN = MINVAL(A)
PRINT *, 'Minimum:', AMIN
END
```

(d)
```
REAL, DIMENSION(100,100) :: A
PRINT *, 'Enter scalar:'
READ *, S
A = A-S
END
```

6.6 Trace the following program segments and predict the output of each one. Line numbers are provided for your convenience and are not part of the program. They will be used in the tracing to demonstrate the sequence in which they are used.

(a)
```
01 INTEGER II(100)
02 DO I=1, 100
03    II(I)=I*2
04 END DO
05 PRINT*,II(II(II(1)))
06 END
```

(b)
```
01 REAL X(2), Y(2), NUM
02 DATA X,Y/1.0,2.0,3.0,4.0/
03 DATA NDIM,Z,P/2,2.0,0.0/
04 DO I = 1, NDIM
05   TERM = 1.0
06   DO J=1, NDIM
07     IF(I/=J) THEN
08        DEN=X(I)-X(J)
09        NUM=Z-X(J)
10        TERM=TERM*NUM/DEN
11     END IF
12   END DO
13   TERM=TERM*Y(I)
14   P=P+TERM
15 END DO
16 PRINT *, P
17 END
```

(a) Each element in the II array has a value equal to its index times 2. So, let's use this shortcut to examine the PRINT statement:

PRINT *, II(II(II(1)))
PRINT *, II(II(2))
PRINT *, II(4)
PRINT *, 8   OUTPUT → 8

(b) Trace Table:

X(1):	1.0	Z:	2.0
X(2):	2.0	P:	0.0, 0.0, 0.0, 4.0
Y(1):	3.0	I:	1, 2, 3
Y(2):	4.0	TERM:	1.0, 0.0, 0.0, 1.0, 1.0, 4.0
NDIM:	2	J:	1, 2, 3, 1, 2, 3
NUM:	0.0, 1.0	DEN:	−1.0, 1.0

Trace Steps:

01: Declare X and Y arrays and NUM.

02: DATA statement assigns X(1)=1.0, X(2)=2.0, Y(1)=3.0, and Y(2)=4.0.

03: DATA statement assigns NDIM=2, Z=2.0, and P=0.0.

04: Enter DO loop: initialize I to 1, check if it exceeds 2 — false, execute loop.

05: TERM=1.0.

06: Enter DO loop: initialize J to 1, check if it exceeds 2 — false, execute loop.

07: IF (I/=J) — (1/=1) is false, do not execute THEN block.

08: Increment J by 1 (J=2) and go to line 06.

06: Check if J exceeds 2 — false, execute loop.

07: IF (I/=J) — (1/=2) is true, execute TERM=TERM*(Z−X(J))/(X(I)−X(J)).
   TERM=1.0*(2.0−2.0)/(1.0−2.0), TERM=0.0.

08: Increment J by 1 (J=3) and go to line 06.

06: Check if J exceeds 2 — true, skip loop.

09: TERM=TERM*Y(1), TERM=0.0.

10: P=P+TERM, P=0.0+0.0, P=0.0.

11: Increment I by 1 (I=2) and go to line 04.

04: Check if I exceeds 2 — false, execute loop.

05: TERM=1.0

06: Enter DO loop: initialize J to 1, check if it exceeds 2 — false, execute loop.

07: IF (I/=J) — (2/=1) is true, execute TERM=TERM*(Z−X(J))/(X(I)−X(J))
   TERM=1.0*(2.0−1.0)/(2.0−1.0), TERM=1.0

08: Increment J by 1 (J=2) and go to line 06.

06: Check if J exceeds 2 — false, execute loop.

07: IF (I/=J) — (2/=2) is false, do not execute THEN block.

08: Increment J by 1 (J=3) and go to line 06.

06: Check if J exceeds 2 — true, skip loop.

09: TERM=TERM*Y(2), TERM=1.0*4.0, TERM=4.0

10: P=P+TERM, P=0.0+4.0, P=4.0.

11: Increment I by 1 (I=3) and go to line 04.

04: Check if I exceeds 2 — true, skip loop.

16: PRINT *, P.

13: STOP.

Output:

4.00000

6.7   Two vectors are said to be *orthogonal* if they are perpendicular to each other. One way of checking orthogonality of two vectors is to take their dot product and see if it is zero (or very close to zero taking into account roundoff errors). The dot product between vectors x and y is defined by:

$$dot\ product\ (x,y) = \sum_{i=1}^{i=3} x_i y_i$$

Write a program which reads in two vectors and determines if they are orthogonal.

```
REAL, DIMENSION (3) :: A, B
PRINT *, 'Components of A and B'
READ *, A, B
PRINT *, 'Enter allowable error:'
READ *, EPS
DOT = SUM(A*B)
IF(ABS(DOT) <= EPS) THEN
  PRINT*, 'The vectors are orthogonal'
ELSE
  PRINT *, 'The vectors are not orthogonal'
END IF
END
```

6.8   Write a program that reads in a list of values, stores them in an array, and returns the minimum value and its position in the array.

```
REAL X(1000)
INTEGER IMIN(1)
PRINT *, 'Number of items?'
READ *, N
PRINT *, 'Enter data'
READ *, (X(I), I=1, N)
AMIN=MINVAL(X)
IMIN=MINLOC(X)                      ! Location must be an array
PRINT *, 'Min value = ', AMIN
PRINT *, 'Found at ', IMIN
END
```

6.9   A list of real numbers whose values range from 0 to 100 is read in from the keyboard. Write a program that creates a list showing how many numbers are in each of the following ranges. (HINT: Consider integer conversion of the real values.)

Range 1:	0	≤ Number	< 10
Range 2:	10	≤ Number	< 20
⋮			
Range 10:	90	≤ Number	≤ 100

```
INTEGER, DIMENSION (10) :: N
! Set up X as allocatable, since there is an unknown number
! of data points.
REAL, DIMENSION(:), ALLOCATABLE :: X
DATA N/10*0/
PRINT *, 'Enter number of items:'
READ *, M
ALLOCATE (X(M))                    ! set up X once M is known
```

```
        PRINT *, 'Enter data:'
        READ *, X
        ! To generate the statistics, we convert the element of X
        ! into a value between 1 and 10. Then we increment the
        ! counter N(J) by one in the appropriate range.
        DO I = 1, M
            J = INT(X(I))/10.0+1
            N(J) = N(J)+1
        END DO
        PRINT 20, (I, N(I), I=1, 10)
    20  FORMAT(' ', 'Range', I2, ':', I3)
        END
```

6.10   We've seen two-dimensional arrays used as tables. Another use of two-dimensional arrays is to create graphical images where the rows and columns of the array can be considered as the (x,y) coordinates. Write a program to plot a curve according to the following steps:

- Initialize all elements of a two-dimensional array to 0.0.
- Set up a variable J that represents the 41 columns in an array of size $(-20:20, -20:20)$. For each row, calculate the position from -20 to 20 where we wish to print a symbol (1 for example). The position will represent the value of the sine function from -2π to 2π.

```
        INTEGER, DIMENSION(-20:20, -20:20) :: PLOT
        DATA PLOT, PI/1681*0, 3.14159/
        DO I = -20, 20
            PLOT(I, NINT(20*SIN(PI*I/10.0))) = 1
        END DO
        PRINT 15, ((PLOT(I, J), J = -20, 20), I = -20, 20)
    15  FORMAT(' ', 41I1)
        END
```

To show you how this program works, let's select a single column (the fourth column for example) in the graph. This will correspond to a J value of -17 in PLOT(I, J), since we started with $J=-20$. Inside the array constructor, when $J=-17$, Y will be $\sin(-17\pi/10.0)$ or approximately -0.81. I then becomes 16. Thus, the number 1 will be placed into PLOT$(16, -17)$. All the other elements in that column will be zero.

6.11   Based on Examples 6.22 and 6.23, write program segments to accomplish the following:
   (a) Percentage of freshmen in the survey.
   (b) Percentage of sophomores in the survey.
   (c) Percentage of juniors in the survey.
   (d) Percentage of seniors in the survey.
   (e) Total number of most experienced programmers (> 3 years experience).
   (f) Total number of intermediate level programmers (2 to 3 years of experience).
   (g) Total number of programmers.
   (h) Percentage of nonprogrammers.
       (You may use the variables defined in Examples 6.22 and 6.23.)

(a) PER_FRESHMEN=REAL(SUM(SURVEY(:,1)))/SUM(SURVEY)*100.0
(b) PER_SOPHOMORES=REAL(SUM(SURVEY(:,2)))/SUM(SURVEY)*100.0
(c) PER_JUNIORS=REAL(SUM(SURVEY(:,3)))/SUM(SURVEY)*100.0
(d) PER_SENIORS=REAL(SUM(SURVEY(:,4)))/SUM(SURVEY)*100.0
(e) NUM_MOST_EXPERIENCED=SUM(SURVEY(5,:))
(f) NUM_INTERMEDIATE=SUM(SURVEY(4,:))
(g) NUM_PROGRAMMERS=SUM(SURVEY(2:5,1:4))
(h) PER_NON_PROGRAMMERS=REAL(SUM(SURVEY(1,:)))/SUM(SURVEY)

6.12 Based on the search method illustrated in Example 6.11 for a one-dimensional array, modify the program to search for a value in a two-dimensional array. Have the program return the row and column subscripts when it locates the desired value. Assume that the maximum limits for rows and columns are 20 and 10, respectively.

```
REAL, DIMENSION(20, 10):: X
INTEGER, DIMENSION(2) :: LOC
PRINT *, 'Enter data by columns:'
READ *, ((X(I, J), I=1, N), J=1, M)
PRINT *, 'Search Value?'
READ *, VALUE
LOC=MAXLOC(X, MASK = X == VALUE)
PRINT*, 'Value at', LOC(1), LOC(2)
END
```

The program requires some discussion since we have used a built-in function (MAXLOC) that we have not yet discussed. This function locates the first position within X where the MASK occurs. In this example, the MASK is (X == VALUE). So, when the computer scans the table named X, it checks each element and whenever the value equals VALUE, its position will be stored in the one-dimensional array LOC.

6.13 For each of the following DATA statements, determine the values that will be assigned to each array element.

(a) `INTEGER A(10)`
    `DATA (A(I),I=10,1,-1)/1, 2, 3, 4, 5, 6, 7, 8, 9, 10/`
(b) `INTEGER A(3, 3)`
    `DATA ((A(I,J),I=1,3),J=1,3)/1, 2, 3, 4, 5, 6, 7, 8, 9/`
(c) `INTEGER A(2, 2, 2)`
    `DATA A/1, 2, 3, 4, 5, 6, 7, 8/`
    (Note that this is the first demonstration of a three-dimensional array.)
(d) `REAL, DIMENSION(5)::A`
    `A = (/(I, I=1,10,2)/)`
(e) `INTEGER, DIMENSION(3,3)::N`
    `N = RESHAPE((/1,2,3,4,5,6,7,8,9/),(/3,3/))`
(f) `INTEGER, DIMENSION(3,3)::A`
    `A(1,:)=(/1,2,3/)`

```
            A(2,:)=(/10,20,30/)
            A(3,:)=(/100,200,300/)
      (g)   INTEGER, DIMENSION(4,4)::A
            A(1:2,1:2)=RESHAPE((/1,2,3,4/),(/2,2/))
            A(3:4,3:4)=RESHAPE((/1,1,1,1/),(/2,2/))
            A(1:2,3:4)=RESHAPE((/2,2,2,2/),(/2,2/))
            A(3:4,1:2)=RESHAPE((/(I, I=10,40,10)/),(/2,2/))
```

(a)   A(1)=10, A(2)=9, A(3)=8, A(4)=7, A(5)=6, A(6)=5, A(7)=4, A(8)=3,
      A(9)=2, A(10)=1

(b)   A(1,1)=1, A(1,2)=4, A(1,3)=7
      A(2,1)=2, A(2,2)=5, A(2,3)=8
      A(3,1)=3, A(3,2)=6, A(3,3)=9

(c)   A(1,1,1)=1, A(2,1,1)=2, A(1,2,1)=3, A(2,2,1)=4, A(1,1,2)=5, A(2,1,2)=6,
      A(1,2,2)=7, A(2,2,2)=8

(d)   A(1)=1.0, A(2)=3.0, A(3)=5.0, A(4)=7.0, A(5)=9.0

(e)   N(1,1)=1, N(2,1)=2, N(3,1)=3
      N(1,2)=4, N(2,2)=5, N(3,2)=6
      N(1,3)=7, N(2,3)=8, N(3,3)=9

(f)   A(1,1)=1, A(2,1)=10, A(3,1)=100
      A(1,2)=2, A(2,2)=20, A(3,2)=200
      A(1,3)=3, A(2,3)=30, A(3,3)=300

(g)   A(1,1)=1, A(2,1)=2, A(3,1)=10, A(4,1)=20
      A(1,2)=3, A(2,2)=4, A(3,2)=30, A(4,2)=40
      A(1,3)=2, A(2,3)=2, A(3,3)=1, A(4,3)=1
      A(1,4)=2, A(2,4)=2, A(3,4)=1, A(4,4)=1

6.14   Write program segments to perform the following tasks:
(a)   Change each negative values in a two-dimensional array A to its negative reciprocal value.
(b)   A real array A(40, 40) has values ranging from 0 to 100. Write a program segment to create a new integer array B according to the following rules:
      – if the element of A is < 50.0, then the corresponding value of B is 0
      – if the element of A is ≥ 50.0, then the corresponding value of B is 1

```
(a)   WHERE(A < 0) A=-1.0/A
(b)   WHERE(A < 50.0)
         B=0
      ELSEWHERE
         B=1
      END WHERE
```

6.15   Trace through the following program and predict its output. Line numbers are provided for your convenience and are not part of the program.

```
01        REAL A(3,3), B(3), C(3)
02        DATA A/1, 2, 3, 4, 5, 6, 7, 8, 9/
```

```
03          DATA B/1, 2, 3/
04          DO I = 1, 3
05              C(I) = 0.0
06              DO J = 1, 3
07                  C(I) = C(I) + A(I, J)*B(J)
08              END DO
09          END DO
10          PRINT 30, C
11      30  FORMAT(' ', 3(F6.1, 1X))
12          END
```

Trace Table:

A:

1.0	4.0	7.0
2.0	5.0	8.0
3.0	6.0	9.0

B:

1.0	2.0	3.0

I: 1, 2, 3, 4   J: 1, 2, 3, 4, 1, 2, 3, 4, 1, 2, 3, 4
C(1):0.0, 1.0, 9.0, 30.0   C(2):0.0, 2.0, 12.0, 36.0   C(3):0.0, 3.0, 15.0, 42.0

OUTPUT
         30.0   36.0   42.0

Supplementary Problems

6.16   Locate the syntax and run-time errors in the following program segments:

(a)
```
REAL A(1:100)
DO I = 1, 10
   A(I-5) = I**2
END DO
```

(b)
```
REAL SIN(10)
PI=3.14159
DO I = 1, 10
     SIN(I) = SIN(I*PI)
END DO
```

(c)
```
REAL X(100)
DATA X/100*2.0/
DO I = 1, INT(X(I))
   I=INT(X(I))
END DO
```

(d)
```
PARAMETER (N=5, M=10)
REAL X(N, M)
READ *,N, M
```

(e)
```
REAL, DIMENSION(:)::Y
READ *,M
ALLOCATE (Y(M))
```

(f)
```
REAL, ALLOCATABLE::A(M,N)
READ *,M, N
ALLOCATE (A(M,N))
```

(g)
```
REAL A(10),B(10,10)
READ *,A,B
PRINT *,DOT_PRODUCT(A,B)
```

(h)
```
REAL A(-100:0), AVG(0:-100)
READ *,A, AVG
```

6.17   Write program segments to accomplish the following:

   (a)   Read in a series of numbers and then determine their sum.
   (b)   The recurrence series is defined as 1, 3, 5, 11, 21, 43, . . . The first two numbers in
         the series are 1 and 3. All other numbers in the series s_i $(i \geq 3)$ are generated by $s_i =$
         $s_{i-1} + 2s_{i-2}$. Write a program to determine the first 50 terms of this series.
   (c)   For a given array X determine the repeated fraction:

$$X(10) + \cfrac{1}{X(9) + \cfrac{1}{X(8) + \cfrac{1}{\ldots + X(2) + \cfrac{1}{X(1)}}}}$$

   (d)   Merge two one-dimensional arrays A and B into a new one-dimensional array C, such
         that the even subscripts of C are generated from consecutive elements of A and the
         odd subscripts are generated by successive elements of B. For example, if A=(7, 3,
         9, 13) and B=(5, 8, 10, 2), then C=(5, 7, 8, 3, 10, 9, 2, 13).

6.18   Write program segments to accomplish the following:

   (a)   Assign the values of a real 10 × 10 array so that each element has a value equal to
         the sum of its subscripts (e.g.,   A(4, 6) = 10.0).
   (b)   Set all the elements of a real 10 × 10 array to 0 if they were originally less than 0.
   (c)   Declare an integer array of rank 4 and have the user enter all four dimensions during
         execution.
   (d)   Declare a real array of rank 2 and have the user enter the lower and upper bounds for
         each index during execution.
   (e)   Use an array constructor to assign the values of a real 10 × 10 array, so that each
         element has a value equal to the sum of its indices (e.g., A(4,6) = 10).

6.19   Write program segments to perform the following tasks on the arrays A(10, 10) and B(10,
         10):

   (a)   Sum a row in A.
   (b)   Determine the maximum value within each array.
   (c)   Transpose an array. The transposed array (B) is the original array (A) with rows and
         columns switched.
   (d)   Subtract each element in the array B from the corresponding element of the A array.
         Have the results returned in the A array.

6.20   Trace through the following program segments and predict their outputs. Line numbers are provided for your convenience and are not part of the program.

```
(a)  01     REAL A(10)            (b)  01     INTEGER A(10)
     02     DO I=1, 10                 02     DO I=1, 9, 2
     03        A(I)=I**2               03        A(I)=I**2
     04     END DO                     04     END DO
     05     DO I=2, 10, 2              05     DO I=2, 8, 2
     06        PRINT *, A(I/2+1)       06        A(I)=A(I-1)-A(I+1)
     07     END DO                     07     END DO
     08     STOP                       08     PRINT 3,(A(I),I=1,10)
     09     END                        09  3  FORMAT(' ',2(I7,3x),/)
                                       10     STOP
                                       11     END
```

6.21   Write a program that reads in a list of values, stores them in an array, and returns the maximum absolute value.

6.22   Modify the min/max sort program (Example 6.9) so a second array B will be sorted based on the sorting sequence for the array A. For example, if the first and third values in A are swapped, then the first and third values in B will also be swapped:

A	B	After Sorting on A:	A	B
5	5000		1	45
4	2347		2	247
1	45		4	2347
2	247		5	5000

Your program should read in a maximum of 100 pairs of numbers. Have the first number in the pair stored in the A array and the second in the B array. Sort the numbers as described and print the results.

6.23   A list of real numbers ranges in value from 0.0 to 100.0. Write a program that reads in the upper limits for five possible ranges into which the data can be grouped as illustrated below. Have the program create a list showing how many numbers exist in each of the ranges. Stop reading in numbers when any value is less than 0.

Range 1:   0   ≤ number < upper limit 1
Range 2:   lower limit 2   ≤ number < upper limit 2
Range 3:   lower limit 3   ≤ number < upper limit 3

Range 4:   lower limit 4   ≤ number < upper limit 4
Range 5:   lower limit 5   ≤ number ≤ upper limit 5

6.24 A national survey of smoking habits as a function of age was taken. Age values range from 10 years old to 100. Smoking levels ranged from nonsmoker, to intermediate smoker (1–2 packs per day), to heavy smoker (3 or more packs per day). Smoking habits were then rated as 1 for nonsmoker, 2 for intermediate level smoker, and 3 for heavy smoker. Additional questions of gender and state residence were also added. Responses were given a list of code numbers. For gender, the data were coded 1 for male and 2 for female. The states were given code numbers ranging from 1 to 50. If we store this information in an array,

(a) How many dimensions must this array have?
(b) Write a program to read the survey results and analyze the data to generate a statistics table (number of 25-year-old women who live in state #5 and are nonsmokers, etc.).
(c) Write a program segment to calculate total number of respondents.
(d) Write a program segment to report total number of nonsmokers.
(e) Write a program segment to report percentage of male and female smokers. For example, assuming there were 100 smokers in the survey, the output would look like this: Of the 100 smokers, 46% were women and 54% were men.

6.25 The operation of scalar multiplication of an array is the process of multiplying each element in the array by the desired scalar value. For example, if we multiply an array by the constant 2, we would multiply each element of the array by this constant. Write a program that reads in an array of size N × M, requests a scalar value, and returns the result of the scalar multiplication.

6.26 Given the following data statements, determine what values will be assigned to each array element:

```
(a)  INTEGER A(3,3)
     DATA A/3*1,3*2,3*3/
(b)  INTEGER A(3,3)
     DATA ((A(I,J),J=1,3),I=1,3)/1,2,3,4,5,6,7,8,9/
(c)  INTEGER A(2,2,2)
     DATA(((A(I,J,K),I=2,1,-1),J=1,2),K=2,1,-1)/1,2,3,4,5,6,7,8/
(d)  REAL, DIMENSION(10)::A
     A=(/(SIN(3.1416/2*I),I=0,9)/)
(e)  REAL, DIMENSION(10)::A
     A=(/(2.5*I, I=1,5),(0.5*I, I=5,1,-1)/)
(f)  INTEGER, DIMENSION(6,6)::A
     DATA A/36*0/
     A(2:6,2:6)=RESHAPE((/(I, 1, 25)/),(/5, 5/))
     A(5:6,:)=RESHAPE((/(I, I=100, 111)/),(/2, 6/))
(g)  INTEGER, DIMENSION(11,11)::PLOT
     DATA PLOT/121*0/
```

```
PLOT(5,:)=(/11*1/)
PLOT(:,5)=(/11*2/)
```

6.27 Modify the program presented in Example 6.29 (printing a sine wave) so that it prints using a width of 100 characters and a length of 60 lines.

6.28 Write program segments to perform the following tasks.

(a) Change all positive values of a two-dimensional array to the $\log_e$ of their value and all negative values to 0.

(b) An integer array has elements that have both even and odd values. Change all even values to 0 and all odd values to the value $+1$.

6.29 Trace through the following program and predict its output. Line numbers are provided for your convenience and are not part of the program.

```
01          INTEGER MAT(10, 10)
02          DATA ((MAT(I, J), I=1, 3), J=1, 4)&
03             /1, 2, 3, 4, 5, 6, 7, 8, 9, 10, 11, 12/
04          DO I=1, 2
05            DO J=1, 4
06              MAT(I+1, J)=MAT(I+1, J)+MAT(I, J)
07            END DO
08          END DO
09          PRINT *, ((MAT(I, J), I=1, 3), J=1, 3)
10          END
```

Answers to Selected Supplementary Problems

6.16 (a) The array element $A(I-5)$ is out of bounds when I is less than or equal to 5.

(b) By declaring SIN to be an array, the intrinsic function is no longer available. Consequently, $SIN(i*\pi)$ will be in error due to a real subscript in what the compiler thinks is a one-dimensional array.

(c) The control variable of the loop cannot change while the loop is operating.

(d) Once the variables N and M are named in a PARAMETER statement, they cannot be changed by any other statement, including the READ statement.

(e) Array Y was not declared ALLOCATABLE. Therefore, Y may not be adjustable.

(f) The variable limits (M and N) should not appear in the declaration statement.

(g) The dot product can only be calculated for vectors (one-dimensional arrays). Two-dimensional arrays are not allowed.

(h) A is declared correctly, but AVG is not. The lower limit on the subscript comes first.

6.17 (a)
```
REAL X(1000)
READ *, N, (X(I), I=1, N)
TOT = SUM(X)
PRINT *, TOT
```

(b)
```
INTEGER S(50)
DATA S(1), S(2)/1, 3/
DO I=3, 50
      S(I)=S(I-1)+2*S(I-2)
END DO
PRINT *, (S(I), I=1, 50)
```

(c)
```
REAL X(10)
READ *, (X(I), I=1, 10)
TERM=X(1)
DO I = 1, 9
  TERM=1/TERM
  TERM=TERM+X(I+1)
END DO
PRINT *, TERM
```

(d)
```
REAL A(50),B(50),C(100)
READ *, N, A, B
DO I = 1, N
   C(2*I) = A(I)
   C(2*I-1) = B(I)
END DO
PRINT *, C
```

6.18 (a)
```
REAL A(10,10)
DO I = 1, 10
   DO J = 1, 10
     A(I,J) = I + J
   END DO
END DO
```

(b)
```
REAL A(10,10)
READ *, A
WHERE(A < 0.0) A=0.0
```

(c)
```
INTEGER, DIMENSION(:,:,:,:), ALLOCATABLE::A
PRINT *,'Enter size of each of four dimensions'
READ *,I, J, K, L
ALLOCATE (A(I, J, K, L))
```

(d)
```
REAL, DIMENSION(:,:), ALLOCATABLE::X
PRINT *,'Enter Lower/Upper limits of 1st dimension'
READ *,IL, IU
PRINT *,'Enter Lower/Upper limits for 2nd dimension'
READ *,JL, JU
ALLOCATE (X(IL:IU,JL:JU))
```

(e)
```
REAL, DIMENSION(10,10)::A
A=RESHAPE((/((I+J, I=1,10), J=1,10)/), (/10,10/))
```

6.19 (a)
```
REAL A(10,10)
READ *, A
PRINT *, 'Row Number?'
READ *, I
TOT=SUM(A(I,:))
PRINT *, 'Sum of row:', TOT
END
```

(b)
```
REAL A(10,10), B(10,10)
READ *, A, B
AMAX = MAXVAL(A)
BMAX = MAXVAL(B)
PRINT *, 'Maximum values of A and B:', AMAX, BMAX
END
```

(c)
```
REAL A(10,10), B(10,10)
READ *, A
B=TRANSPOSE(A)
PRINT *, B
```

```
        END
(d)     REAL A(10,10), B(10,10)
        READ *, A, B
        A=A-B
        PRINT *, A
        END
```

6.20 (a) Trace Table:

A:	1.0	4.0	9.0	16.0	25.0	36.0	49.0	64.0	81.0	100.0

I: 1, 2, 3, 4, 5, 6, 7, 8, 9, 10, 11, 2, 4, 6, 8, 10, 12

Output:
    4.0 9.0 16.0 25.0 36.0 (on separate lines)

(b) Trace Table:

A:	1	−8	9	−16	25	−24	49	−32	81	(blank)

I: 1, 3, 5, 7, 9, 11, 2, 4, 6, 8, 10, 1, 2, 3, 4, 5, 6, 7, 8, 9, 10, 11

Step by Step Trace (Summary):

Elements 1, 3, 5, 7, and 9 are assigned values equal to their index squared. Elements 2, 4, 6, and 8 are assigned the value equal to their preceding neighbor, minus their following neighbor. The last element is never assigned a value.

Output:
```
    1    -8
    9    -16
   25    -24
   49    -32
   81    **** Last value could be anything, but most likely 0.
```

6.21
```
REAL X(100)
PRINT *, 'Enter number of items and data:'
READ *, N, (X(I), I = 1, N)
PRINT *, 'Maximum value:', MAXVAL(ABS(X))
END
```

6.22
```
REAL, DIMENSION(:), ALLOCATABLE :: A, B
INTEGER INDEX(1)
PRINT *, 'Number of items:'
READ *, N
ALLOCATE (A(N), B(N))
PRINT *, 'Enter A and B arrays:'
```

```
      READ *, (A(I), B(I), I = 1, N)
      DO I=1, N-1
         INDEX = MINLOC(A(I:N))
      ! Switch values in A
         SWAP1 = A(I)
         A(I) = A(INDEX(1))
         A(INDEX(1)) = SWAP1
      ! Now switch values in B
         SWAP2 = B(I)
         B(I) = B(INDEX(1))
         B(INDEX(1)) = SWAP2
      END DO
      DO I = 1, N
         PRINT *, A(I), B(I)
      END DO
      END
```

6.23
```
      INTEGER, DIMENSION(5) :: COUNT
      INTEGER X
      DATA COUNT/5*0/
      DO WHILE (X >= 0 .AND. X <= 100)
         READ *, X
         SELECT CASE(X/5)
            CASE(0:4)
               COUNT(1) = COUNT(1) + 1
            CASE(5:8)
               COUNT(2) = COUNT(2) + 1
            CASE(9:12)
               COUNT(3) = COUNT(3) + 1
            CASE(13:16)
               COUNT(4) = COUNT(4) + 1
            CASE(17:20)
               COUNT(5) = COUNT(5) + 1
         END SELECT
      END DO
      DO I = 1, 5
         PRINT *, 'Number within range ', I, ' was ', COUNT(I)
      END DO
      END
```

6.24 (a) The array must have four dimensions: age, smoking level, gender, and state.

(b)
```
      INTEGER RESPOND(10:100, 3, 2, 50)
      INTEGER AGE, SMOKE, GEN, STATE
      DATA RESPOND/27300*0/
      PRINT *, 'Number of respondents?'
      READ *, N
      DO I = 1, N
         READ *, AGE, SMOKE, GEN, STATE
         RESPOND(AGE,SMOKE,GEN,STATE) =&
         RESPOND(AGE,SMOKE,GEN,STATE)+1
      END DO
```

(c) If the total number of respondents is not read in, this is the code that would be needed:

```
      NTOTAL = 0
      DO AGE = 10, 100
        DO SMOKE = 1, 3
          DO GEN = 1, 2
            DO STATE = 1, 50
              NTOTAL = NTOTAL + RESPOND(AGE, SMOKE, GEN, STATE)
            END DO
          END DO
        END DO
      END DO
      !*********************************************************
      ! This could also be done with an array operator such as
      !        NTOTAL = SUM(RESPOND(10:100, 1:3, 1:2, 1:50))
      !*********************************************************
  (d) NONSMK = 0
      DO AGE = 10, 100
        DO GEN = 1, 2
          DO STATE = 1, 50
            NONSMK = NONSMK + RESPOND(AGE, 1, GEN, STATE)
          END DO
        END DO
      END DO
      !*********************************************************
      ! This could also be done with an array operator such as
      !        NTOTAL = SUM(RESPOND(10:100, 1:1, 1:2, 1:50))
      !*********************************************************
  (e) NUMFEMSMK = 0
      NUMMALSMK = 0
      DO AGE = 10, 100
        DO SMOKE = 1, 3
          DO STATE = 1, 50
            NUMFEMSMK = NUMFEMSMK + RESPOND(AGE,SMOKE,2,STATE)
            NUMMALSMK = NUMMALSMK + RESPOND(AGE,SMOKE,1,STATE)
          END DO
        END DO
      END DO
      PFEMSMK = NUMFEMSMK/NTOTAL      ! NTOTAL comes from (c) above
      PMALSMK = NUMMALSMK/NTOTAL
      !*********************************************************
      ! This could also be done with an array operator such as
      !     PFEMSMK=SUM(RESPOND(10:100, 1:3, 2:2, 1:50))/NTOTAL
      !     PMALSMK=SUM(RESPOND(10:100, 1:3, 1:1, 1:50))/NTOTAL
      !*********************************************************
```

6.25
```
      REAL, DIMENSION (:,:) :: X
      PRINT *, 'Number of rows and columns?'
      READ *, N, M
      ALLOCATE (X(N,M))
      PRINT *, 'Enter data values:'
      READ *, ((X(I, J), J=1, M), I=1, N)
      PRINT *, 'Enter scalar value:'
      READ *, S
      X = X*S
```

```
          PRINT *, 'Resulting array is:'
          PRINT *, ((X(I, J), J=1, M), I=1,N)
          END
```

6.26 (a) A(1, 1)=1, A(1, 2)=2, A(1, 3)=3, A(2, 1)=1, A(2, 2)=2, A(2, 3)=3, A(3, 1)=1, A(3, 2)=2, A(3, 3)=3

(b) A(1,1)=1, A(1, 2)=2, A(1, 3)=3, A(2, 1)=4, A(2, 2)=5, A(2, 3)=6, A(3, 1)=7, A(3, 2)=8, A(3, 3)=9

(c) A(2, 1, 2)=1, A(1, 1, 2)=2, A(2, 2, 2)=3, A(1, 2, 2)=4, A(2, 1, 1)=5, A(1, 1, 1)=6, A(2, 2, 1)=7, A(1, 2, 1)=8

(d) A=(0.0,1.0,0.0,−1.0,0.0,1.0,0.0,−1.0,0.0,1.0)

(e) A=(2.5,5.0,7.5,10.0,12.5,2.5,2.0,1.5,1.0,0.5)

(f)
```
                0,0,0,0,0,0
                0,1,6,11,16,21
    A =         0,2,7,12,17,22
                0,3,8,13,18,23
                100,102,104,106,108,110
                101,103,105,107,109,111
```

(g) (no commas are shown to separate values)
```
                00000100000
                00000100000
                00000100000
                00000100000
                00000100000
    PLOT=       22222222222
                00000100000
                00000100000
                00000100000
                00000100000
                00000100000
```

6.27
```
     DO I = 0, 60
        X = I*2*3.14159/60.0
        Y = SIN(X)
        N = NINT(50+Y*50+1)
        PRINT *, ("*", J = 1, N)
     END DO
```

6.28 (a)
```
        WHERE (A > 0.0)
            A=LOG(A)
        ELSEWHERE
            A=0
        END WHERE
```
(b)
```
        WHERE (MOD(A,2) == 0)
            A=0
        ELSEWHERE
```

```
        A=1
    END WHERE
```

6.29   <u>Trace Table:</u>

Notes: 1) "*" indicates undefined value

              2) the following table shows the sequential values for each array element

M

1	4	7	10	*	*	*	*	*	*
2, 3	5, 9	8, 15	11, 21	*	*	*	*	*	*
3, 6	6, 15	9, 24	12, 33	*	*	*	*	*	*
*	*	*	*	*	*	*	*	*	*
*	*	*	*	*	*	*	*	*	*
*	*	*	*	*	*	*	*	*	*
*	*	*	*	*	*	*	*	*	*
*	*	*	*	*	*	*	*	*	*
*	*	*	*	*	*	*	*	*	*
*	*	*	*	*	*	*	*	*	*

I: 1, 2, 3, 1, 2, 3   J: 1, 2, 3, 4, 5, 1, 2, 3, 4, 5

<u>Output:</u>

    1.00000   3.00000   6.00000   4.00000   9.00000   15.00000   7.00000   15.00000   24.00000

Chapter 7

Subprograms

7.1 MODULARITY — THE KEY TO PROGRAMMING SUCCESS

If we ask ten professional programmers the question, "What is the best strategy to write a complex program?" all ten would probably answer "Modularize!" In effect, the professionals are telling us that if we break the complex problem down into several smaller problems (subprograms), we stand a better chance of being successful. A "divide and conquer" approach is the key to success.

What do we mean by "modularize"? Most programmers agree that to modularize a task is to break it into individual, well-focused *subtasks*. If you concentrate on solving one small subtask at a time, the overall task is simpler to solve. There is nothing unique about this approach since we do it all the time in our personal lives. How often have you heard "I can only do one thing at a time!" Well, that's what modularization is all about — concentrating on one thing at a time.

In this chapter, we will not learn any new ideas about programming, other than how to package programs differently. We will break long programs into several smaller subprograms, all held together by a main program, whose primary function is to oversee all the subtasks. Each of the subprograms will have only a single task to perform.

The best way for us to introduce the need for modularization is to introduce a simple problem. One type of program that is a candidate for modularization is one that repeats the same type of calculation a number of times. This occurs quite often when you need to use a mathematical operation that is not built into the compiler, so that you are forced to do it yourself. The factorial function $[n! = (n-1)(n-2)...(2)(1)]$ is such an example.

EXAMPLE 7.1

Suppose that a laboratory instructor wants to divide 12 students into two groups with 7 and 5 students. We can show that the number of possible combinations c that can occur is

$$c = \frac{12!}{5!\,7!} = 792$$

To generalize this to a class of n students and groups of i and $n-i$, we use the formula:

$$c = \frac{n!}{i!\,(n-i)!}$$

A program to calculate c would require three separate loops to calculate $n!$, $i!$, and $(n-i)!$ as shown in the following program and flowchart:

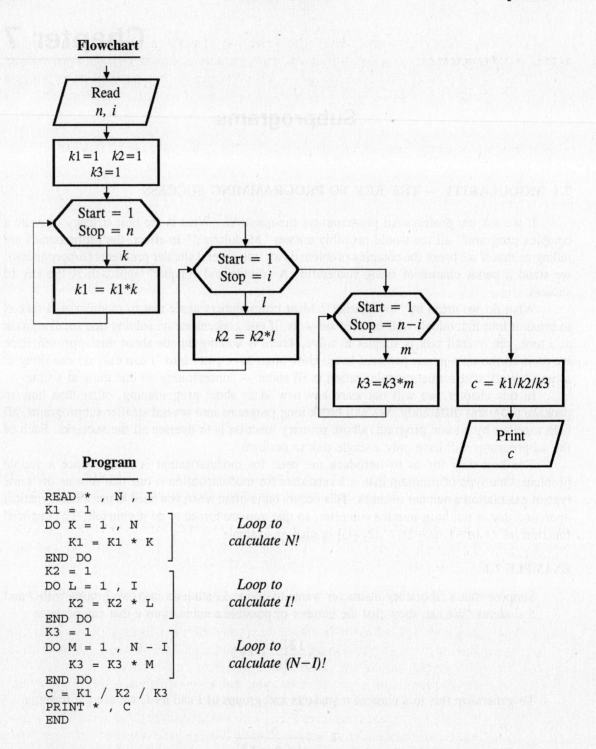

Flowchart

Program

```
READ * , N , I
K1 = 1
DO K = 1 , N
   K1 = K1 * K        Loop to
END DO                calculate N!
K2 = 1
DO L = 1 , I
   K2 = K2 * L        Loop to
END DO                calculate I!
K3 = 1
DO M = 1 , N - I
   K3 = K3 * M        Loop to
END DO                calculate (N−I)!
C = K1 / K2 / K3
PRINT * , C
END
```

Although this program works, it is an awkward structure, since we use the loops for calculating the factorial three times, with only small changes each time. Thus, we needlessly wrote extra code for the factorials. Hopefully, there is a better way so that we won't have to write the same code over and over again.

Fortunately, most programming languages have a way to avoid unnecessary repetition such as this. A *subprogram* can be set up outside the main program to calculate the factorial for any value of *n*. The subprogram worries about the details of calculating *n*!, while the main program controls sending the right values to the subprogram and decides what to do with the results.

.MAIN. program   Subprogram for factorial

```
READ *, N, I
      ⋮
      ⋮
(calculate K1=N!)
      ⋮
      ⋮
(calculate K2=I!)
      ⋮
      ⋮
(calculate K3=(N-I)!)
      ⋮
      ⋮
C = K1 / K2 / K3
PRINT *, C
END
```

How to calculate the factorial of any number

Every time that the main program needs to calculate the factorial, the value of N, I, or (N−I) is sent to the subprogram for the calculation. One advantage of programming this way is that we write the subprogram <u>only once</u>. If set up correctly, the subprogram can calculate the factorial for any number sent to it. Notice that the main program controls what to send and what to do with the results. However, the main program leaves all the details of the calculation to the subprogram.

There are several major advantages to breaking programs into smaller subprograms:

- You can simplify your job by focusing on a small task assigned to the subprogram.
- You can reuse the code in the subprogram as often as needed.
- Subprograms are *portable*, which means that they can be saved in a library and used in other programs or by other programmers. Thus, the factorial subprogram written here can be used in a different program.
- In addition to your own libraries, you can also use libraries created by others. Some of these contain thousands of mathematical functions.
- Subprograms make it easier to debug your programs. Ten subprograms of 20 lines each are much easier to correct than a 200-line program with the same code embedded in it.

As we will see shortly, subprograms can contain all the elements that we have already discussed, such as control structures, arrays, and I/O commands. The only new concept that we introduce here is that the subprogram will work in concert with, and under the control of, a main program or another subprogram.

7.2 THE FUNCTION SUBPROGRAM

The simplest type of subprogram is the *function subprogram* whose purpose is to calculate a *single numerical* answer and return the result. You have already seen many examples of functions when you used *intrinsic* or *built-in functions* such as:

```
Y = SQRT(X)
```

The execution of this statement is so automatic that you didn't give it much thought. But it is important that we review the process for using functions and how to transfer the data. The statement Y = SQRT(X) is a *calling* statement, which tells the computer to use the function built into the compiler for calculating the square root. The computer transfers the value of X to the appropriate function and stores the answer $\sqrt{X}$ in the variable Y.

Even though Fortran has many built-in functions, there are still many that are missing. The factorial $n!$ is one of these. Therefore, we need a way to construct other functions that can be called just like the SQRT function. The principal difference, though, is that we now need to supply the necessary instructions in the form of a *function subprogram*, with the syntax

```
type FUNCTION name (list of variables )
        subprogram instructions
RETURN
END
```

The first line of the subprogram states that this is a function and gives it a name, which is the same as the one to be used in the main program calling statement. Within the subprogram, this name is also used as a variable to which the desired value will be assigned. Because the function name is also a variable inside the function, the type of the variable may need to be declared. That is why there is a typing option at the beginning of the function statement. Following the name is an optional list of variables that the function needs for the calculation.

EXAMPLE 7.2

Since the function name will be used as a variable, we sometimes need to declare the type (real, integer, character, and so forth) at the beginning of the function. This typing is optional, though, if implicit typing rules are sufficient. Thus, the following are equivalent:

```
INTEGER FUNCTION IFACT(N)        or        FUNCTION IFACT(N)
```

Since the variable IFACT is implicitly integer, we do not need to redeclare it. In the subsequent examples, we will always assume implicit typing. However, this option is only available with real or integer data. With character, double precision, logical, or complex data, the type declaration is required in the function statement as shown in this example:

```
DOUBLE PRECISION FUNCTION COMPUTE(A, B, C)
```

In this example, we did not have a choice. Since real and integer are the only implicit data types, we had to declare the variable COMPUTE to be double precision.

The function subprogram body is similar to any other program in that it can contain declaration and assignment statements, loops, branches, and so on. At the end of the subprogram are the RETURN and END statements. The computer uses an optional RETURN statement at execution time to return control back to the program segment that called it. The END statement indicates the physical end of the specific segment and separates it from the other segments.

EXAMPLE 7.3

Let's return to Example 7.1 to compute the number of possible combinations of groups with size i and $n-i$. But we will replace the code that was repeated three times with a function. Since the factorial function ($i!$) does not exist on most compilers, we must write our own.

Flowchart

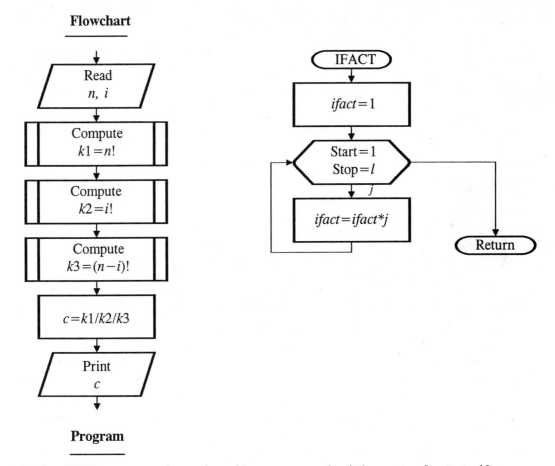

Program

```
! The MAIN program is primarily concerned with control. Details
! of the factorial calculation are handled in the function.
!*************************************************************
PRINT *, 'ENTER N and I:'
READ *, N, I
```

(Program continues on next page)

```
! Three calls to the function to compute N!, I! and (N-I)!
!***************************************************************
K1 =   IFACT ( N )
K2 =   IFACT ( I )
K3 =   IFACT ( N-I )
C = K1 / K2 / K3
PRINT *, 'C= ', C
END
!***************************************************************
! The function is written as a stand-alone subprogram.
!***************************************************************
FUNCTION IFACT ( L )
  IFACT = 1
  DO J = 1 , L
     IFACT = IFACT * J
  END DO
  RETURN
END
```

The function follows the end of the main program. The computer will know where the main program ends and the function subprogram begins by their respective END and FUNCTION statements. When the computer comes to the assignment statement in the main program

$$K1 = IFACT(N)$$

it seeks out the function IFACT. The computer then transfers the value inside the parentheses (N in this case) to the subprogram where it is matched to the variable L. The function then computes N! and returns its value to the variable K1. When the main program comes to the next call

$$K2 = IFACT(I)$$

the same thing will happen, except that the computer now transfers the value of I to the subprogram and returns the result to K2. Finally, the third call to the function subprogram sends (N−I) to the function for computation, and (N−I)! is returned. Note how we use the same function subprogram three times, but with different values transferred each time.

The subprogram IFACT computes the factorial of the value within the parentheses in the calling statement with the aid of a *dummy variable* (L in Example 7.3). The value transferred to L is used locally within the subprogram for the computation of the factorial.

There were two new flowchart symbols that we introduced in this last example. Within the main program, we used a rectangular box with double lines to indicate that an *off-page process* is being used. An off-page process is a stand-alone unit (such as a function) that contains details about how to perform the required operation. In the example, we used this symbol three times to indicate the number of times we are calling this function. The start of the function itself is indicated by the elliptical flowchart symbol. We place the ellipse at the beginning and place the name of the routine inside. Also, we place an ellipse at the end of the function to indicate its end. Note that the function stands alone, and could have been placed on another piece of paper for convenience: hence its name *off-page* process.

Variables in Fortran are *local*. They exist only in the program segment in which they explicitly appear. Thus, if we had two variables with the same name within a main program and a function, they would not be the same. In some other computer languages such as BASIC, where variables are *global*, they would have the same value.

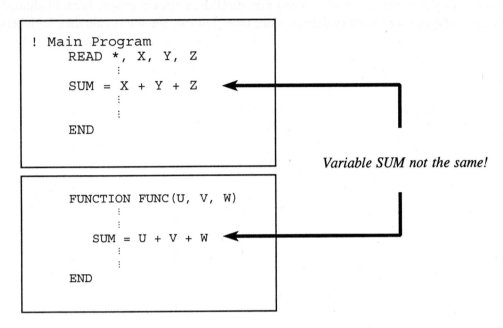

```
! Main Program
    READ *, X, Y, Z

    SUM = X + Y + Z


    END
```

Variable SUM not the same!

```
    FUNCTION FUNC(U, V, W)

        SUM = U + V + W

    END
```

The fact that variables in Fortran are <u>local</u> is very important when constructing large programs with many subprograms. Without this feature, you would find it difficult to use subprograms written by others, and you would lose the portability that is so important.

EXAMPLE 7.4

Trace through the following program segment to see what the output of the program will be:

```
X = 1.2345
Y = 9.8765
SUM = X + Y
PRINT *, SUM
PRINT *, FUNC(X, Y)
PRINT *, A, B
END
!*************************************************************
! The values of X and Y are transferred to the local variables
! A and B. The function computes A + B and returns the result.
!*************************************************************
FUNCTION FUNC(A, B)
  FUNC = A + B
  RETURN
END
```

The first PRINT statement in the main program prints out the value of SUM, or 11.11100. When the second PRINT statement executes, it will call the function subprogram FUNC and transfer the values 1.2345 and 9.8765 to A and B, respectively. Inside the function, A and B are added and their sum assigned to the variable FUNC. This value (11.11100) is then returned to the main program and printed. Now, when the computer executes the third print statement (PRINT *, A, B), it will find that A and B have not been assigned values in the main program (only in the function!), so you may receive an error message. In all likelihood though, the computer will print two zeros since most Fortran compilers initialize variables to zero. The point of this exercise is to show that variables are local to the segment in which they are defined and assigned values.

The local feature is very useful because it allows different sets of input data to use the same function repeatedly with a minimum of effort. To send new data, you write another calling statement and include the data within the argument list. The figure below schematically shows the most common way of transferring data to a function.

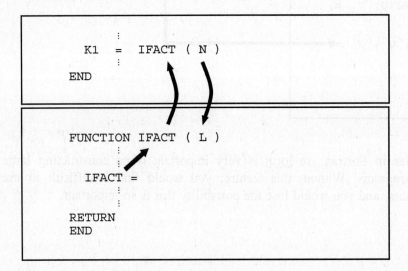

The value of the variable N inside the parentheses in the main program calling statement goes to L in the subprogram, even though the two variables do not have the same name. This feature makes it easy to transfer different values to the subprogram. The result of the calculation returns to the main program through the name of the function (IFACT). Notice first, though, that the subprogram uses the function name as a variable to store the result. Thus the function name IFACT occurs at least three different times:

- In the calling statement in the main program
- In the name of the function subprogram
- As a variable within the subprogram

An important point about subprograms is that the <u>type</u> of the corresponding variables in the main program and the subprogram argument lists must match. Thus, in the above figure, the variables sent to the subprogram are integers, as are the dummy variables set up to receive them. Similarly, IFACT is implicitly integer in both segments. You must pay special attention to the type of the variables since it is easy to create a mismatch. Also, you must be careful that the argument list in the calling statement and the function statement match in the <u>number</u> of variables and in their <u>order</u>. If you send four values, you must have four variables to receive them. Finally, there is a one-to-one correspondence between the position of the variables within the two lists. The third value in one list will be sent to the third variable in the other list, for example.

EXAMPLE 7.5

Assume that we wish to send three variables to a function called ADD. The first two variables, X and Y, are real, but the third, J, is an integer:

$$\begin{array}{ccc} real & real & integer \\ \updownarrow & \updownarrow & \updownarrow \end{array}$$
$$Y = ADD\ (\ X,\quad Y,\quad J\ )$$

The corresponding function statement variables must match in number, order and type:

$$\begin{array}{ccc} real & real & integer \\ \updownarrow & \updownarrow & \updownarrow \end{array}$$
$$FUNCTION\ ADD\ (\ A\ ,\ X\ ,\ I\ )$$

Note that X from the main will be assigned to A in the function, not to X in the function, even though they have the same variable name. <u>Position within the list</u> determines the assignment, not similarity of variable names!

EXAMPLE 7.6

If necessary, you may have to explicitly declare some variables in the function subprogram to satisfy the requirement that variables must match in type. For example, if we had used W instead of the variable I in Example 7.5, we would need to redeclare one of the variables. Note that W is an implicitly real, while I is implicitly integer.

```
!*********************************************************
! The variable J is implicitly integer in the main program
!*********************************************************
       ⋮
Y = ADD ( X, Y, J )
       ⋮
END
!*********************************************************
! The variable W must be declared as integer to match data sent
!*********************************************************
FUNCTION ADD ( A , B, W )
  INTEGER W
       ⋮
  RETURN
END
```

Under normal circumstances (using implicit typing), the variable W would be real. But the data item being sent (stored in J) is an integer, so there will be a type mismatch unless we change the variable type. That is the reason for the declaration statement inside the function.

Function subprograms are easy to use. You may use them in assignment statements, as part of mathematical expressions, or inside PRINT statements. For this reason, they are the preferred method for simple mathematical calculations. But there are other times when we need more complex operations. For these we will need another type of subprogram, which is described in the next section.

7.3 SUBROUTINES

The second type of subprogram is the *subroutine*. Like the function, it stands outside the main program and uses local variables. The difference is that the subroutine can do more sophisticated things than the simple function. Whereas the function can give only single numerical answers such as the square root of a number, subroutines can return more than a single numerical answer. For example, we can use the subroutine to sort an entire array or to carry out a curve fitting procedure on a large data set. There is no limit to the amount of data that the subroutine can return. Therefore, it is a more powerful tool than the function.

As with functions, the use of a subroutine requires a three-step process:

- Call the subroutine from the main program
- Pass data to the subroutine
- Set up the subroutine to receive the passed data, process it, and return the results

The procedure for calling a subroutine is a little different from that for a function. We used functions when a single numerical answer was sufficient. But with subroutines, we can return any amount of data, including nothing. Therefore, the subroutine is more versatile. With subroutines, we pass data to and from the subroutine with the calling statement:

CALL *subroutinename* (*variable1* , *variable2* , . . . , *variableN*)

where *subroutinename* is the name of the specific subroutine that you want to use and *variable1* ... *variableN* is a list of variables passing back and forth between the main and the subroutine. These variables are *two-way* variables. They may pass data to the subroutine or they may receive results, depending upon the context. The corresponding statements which set up the subroutine are:

SUBROUTINE *subroutinename* (*variable1* , *variable2* , . . . , *variableN*)
       ⋮
       ⋮
   RETURN
END

The identifier *subroutinename* must be identical with the one in the calling statement and must follow the standard rules for any variable name. The argument list in the calling statement and in the SUBROUTINE statement must have the same number of variables, and each must agree in type with its counterpart. They need not have the same variable names. Thus:

```
                    ⋮
        CALL ADD ( X , Y , Z , I , SUM )
                    ⋮



    SUBROUTINE ADD (  A , B , C , L ,TOT  )
                    ⋮
    RETURN
    END
```

In this example, the first variable in the subroutine argument list A receives the value of the first variable X in the calling argument list. Similarly, B receives the value of Y, C receives the value of Z, and so forth. Also, the variables sending and receiving the data must match in type. Thus, if X is real, A must be real, and if I is an integer, then L must also be an integer.

The variables in the argument lists can either send or receive data. Usually, this will be obvious from the context of the problem. In the example given, X, Y, Z, and I are sending data to the subroutine, while SUM is the variable where the returned answer is stored. But each variable is also a two-way variable. Thus, we may use X to send data down to the subroutine, but if the subprogram modifies the corresponding variable A, then X will change also.

EXAMPLE 7.7

The following main program calls the subroutine ADD, transfers the values of X, Y, Z, and I, and assigns them to their corresponding variables in the subroutine, A, B, C, and L:

```
                    ⋮
        DATA X, Y, Z, I/2.0, 3.0, 4.0, 3/
        CALL ADD ( X , Y , Z , I , SUM )
        PRINT *, SUM
                    ⋮
```

```
        SUBROUTINE ADD (A , B , C , L , TOTAL)
          TOTAL = 0.0
          DO K = 1 , L
             TOTAL = TOTAL  + A / B
          END DO
          A = TOTAL/C
          RETURN
        END
```

The values in the main program are X=2.000000, Y=3.00000, Z=4.00000, and I=3. These are transferred to the variables A, B, C, and L, respectively, in the subroutine. There, a value of TOTAL=2.00000 is computed, returned to the variable SUM in the main program, and printed. Also note that the subroutine changes the value of A with the statement A=TOTAL/C. Since A is equivalent to X in the main program, X will change also.

The subroutine must physically follow the last line of the main program. If there are several subroutines and functions, they may go in any order. In the following example, we place periods around the name of each module to highlight the fact that these are individual units.

```
.MAIN.                          or        .MAIN.
SUBROUTINE .TWO.                          FUNCTION .ONE.
FUNCTION .ONE.                            SUBROUTINE .ONE.
SUBROUTINE .ONE.                          SUBROUTINE .TWO.
```

The order in which you list the various subprograms is unimportant, since the computer will seek them out by <u>name</u> when it needs them. It may help in debugging, though, if you list them in a logical order — for instance, the order in which you call them.

7.4 ARRAYS AND SUBPROGRAMS

Our discussion has focused on passing single-valued variables to subprograms. But we can pass arrays also if we declare the arrays in both program segments. While this sounds like a duplication of effort, recall that subprograms are stand-alone segments. Thus, if we are going to use an array in the subprogram we must declare it in both modules where it is used.

EXAMPLE 7.8

When we pass the entire array A to the subroutine SUM, we have to declare the array twice:

```
REAL A(100)
   ⋮
CALL SUM ( A, TOT )
   ⋮
END
```

```
SUBROUTINE SUM( X , TOTAL )
  REAL X(100)
     ⋮
  RETURN
END
```

The array A is declared in the main program as a one-dimensional array with 100 elements. When we pass the array to the subroutine, all we need do is give the array name in the calling statement. Since we have already declared A as an array, the computer understands that the calling statement sends all 100 array elements. Finally, note that the variable receiving the array in the subroutine is X. Since we are sending down a real array with 100 elements, X must also be a real array with 100 elements.

One of the most important results of the ability to pass arrays is the possibility of using a subprogram with variable-sized arrays. Recall that in a main program we had to specify explicitly the maximum size of an array in the declaration statement. Fortran does not permit variable-sized arrays in main programs, unless you use the ALLOCATBLE option in the declaration statement. Inside subprograms, though, variable-sized arrays are allowed.

EXAMPLE 7.9

Assume that we have two arrays declared as A(100) and B(10). We wish to send A to a subroutine for processing first, followed by a second call with B. First, we send the array A with its size of 100. Then we send B with its size of 10. We set up the subroutine so that the local array X has a variable size M. When the computer receives the value of M (either 100 or 10) it will set up the required amount of memory space.

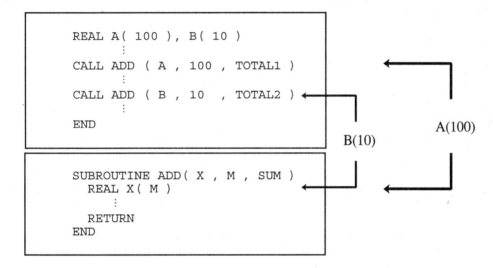

A key point to observe is that the array in the subroutine is a *variable*-sized array. Only when a value is transferred to M will the computer set up the array X with the requested number of elements. With the first calling statement in the main program, we are sending the A array with M=100; the second time M=10, so the array X is set up with 10 elements.

Besides sending entire arrays, it is also possible to transfer individual elements. But, of course, the data types must match.

EXAMPLE 7.10

In the program below, array A is declared in the main program to have 25 elements, but we are sending only two of the elements, A(1) and A(2), to the subroutine. Since each array element is a single value, the variables receiving the data must be single-valued variables.

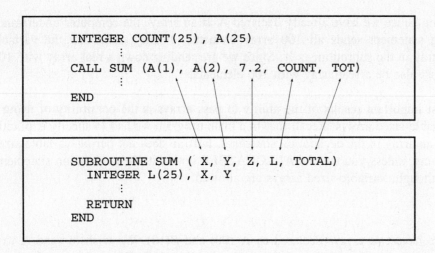

A(1) and A(2) are individual elements of the array A. These elements are assigned to the single-valued variables X and Y in the subroutine. Also, we have sent down a constant 7.2 to the variable Z, and the whole array COUNT to the array L. Note in this case that COUNT and L are declared as the same type (integer) and size (25 elements).

7.5 CREATING GLOBAL DATA — THE COMMON STATEMENT

We have stressed several times that Fortran uses variables which are local; these local variables exist only in the program segments in which you explicitly use them. Thus, the variable X in the main is different from the variable X in a subprogram. This is a very important feature since it allows you to reuse subprograms with few changes. Still, there are times when you may wish to have *global variables*, or variables that exist in several modules <u>simultaneously</u>. Fortran has such a feature, called the *COMMON block*, that allows you to declare selected variables as global.

Before we show you how to use the COMMON block, we want to show you why the need exists. Suppose that you have a lengthy program that makes many calls to subroutines and that each call transfers many items in the argument list:

```
CALL DUMMY(A, B, I, J, C, U)
CALL DUMMY(A, B, I, J, C, V)
CALL DUMMY(A, B, I, J, C, W)
```

In all three call statements, we have sent many of the same variables. The only difference in the three calling statements was the last item in the list, U, V, or W. The first five variables were all the same and resulted in extra typing that could easily result in errors if you were not careful. If we could turn these five into *global* variables there would be no need to explicitly transfer them to the subroutine — they would already be there.

The COMMON block structure allows us to declare a list of variables to be global in several program segments. The syntax of the statement is:

COMMON *variable1, variable2, . . ., variableN*

The COMMON statement contains a list of variables to be stored in common memory for use by each module given access to it. If a module will need these variables, then the COMMON statement must be included. If a subprogram will not use the common data, then you do not need the COMMON statement and may omit it. When the COMMON statement appears in a subprogram, the variable names need not be the same as the ones in the main program. Instead, the data are matched by their location in the variable list. For example, the first variable listed inside the parentheses of the main program COMMON statement is assigned to the first variable in the subprogram COMMON statement, regardless of its name. Similarly, the second variable in the main program COMMON statement is matched with the second variable, and so forth.

EXAMPLE 7.11

To demonstrate how to use the COMMON statement, let's work on the program where we have three CALL statements, each with the same five variables plus one different variable. We will put the five variables into the COMMON statement and send down only the variable that is not common.

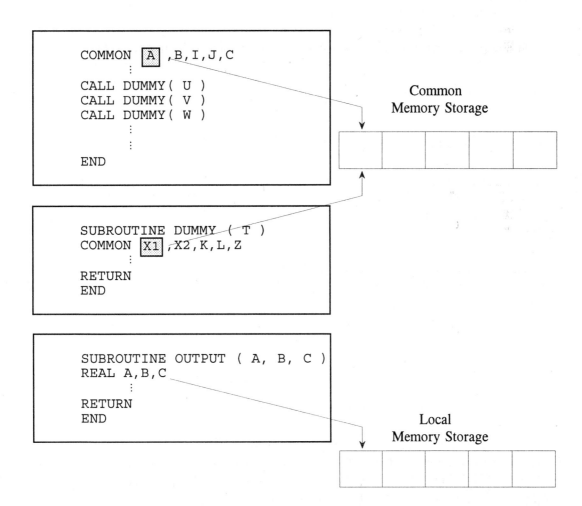

The variables A (in the main) and X1 (in the first subroutine) share the same memory block because of the COMMON statement. Therefore, they will always have the same value. Note that in the second subroutine (OUTPUT), which does not have a COMMON statement, there are only local variables. Thus, the variable A in subroutine OUTPUT is different from A in the main.

   This example shows that you can have a mixture of local and global variables. By default, variables are local. So if you want global variables, you must set up a COMMON block and specify it in each subprogram that will use it. We must warn you though, that global variables can cause many problems if you are not careful. Overuse of COMMON blocks will greatly increase the difficulty of debugging programs containing them.

   There is a second type of COMMON block called the *named COMMON block*. We can give each COMMON block a name, which will allow us to break all the shared data into smaller packages. This will allow us to share some data with one subprogram and other data with another subprogram. The syntax of the named COMMON block is:

   COMMON */name/ variable1, variable2, . . ., variableN*

We give the block a name by specifying it inside the slash marks, and we list the variables to be associated with that block. To transfer this block of variables to the subroutine, all we need do is to specify the same block name in the subroutine.

   Suppose we wanted to share variables A, B, C, D, and E with one group of subroutines, and T, U, V, W, and X with a second set of subroutines. We would do it as shown below.

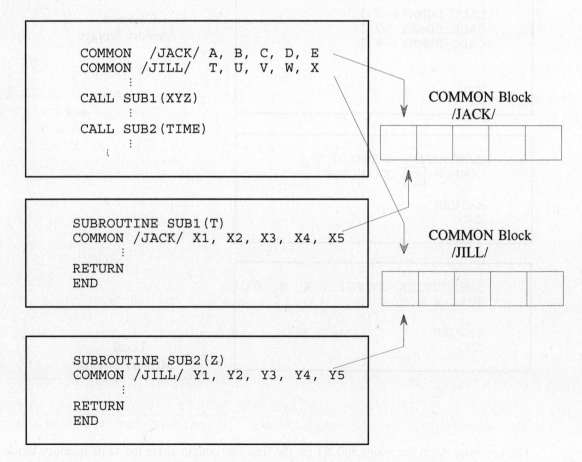

```
COMMON   /JACK/ A, B, C, D, E
COMMON /JILL/  T, U, V, W, X
   :
CALL  SUB1(XYZ)
   :
CALL  SUB2(TIME)
   :
```

COMMON Block
/JACK/

```
SUBROUTINE SUB1(T)
COMMON /JACK/ X1, X2, X3, X4, X5
   :
RETURN
END
```

COMMON Block
/JILL/

```
SUBROUTINE SUB2(Z)
COMMON /JILL/ Y1, Y2, Y3, Y4, Y5
   :
RETURN
END
```

The named COMMON block /JACK/ shares the variables A, B, C, D, and E with the SUBROUTINE SUB1 variables X1, X2, X3, X4, and X5. The second named COMMON block /JILL/ shares only the variables, T, U, V, W, and X with the variables Y1, Y2, Y3, Y4, and Y5 in SUBROUTINE SUB2.

One requirement of the named COMMON block (but not unnamed blocks) is that it must be the same length (four, or five, or however many variables) in every module in which it appears. Even if you will not use all the variables in the block, you must provide a variable to receive the data. For example, in SUBROUTINE SUB2, you may not need the variables Y2 and Y4 for any calculations. Yet, you must provide these two variables. Finally, variables listed in the COMMON blocks cannot be initialized with the DATA statement. Each variable must be explicitly assigned a value with either a READ statement or a direct assignment.

One problem with COMMON blocks is that you may pass character data in either a named or unnamed COMMON block. But if you do so, you cannot pass other types of data such as reals, integers, and so forth. You must use a separate named COMMON block for these. In these blocks, though, you can mix different types, provided that there is no character data.

In spite of its apparent usefulness, we strongly recommend that you avoid COMMON blocks if possible. Sometimes, they can be used to good effect, as we will show in the section on debugging. In general, though, they compromise the safety of the individual modules. We go to great lengths to set up subprograms that are independent of each other to ensure that there is no "crosstalk." Common blocks directly attack this structure and may produce errors that are very difficult to locate and then eliminate.

7.6 MODULES

Fortran 90 offers a second, more convenient way to declare global data. This is done with a *module* that consists of declaration statements and assignment statements. Inside the module, we can declare any variables or named constants that can be used by any other module such as a subroutine or a function. But in order to access this data, the subprogram requesting access must contain the command *USE*. The form for the module is as follows:

> MODULE *module_name_of_your_choice*
>   *declaration and intialization statements*
> END MODULE *module_name_of_your_choice*

and the corresponding statement within the module to access this data is as follows:

> USE *module_name_of_your_choice*

The module is given a convenient name such as CONSTANTS or anything else that you choose, provided that it follows the Fortran naming convention. This name is then repeated with every USE instruction to give access to the data that is to be shared.

EXAMPLE 7.12

Here is an example in which we define a module to contain the value of PI and allow several modules to have access to the value:

```
MODULE CONSTANTS
   REAL, PARAMETER :: PI=3.14159
END MODULE CONSTANTS
!
! First module that uses the value of PI
!
SUBROUTINE A()
   USE CONSTANTS
      ⋮
   (instructions that use the value of PI)
      ⋮
END
!
! Second module that uses the value of PI
!
REAL FUNCTION B()
   USE CONSTANTS
      ⋮
   (instructions that use the value of PI)
      ⋮
END
```

In this example, PI is declared in the module as a named constant with the value shown. Then in each of the subprograms, this value is retrieved through the USE instruction that gives that subprogram access to the global data. Notice that both subroutines and functions can retrieve this data, but that each subprogram must use a separate USE instruction.

In this example, there was not much advantage to using the module. But in those situations where many more named constants and global data are used, you will find this structure to be more useful than the COMMON blocks previously discussed.

7.7 RECURSIVE PROCEDURES

A *recursive procedure* is a function or a subroutine that calls itself. In order to do this, however, we must modify the subprogram definition statements. To create a recursive function, for example, we must modify the function by specifying that it is recursive and we must also provide a mechanism to return the result of the computation. We do all of this in the first line of the recursive function as follows:

RECURSIVE FUNCTION (*variable list*)   RESULT (*answer to be returned*)

Within the first set of parentheses, we place the input data for the computation. The RESULT clause, on the other hand, provides the means for returning the answer.

EXAMPLE 7.13

Recall in Example 7.3 that the factorial *n!* is defined by:

$$n! = (n)(n-1)(n-2)\cdots(2)(1)$$

But, we can also write it as

$$n! = (n)(n-1)! \qquad for \ \ n > 0$$

Notice that this second definition is recursive since we must go back to the factorial calculation to complete the computation as in this example to compute 3!:

$$3! = (3)(2!)$$
$$2! = (2)(1!)$$
$$1! = (1)(0!)$$
$$0! = 1$$

We start off by setting up 3! by the recursive definition, which is (3)(2!). Now, in order to compute 2!, we reuse the definition, which is 2!=(2)(1!). Finally, 1!=(1)(0!), where 0!=1 by definition. Once we get to 0!, we stop the recursive procedure. Now we work backward to produce the results: 0!=1, 1!=1, 2!=2, 3!=6:

```
RECURSIVE FUNCTION IFACT(L)    RESULT(FACTORIAL_L)
    INTEGER :: FACTORIAL_L
    IF (L == 0) THEN
       FACTORIAL_L=1
    ELSE
       FACTORIAL_L=L*IFACT(L-1)
    END IF
    RETURN
END
```

We can also create recursive subroutines by adding the RECURSIVE qualifier to the subroutine definition statement:

RECURSIVE SUBROUTINE *name (variable list)*

In this case, the answer to be returned is contained within the single set of parentheses as a separate variable. To demonstrate this, we will rework the factorial example as a recursive subroutine.

EXAMPLE 7.14

Here is the factorial calculation from Examples 7.3 and 7.13 rewritten as a recursive subroutine.

```
RECURSIVE SUBROUTINE IFACT(L, FACTORIAL_L)
   INTEGER :: FACTORIAL_L
   IF (L == 0) THEN
      FACTORIAL_L=1
   ELSE
      CALL IFACT(L-1, FACTORIAL_L)
      FACTORIAL_L=L*FACTORIAL_L
   END IF
   RETURN
END
```

Notice that each time through the subroutine, the value of L will be reduced by 1 and the subroutine will be summoned for another calculation. After the value is returned in the form of the variable FACTORIAL_L, its value is multiplied by L.

There is one special case that we did not take care of in these two examples. This is where the value of L is negative. In this case, the factorial of a negative number is undefined and we would have to add code to take care of this situation. When constructing recursive procedures, you may have to take care that special cases are considered.

Recursive functions and subroutines are called from the main program exactly as before. In fact, in the main program, there is no way of knowing whether a subprogram is recursive or nonrecursive. Therefore, there will be no change in the calling statement.

7.8 ENGINEERING AND SCIENCE APPLICATIONS

We began this chapter by stating there is nothing new about subprograms. They are simply a different way of packing the same goods. Therefore, it seems appropriate here to begin the discussion by "repackaging" three engineering related algorithms as subprograms. These include:

- Dot product of two vectors
- Determining the angle between two vectors
- Vector transformation

The first two can be implemented with a function subprogram only. The third will be done with subroutines. Sometimes, you can implement the desired program with either functions or subroutines. This is certainly true in these examples. So, as an additional exercise, you may want to convert functions to subroutines and vice versa.

EXAMPLE 7.15

Assume that we have two vectors, f^1 and f^2, each with three components. The *dot product* of the two vectors (indicated by the symbol •) is defined by summing the products of the components of each vector:

$$f^1 \cdot f^2 = \sum_{i=1}^{i=3} f_i^1 f_i^2 = f_1^1 f_1^2 + f_2^1 f_2^2 + f_3^1 f_3^2$$

This equation tells us to multiply the two x components of the vectors together, the two y components together, and the two z components together. The sum of all these products is the dot product. For example, if f^1 has components (3, 4, 7) and f^2 has components (0, 1, 3), then the dot product is given by $(3 \cdot 0 + 4 \cdot 1 + 7 \cdot 3) = 4 + 21 = 25$. The result of this calculation is a *scalar* quantity, which means that it has only a magnitude and lacks direction. The vectors themselves, on the other hand, have both magnitude and direction. This procedure is shown in the following flowchart and main program.

Flowchart

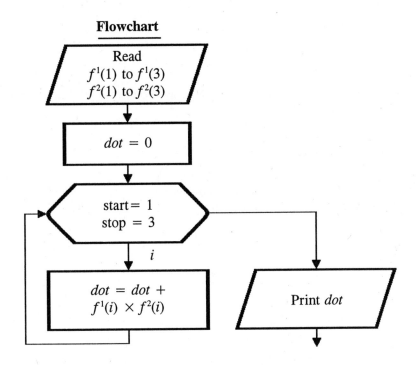

Program

```
! Declare the two vectors as one-dimensional arrays.
!****************************************************************
REAL F1(3), F2(3)
READ *, (F1(I), I=1,3), (F2(J), J=1,3)
!****************************************************************
! Now compute the dot product by summing the product of
! the individual components of the two vectors.
!****************************************************************
DOT = 0.0
DO I=1,3
   DOT = DOT + F1(I)*F2(I)
END DO
!****************************************************************
! Print the results. Note that DOT is a scalar quantity.
!****************************************************************
PRINT *, DOT
END
```

In this version of the dot product, we have written it as a main program. We will now convert the dot product into a function subprogram called DOT. We could also convert it into a subroutine, but as you will see shortly the function is more convenient.

We can convert this into a function subprogram almost directly. There are only a few changes and additions that we need to make:

- Create a main program to call the function
- Keep the READ statement in the main program
- Make the arrays variable size to improve the flexibility
- Make the loop control variable correspond to the size of the arrays
- Give the name DOT to the function

Once we make these changes, the function will be a general one that we can reuse without modifications.

Flowchart

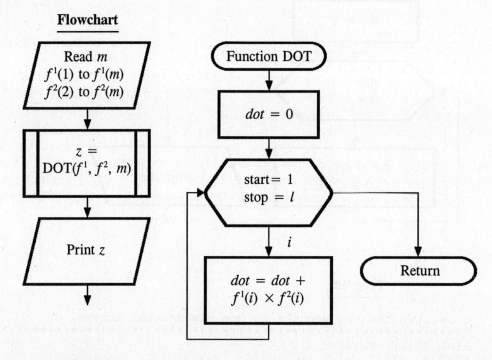

Program

```
!*************************************************************
! Main program reads in A and B vectors and calls function DOT
! to compute the dot product of A and B
!*************************************************************
REAL A(100), B(100)
PRINT *, 'Enter number of components, and A & B vectors:'
READ *, M, (A(I), I = 1, M), (B(I), I = 1, M)
Z = DOT(A, B, M)
PRINT *, 'DOT PRODUCT = ', Z
END
```

```
!*********************************************************
! Function subprogram to calculate the dot product of two vectors
! of arbitrary size (L)
!*********************************************************
FUNCTION DOT(F1, F2, L)
  REAL F1(L), F2(L)
  DOT = 0.0
  DO I = 1, L
     DOT = DOT + F1(I)*F2(I)
  END DO
  RETURN
END
```

The main program sets up the two arrays and reads in their values. Notice that the declaration statements there must specify an actual size for the arrays. Therefore, we usually set the size of the arrays arbitrarily high so that it is unlikely that we will exceed the reserved memory space. In this case, we set each vector to have 100 elements. Then we read in M, which is the actual number of elements in the array. This is usually 3 for real space vectors. Once the program reads in the arrays, their values transfer to the function along with the value of M. The function then uses the value of M to set up the arrays and to control the loop that computes the dot product. Finally, the function name DOT is a variable within the function and contains the desired scalar result.

Note carefully how the main program must send down an integer value to the local variable L that can be used to size the arrays. Study this example carefully since you will use it frequently.

A key point about setting up a subprogram is that you should make an effort to have the subprogram as flexible as possible so that you will not have to edit it each time you want to use it. For instance, we could use this function for dotting two vectors with 3, 10, 100, or any number of elements. The critical step is to set up the arrays as *variable* arrays. Also, you must set up any associated DO loops to run with variable limits. Finally, notice that we kept the I/O statements in the main program rather than in the subprogram.

EXAMPLE 7.16

Consider two vectors, F^1 and F^2, where we wish to know the angle between them:

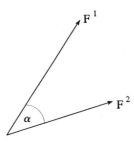

We can find the angle α between the two vectors, F^1 and F^2, with the formula:

$$\cos(\alpha) = \frac{F^1 \cdot F^2}{|F^1| |F^2|}$$

where $F^1 \bullet F^2$ = the dot product of the two vectors, and $|F^1|$ and $|F^2|$ are the lengths of the vectors respectively. The length can be computed by

$$|F| = [(F_1)^2 + (F_2)^2 + (F_3)^2]^{1/2}$$

For example, if we had two vectors, $F^1 = (12, 5, 6)$ and $F^2 = (3, 2, 0)$, we calculate the angle as follows:

$$
\begin{aligned}
F^1 \bullet F^2 &= 12 \times 3 + 5 \times 2 + 6 \times 0 &= 46 \\
|F^1| &= \sqrt{12^2 + 5^2 + 6^2} &= \sqrt{205} \\
|F^2| &= \sqrt{3^2 + 2^2 + 0^2} &= \sqrt{13} \\
\cos(\alpha) &= 46/\sqrt{205 \times 13} &= 0.891065 \\
\alpha &= \cos^{-1}(0.891065) &= 26.992770^\circ
\end{aligned}
$$

We will convert this calculation to a function called ANGLE that receives the two vectors and returns the single numerical value that is α. Keep in mind that when a computer does trigonometric calculations, all answers appear in radians, not degrees! So we will have to convert the answer (by multiplying by 57.296) before printing any results.

Flowchart

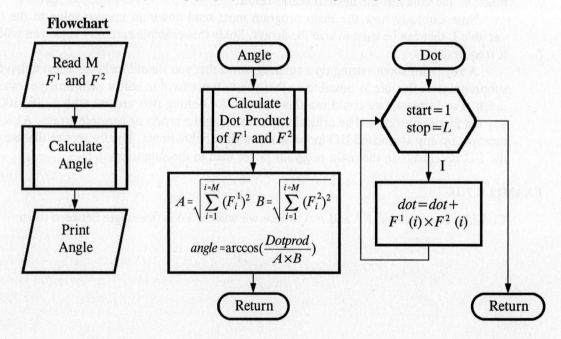

Program

```
! In the main program, we read in the vectors and call the
! appropriate functions. We use the main program to control the
! sequence of operations and leave the details to the functions.
!*****************************************************************
REAL F1(100), F2(100)
PRINT *, 'Enter number of elements and F1 and F2:'
```

(Program continues on next page)

```
READ *, M, (F1(I), I=1,M), (F2(I), I=1,M)
ANS = ANGLE(F1, F2, M)
PRINT *, 'Angle = ', ANS * 57.296
END
!**************************************************************
! Function Angle to compute the angle between two vectors. This
! function calls another function (DOT) to compute the dot
! product that is needed for the computation of the angle.
!**************************************************************
FUNCTION ANGLE(F1, F2, M)
  REAL F1(M), F2(M)
  A = 0.0
  B = 0.0
  DO I = 1, M
     A = A + F1(I)**2
     B = B + F2(I)**2
  END DO
  DOTPROD = DOT(F1, F2, M)
  ANGLE = ACOS(DOTPROD/SQRT(A*B))
  RETURN
END
!**************************************************************
! Function to compute the dot product of two vectors of
! arbitrary size (L) from Example 7.15
!**************************************************************
FUNCTION DOT(F1, F2, L)
  REAL F1(L), F2(L)
  DOT = 0.0
  DO I = 1, L
     DOT = DOT + F1(I)*F2(I)
  END DO
  RETURN
END
```

The main program first transfers the arrays F1 and F2 to function ANGLE. The way that we have set this up though requires this function to call another function (DOT) before completing its calculations. Thus, the sequence of transfer is as follows:

- Main program sends F1, F2, and M to ANGLE
  - Function ANGLE sends F1, F2, and M to the function DOT to compute F1•F2
  - Function DOT computes the dot product and return the answer with DOT
  - Function ANGLE then uses the variable DOT to compute the angle, which is sent back to the MAIN program

- MAIN program prints out the value of the angle

A function may call another function or any other subprogram. The only restriction is that it may not call itself. Any function that calls itself must use the RECURSIVE qualifier in the subprogram definition statement as discussed in Section 7.7 of this chapter.

Before we leave this example, you should note that we could have incorporated the code for the function DOT into the function ANGLE, thus minimizing the number of transfers. But then we could not use the function subprogram DOT, which we have already written and debugged. The goal of the modular approach to programming is to break the problem into smaller, more manageable parts. This is exactly what we have done here. Yes, we could have written the entire program as a main program, without any calls to subprograms, but then we would have to reinvent the algorithms every time we need to do vector calculations.

EXAMPLE 7.17

If we have a vector F in the X-Y-Z coordinate system, it is sometimes easier to work in a different coordinate system such as X'-Y'-Z' shown below (Z and Z' axes not shown for clarity). The new, transformed coordinate system might be more desirable due to the fact that the mathematics might be simpler. The simplest transformation is a rotation about one axis:

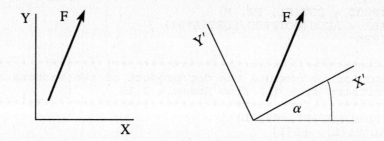

In this transformation, we have taken a rotation through an angle α about the axis perpendicular to the page. Notice that the vector has not changed position, nor has its length changed. But the *components* in the new X'-Y'-Z' coordinate system have changed. If the vector coordinates in the old X-Y-Z system were $F = (F_1, F_2, F_3)$, then we can calculate the components of the new vector as (F'_1, F'_2, F'_3) with the aid of the equation:

$$\begin{bmatrix} F'_1 \\ F'_2 \\ F'_3 \end{bmatrix} = \begin{bmatrix} \cos(\alpha) & -\sin(\alpha) & 0 \\ \sin(\alpha) & \cos(\alpha) & 0 \\ 0 & 0 & 1 \end{bmatrix} \begin{bmatrix} F_1 \\ F_2 \\ F_3 \end{bmatrix}$$

As an example, if we rotate the vector $F = (2, 4, -1)$ by $30°$, we have:

$$\begin{bmatrix} F'_1 \\ F'_2 \\ F'_3 \end{bmatrix} = \begin{bmatrix} \cos(30) & -\sin(30) & 0 \\ \sin(30) & \cos(30) & 0 \\ 0 & 0 & 1 \end{bmatrix} \begin{bmatrix} 2.0 \\ 4.0 \\ -1.0 \end{bmatrix}$$

Following the rules for multiplication of two matrices, we obtain $F' = (-0.268, 4.464, -1.0)$. The Z component has not changed but the other two components have. To carry out the desired coordinate transformation, we need to multiply the original vector by a square matrix containing the values of the trigonometric functions. This problem is somewhat different from the previous algorithm (Example 6.24), where we considered the multiplication of a L $\times$ M by a M $\times$ N matrix to produce a L $\times$ N matrix. In this example, the vector is an L $\times$ 1 matrix, or a matrix with only one row. Therefore, we can simplify the algorithm for this special case.

In the flowchart below, notice that the subroutine for the matrix multiplication has eliminated one loop from the algorithm shown in Example 6.24. We leave it as an exercise for you to show that this is correct for multiplication of a vector by a square matrix.

Flowchart

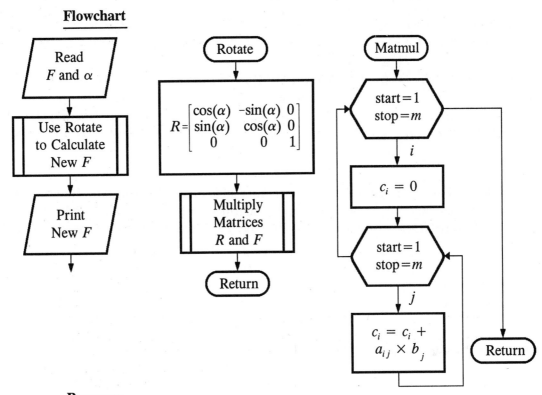

Program

```
! Main program reads in F and angle alpha, then calls the
! subroutine ROTATE to perform the transformation.
!****************************************************************
REAL F(3), F2(3)
PRINT *, 'ENTER THE VECTOR AND THE ROTATION ANGLE:'
READ *, (F(I), I = 1, 3), ANGLE
CALL ROTATE (F, ANGLE, F2)
PRINT *, 'Vector after rotation: ', (F2(I), I = 1, 3)
END
!****************************************************************
!  Subroutine rotate for a simple rotation about the Z axis
!****************************************************************
SUBROUTINE ROTATE (F, ANGLE, F2)
  REAL F(3), F2(3), R(3,3)
  ANGLE=ANGLE/57.2958
  R = 0.0
  R(1,1) = COS(ANGLE)
  R(1,2) = -SIN(ANGLE)
  R(2,1) = SIN(ANGLE)
```

(Program continues on next page)

```
      R(2,2) = COS(ANGLE)
      R(3,3) = 1.0
      CALL MATMUL( R, F, F2, 3, 3)
      RETURN
END
!**************************************************************
! Subroutine MATMUL performs multiplication of two matrices
! (A and B) and stores the result in array C.
!**************************************************************
SUBROUTINE MATMUL( A, B, C, M, N)
  REAL A(M,N), B(N), C(M)
  DO I = 1, M
     C(I) = 0.0
     DO J = 1, N
        C(I) = C(I) + A(I,J)*B(J)
     END DO
  END DO
  RETURN
END
```

The main program takes the values of F and ANGLE and sends them to the first subroutine. There the rotation matrix R is prepared, after which F is sent along with R to MATMUL for matrix multiplication. Note in the calling statement of MATMUL that we list F as the input array as input to the subroutine and the array F2 to receive the transformed matrix.

7.9 DEBUGGING TIPS

Subprograms are one of the most useful and desirable features of any programming language. They allow programmers to:

- Modularize their code to take advantage of repetitive occurrence of operations
- Break the problem down into several smaller, more manageable steps
- Allow the creation of libraries of commonly used operations and functions

By creating libraries of subprograms that you will use frequently, you indirectly test and debug the subprograms repetitively, resulting in high-quality code. You have probably heard the saying, "Don't reinvent the wheel." By using subprograms in the fashion just outlined, you avoid reinventing the wheel, and in addition, you take out the flat spots over time.

Now, we must talk about the downside of modular programming. By modularizing the code to this extent, it can become more difficult to determine where an error originates. Since we must transfer data values between a main program and one or more subprograms, there may be conflicts in how the data are defined in each (real in one but integer in the other, for example). Also, there is sometimes difficulty in locating logic errors because of the many transfers of control to one of the subprograms. This poses a special problem. For example, if your program calls a function 10 times in the main program, and 4 times in a subprogram, how do you know which of the 14 calls produces the error? Also, we tend to nest subprograms (as with the example of a subroutine calling a function). After several levels of nesting, you may need a road map to keep track of what's happening.

There are two types of errors that are unique to subprograms. These are:

- Incorrect data transfers between the calling statement and the subprogram
- Difficulty in following the multiple transfers between the main program and the subprogram(s).

Of course, other types of problems, such as syntax errors, will occur. But these will be the same as those discussed in previous chapters, and the strategies to remove them are the same. For example, an improperly declared array may produce the same message whether the error occurs in the main program or the subprogram. So we will not discuss these errors any further. What we are more concerned with here are those errors unique to subprograms. Unfortunately, your compiler will not give you much help in locating these types of errors. Therefore, we must develop our own strategies.

Incorrect Data Transfers

One common problem that occurs with subprograms is that the variables being sent to a subprogram are mismatched with the variables in the argument list of the subprogram. You may inadvertently send down too many or too few variables, the types may mismatch, or one variable may be an array while the receiving variable is not. The best way to detect these types of errors is to use a PRINT statement before the transfer to the subprogram and after the result is returned.

EXAMPLE 7.18

If the type of each variables being sent through a calling statement does not match with the corresponding variables in the subprogram argument list, a run-time error will result. We will add PRINT statements at key points to detect these types of errors.

```
!*********************************************************
! The variables X and Y in the main program will be real. But
! the variable I will be an integer. We will then send all
! three to the subroutine, which is expecting three real
! variables.
!*********************************************************
X = 2.0
Y = 3.0
I = 4
PRINT *,'In main program, X,Y,I=', X, Y, I
CALL COMPUTE ( X, Y, I)
END
!*********************************************************
! The subroutine is expecting three real variables, but it is
! being sent two reals and one integer. Thus, there is a type
! mismatch.
!*********************************************************
SUBROUTINE COMPUTE ( A, B, C)
  PRINT *, A, B, C
    :
  RETURN
END
```

When you run this program, the values in the main program are 1.000000, 2.000000, and 4. But after transfer to the subprogram, they become 1.000000, 2.000000, and 0.000000. The integer value in the main program is "lost" when we transfer it to a different type (a real variable) in the subprogram.

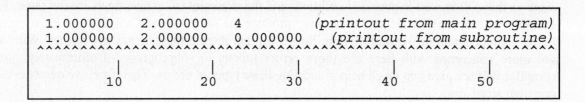

```
1.000000    2.000000    4          (printout from main program)
1.000000    2.000000    0.000000    (printout from subroutine)
^^^^^^^^^^^^^^^^^^^^^^^^^^^^^^^^^^^^^^^^^^^^^^^^^^^^^^^^^^^^^^^^^
     |           |          |          |          |
     10          20         30         40         50
```

Notice that the program compiles and runs, but that it produces the wrong answer. Therefore, these types of errors can easily creep into your programs if you are not careful. As we show in this example, we printed the data from the module that calls the subprogram, and then we print them a second time from within the subprogram to make sure that data are transferred correctly. In the printout shown, it would then be obvious that there is a problem. So use the PRINT statement liberally throughout your programs when debugging.

Tracing Transfers Between Subprograms

Tracing through a series of calls to subprograms can become confusing, because control is transferred many times and it is sometimes difficult to determine where the call came from. As a result, it may not be clear that the subprograms are being executed in the proper order. One way to handle this is to use PRINT statements that produce a path of all transfers. The messages to add to your subprograms should indicate when you enter or leave a particular module, and its name.

EXAMPLE 7.19

The following program contains three subroutines, some of which call each other. Thus, it may be difficult to follow the transfers. But by adding PRINT statements at the beginning and end of each of the subroutines, the computer will construct a record of all the transfers.

```
PRINT *,' Starting the Main program'
CALL A
CALL B
END
!*************************************************************
! First subroutine
!*************************************************************
SUBROUTINE A
  PRINT *,' Entering Subroutine A'
       ⋮
  PRINT *,' Leaving Subroutine A'
  RETURN
END
```

(Program continues on next page)

```
!******************************************************************
! Second Subroutine
!******************************************************************
SUBROUTINE B
  PRINT *,' Entering Subroutine B'
        :
  CALL C
  PRINT *,' Leaving Subroutine B'
  RETURN
END
!******************************************************************
! Third Subroutine
!******************************************************************
SUBROUTINE C
  PRINT *,' Entering Subroutine C'
        :
  PRINT *,' Leaving Subroutine C'
  RETURN
END
```

When you run this program, the following output will appear on the screen:

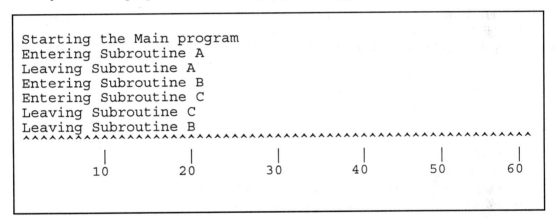

This output is useful for two reasons. First, it identifies the exact path the computer followed in executing the program. By comparing it to your algorithm or flowchart, you can determine if the transfer logic is correct. The second important feature of this type of output is that it can help identify where run-time errors are occurring. For example, suppose we had the following printout for the same program:

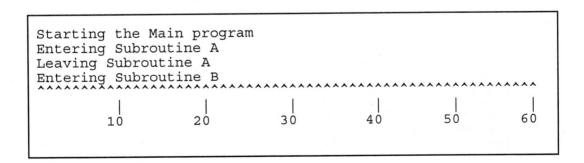

Since subroutine B never transferred to C or the error occurred in the transfer, we can conclude that there was an error in subroutine B. Without the path trace shown here, we would not know exactly where the error occurred. Consequently, it is important to isolate each of the subprograms and try to determine which of them is faulty by using PRINT statements.

Tracing Subprograms

When tracing subprograms, you need to perform two additional steps beyond those used when tracing a program without subprograms. First, the data in the argument list must be transferred to the appropriate variables in the subprogram at the beginning of the trace. Then, the second step is to trace the subprogram like any other program. After completing the trace, data returns to the appropriate variables in the calling program. The only additional information that you need are the names of the variables being passed from the calling program.

EXAMPLE 7.20

Consider the following program that uses both a function subprogram and a subroutine. You must execute three separate traces, one each for the .MAIN., the function, and the subroutine.

```
! Program to demonstrate tracing of subprograms
!*************************************************************
INTEGER A, B, C, D
READ *, A, B, C, D
PRINT *, 'Maximum value entered is', MAXI(A, B, C, D)
CALL SWAP(A, B)
CALL SWAP(C, D)
PRINT *, 'A,B,C, and D now have values ' , A, B, C, D
END
!*************************************************************
! Determine the largest value in a list of four variables
!*************************************************************
FUNCTION MAXI(X1, X2, X3, X4)
  INTEGER X1, X2, X3, X4
  MAXI = X1
  IF (X2 > MAXI) MAXI = X2
  IF (X3 > MAXI) MAXI = X3
  IF (X4 > MAXI) MAXI = X4
  RETURN
END
!*************************************************************
! Swap the values of the variables X and Y
!*************************************************************
SUBROUTINE SWAP(X, Y)
  INTEGER X, Y, TEMP
  TEMP = X
  X = Y
  Y = TEMP
  RETURN
END
```

Assume that we have 2, 1, 4, 3, as the initial input. The trace table will then consist of three separate columns, one for each of the modules:

.MAIN.		Function .MAXI.		Subroutine .SWAP.			
A	2, 2, 1	MAXI	2, 4	X↔A	2, 1	X↔C	4, 3
B	1, 1, 2	X1↔A	2	Y↔B	1, 2	Y↔D	3, 4
C	4, 4, 3	X2↔B	1	TEMP	2	TEMP	4
D	3, 3, 4	X3↔C	4				
MAXI	4	X4↔D	3				

We have introduced a new notation in tracing the function and the subroutine. Since variables are <u>local</u> to the subprogram, we show these variables with the corresponding variables from the calling routine, which may have a different name. Thus, in the function MAXI, the computer associates the local variable X1 with the variable A from the main program. Similarly, the program calls the subroutine SWAP twice. Thus, we show the local variable X with A for the first transfer, and with C for the second transfer. Follow this example closely to make sure that you understand how we traced this simple program. To help you, we show below the trace documentation:

Program Trace:

.MAIN. Trace
    READ values for A, B, C, D (2, 1, 4, 3)
    Call function MAXI(A, B, C, D) or MAXI(2, 1, 4, 3)

.MAXI. Trace
    Transfer variable names and values to dummy variables
    Assign X1 to MAXI, MAXI=2
    X2>MAXI? 1>2? false
    X3>MAXI? 4>2? true, then MAXI=4
    X4>MAXI? 3>4? false
    Return MAXI to MAIN
    Return argument values to MAIN
    A=2, B=1, C=4, D=3

.MAIN. Trace
    Print MAXI value (4)
    Call subroutine SWAP(A, B) or SWAP(2, 1)

.SWAP. Trace
   Transfer variable names and values to dummy variables
   Assign TEMP value of X, or TEMP=2
   Assign X value of Y, or X=1
   Assign Y value of TEMP, or Y=2
   Return argument values to MAIN, or X=A=1, Y=B=2
   A=1, B=2

.MAIN. Trace
   Call SWAP(C, D), or SWAP(4, 3)

.SWAP. Trace
   Transfer variable names and values to dummy variables (X=C=4 and Y=D=3)
   Assign TEMP value of X, or TEMP=4
   Assign X value of Y, or X=3
   Assign Y value of TEMP, or Y=4
   Return argument values to MAIN, or X=C=3, Y=D=4
   C=3, D=4

.MAIN. Trace
   Print A, B, C, D, or 1, 2, 3, 4

Output: The maximum value entered was 4
          A, B, C, D have values 1   2   3   4

We should point out a few things about this trace. First, each program module requires its own variable table. Second, when tracing a function, the function name is also a variable that you must consider. Finally, you must be careful that when the dummy variable in the subprogram changes, its corresponding variable in the calling routine also changes.

In summary, our advice for tracing subprograms is:

- Create a variable table for each program module.
- When tracing a function also include its name as a variable.
- Show dummy arguments and the names of the corresponding calling variables together.

As we found in previous chapters, there is no substitute for tracing a program to detect logic errors. Although tracing a program with subroutines and functions is more involved than tracing programs without subprograms, it is even more important now. Some of the ideas presented here should make that job a little bit easier.

Some commercial compilers offer a debugger included with the compiler. Many of these debuggers offer features such as automated tracking of each variable and recording control transfers between modules. If you have such a debugger available on your system, you can reproduce many of the features shown here.

Solved Problems

7.1   Locate syntax and run-time errors in each of the following program segments.

```
(a) INTEGER I,J              (b) REAL A(10)
    CALL MULT(I,J,K)             CALL SUB1(A(10))
       ⋮                            ⋮
    END                          END
    SUBROUTINE MULT(A,B,C)       SUBROUTINE SUB1(A(10))
       ⋮                         REAL A
    END                             ⋮
                                 END
(c) REAL A, B                (d) REAL IFACT
       ⋮                         I = 5
    ANS = 2.0*SUB3(A,B,1)        PRINT *, IFACT(I)
       ⋮                         END
    END                          REAL FUNCTION IFACT(I)
    REAL FUNCTION SUB3(X,Y,1)    IF(I <= 1) THEN
    REAL X, Y                        IFACT = 1
       ⋮                         ELSE
    END                              IFACT = I*IFACT(I-1)
                                 END IF
                                 RETURN
                                 END
(e) READ *, X                (f) REAL A(5), B(5)
    CALL SUBROUTINE SUB(X, ANS)  CALL SUB4(A,B)
    PRINT *, ANS                 END
    END                          SUBROUTINE SUB4(A,B,I)
    SUBROUTINE SUB(X, ANS)       REAL A(I), B(I), C(I)
    ANS = SQRT(SIN(X)**2)           ⋮
    RETURN                       END
    END
```

(a) Type mismatch since I, J, and K are integers, but A, B, and C are real (this may only produce a warning on some compilers).
(b) The array A in the subroutine is not declared, but the argument list uses an array element.
(c) Attempt to transfer a constant (1) to another constant (1).
(d) The function attempts to call itself. Must use RECURSIVE qualifier and RESULT clause to do this.
(e) Calling statement in the main program should be CALL SUB(X, ANS).
(f) Mismatch in number of arguments between CALL statement and subroutine.

7.2   Program segments generally must have unique names. Some compilers, though, will allow a subroutine, a built-in function, or a user-defined function to share the same name. In the following program, we use SIN as both an intrinsic function and a subroutine. Run the following to see how your compiler responds.

```
      X = 0.145
      PRINT *, SIN(X)              ! Here, SIN is a built-in function
      CALL SIN(X)                  ! But here, SIN is a subroutine.
      END
      SUBROUTINE SIN(X)
         PRINT *, X
         RETURN
      END
```

7.3 Write program segments to accomplish the following using either built-in functions or user-defined functions:

(a) Read in a number and determine its square root. Keep in mind that the number may be negative. (Use ABS function to handle such situations.)

(b) Read in five numbers and determine which is the largest.

(c) Examine the elements of the 100-element array A two at a time and determine which is larger. Then repeat this process for all the remaining pairs of array elements.

(d) Read in an array with 100 elements and determine the sum of all elements in the array. Print out the results in the main program.

(e) Repeat exercise (d) but for an arbitrary size array.

```
(a)  !***********************************************************
     ! We can use the SQRT built-in function, either in an
     ! assignment statement or in a PRINT statement.
     !***********************************************************
     PRINT *, 'Enter a number:'
     READ *, X
     PRINT *, 'Square root of X is:', SQRT(ABS(X))
     END
(b)  !***********************************************************
     ! The MAX function can take any number of variables in the
     ! argument list.
     !***********************************************************
     PRINT *, 'Enter five numbers:'
     READ *, A, B, C, D, E
     PRINT *, 'Largest value is:', MAX(A, B, C, D, E)
(c)  !***********************************************************
     ! We can also send individual elements of an array
     ! to the MAX built-in function.
     !***********************************************************
     REAL A(100)
     PRINT *, 'Enter A:'
     READ *, (A(I), I=1, 100)
     DO I=1, 99, 2
        PRINT *, MAX(A(I), A(I+1)), 'is larger'
     END DO
(d)  !***********************************************************
     ! We can use the SUM built-in function to compute the sum
     ! of the array. The main program reads in the list
     ! and then calls the function SUM to add the numbers.
     !***********************************************************
```

```
        REAL A(100)
        PRINT *, 'Enter A:'
        READ *, (A(I), I = 1, 100)
        PRINT *, SUM(A)
        END
(e) !*******************************************************
        ! In the previous example, we knew in advance how many
        ! array elements there were. In this example, we use a
        ! variable-sized array to handle the situation where we
        ! read in the number of elements at execution time.
        !*******************************************************
        REAL, ALLOCATABLE :: A(:)
        PRINT *, 'Number of elements?'
        READ *, N
        ALLOCATE (A(N))
        PRINT *, 'Enter A:'
        READ *, (A(I), I = 1, N)
        PRINT *, SUM(A)
        END
```

7.4   Write a main program to read in a value x. Then create a subprogram to compute the number x raised to the nth power. Then using this function, compute the repeated fraction:

$$\cfrac{1}{x^5 + \cfrac{1}{x^4 + \cfrac{1}{x^3 + \cfrac{1}{x^2 + \cfrac{1}{x^1}}}}}$$

In this example, compute the approximation for only five terms, as shown above.

```
PRINT *, 'Enter X:'
READ *, X
PRINT *, APPROX(X)
END
!***************************************************************
! After each term in the series is computed, we take the
! reciprocal of that term and add it to X**I to compute the
! next term.
!***************************************************************
FUNCTION APPROX(X)
    APPROX = 0.0
    DO I = 1, 5
        APPROX=1.0/(APPROX + POWER(X,I))
    END DO
END
!***************************************************************
! Function to compute X to the N power.
!***************************************************************
```

```
FUNCTION POWER(X, N)
   POWER = X**N
   RETURN
END
```

7.5   Write program segments to accomplish the following, using subroutines.

(a) Transfer the one-dimensional array A to a subroutine that computes a new B array such that $B(I) = A(I)$ when I is odd, but $B(I) = 2A(I)$ when I is even.

(b) Transfer the two one-dimensional arrays A and B to a subroutine that performs matrix addition. Matrix addition is defined by according to the formula $C(I) = A(I) + B(I)$. When C is computed, return it to the main program.

(c) Transfer a one-dimensional array A to a subroutine where each element of the array is multiplied by a constant K defined by $K = 1.0/A(1)$. Inside the subroutine, store the result back into A.

(d) Transfer a one-dimensional array to a subroutine that determines the maximum value in the array and then divides all elements of the array by that value.

(a)
```
!************************************************************
! We assume arrays A and B have 100 elements each. After
! reading in A, we summon CREATE where B is created.
!************************************************************
REAL A(100), B(100)                        (Assuming 100 elements)
PRINT *, 'Enter array:'
READ *, (A(I), I = 1, 100)
CALL CREATE(A, B)
PRINT *, 'The B array is:'
PRINT *, (B(I), I = 1, 100)
END
!************************************************************
! One easy way to handle the even/odd decision is to set up
! a loop with a step count of 2.
!************************************************************
SUBROUTINE CREATE(A, B)
   REAL A(100), B(100)
   DO I = 1, 99, 2
      B(I) = A(I)
      B(I+1) = 2.0*A(I+1)
   END DO
   RETURN
END
```

(b)
```
!************************************************************
! We read in A and B in the main program and send them
! to the subroutine where C is created.
!************************************************************
REAL A(100), B(100), C(100)                (Assuming 100 elements)
PRINT *, 'Enter A and B values:'
READ *, (A(I), I = 1, 100), (B(I), I = 1, 100)
CALL CREATEC(A, B, C)
PRINT *, 'C array is:'
PRINT *, (C(I), I = 1, 100)
END
```

```
!**********************************************************
! Note that all the arrays have to be declared in the
! subroutines also. C is created by adding the corresponding
! elements of A and B.
!**********************************************************
SUBROUTINE CREATEC(A, B, C)
  REAL A(100), B(100), C(100)
  C=A+B
  RETURN
END
```

(c)
```
!**********************************************************
! This program divides all elements of the array A by the
! first value. If A(1)=0.0, however, the program will stop.
! The main program is concerned with I/O of the array A and
! leaves all the details to the subroutine.
!**********************************************************
REAL A(100)                              (Assuming 100 elements)
PRINT *, 'Enter array A:'
READ *, (A(I), I = 1, 100)
DENOM=A(1)
IF(DENOM /= 0.0) THEN
    CALL DIVIDE(A, DENOM)
    PRINT *, 'Normalized array is:'
    PRINT *, (A(I), I = 1, 100)
ELSE
    STOP 'ERROR IN A(1)'
END IF
END
!**********************************************************
! This subroutine divides all elements of A by DENOM=A(1).
!**********************************************************
SUBROUTINE DIVIDE(A, DENOM)
  REAL A(100)
  A = A/DENOM
END
```

(d)
```
!**********************************************************
! This program normalizes the array by first searching
! through A and finding the largest value. Then it divides
! all the elements by this maximum value. The main is
! primarily concerned with I/O of the array A. The details
! of the normalization are done in the subroutine.
!**********************************************************
REAL A(100)                              (Assuming 100 elements)
PRINT *,'Enter A array:'
READ *, (A(I), I = 1, 100)
CALL NORMAL(A)
PRINT *, 'A array after normalization is:'
PRINT *, (A(I), I = 1, 100)
END
!**********************************************************
! The MAXVAL function determines the maximum value within the
! array A. Once this is determined, each element of A is
! divided (or normalized) by the maximum value.
!**********************************************************
SUBROUTINE NORMAL(A)
```

```
      REAL A(100), MAX
      MAX = MAXVAL(A)
      A=A/MAX
      RETURN
END
```

7.6   Find the errors in the following code designed to print the sum of the elements in array A and the sum of the elements in array B.

```
      REAL, DIMENSION(10) :: A, B
      PRINT *, 'Enter A and B:'
      READ *, (A(I), I = 1, 10), (B(I), I = 1, 10)
      PRINT *, SUM(A), SUM(B)
END
FUNCTION SUM(MAT)
   REAL MAT(N)
   DO I = 1, N
      SUM = SUM + MAT(I)
   END DO
   RETURN
END
```

Solution: We start by tracing the program. Let's assign values for A and B such as:

A	1.0	2.0	3.0	4.0	5.0	6.0	7.0	8.0	9.0	10.0
B	2.0	4.0	6.0	7.0	8.0	9.0	2.0	6.0	7.0	9.0

<u>Program Trace:</u>

.MAIN. Trace:
   READ in the 10 values of the arrays A and B
   Transfer values of A to function SUM

.SUM. Trace:
   The array A is assigned to the local array MAT

At this point, one of the errors has occurred. Notice that we cannot set up the array MAT in the function since the value of N is undefined and assumed to be 0 by the computer. So, let's change N to 10 and restart the trace.

.MAIN. Trace:
   READ in the ten values of the arrays A and B
   Transfer values of A to function SUM

.SUM. Trace:
   The array A is assigned to the local array MAT
   Begin the loop
   I=1, SUM = 0.0 + A(1)=1.0

I=2, SUM = 1.0 + A(2)=3.0

$\vdots$

I=10, SUM = 45.0 + A(10)=55.0
Return value of 55.0 to .MAIN.

.MAIN. Trace:
Print out value of SUM(A), which is 55.0
Transfer values of B to function SUM

.SUM Trace:
The array B is assigned to the local array MAT
Begin the loop
I=1, SUM+SUM+B(1)=55.0+2.0=57.0

When we go to compute the sum of the second array B, an error occurs in the function. Note that when we add the first element of MAT(1), which is equivalent to B(1), the old value of SUM is not reset. Thus, the value of SUM=55.0 was left over from the first use of the function for the array A. To solve this problem, we should add an initialization statement, SUM=0.0, before the DO loop.

7.7 Trace through the following program segments and predict their output:

(a)
```
REAL F
Y = 2.0
PRINT*, F(F(F(Y)))
STOP
END
FUNCTION F(X)
  F = X**2
  RETURN
END
```

(b)
```
DATA A/1.0/
DATA B/2.0/
CALL SUB(A, B, C)
PRINT*, A, B, C
END
SUBROUTINE SUB(X, Y, Z)
  X = 2.0*X*Y
  Y = -Y
  Z = X/Y
  RETURN
END
```

(a) Program Trace:
.MAIN. Trace:
Y = 2.0
Compute F(2.0)

.F. Trace:
X = 2.0
F = X**2= 4.0
Return value of 4.0 to MAIN

.MAIN. Trace:
Compute F(4)

.F. Trace:

(b) Program Trace:
.MAIN. Trace:
DATA: A=1.0, B=2.0
Print A, B, C (1.0, 2.0, −2.0)
Transfer to SUB

.SUB. trace:
X = 2.0*X*Y = 4.0
Y = −Y = −2.0
Z = X/Y = −2.0
Return to .MAIN.

.MAIN. Trace:
Print values of A, B, C

X = 4.0
F = X**2 = 16.0   Variable Listing:
Return value of 16.0 to MAIN   .MAIN.
                                                 A: 1.0, 4.0
.MAIN. Trace: B: 2.0, −2.0
  Compute F(16)   C: −2.0

.F. Trace: .SUB.
  X = 16.0   A⇔X: 1.0, 4.0
  F = X**2 = 256.0   B⇔Y: 2.0, −2.0
  Return value of 256.0 to MAIN   C⇔Z: −2.0

Output: Output:
     256.0000   4.00000 −2.00000 −2.00000

7.8   One of the most important reasons that we write subprograms is to create libraries of
        common mathematical operations. Once we have created these libraries, we can then
        extract any of the subprograms stored there and use them in other programs, thereby
        greatly reducing our programming efforts. But to be effective, each of the subprograms
        should execute a single task. Therefore, libraries tend to be large, with several hundred
        common functions. To help you begin creating your own personalized library, write
        subprograms to perform the following simple mathematical tasks:

(a) FACT   computes the factorial ($n! = n(n-1)$. . .$(2)(1)$) for any positive integer.
(b) SUMLIS   computes the sum of all elements in a list of arbitrary size.
(c) SUMCOL   computes the sum of all elements in column I of a table with m rows and
               n columns.
(d) MAXSRC   searches for the maximum value in a list of arbitrary size.
(e) DERIV   calculates a numerical approximation to the derivative of a function $f(x)$ at
               a point x. One approximation (known as the central difference method) is
               given by the formula:

$$DERIV \approx \frac{f(x + \Delta x) - f(x - \Delta x)}{2 \Delta x}$$

               where x is the point of evaluation of the derivative, Δx is a small number,
               and $f(x)$ is the function at point x. The accuracy of the approximation
               improves as Δx becomes smaller.
(f) SWITCH   switches two numbers.
(g) MATADD   adds two matrices element by element.
(h) SORT   sorts a one-dimensional array in ascending order.

(a) !***
     ! The factorial of N<0 is not defined, so we must check for

```
      ! this special case first. The STOP 'ERROR' command will
      ! terminate execution and print an error message. To compute
      ! the factorial of N, we first set FACT=1.0 and then multiply
      ! FACT by all integers between 2 and N.
      !*****************************************************************
      FUNCTION FACT(N)
        IF(N < 0) STOP 'ERROR'
        FACT = 1.0
        DO I = 2, N
           FACT = FACT * I
        END DO
        RETURN
      END
(b) !*****************************************************************
      ! We transfer the list X and the number of items, N. N sets
      ! up the variable-sized array and also controls the loop to
      ! add the items in the list. The result is returned in the
      ! variable SUMLIS.
      !*****************************************************************
      FUNCTION SUMLIS(X, N)
        REAL X(N)
        SUMLIS = 0.0
        DO I = 1, N
          SUMLIS = SUMLIS + X(I)
        END DO
        RETURN
      END
(c) !*****************************************************************
      ! The function assumes a table with M rows and N columns.
      ! The variable J is the column that we wish to sum. The
      ! sum of that column is returned via SUMCOL.
      !*****************************************************************
      FUNCTION SUMCOL(X, J, M, N)
        REAL X(M, N)
        SUMCOL = SUM(X(:,J))
        RETURN
      END
(d) !*****************************************************************
      ! The list to be searched, X, has N elements. We can use
      ! use the array function MAXVAL to search the array and
      ! find the maximum value.
      !*****************************************************************
      REAL FUNCTION MAXSRC(X, N)
        REAL X(N)
        MAXSRC = MAXVAL(X)
        RETURN
      END
(e) !*****************************************************************
      ! We send X and DELTAX to the function to compute the
      ! derivative at X. DELTAX should be a very small value.
      ! We must also supply a function for F(X).
      !*****************************************************************
      FUNCTION DERIV(X, DELTAX)
        DERIV = (F(X+DELTAX)-F(X-DELTAX))/(2.0*DELTAX)
        RETURN
```

```
     END
     !***********************************************************
     ! You must also fill in the equation for F(X).
     !***********************************************************
     REAL FUNCTION F(X)
        F = .......            (Reader fills in the function to be evaluated here)
        RETURN
     END
(f)  !***********************************************************
     ! To switch two numbers, we must set up a dummy variable
     ! TEMP. Once we store A in TEMP, we free up A to receive
     ! the value of B. Then B is free to receive the value in TEMP
     !***********************************************************
     SUBROUTINE SWITCH(A, B)
        TEMP = A
        A = B
        B = TEMP
        RETURN
     END
(g)  !***********************************************************
     ! All three arrays must be declared with the same size: M
     ! rows and N columns. Both M and N are sent down at execution
     ! time. C is then generated by adding A and B. A simpler way
     ! to do this is to simply write C=A+B without the loops. But
     ! we did it the long way to illustrate how the indices change
     ! and to show the correspondence between the elements being
     ! added.
     !***********************************************************
     SUBROUTINE MATADD(A, B, C, M, N)
        REAL A(M, N), B(M, N), C(M, N)
        DO I = 1, M
           DO J = 1, N
              C(I, J) = A(I, J) + B(I, J)
           END DO
        END DO
        RETURN
     END
(h)  !***********************************************************
     ! See Example 6.9 for a discussion of a sorting method. We
     ! have modified that main program by converting the array
     ! into a variable-sized array. Also, we perform the
     ! switching by calling the subroutine SWITCH from (f) above.
     !***********************************************************
     SUBROUTINE SORT(X, N)
        REAL X(N)
        DO L = 1, N-1
           BIG = X(L)
           DO I = L, N
              IF(X(I) > BIG) THEN
                 CALL SWITCH(X(I), X(L))
                 BIG=X(L)
              END IF
           END DO
        END DO
     END
```

7.9   Write a subroutine that computes the average *avg*, the variance *var,* and the standard deviation *std* of a list of numbers using the formulas shown below. Use a main program to read in the data, and separate subprograms to perform the computations.

$$avg = \bar{x} = \frac{\displaystyle\sum_{i=1}^{i=n} x_i}{n}$$

$$var = \sigma^2 = \frac{\displaystyle\sum_{i=1}^{i=n} (avg - x_i)^2}{(n-1)}$$

$$std = \sigma = \sqrt{\sigma^2}$$

Use a main program to read in the data, and the subprogram to perform the computations.

```
!************************************************************
! Main program to read in all X values
!************************************************************
REAL X(1000)
PRINT *, 'How many data points?'
READ *, N
PRINT *, 'Enter data points:'
READ *, (X(I), I = 1, N)
CALL STAT(X, N, AVG, VAR, STD)
PRINT *, 'Avg= ', AVG, 'Var= ', VAR, 'Std Dev= ', STD
END
!************************************************************
! Subroutine STAT to compute statistics of a group of data.
! We calculate the average first, because we need it to compute
! the variance. Then we compute the standard deviation.
!************************************************************

SUBROUTINE STAT(X, N, AVG, VAR, STD)
   REAL X(N)
   AVG = SUM(X)/N
!************************************************************
! Once the AVG is known, we can use it to compute the variance
!************************************************************
   TOT=SUM((AVG-X)**2)
   VAR = TOT/(N-1)
!************************************************************
! The standard deviation is just the square root of the variance
!************************************************************
   STD = SQRT(VAR)
   RETURN
END
```

7.10 The *determinant of a matrix A*, indicated by $|A|$, is a frequent calculation needed in many fields. For a 3×3 matrix, the determinant is given by:

$$\begin{vmatrix} a_{11} & a_{12} & a_{13} \\ a_{21} & a_{22} & a_{23} \\ a_{31} & a_{32} & a_{33} \end{vmatrix} = a_{11}(a_{22}a_{33} - a_{23}a_{32}) - a_{12}(a_{21}a_{33} - a_{23}a_{31}) + a_{13}(a_{21}a_{32} - a_{22}a_{31})$$

Write a function subprogram to calculate the determinant of a 3×3 matrix.

```
!***************************************************************
! We set up the array as a fixed, not a variable size.
!***************************************************************
REAL A(3, 3)
PRINT *, 'Enter the array A by rows:'
READ *, ((A(I,J), J=1,3), I=1,3)
PRINT *, 'Determinant of A is: ', DET(A)
END
!***************************************************************
! The determinant of a 3 x 3 matrix is rather simple, so we can
! evaluate it in a single assignment statement. Note that the
! array size is fixed, and that the value of the determinant of
! A is returned via DET. For matrices larger than 3 x 3, the
! mathematical definition is more complicated and we cannot use
! this function.
!***************************************************************
FUNCTION DET(A)
  REAL A(3,3)
  DET = A(1,1)*(A(2,2)*A(3,3)-A(2,3)*A(3,2))- &
        A(1,2)*(A(2,1)*A(3,3)-A(2,3)*A(3,1))+ &
        A(1,3)*(A(2,1)*A(3,2)-A(2,2)*A(3,1))
  RETURN
END
```

7.11 One of the best-known methods for solving a system of simultaneous equations (called Cramer's rule) uses the determinant. Assume that we have the following series of equations:

$$a_{11}x_1 + a_{12}x_2 + a_{13}x_3 = b_1$$
$$a_{21}x_1 + a_{22}x_2 + a_{23}x_3 = b_2$$
$$a_{31}x_1 + a_{32}x_2 + a_{33}x_3 = b_3$$

where the a_{ij} and b_i are constants, and x_i are the unknowns. An example of such a system of equations would be:

$$7x_1 \;+\; 2x_2 \;+\; 3x_3 \;=\; 45$$

$$-1x_1 \;+\; 4x_2 \;+\; 8x_3 \;=\; 44$$

$$2x_1 \;-\; 3x_2 \;+\; 2x_3 \;=\; 28$$

with a solution $x_1=4$, $x_2=-2$, and $x_3=7$. We can solve these equations by using determinants as defined in the previous solved problem (7.10).

$$x_1 = \frac{\begin{vmatrix} b_1 & a_{12} & a_{13} \\ b_2 & a_{22} & a_{23} \\ b_3 & a_{32} & a_{33} \end{vmatrix}}{\begin{vmatrix} a_{11} & a_{12} & a_{13} \\ a_{21} & a_{22} & a_{23} \\ a_{31} & a_{32} & a_{33} \end{vmatrix}} \quad x_2 = \frac{\begin{vmatrix} a_{11} & b_1 & a_{13} \\ a_{21} & b_2 & a_{23} \\ a_{31} & b_3 & a_{33} \end{vmatrix}}{\begin{vmatrix} a_{11} & a_{12} & a_{13} \\ a_{21} & a_{22} & a_{23} \\ a_{31} & a_{32} & a_{33} \end{vmatrix}} \quad x_3 = \frac{\begin{vmatrix} a_{11} & a_{12} & b_1 \\ a_{21} & a_{22} & b_2 \\ a_{31} & a_{32} & b_3 \end{vmatrix}}{\begin{vmatrix} a_{11} & a_{12} & a_{13} \\ a_{21} & a_{22} & a_{23} \\ a_{31} & a_{32} & a_{33} \end{vmatrix}}$$

Notice that the denominator in all three cases is the same (determinant of A or $|A|$), where A is the square matrix formed by the coefficients of the unknowns. The numerators consist of $|A'|$, where the matrix A' is formed by replacing one of the columns of A by the vector B, which is an array of the constants in the equations to be solved.

Write a main program that reads in the coefficient matrix A and the constant vector B to form the matrices A'. Then use the function DET from solved problem 7.10 to solve for the three unknowns.

```
! Main program to read in the coefficients and the equation
! constants into A and B respectively
!*************************************************************
REAL A(3, 3), X(3), B(3)
DO I = 1, 3
   PRINT *,'Enter coefficients and constant for eq',I
   READ *, (A(I, J), J = 1, 3), B(I)
END DO
CALL CRAMER(A, X, B)
PRINT *, 'The unknowns are:', (X(I), I = 1,3)
END

!*************************************************************
! Cramer forms the matrices A1, A2, and A3 (A' in the problem
! statement) by successively substituting the vector B into the
! first, second, and third column of A. The function DET is then
! used to compute the determinant of each of these matrices to
! solve for the unknowns.
!*************************************************************
SUBROUTINE CRAMER(A, X, B)
   REAL A(3,3), X(3), B(3), A1(3,3), A2(3,3), A3(3,3)
!*************************************************************
! Since the denominator is the same, calculate that first
```

```
!*************************************************************
  DENOM = DET(A)
!*************************************************************
! Loop computes the matrices A1, A2, and A3 in which the B
! vector substitutes into 1st, 2nd, and 3rd column of A.
!*************************************************************
  A1 = A
  A2 = A
  A3 = A
  DO I = 1, 3
     A1(I, 1) = B(I)
     A2(I, 2) = B(I)
     A3(I, 3) = B(I)
  END DO
!*************************************************************
! Once A1, A2, and A3 are formed, we take the determinant of
! each and divide by DET(A) to obtain the unknowns - X(1), X(2),
! and X(3). The determinant function DET is given in solved
! problem 7.10 and must be included.
!*************************************************************
  X(1) = DET(A1)/DENOM
  X(2) = DET(A2)/DENOM
  X(3) = DET(A3)/DENOM
RETURN
END
```

7.12 Mesh analysis is often used for solving complex resistor networks to calculate the currents flowing in different legs of an electrical circuit. Consider the following network with a single voltage source and eight resistors arranged as shown:

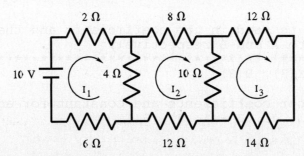

Because the voltage drop around each loop must be zero, it can be shown that the following set of simultaneous equations describes the current flow in each leg:

$$
\begin{aligned}
12 I_1 \;-\; 4 I_2 \qquad\qquad &= 10 \\
-4 I_1 \;+\; 34 I_2 \;-\; 10 I_3 &= 0 \\
-\; 10 I_2 \;+\; 36 I_3 &= 0
\end{aligned}
$$

Use the subprogram for Cramer's method from the previous problem to solve for the current I_j in each of the three legs of the circuit.

Solution: The coefficient matrix A and the constant vector B are given by:

$$A = \begin{bmatrix} 12 & -4 & 0 \\ -4 & 34 & -10 \\ 0 & -10 & 36 \end{bmatrix} \qquad B = \begin{bmatrix} 10 \\ 0 \\ 0 \end{bmatrix}$$

When you run the program given in the previous problem (7.11), enter the values for A by rows (12, −4, 0, etc.) along with the values for B (10, 0, 0). The results will be approximately $I(1) = 0.8705$, $I(2) = 0.1115$, and $I(3) = 0.03097$.

7.13   One of the most famous series in mathematics is named in honor of Leonardo Fibonacci (b.1175). This series seems to describe many different phenomena in nature and has fascinated scientists for almost 800 years. The series is a simple one:

$$1 \quad 1 \quad 2 \quad 3 \quad 5 \quad 8 \quad 13 \quad 21 \quad 34 \quad 55 \ \ldots$$

Notice that any term in the series is simply the sum of the two previous terms, or $T_n = T_{n-1} + T_{n-2}$. An interesting feature of this series is that the determinant of a matrix made from consecutive terms in this series is always zero. For example, look at the determinant of the matrix made from the first nine terms, or the determinant of the matrix made from later terms in the series; the result is always the same:

$$\begin{vmatrix} 1 & 1 & 2 \\ 3 & 5 & 8 \\ 13 & 21 & 34 \end{vmatrix} = 0 \qquad \begin{vmatrix} 13 & 21 & 34 \\ 55 & 89 & 144 \\ 233 & 377 & 610 \end{vmatrix} = 0$$

This can be proven by a mathematical analysis of the sequence of terms. But it is also instructive for you to try to "prove" this numerically by substituting the numbers and calculating the determinant. This does not rigorously prove the hypothesis but it does help to support it. Sometimes, a rigorous mathematical proof does not exist for a particular problem, and you will have to try this numerical approach.

In this problem you are to examine the first ten matrices formed in this way and then evaluate the determinant. Here is the approach that you should use:

(a)   Generate the first 50 terms in the Fibonacci series and store them in an array.
(b)   Create a matrix of terms in the series using the first through the ninth terms.
(c)   Calculate the determinant of the matrix thus formed.
(d)   Repeat (b) and (c) nine times, but each time form the matrix with the second through the tenth terms in the series, then the third through the eleventh, and so forth.
(e)   If any of the determinants are not zero, print out an appropriate message.

(f) Take special care that the determinant may not be *exactly* equal to zero because of round-off errors associated with real numbers. It is better to use real numbers for this problem because real numbers allow you to store larger values.

```
!*****************************************************************
! Create the first 50 terms in the series and store in the one-
! dimensional array FIB
!*****************************************************************
REAL FIB(50), A(3,3)
FIB(1) = 1.0
FIB(2) = 1.0
DO I = 3, 50
   FIB(I) = FIB(I-1) + FIB(I-2)
END DO
!*****************************************************************
! The outer loop executes 10 times, each time setting the value
! of INDEX and performing the following instructions:
!         1) form the matrix starting with the INDEX'th term
!         2) calculate the determinant of the matrix formed
!         3) if the determinant is less than 0.001, then the
!            program concludes that the identity holds.
!*****************************************************************
DO INDEX = 1, 10
   DO I = 1, 3
      DO J = 1, 3
         A(I, J) = FIB(J+(I-1)*3+INDEX-1)
      END DO
   END DO
   IF(ABS(DET(A)) < 0.001) THEN
      PRINT *, 'Test #', INDEX, 'OK'
   ELSE
      PRINT *, 'Test #', INDEX, 'Invalid'
   END IF
END DO
END
!*****************************************************************
! See solved problem 7.10 for the DET function
!*****************************************************************
```

7.14 We presented a program (Example 7.17) for calculating the components of a vector after a rotation about the z axis. There are many times, however, where we need to apply more complex rotations. Therefore, in this problem, you are to rewrite the subprogram given in Example 7.13 to allow a rotation about *any* axis. The equations for the rotation matrix are (r_x, r_y, r_z = matrix for rotation about the x, y, and z axes, respectively):

$$r_x = \begin{bmatrix} 1 & 0 & 0 \\ \cos(\alpha) & -\sin(\alpha) & 0 \\ \sin(\alpha) & \cos(\alpha) & 1 \end{bmatrix} \quad r_y = \begin{bmatrix} \cos(\alpha) & 0 & \sin(\alpha) \\ 0 & 1 & 0 \\ -\sin(\alpha) & 0 & \cos(\alpha) \end{bmatrix} \quad r_z = \begin{bmatrix} \cos(\alpha) & -\sin(\alpha) & 0 \\ \sin(\alpha) & \cos(\alpha) & 0 \\ 0 & 0 & 1 \end{bmatrix}$$

Rewrite the program and subprogram from Example 7.13 so that you may take three rotations about each of the axes in succession. Use an initial vector of (2.5, 3.0, 0.0) and rotate it 25° about x, $-45°$ about y, and 90° about z. To double check your program, take the new vector that you get from these calculations and put it back into the program. This time, however, rotate the vector in the reverse direction $(-90°$ about z, 45° about y, and $-25°$ about x). Did you get the original vector back?

```
!****************************************************************
! We define three rotation matrices, RX, RY, and RZ, for each
! rotation desired. Then we will send the vector A to the
! subroutine MATMUL along with RX for the first transformation
! (answer stored back into A). Then we will send the vector A
! down to MATMUL a second time with RY to compute the effect of
! the second rotation. Finally, we send A down to MATMUL with
! RZ for the third transformation. The rotation matrices are
! evaluated in the subroutine ROTATE, which we will use twice
! — once for the forward transformations, once for the reverse
! transformations.
!****************************************************************
REAL A(3), A2(3), A3(3), A4(3), RX(3,3), RY(3,3), RZ(3,3)
PARAMETER (RAD=57.295827)
PRINT *, 'Enter vector components'
READ *, (A(I), I = 1,3)
PRINT *, 'Enter rotations about x, y, z axes:'
READ *, ANGLEX, ANGLEY, ANGLEZ
ANGLEX=ANGLEX/RAD
ANGLEY=ANGLEY/RAD
ANGLEZ=ANGLEZ/RAD
!****************************************************************
! Once the rotation angles have been read in, compute the
! components of the three rotation matrices.
!****************************************************************
CALL ROTATE(RX, RY, RZ, ANGLEX, ANGLEY, ANGLEZ)
!****************************************************************
! Send A down to MATMUL with RX for the first transformation.
! Then send the modified A to MATMUL with RY for the
! second transformation. Finally, send the twice modified A
! down to MATMUL with RZ for the third transformation.
!****************************************************************
CALL MATMUL(RX, A, A2, 3, 3)
CALL MATMUL(RY, A2, A3, 3, 3)
CALL MATMUL(RZ, A3, A4, 3, 3)
PRINT *, 'After 3 rotations, the vector is:'
PRINT *, (A4(I), I = 1, 3)
!****************************************************************
! Now, reverse the rotations and repeat the calculations
!****************************************************************
CALL ROTATE(RX, RY, RZ, -ANGLEX, -ANGLEY, -ANGLEZ)
CALL MATMUL(RZ, A4, A3, 3, 3)
CALL MATMUL(RY, A3, A2, 3, 3)
CALL MATMUL(RX, A2, A, 3, 3)
PRINT *, 'After reversing, the vector is:'
PRINT *, (A(I), I = 1, 3)
END
!****************************************************************
! Subroutine to compute the rotation matrices
```

```
!*************************************************************
SUBROUTINE ROTATE(RX, RY, RZ, ANGLEX, ANGLEY, ANGLEZ)
   REAL RX(3, 3), RY(3, 3), RZ(3, 3)
   RX = 0.0
   RY = 0.0
   RZ = 0.0
   RX(1,1) = 1.0
   RX(2,1) = COS(ANGLEX)
   RX(2,2) = -SIN(ANGLEX)
   RX(3,1) = SIN(ANGLEX)
   RX(3,2) = COS(ANGLEX)
   RX(3,3) = 1.0
   RY(1,1) = COS(ANGLEY)
   RY(1,3) = SIN(ANGLEY)
   RY(2,2) = 1.0
   RY(3,1) = -SIN(ANGLEY)
   RY(3,3) = COS(ANGLEY)
   RZ(1,1) = COS(ANGLEZ)
   RZ(1,2) = -SIN(ANGLEZ)
   RZ(2,1) = SIN(ANGLEZ)
   RZ(2,2) = COS(ANGLEZ)
   RZ(3,3) = 1.0
   RETURN
END
```

7.15 Write a function or a subroutine that computes a power function such as $y = x^n$ using the following recursive process:

$$x^n = (x)(x^{n-1})$$
$$x^0 = 0$$

As an example, consider this process for evaluating 4^3:

$$4^3 = (4)(4^2)$$
$$4^2 = (4)(4^1)$$
$$4^1 = (4)(4^0)$$
$$4^0 = 1$$

We begin the evaluation process from the top down until we reach a value raised to the 0 power. Then, we reverse the process to compute the result:

$$4^3 = (4)(4^2) = (4)(16) = 64$$
$$4^2 = (4)(4^1) = (4)(4) = 16$$
$$4^1 = (4)(4^0) = (4)(1) = 4$$
$$4^0 = 1 \qquad\qquad = 1$$

```
!*************************************************************
! In the main program, we read in the number and the exponent.
! Then, we call the recursive function. Note that we answer will
! be returned in the same way as nonrecursive functions.
```

```
!**************************************************************
PRINT *, 'Enter number and exponent:'
READ *, X, N
ANSWER = POWER(X, N)
PRINT *, 'X ** N = ', ANSWER
END
!**************************************************************
! To use a recursive function, we must set up a RESULT clause
! containing the answer. In this example, the variable XN
! contains the final result. Notice that each time the recursive
! function is called N is decreased by 1 until N equals 0.
!**************************************************************
RECURSIVE FUNCTION POWER(X, N)   RESULT(XN)
  IF(N == 0) THEN
    XN = 1.0
  ELSE
    XN = X * POWER(X, N-1)
  END IF
  RETURN
END
```

Supplementary Problems

7.16 Locate syntax and run-time errors in each of the following program segments:

(a)
```
READ *, A
CALL SUB(A)
   ⋮
END
REAL SUBROUTINE SUB(A)
PRINT *, A
RETURN
END
```

(b)
```
CALL JACK(A, B)
END
REAL FUNCTION JACK(A, B)
JACK = A*B
RETURN
END
```

(c)
```
COMMON Y
X = 4.0
CALL SUB(X)
END
SUBROUTINE SUB(X)
COMMON X
PRINT *, X
RETURN
END
```

(d)
```
REAL F, X, Y, Z
READ *, X, Y, Z, I
   ⋮
PRINT *, F(X, Y, Z, I)
END
FUNCTION F(X, Y, I)
F = SIN(X)*EXP(-Z*Y)**I
RETURN
END
```

(e)
```
DOUBLE PRECISION A, B
CALL SUB3(A, B)
   ⋮
END
SUBROUTINE SUB3(A, B)
   ⋮
RETURN
END
```

(f)
```
INTEGER DOT, A(3), B(3)
DATA A/1,2,3/, B/1,2,6/
C=DOT(A,B)
   ⋮
END
FUNCTION DOT(A, B)
INTEGER A(3), B(3)
DOT = ...
END
```

7.17 Variable dimensioning of arrays in a subprogram is really a misnomer. The storage location has been set up in the calling module and this can't change, no matter what you use to dimension the array in the subprogram. Run these two examples to see how your compiler handles variable-sized arrays.

```
REAL A(1)                          REAL A(100)
A(1) = 100                         DO I = 1, 100
CALL SUB1(A,1)                        A(I) = I
END                                END DO
SUBROUTINE SUB1(A,I)               CALL SUB1(A, 100)
   REAL A(I)                       END
   PRINT *, A                      SUBROUTINE SUB1(A, I)
   RETURN                             REAL A(I)
END                                   PRINT *, (A(J), J=1,100)
                                      RETURN
                                   END
```

7.18 Write program segments to accomplish the following, using either built-in functions or user-defined functions.

(a) Read in a two-dimensional array of size N × M and compute the sum of all elements.
(b) Read in a two-dimensional array of size N × M and compute the sum of any row I.
(c) Read in an M × N two-dimensional array. Then compute and print the sum of each row.
(d) Read in a one-dimensional array A of size N, a two-dimensional array Y of size M × N (M > N), and compute the elements of the new array Z defined by Z(I)=A(I)/Y(M−N, I)

7.19 Write a function that computes the factorial ($i!$) of a number i. Then use that function in a second subprogram to compute the series shown below.

$$\sum_{i=1}^{i=n} (-1)^{(i+1)} \frac{1}{i!}$$

The main program should read in the value of n, then call the subprograms to compute the series for the appropriate number of terms, and print out the sum of the series terms. All computations should be done in the function subprograms.

7.20 Write program segments to accomplish the following using subroutines.

(a) Read in a one-dimensional array of arbitrary size (up to 1000 elements) and send it to a subroutine that searches for the largest number. Then have the subroutine report how many elements are larger than 0.5 times the maximum value.
(b) Compute the average *xavg* of an array X and then determine the deviation d of each

element of X from the average according to the formula $d_i = X_i - xavg$.

(c) The dot product ($\bullet$) of two vectors a and b (each containing three elements) is defined by $a \bullet b = a_1 b_1 + a_2 b_2 + a_3 b_3$. Write a function to implement the dot product. Then write a subroutine to compute the magnitude of $(a \bullet b)(b \bullet d)(b \bullet c)$.

(d) The cross product ($\otimes$) of two vectors a and b (each containing three elements) is defined by $c = a \otimes b = [(a_2 b_3 - a_3 b_2), (a_3 b_1 - a_1 b_3), (a_1 b_2 - a_2 b_1)]$. Note that c is a vector whose components are given by the terms in parentheses. Write a subroutine to compute the cross product of two vectors a and b.

(e) Use the function for the dot product and the subroutine for the cross product to verify the identity $(a \otimes b) \bullet (c \otimes d) = (a \bullet b)(b \bullet d)(b \bullet c)$.

7.21 The following program was supposed to print out the elements of an array in a sequential manner (that is, A(1), A(2), A(3), . . ., A(10)). What went wrong?

```
REAL A(10)
PRINT *, 'Enter the array A:'
READ *, (A(I), I = 1, 10)
DO INDEX = 1, 10
   CALL TEST(A)
END DO
END
SUBROUTINE TEST(A)
   DATA I/1/
   PRINT *, A(I)
   I=I+1
   RETURN
END
```

7.22 One of the most important reasons that we write subprograms is that we can create libraries of common mathematical operations. Once we have created these libraries, we can then use any of the subprograms stored there in other programs and greatly reduce our programming efforts. But to be effective, each of the subprograms should execute only a single task or a few very closely related tasks. Therefore, libraries tend to be large, with several hundred common functions. To help you begin creating your own personalized library, write subprograms to perform the following simple mathematical tasks:

(a) TABSRC   searches a table for the maximum value
(b) ROWSUM   sums all elements in the ith row in a table
(c) TABSUM   sums all elements in a table
(d) VECADD   adds two vectors
(e) MATMUL   multiplies two matrices
(f) TRANSP   generates the transpose of a matrix. A transpose is generated by placing A(I, J) into B(J, I)
(g) VECLEN   calculates the length of a vector (see Example 7.12 for definitions)

7.23 Write a program to approximate the value of the infinite series for $R(x)$ given by

$$R(x) = J_0(x) + \frac{J_0(x^2)}{2!} + \frac{J_0(x^3)}{3!} + \cdots$$

where J_0 is known as the zero-order Bessel function defined by

$$J_0(x) = 1 - \frac{x^2}{2^2} + \frac{x^4}{2^2 \, 4^2} - \frac{x^6}{2^2 \, 4^2 \, 6^2} + \cdots$$

When computing the Bessel function, terminate the series when the absolute value of any new term changes the approximation by no more than 0.1%. In a similar way, terminate the approximation for $R(x)$ when the absolute value of any new term adds no more than 0.1% to the series total.

7.24 The functions presented in this chapter for finding the maximum value (Solved Problems 7.8d and Supplementary Problem 7.22a) are only useful for examining a list or table of discrete data values. They cannot be used to find the maximum value of a continuous function. For such a function, we must use a different approach. Write a program that utilizes the following algorithm:

(a) Read in a starting point x, a step size Δx, and an allowable error Φ
(b) Start the search by calculating $f(x)$ and $f(x+\Delta x)$
(c) If $f(x) < f(x+\Delta x)$, then increase x by Δx and repeat step (b)
(d) Otherwise, reduce the step size Δx by half and repeat step (b)
(e) Repeat until $|f(x) - f(x+\Delta x)| < \Phi$.
(f) Report $(x+x+\Delta x)/2$ as the position of the maximum value of the function.

Apply the above algorithm to the function $y(x) = \sin(x)e^{-x}$. Start your search at $x=0.7$ with an initial $\Delta x=0.1$ with Φ to 0.001.

7.25 Write a recursive function or subroutine to compute the sum of integers between 1 and N.

Answers to Selected Supplementary Problems

7.16 (a) Typing (REAL) is not used with subroutines.
(b) Calling statements are used with subroutines, not functions.
(c) The variable X is sent to the subroutine via both the COMMON statement and the argument list. This is not allowed.
(d) There is a mismatch in the number of arguments in the calling statement and the FUNCTION statement.

(e) A and B must be declared in the subroutine as double precision.

(f) DOT is declared as an integer variable in the main program. Therefore, the function should be declared as an integer also.

7.18 (a)
```
!********************************************************
! Use the main program to read in the two-dimensional array
! and the number of columns (M) and rows (N).
!********************************************************
REAL, DIMENSION(:), ALLOCATABLE :: A
PRINT *, 'Enter size of array (no more than 100 x 100):'
READ *, M, N
ALLOCATE (A(M,N))
PRINT *, 'Enter the array by rows:'
READ *, ((A(I, J), J = 1, M), I = 1, N)
PRINT *, TOT(A)
END
!*********************************************************
! To sum the table, we use the SUM function.
!*********************************************************
FUNCTION TOT(X)
   REAL, DIMENSION(:,:) :: X
   TOT = SUM(X)
   RETURN
END
```
(b)
```
!*********************************************************
! We enter a specific row for summing through the variable
! I. We send this to the subroutine along with the table, the
! number of columns (M), and the number of rows (N).
!*********************************************************
REAL, DIMENSION(:,:), ALLOCATBLE :: A
PRINT *, 'Enter size of array (less than 100 x 100):'
READ *, M, N
ALLOCATE(A(M,N))
PRINT *, 'Enter the array by rows:'
READ *, ((A(I, J), J = 1, M), I = 1, N)
PRINT *, 'Which row is to be summed?'
READ *, I
PRINT *, TOT(A, I)
END
!**********************************************************
! We use a subarray combined with the SUM function to
! sum all the elements in the Lth row.
!**********************************************************
FUNCTION TOT(X, I, J, L)
   REAL, DIMENSION(:,:) :: X
   TOT = SUM(X(L,:))
   RETURN
END
```
(c)
```
!**********************************************************
! We will use the function from problem (b) above. But this
! time, the variable that fixes the row for summing will be
! controlled by the main program.
!**********************************************************
```

```
      REAL A(100, 100)
      PRINT *, 'Enter size of array (less than 100 x 100):'
      READ *, N, M
      PRINT *, 'Enter the array by rows:'
      READ *, ((A(I, J), J = 1, M), I = 1, N)
      DO I = 1, N
         PRINT *,'Sum of row', I, 'is', TOT(A, N, M, I)
      END DO
      END
      !***********************************************************
      ! The main program will send down a different value of L
      ! each time the function is called. But during this
      ! calculation, L is fixed until all elements in that row are
      ! added with the SUM function.
      !***********************************************************
      FUNCTION TOT(X, I, J, L)
         REAL X(I, J)
         TOT = SUM(X(L,:))
         RETURN
      END
(d)   !***********************************************************
      ! Use the main program to read in the data. But leave the
      ! computation to the subprogram.
      !***********************************************************

      REAL A(100), Y(100,100), Z(100)
      PRINT *, 'Enter size of A (no more than 100):'
      READ *, N
      PRINT *, 'Enter number of rows in Y:'
      READ *, M
      PRINT *, 'Enter A:'
      READ *, (A(I), I = 1, N)
      PRINT *, 'Enter Y by rows:'
      READ *, ((Y(I,J), J = 1, N), I = 1, M)
      DO I = 1, N
         Z(I) = COMPUTE(A, Y, N, M, I)
      END DO
      PRINT *, 'Z values:', (Z(I), I = 1, N)
      END
      !***********************************************************
      ! The computation is a single assignment statement. The main
      ! program controls which element is being computed.
      !***********************************************************
      FUNCTION COMPUTE(X, Y, N, M, I)
         REAL X(N), Y(M, N)
         COMPUTE = X(I)/Y(M-N,I)
         RETURN
      END


7.19  PRINT *, 'Enter number of terms in the series:'
      READ *, N
      PRINT *, 'Series total = ', SERIES(N)
      END
```

```
!*********************************************************
! The loop computes one term in the series at a time and adds
! it to the total. The sign of each term alternates. One way to
! do this is with (-1)**(I + 1) where I is the LCV. The
! denominator is computed by the factorial function IFACT.
!*********************************************************
FUNCTION SERIES(N)
   SERIES = 0.0
   DO I = 1, N
      SERIES = SERIES + (-1.0)**(I + 1)/IFACT(I)
   END DO
   RETURN
END
!*********************************************************
! The factorial function from Example 7.3
!*********************************************************
FUNCTION IFACT(I)
   IFACT = 1
   DO K = 2, I
      IFACT = IFACT * K
   END DO
   RETURN
END
```

7.20 (a)
```
REAL A(1000)
PRINT *, 'Enter Number of items:'
READ *, N
PRINT *, 'Enter Data:'
READ *, (A(I), I = 1, N)
CALL MIDDLE(A, N, J)
PRINT *, J, 'data points were above 0.5*(max value)'
END
!*********************************************************
! Array A is searched to find the largest value.
!*********************************************************
SUBROUTINE MIDDLE(A, N, J)
   REAL A(N)
   BIG = MAXVAL(A)
!*********************************************************
! The variable J is the number of elements that exceed
! BIG/2. We examine each element in the array to see if
! it exceeds BIG/2. If it does, J is increased by 1.
!*********************************************************
   J = 0
   DO I = 1, N
      IF(A(I) > BIG/2.0) J = J + 1
   END DO
   RETURN
END
```

(b)
```
REAL X(1000), D(1000)
PRINT *, 'Enter number of items:'
READ *, N
PRINT *, 'Enter data:'
READ *, (X(I), I = 1, N)
```

```
      CALL DEV(X, D, N)
      PRINT *,'Input data and deviations:'
      PRINT *, (X(I), D(I), I = 1, N)
      END
      !**********************************************************
      ! DEV computes the average error between each data point and
      ! the average of all the data.
      !**********************************************************
      SUBROUTINE DEV(X, D, N)
        REAL X(N), D(N)
        AVG = SUM(X)/N
      !**********************************************************
      ! Once the average has been determined, it is subtracted
      ! from each of the elements to determine the D array.
      !**********************************************************
        D = X-AVG
        RETURN
      END
  (c) REAL A(3), B(3), C(3), D(3), MAG
      PRINT *, 'Enter A, B, C, and D vectors:'
      READ *,(A(I), I = 1, 3), (B(I), I = 1, 3), &
             (C(I), I = 1,3), (D(I), I = 1, 3)
      CALL COMPUTE(A, B, C, D, MAG)
      PRINT *, 'Triple scalar product = ', MAG
      END
      !**********************************************************
      ! DOT(A,B) is a scalar quantity. So when we compute the
      ! three dot products, we can multiply them directly to
      ! obtain the value of MAG
      !**********************************************************
      SUBROUTINE COMPUTE(A, B, C, D, MAG)
        REAL A(3), B(3), C(3), D(3), MAG
        MAG = DOT(A, B)*DOT(B, D)*DOT(B, C)
        RETURN
      END
      !**********************************************************
      ! DOT function from Example 7.15
      !**********************************************************
      FUNCTION DOT(X, Y)
        REAL X(3), Y(3)
        DOT = 0.0
        DO I = 1, 3
           DOT = DOT + X(I)*Y(I)
        END DO
        RETURN
      END
  (d) REAL A(3), B(3), C(3)
      PRINT *, 'Enter A and B vectors:'
      READ *, (A(I), I = 1, 3), (B(I), I = 1, 3)
      CALL CROSS(A, B, C)
      PRINT *, 'Cross product ='
      PRINT *, (C(I), I = 1, 3)
      END
      !**********************************************************
      ! The cross product of two vectors is itself a vector.
```

```
    ! Therefore, we must calculate the components individually.
    !************************************************************
    SUBROUTINE CROSS(A, B, C)
      REAL A(3), B(3), C(3)
      C(1) = A(2)*B(3)-A(3)*B(2)
      C(2) = A(3)*B(1)-A(1)*B(3)
      C(3) = A(1)*B(2)-A(2)*B(1)
      RETURN
    END
(e) REAL A(3), B(3), C(3), D(3), E(3), F(3)
    PRINT *, 'Enter A, B, C, and D vectors'
    READ *, A, B, C, D
    !************************************************************
    ! Take the cross product of A and B and store in E. Then
    ! take the cross product of C and D and store in F. This
    ! enables us to evaluate the left-hand side (LHS) of the
    ! identity by taking the dot product of E and F. The right-
    ! hand side (RHS) is evaluated by a series of dot products.
    !************************************************************
    CALL CROSS(A, B, E)
    CALL CROSS(C, D, F)
    LHS = DOT(E, F)
    RHS = DOT(A, B)*DOT(B, D)*DOT(B, C)
    !************************************************************
    ! The RHS may not be exactly equal to the LHS because of
    ! round-off errors. So we allow for a small residual.
    !************************************************************
    IF(ABS(LHS-RHS) < 0.001) THEN
        PRINT *, 'Identity valid'
    ELSE
        PRINT *, 'Identity not valid'
    END IF
    END
    !************************************************************
    ! DOT product from Example 7.15
    !************************************************************
    FUNCTION DOT(X, Y)
      REAL X(3), Y(3)
      DOT = 0.0
      DO I = 1, 3
        DOT = DOT + X(I)*Y(I)
      END DO
      RETURN
    END
    !************************************************************
    ! Cross product subroutine
    !************************************************************
    SUBROUTINE CROSS(A, B, C)
      REAL A(3), B(3), C(3)
      C(1) = A(2)*B(3)-A(3)*B(2)
      C(2) = A(3)*B(1)-A(1)*B(3)
      C(3) = A(1)*B(2)-A(2)*B(1)
      RETURN
    END
```

7.21   Trace through the program.

Program Trace:
.MAIN. Trace:
    READ in values into the array A. Assume that A(1)=10., A(2)=20., ... A(3)=100.
    Begin Loop, INDEX=1
    Send array A to the subroutine TEST

.TEST. Trace:
    Execute the DATA statement. I = 1
    PRINT value of A(1) → error, since A is not declared as an array in the subroutine.

We must declare A as an array in the subroutine by adding a statement REAL A(10) before
the DATA statement. Note that once this is done, the program will work correctly. The
DATA statement will provide only _initial_ values to the indicated variables. Thus, I will be
assigned a value of 1 during the first call to the function. But subsequent calls will ignore
the DATA statement and will use the updated values of I through the I=I+1 statement.

7.22   (a)
```
!*********************************************************
! We assume that X(1,1) is the largest value and then
! compare each of the remaining elements to the maximum
! value. When a larger value is found, this becomes the
! new max value.
!*********************************************************
FUNCTION TABSRC(X, M, N)
  REAL X(M, N)
  TABSRC = X(1, 1)
  DO I = 1, M
    DO J = 1, N
      IF(X(I, J) > TABSRC) TABSRC = X(I, J)
    END DO
  END DO
  RETURN
END
```
(b)
```
!*********************************************************
! The table is set up as a variable-sized array. The row
! to be summed is stored in the variable I. Each element
! in that row is then added to the variable ROWSUM by the
! SUM built-in function.
!*********************************************************
FUNCTION ROWSUM(X, M, N, I)
  REAL X(M, N)
  ROWSUM = SUM(X(I,:))
  RETURN
END
```
(c)
```
!*********************************************************
! Add every element in the array for M rows and N columns
!*********************************************************
FUNCTION TABSUM(X, M, N)
  REAL X(M, N)
  TABSUM = SUM(X)
```

```
      RETURN
    END
(d) !********************************************************
    ! To add two vectors, you add the corresponding elements of
    ! each vector and store the results in a new vector RESULT.
    !********************************************************
    FUNCTION VECADD(X, Y, RESULT, N)
      REAL X(N), Y(N), RESULT(N)
      RESULT=X+Y
      RETURN
    END
(e) !**********************************************************
    ! To multiply, you take the row of one matrix and multiply it
    ! by the corresponding column of the other matrix. The sum
    ! of the products is a single element of C. See Example 6.24
    ! for an in-depth discussion.
    !**********************************************************
    SUBROUTINE MATMUL(A, B, C, M, N)
      REAL A(M, N), B(N, M), C(M, M)
      DO I = 1, M
         DO J = 1, M
            C(I, J) = 0.0
            DO K = 1, N
               C(I, J) = C(I, J) + A(I, K)* B(K, J)
            END DO
         END DO
      END DO
      RETURN
    END
(f) !**********************************************************
    ! The transpose of a matrix is generated by switching the
    ! row and column indices. A(I,J) becomes B(J,I) for example.
    !**********************************************************
    SUBROUTINE TRANSP(A, B, M, N)
      REAL A(M, N), B(N, M)
      DO I = 1, M
         DO J = 1, N
            B(I, J) = A(J, I)
         END DO
      END DO
      RETURN
    END
(g) !**********************************************************
    ! The length of a vector is a scalar quantity. It is the
    ! square root of the sum of the squares of all the elements
    ! of that vector.
    !**********************************************************
    FUNCTION VECLEN(X, N)
      REAL X(N)
      VECLEN = 0.0
      DO I = 1, N
         VECLEN = VECLEN + X(I)**2
      END DO
      VECLEN = SQRT(VECLEN)
    END
```

7.23
```
!****************************************************************
! Enter the key parameters, X, JLIMIT, and RLIMIT. X is the
! value at which the function is to be evaluated, while JLIMIT
! is the acceptable limit for terminating the Bessel function
! computation. JLIMIT is passed to the function via a COMMON
! statement, but it could also be transferred in the calling
! statement. RLIMIT is the corresponding value for terminating
! the computation of R(x).
!****************************************************************
REAL J0, JLIMIT
COMMON JLIMIT
PRINT *, 'Enter X, JLIMIT, RLIMIT'
READ *, X, JLIMIT, RLIMIT
!****************************************************************
! Initialize the approximation to the series R to J0(X). We must
! also keep track of the number of the term since we must use
! it to compute the argument for J. We initialize N (the term
! counter to 2 and increment it by 1 each time through the loop.
!****************************************************************
R = J0(X)
N = 2
!****************************************************************
! Use a conditional loop to compute the series approximation for
! R. Whenever any ABS(TERM)/R becomes less than RLIMIT, we stop.
!****************************************************************
TERM = R
DO WHILE(ABS(TERM)/R > RLIMIT)
   TERM = J0(X**N)/IFACT(N)
   R = R + TERM
   N = N + 1
END DO
PRINT *, 'Series Approximation = ', R
END
!****************************************************************
! Function to approximate the Bessel function. The limit to
! decide when to terminate the approximation is passed
! through a COMMON statement.
!****************************************************************
REAL FUNCTION J0(X)
   REAL JLIMIT
   COMMON JLIMIT
!****************************************************************
! Variables: TERM = individual power term (X**2N) in the series
!            N    = number of the term
!            SIGN = +1 or -1
!            DENO = denominator (2**2, (2**2*4**2), etc.)
!****************************************************************
   J0 = 1.0
   TERM = 1.0
   N = 0
   SIGN = 1
   DENO = 1
!****************************************************************
! Continue the series evaluation until any term contributes
! so little that there is no sense continuing the computation.
```

```
   ! This is done by noting whether ABS(TERM)/JO <= JLIMIT.
   !*****************************************************************
     DO WHILE (ABS(TERM)/JO > JLIMIT)
        SIGN = -SIGN
        N = N+2
        DENO = DENO*N**2
        TERM = X**N/DENO
        JO = JO + SIGN*TERM
     END DO
   END
   !*****************************************************************
   ! Use the function subprogram for the factorial from Example 7.3
   !*****************************************************************
   FUNCTION IFACT(L)
     IFACT = 1
     DO J = 1, L
        IFACT = IFACT*J
     END DO
     RETURN
   END
```

7.24
```
   !*****************************************************************
   ! In the main program, we read in X, DX, and PHI and then call
   ! the function before printing out the results.
   !*****************************************************************
   PRINT *, 'Enter starting value, step size, and error:'
   READ *, X, DX, PHI
   PRINT *,'Maximum Value of function:', FMAX(X, DX, PHI)
   PRINT *,'Maximum Value is at:', (2*X+DX)/2.0
   END
   !*****************************************************************
   ! Function to conduct search for maximum value in a function.
   !*****************************************************************
   FUNCTION FMAX(X, DX, PHI)
     CHECK = F(X+DX)-F(X)
     IF(CHECK < 0) STOP 'Bad start point'
     DO WHILE (CHECK > PHI)
        IF(F(X) < F(X+DX)) THEN
           X = X + DX
        ELSE
           DX = DX/2
        END IF
        CHECK = ABS(F(X) - F(X + DX))
     END DO
     FMAX = F(X+DX)/2.0
   END
   !*****************************************************************
   ! Function to be evaluated which will vary for each problem.
   ! Here is an example.
   !*****************************************************************
   FUNCTION F(X)
     F = SIN(X) * EXP(-X)
   END
```

7.25
```
!****************************************************************
! In the main program, we read in the value of N and call the
! recursive function. Notice that the answer is returned to
! the variable IANS just as with a nonrecursive function.
!****************************************************************
PRINT *, 'Enter N:'
READ *, N
IANS = INT_ADD(N)
PRINT *, ANS
END
!*****************************************************************
! Each time through the recursive function, we add the current
! value of N. Notice though, that we reduce N by 1 before
! sending it back to the function. When N reaches 1, we stop and
! complete the summation.
!*****************************************************************
RECURSIVE FUNCTION INT_ADD(N)   RESULT(ITOTAL)
   IF(N == 1) THEN
      ITOTAL = 1
   ELSE
      ITOTAL = N + INT_ADD(N-1)
   END IF
   RETURN
END
```

Chapter 8

Character and Logical Data

8.1 OVERVIEW

Most engineering and scientific applications deal with the processing of numerical data, but there are occasions when character data (text) is also a consideration. In previous chapters, we presented only limited examples of character data. This chapter will take a closer look at character data and some applications that require their use. Topics to be covered in this chapter include:

- The need for character data
- Declarations and assignment statements
- Character processing
- Formatted and unformatted input/output
- Internal files
- Character-based library functions
- Logical data
- Debugging tips.

8.2 THE NEED FOR CHARACTER DATA

There are many reasons for creating programs. One is to save time through increased productivity. By computerizing the solution to a common problem, the time it takes to solve that problem can be dramatically reduced. With computerization comes an even bigger advantage: consistency. Once a program is written to solve a problem, the computer will faithfully execute the same procedure every time (as long as the program isn't changed). This means that, right or wrong, the answer will always be the same, given the same input. Assuming the program has been properly validated, the only cause of an error would be improper input. One way to help prevent improper I/O, or a misunderstanding about what your data mean is through the use of character data, which is the subject of this chapter. For example, you may want to include identifying information with your input. This might include sample identification, processing history, testing date, and identification of personnel that is to be kept with the numerical data used for analysis. With proper use of nonnumeric data, your programs will become easier to use, both by yourself and others. While this is a simple matter, it is an important one. Character data can be used to add a level of versatility to your programs. Up to this point the programs presented have been mostly procedural. This means that you run a particular program to perform a particular task. Some programs, however, require a dialog and are designed to be more general. For example, you may want your program to give a long list of options that trigger a series of calculations. The program may be required to interpret all these responses, store some of them, and direct the operation of the program based on these inputs. Sometimes, the input data will consist of a mixture of numeric and nonnumeric data, and your program may have to sift through these data to extract the essential information needed for execution.

While most engineering problems focus on the manipulation of numerical data, there is a vast area of applications that requires textual data instead. Consider the problems of sorting a list of names in alphabetical order, or counting the number of words in a passage. When looking up information in data tables, it is convenient to construct tables such that the row and column headings mean something significant. For example, assume that a table of material properties exists and can be accessed through a function named PROPERTY. To retrieve the modulus of elasticity E (a measure of the material's stiffness) for a common stainless steel (SA-240-304) the necessary line of code might look like this:

```
E_STEEL = PROPERTY('SA-240-304', 'E')
```

By using strings such as 'SA-240-304' or 'E', it is much easier to understand what actions are taking place. In the following sections, we will discuss the mechanics of setting up and using character or string data and illustrate how they can be useful in engineering and science applications.

8.3 DECLARATIONS AND ASSIGNMENT STATEMENTS

A group of alphanumeric symbols is known as a *character*, which is declared to be of type CHARACTER. A character variable has a property known as length, which is the number of characters that can be stored in the character variable. The following example illustrates the declaration of a character variable.

EXAMPLE 8.1

This is how to declare the variable NAME to store nonnumeric data up to 20 characters long:

```
CHARACTER (LEN=20) :: NAME
```

You may also declare several variables with the same declaration statement.

```
CHARACTER (LEN=20) :: NAME, ADDRESS, PHONE
```

If all the variables are to be different lengths, you may not use this form. Instead, the length of each character variable must be defined separately:

```
CHARACTER NAME*20, ADDRESS*30, PHONE*20
```

As with any other Fortran data type, an array of character data can be constructed. For a character array, all of the elements <u>must</u> have the same length. Thus, you must specify the number of elements and the length of each.

EXAMPLE 8.2

The following declaration statement creates a two-dimensional array called TABLE of 5 rows and 2 columns with character elements of length 7. Thus, each element in the table can be as many as 7 characters long.

```
CHARACTER (LEN=7) :: TABLE(5, 2)
```

You refer to each element in the table just as with any other array. Thus, TABLE(3,2) refers to the element in row 3, column 2. As we will see shortly, if fewer than 7 characters are used, the compiler will substitute blank spaces as needed.

One application of character arrays is generating printer graphics. If your monitor system does not have graphics capabilities, you can still create low-resolution graphics by using a character array. Some Fortran 90 compilers, however, will have graphics capabilities which eliminate the need for this application of character data.

EXAMPLE 8.3

Most terminal screens measure 80 columns by 20 rows. We will use a character array of this size on which to plot the function . The process involves plotting 80 points from −pi to pi and scaling these points to fit within the array bounds.

```
! Use of character data to graphically display data. The character
! array SCREEN will fit onto a screen of 80 columns by 20 rows.
! each element is one character long (either a '*' or ' ').
!***********************************************************************
INTEGER COLS, ROWS
PARAMETER(COLS=80, ROWS=20, PI=3.1416)
CHARACTER*1 SCREEN(ROWS, COLS)
!***********************************************************************
! Initialize all elements of SCREEN to blank spaces.
!***********************************************************************
DATA SCREEN / 1600*' '/
!***********************************************************************
! From the column value calculate X. From the Y value calculate
! the row number in which to place a '*'.
!***********************************************************************
DO JX = 1, COLS
    X = (-PI + (JX-1)*(PI))/(COLS-1)*-2
    Y = SIN(X)
    IY = 1 + NINT((Y-1.0)/(-2.0)*(ROWS-1))
    SCREEN(IY, JX) = '*'
END DO
!***********************************************************************
! Now print the results by rows to the screen.
!***********************************************************************
DO I = 1, ROWS
    PRINT *, (SCREEN(I,J), J = 1, COLS)
END DO
END
```

The two assignment statements that define X and IY inside the first DO loop normalize these values so that X ranges between $-\pi$ and 0, while IY ranges between 1 and 20, corresponding to the number of rows in the output graph. The purpose of these statements is to determine into which element of the character array SCREEN the star '*' symbol will be placed. The output from the program will look like this:

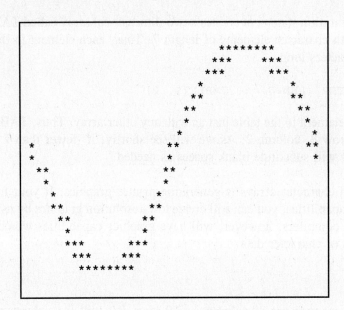

Note: If you find that your computer tries to "wrap" the text rather than print 80 characters on a line, you may need to format to make the program work properly. This type of "plotting" is necessary only if your compiler and monitor do not support graphics. Fortunately, most compilers now support higher resolution graphics, so you won't have to resort to methods such as this.

8.4 CHARACTER PROCESSING

In Fortran a number of operations are available for processing character data. These include assigning values to variables, extracting a portion of a string value, assigning a portion of a string value, appending strings together, and relational operations with strings.

The process of assigning a value to a character variable is similar to that used for numeric variables. The only change is that the assigned value must be enclosed between apostrophes or quotation marks. Here are the rules and simple examples illustrating assignment statements:

Rule 1: Character must be enclosed between apostrophes or quote marks
         (X = 'string value' or X = "string value")

Rule 2: If the string value has a shorter length than the variable, blanks will be added at the end of the string to fill out the missing characters. This is known as *padding*. (Example: If Y has length 5, then Y = 'ABC' results in Y = 'ABC ' with two blanks added.)

Rule 3: If the string value being assigned is longer than the length of the receiving variable, then the overflowing characters are not stored. (Example: If Z has length 3, then

Z='abcde' results in Z='abc'. Note that 'de' is truncated.)

Rule 4:   To include an apostrophe in the string, you must type it twice. (Example: X='It''s an example' results in the value *It's an example*.)

EXAMPLE 8.4

In the table below are examples of character assignment statements using the declaration statement shown below. Refer to Chapter 2 for a listing of the permitted characters.

```
CHARACTER X*5, Y*7, Z*10
```

Statement	Result, Rule, and Comments
X = '123AB'	*123AB (Rule 1)*
Y = '123AB~~'	*123AB (Rule 2 - 2 blank spaces (~) at end)*
X = 'she''s'	*she's (Rule 4)*
Y = "she's"	*When an apostrophe appears inside quote marks, Rule 4 does not apply and the inner apostrophe is printed*
Z = 'X has length 5'	*X has leng (Rule 3)*

Substrings

Fortran also allows for the concept of a substring, where a substring is a consecutive sequence of characters from within a string. Substrings allow us to remove characters from a longer string and perform various operations on them.

EXAMPLE 8.5

Consider the string 'Help'. We can form various length substrings from the characters that make up the total string:

Length 0 substrings:	[null]
Length 1 substrings:	'H', 'e', 'l', 'p'
Length 2 substrings:	'He', 'el', 'lp'
Length 3 substrings:	'Hel', 'elp'
Length 4 substrings:	'Help'

Notice that we could only form substrings from consecutive characters. For example, we could not form a substring of 'Hep' because we would have to skip a letter.

Fortran has a simple notation that allows us to extract substrings from a string. The concept of a character variable having many elements is much like a one-dimensional array. Each character resides in its own element. Substrings allow us to extract or replace a list of characters stored in a string variable. The general form to reference a substring of a variable is as follows:

Character variable(I: J)

where $1 \leq I \leq J \leq$ length of the string variable. If I is omitted, then the default value of 1 is assumed. If J is omitted, then the default value of the string length is assumed.

EXAMPLE 8.6

Assume that ALPHA is a character variable and is declared to have length 26 with the value 'ABCDEFGHIJKLMNOPQRSTUVWXYZ'

Substring	Value and Comments
ALPHA(1:3)	*ABC*
ALPHA(:3)	*ABC* (*Assumed starting index = 1*)
ALPHA(24:)	*XYZ* (*Assumed ending index = 26*)
ALPHA(2:2)	*B* (*Single character substring*)
ALPHA(:)	*ABCDEFGHIJKLMNOPQRSTUVWXYZ* (*Assumed starting index is 1 and assumed ending index is 26*)

Substrings can be used in assignment statements. When placed on the right-hand side of the equals sign, the substring is assigned to the receiving string variable. When placed on the left-hand side of the equals symbol, the substring receives the assigned value. This allows you to modify a portion of a string. The rules for padding (adding blanks) and truncation apply.

EXAMPLE 8.7

Assume that the character variable A has length 3, B has length 5, ALPHA has length 26 with the value 'ABCDEFGHIJKLMNOPQRSTUVWXYZ', and BETA has length 10 with the value '1234567890'. Here are several assignment statements based on these values:

Assignment Statement	Result and Comment
A = ALPHA(1:3)	*A has value from index 1 to 3: ABC*
B = BETA(1:3)	*B has value from 1 to 3: 123~ ~ (2 blanks at the end)*
A = BETA(5:10)	*A has value from index 5 to 10: 567 (890 was truncated)*
BETA(1:3) = ALPHA(1:3)	*The first 3 values of BETA come from the first 3 values of ALPHA. The rest of BETA is unchanged: ABC4567890*
BETA(1:4) = ALPHA(24:26)	*The first 4 values of BETA come from the last 3 values of ALPHA and an additional blank space: XYZ~567890*

Concatenation of Strings

One operation that we commonly perform with strings and substrings is *concatenation*, which is the process of appending one string or substring to another. You can think of this operation as being a string "addition," and it is indicated by //. The strings to be "added" are placed on either side of the // symbol.

EXAMPLE 8.8

In this example, we will read in a person's first name and last name and then form a character variable FULLNAME by use of the concatenation operation.

```
!*************************************************************
! The first and last names will be stored in FIRST and LAST
! respectively. The full name will be created by joining
! these two names.
!*************************************************************
CHARACTER*20 FIRST, LAST
CHARACTER*41 FULLNAME
PRINT *, 'Enter your first name within apostrophes'
READ *, FIRST
PRINT *, 'Enter your last name within apostrophes'
READ *, LAST
!*************************************************************
! Create FULLNAME by joining the first and last names
! (separated by a comma) with two concatenation operations
!*************************************************************
FULLNAME = LAST//','//FIRST
PRINT *, FULLNAME
END
```

This program will print your last name, a comma, and your first name. Note that concatenation is order dependent — meaning that LAST//FIRST and FIRST//LAST will not produce the same strings. Notice also that this may produce several extra blank spaces since we have set up the two variables LAST and FIRST to be of length 20. Thus, if we entered 'Marty' and 'Cwiakala' as the first and last names respectively, this program will produce the output:

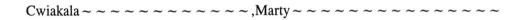

Cwiakala ~ ~ ~ ~ ~ ~ ~ ~ ~ ~ ~ ~ ~ ,Marty ~ ~ ~ ~ ~ ~ ~ ~ ~ ~ ~ ~ ~ ~ ~

Collating Sequence

We have seen in previous chapters the use of relational operations on numerical data. These same operations can be applied to character data. To understand what the outcome of a relational operation will be, it will be necessary to understand the character set's *collating sequence*. The collating sequence is the order in which the characters are arranged from a minimum to a maximum value. For example 'A' is "less" than 'B', 'B' is "less" than 'C', and so on. For the alphabetic symbols, the collating sequence is equivalent to alphabetical order. But how do characters like '!', '*', and even uppercase versus lowercase letters appear in the collating sequence? This will depend on the character set adopted by the computer and the compiler. It was stated earlier that two common character sets are encountered as the default character sets. They are ASCII and EBCDIC. The collating sequences for each of these character sets are different and are illustrated below:

ASCII collating sequence for printable characters:

Blank ! " # $ % & ' ( ) * + , - . /
0 1 2 3 4 5 6 7 8 9 : ; < = > ? @
A B C D E F G H I J K L M N O P Q R S T U V W X Y Z { } ^ _ `
a b c d e f g h i j k l m n o p q r s t u v w x y z { | } ~

EBCDIC collating sequence for printable characters:

Blank] . < (+ ! & [$ *) ; ^ - / , % _ > ? : # @ ' = "
a b c d e f g h i j k l m n o p q r s t u v w x y z
A B C D E F G H I J K L M N O P Q R S T U V W X Y Z
0 1 2 3 4 5 6 7 8 9

The six relational operations ($<$, $<=$, $==$, $/=$, $>$, and $>=$) can be applied to character data. The equals and not equals operations are easily understood in the context that character data either match or they don't. But the issue is not so clear for the $<$ and $>$ operations, which require knowledge of the collating sequence. When comparing single character strings, the order is determined by the position within the collating sequence. For strings of more than one character, the comparison starts with the first character of each string. If those characters are the same, the comparison moves to the second character, and so on. If the string runs out of characters, then the computer interprets the next character to be a blank space. This is the same procedure used when alphabetizing a list. The following example shows the use of relational operations:

EXAMPLE 8.9

Character Set	Expression	Result and Comments
ASCII	'A' $<$ 'B'	True
ASCII	'A' $<$ 'a'	True
EBCDIC	'A' $<$ 'a'	False
ASCII	'AAA' $<$ 'B'	True
ASCII	'AAA' $<$ 'AA'	False (Blank is assumed to come after 'AA')
ASCII	'1' $<$ 'X'	True (Numbers come before letters in ASCII)
EBCDIC	'1' $<$ 'X'	False (Numbers come after letters in EBCDIC)

Because of the collating sequence, procedures to sort a list of numbers can be utilized to sort a list of names. This is the most common way to alphabetize a list of names.

EXAMPLE 8.10

The following example puts a list of names into alphabetical order. The names are stored in an array with 100 elements, and we will swap two names just as we did with numbers. See Example 6.9 for a discussion of the sorting method.

```fortran
! The array LIST stores the 100 names. We search the list for
! the minimum value within the list, where the minimum value
! is decided by the collating sequence. Once found, we will
! switch this value with the one in the target position.
!******************************************************
CHARACTER*20 LIST(100), LISTMIN, SWAP
PRINT *, 'Number of names in the list (100 max.)?'
READ *, N
DO I = 1, N
    PRINT *,'Enter name', I,' between apostrophes'
    READ *, LIST(I)
END DO
!******************************************************
! Start the sorting operation
!******************************************************
DO I = 1, N-1
    LISTMIN = LIST(I)
    INDEX = I
    DO J = I+1, N
        IF(LIST(J) < LISTMIN) THEN
            LISTMIN = LIST(J)
            INDEX = J
        END IF
    END DO
    SWAP = LIST(I)
    LIST(I) = LIST(INDEX)
    LIST(INDEX) = SWAP
END DO
DO I = 1, N
    PRINT *, LIST(I)
END DO
END
```

Dealing with character variables in subprograms is similar to working with any other variable type. You are must declare all variables to match their declaration in the calling program. This is especially problematic with character data, since string length can vary considerably from variable to variable. Fortunately, Fortran allows for *automatic* string length assignment, which means that you are not required to know the length of a string variable. This feature not only makes it easier for you by avoiding errors in declaration statements, but also adds versatility to your subprograms. Since the called subprogram will automatically match the variables, different variables of different lengths can be utilized by the same subprogram.

To have the string length automatically assigned in a subprogram, replace the length parameter with a star enclosed within parentheses (*). This will force the length of the variable to be the same as the argument being passed. With the convenience of automatic string length assignment comes the need to interrogate a variable to determine how long a string it can hold. The LEN function is used for this purpose.

EXAMPLE 8.11

This example illustrates how to determine the length of a string by using the LEN built-in function. In this example, we will use the LEN function to determine the length of a character constant and add a series of stars (*) to fill out the output variable.

```
!**************************************************************
! The character variable INPUT will contain a string which
! will have trailing blank spaces. We will send this to the
! subroutine ADDSTAR, which will replace these blanks by stars
!**************************************************************
CHARACTER*20 INPUT, OUTPUT
PRINT *,'Enter text string enclosed between apostrophes'
INPUT = 'Harry Truman'
CALL ADDSTAR(INPUT,OUTPUT)
PRINT *,'The string with stars (*) replacing trailing blanks'
PRINT *, OUTPUT
END
!**************************************************************
! Variables IN and OUT in the subroutine are declared with the *(*)
! statement. This will allow the subroutine to accept any size string.
! We start by copying IN into the output variable OUT. Then, we use the
! LEN function to determine the length of the character variable. The
! DO loop then starts at the end and works backward to replace the
! blanks with stars. When the first nonblank character is found, the
! loop ends.
!**************************************************************
SUBROUTINE ADDSTAR(IN,OUT)
CHARACTER*(*) IN, OUT
OUT = IN
I = LEN(OUT)
DO WHILE(OUT(I:I) == ' ')
   OUT(I:I) = '*'
   I = I-1
END DO
END
```

When this program executes, the value of INPUT is 'Harry Truman', which is then sent to the subroutine and copied into the variable OUT. Within the subroutine, the LEN function examines this string and determines that it is 12 characters long (remember, the blank space in the middle of the string is included in the count). The loop then works backward and replaces any trailing blank space with a star. The resulting output is:

Harry Truman********

8.5 FREE-FORMATTED AND FORMATTED I/O OF CHARACTER DATA

We have already seen examples of list-directed (also called free-formatted) input and output (I/O) of character strings in Example 2.16. Recall that free-formatting, also known as list-directed formatting, leaves the formatting up to the compiler and is used when the appearance of the output data is generally unimportant. Free-formatted I/O is accomplished by placing a "*" after the READ or PRINT word. In this context, strings are printed out by including them inside single quote marks in the PRINT statement. But, if you want to print out a character variable, all you need do is list the variable in the free-formatted output statement.

EXAMPLE 8.12

Below is a program to read in a name and then echo it to the screen:

```
!***************************************************************
! The variable NAME is declared to be 40 characters long. After
! entering the name, the program will echo the input data via
! free-formatted I/O statements.
!***************************************************************
CHARACTER*40 NAME
PRINT *, 'Enter your name inside single quote marks:'
READ *, NAME
PRINT *,'Name entered was: ', NAME
END
```

In this example, we have printed out both a string ('Name entered was: ') and the contents of a character variable with free-formatted I/O. The only problem that you might encounter is that you need to enter the input data inside apostrophes or quote marks. If you forget to include the quotes, the computer is likely to report a run-time error.

Formatting gives you control over the appearance of your output. By using formatting in an input statement, you can eliminate the restrictions of special characters, spaces, and so on that are present when using free-formatting. By using formatting in an output statement, you can combine numbers and strings in a fashion that is completely under your control. Strings are formatted using the "A" edit descriptor within the FORMAT statement with the following general form:

$$n \text{ A } len$$

where n=a repeat specifier and len=the length of the string. A simple example would be 3A5, where the instruction A5 is to be repeated three times. Refer to Chapter 3 for several examples.

The repeat factor is the same as with all format specifiers. The len is used to indicate how many characters are in the string. If you omit a value for len, then the length of the string variable being referenced is automatically used. But, if len is less than the length of the variable being printed, trailing characters will be truncated. On the other hand, if len is greater than the length of the variable, extra blanks are placed at the front of the string.

EXAMPLE 8.13

For the following examples, assume that the character variable STR1 has length 10 and the value 'ABCDEFGHIJ', and that STR2 has length 5 and the value '12345':

```
CHARACTER STR1*10, STR2*5
STR1 = 'ABCDEFGHIJ'
STR2 = '12345'
```

	Statement	Output	Comments
1	`PRINT 1, STR1` `FORMAT(1X, A10)`	ABCDEFGHIJ	*(Formatting matches exactly)*
2	`PRINT 2, STR1` `FORMAT(1X, A)`	ABCDEFGHIJ	*(Automatic use of variable length)*
3	`PRINT 3, STR1` `FORMAT(1X, A3)`	ABC	*(Only 3 characters can be printed)*
4	`PRINT 4, STR1, STR2` `FORMAT(1X, A11, A5)`	~ABCDEFHIJ12345	*(Padding with blank (~) at beginning of string)*

8.6 INTERNAL FILES

There are instances when the form of the output or input will not be known. For example, you might have an application where you will be reading in one, two, or three numbers, but you do not know in advance how many are present. In such applications internal files are useful.

Internal files allow you to convert one data type to another. Consider the problem in which you are asked to read in an integer of up to 6 digits, multiply the number by 2, and then return the result in reverse order. For example, 123 multiplied by 2 yields 246; but you want to return the result as 642. Multiplication can be easily performed on a number, but swapping digits can be more easily performed on character data. Therefore, it makes sense to do the initial phase of the processing on the numerical data and then convert to character data for the reversal process. The following procedure will be used:

- Multiply the desired number by 2 and store the result as a file in the computer memory (as opposed to a file stored on a hard or floppy disk)
- Reread the result as a string
- Process the string to reverse the digits and then write the new string back into memory as a file
- Finally, reread the file as an integer

By reading and writing to the computer memory, we have created an *internal file*, which is stored only as long as the program that created it is running. We will discuss the other, more permanent type of file (external files), in the next chapter. With internal files, it is possible to interpret the data in any format you wish.

To obtain data from an internal file, we need to use a string variable within the READ statement. To send data to an internal file, we use the WRITE statement. Here are the forms we will use:

READ(*string, format*) *I/O list*   or   WRITE(*string, format*) *I/O list* where string is a character variable indicating the name of the storage location of the internal file, and format is the statement label indicating where formatting instructions are to be found.

EXAMPLE 8.14

This program takes an integer, multiplies it by 2, and then returns the result with the digits reversed as an integer. It does so by storing the integer (after multiplication) in an internal file called 'STRING'. The READ statement then reads in the data from that file as a character array, and prints the characters back to the file in reverse order.

```
!*************************************************************
! The original integer value is stored in INPUT.
!*************************************************************
       CHARACTER*1 FWD(8)
       INTEGER INPUT
       CHARACTER*8 STRING
       PRINT *,'Enter an Integer'
       READ *,INPUT
       INPUT = INPUT*2
!*************************************************************
! Now, write INPUT to the internal file
!*************************************************************
       WRITE(STRING, 1) INPUT
   1   FORMAT(I8)
!*************************************************************
! Reread the internal file as a character string array
!*************************************************************
       READ(STRING, 2) (FWD(I), I = 1, 8)
   2   FORMAT(8A1)
!*************************************************************
! Reverse the string by writing it into the file backward
!*************************************************************
       WRITE(STRING, 2) (FWD(I), I = 8, 1, -1)
!*************************************************************
! Read the file as an integer value
!*************************************************************
       READ(STRING, 1) IOUT
       PRINT *, 'Output is: ', IOUT
       END
```

To demonstrate how this works, let's assume that we enter the integer value 26132791 as input. The program will then proceed as follows:

Step 1 (read in integer value):	26132791
Step 2 (multiply value by 2):	52265582
Step 3 (send as an integer to internal file):	52265582
Step 4 (read from internal file as individual characters):	'5' '2' '2' '6' '5' '5' '8' '2'
Step 5 (send as characters backward to an internal file):	'2' '8' '5' '5' '6' '2' '2' '5'
Step 6 (read the internal file as an integer):	28556225

Internal files provide an easy way to convert character data into integer or real data, and vice versa. They also are useful when you do not know in advance what the input is going to be.

8.7 CHARACTER-BASED LIBRARY FUNCTIONS

There are several built-in functions that operate on or produce character data, and these functions are summarized below. For the following functions, I represents an integer, C is a single character string, STRING is a multicharacter string, and SUB is a substring.

CHAR(I)
Returns a single character at position I of the processor's collating sequence. (Example: If the processor uses the ASCII sequence, then CHAR(65) will produce the character in the 65th position in that sequence, which is the letter 'A'.)

ICHAR(C)
Returns the position in the collating sequence of the desired character. (Example: If the processor uses the ASCII collating sequence, then ICHAR('A') will produce the location in the collating sequence where the letter 'A' is found, in this case 65.)

INDEX(STRING, SUB)
Determines the starting location of the substring SUB within the larger string. (Example: If STRING is 'ABCDEFGHIJ', and SUB is 'DEF', then INDEX(STRING,SUB) returns a value of 4 where the substring begins.)

LEN(STRING)
Returns the length of a string if that string is a constant. But, if the string is a variable, then the reported length will match the declared length. (Example: If STRING is 'ABCDEFGHIJ', then LEN(STRING) returns the value 10.)

LGE(A, B)
Compares the character strings or variables A and B, and determines whether A is lexically greater than or equal to B in the collating sequence being used. (Example: if A='a' and B='B', then LGE(A, B) is .TRUE. in the ASCII sequence.)

LGT(A, B)
Compares the character strings or variables A and B, and determines whether A is lexically greater than B. (Example: if A='a' and B='B', then LGT(A,B) is .TRUE.)

LLE(A, B)
Compares the character strings or variables A and B, and determines whether A is lexically less than or equal to B. (Example: if A='a' and B='B', then LLE(B,A) is .FALSE.)

LLT(A, B)
Compares the character strings or variables A and B, and determines whether A is lexically less than B. (Example: if A='a' and B='B', then LGT(B,A) is .FALSE.)

ADJUSTL(STRING)
Returns a string of the same length as STRING in which all leading blanks are removed and then added to the end (left justification). (Example: ADJUSTL(' abc') produces 'abc '.)

ADJUSTR(STRING)   Returns a string of the same length as STRING in which all
                                trailing blanks are removed and then added to the beginning (right
                                justification). (Example: ADJUSTR('abc   ') produces '   abc'.)

EXAMPLE 8.15

The following program converts all lowercase characters to uppercase assuming that the
ASCII collating sequence is being used. This can be done by noting that lowercase letters are
between 097 and 122 in the ASCII collating sequence, while the uppercase letters are
between 065 and 090. In the program, we will determine the position of each letter in the
ACSII collating sequence. If the position falls between 097 and 122, we will subtract 32 from
it to convert the letter to an uppercase letter. As an example, note that in the ASCII collating
sequence, lower case 'a' is in position 97 while upper case 'A' is in position 65.

```
!******************************************************************
! Program to convert all lowercase letters into uppercase. Read in
! the message as a character array.
!******************************************************************
        CHARACTER (LEN=1) :: MESSAG(128)
        PRINT *,'Enter a string'
        READ 1, (MESSAG(I), I = 1, 128)
   1    FORMAT(128A1)
!******************************************************************
! Determine location in ASCII sequence and see whether the
! character is between the 097 and 122 positions inclusively.
! If it is, subtract 32.
!******************************************************************
        DO I = 1, 128
            J = ICHAR(MESSAG(I))
            IF(J >= 97 .AND. J <= 122) THEN
                J = J-32
                MESSAG(I) = CHAR(J)
            END IF
        END DO
        PRINT 1, (MESSAG(I), I = 1, 128)
        END
```

The above program can be modified easily to code a message. For example, consider the
process of reversing the order of the characters. If the characters abc. . .ABC. . . were mapped
to zyx. . .ZYX. . . a coded message would result. Rerunning the result through the program a
second time would decipher the message. Of course, much more complicated coding algorithms
can be constructed (see Supplementary Problem 8.21).

8.8 LOGICAL DATA

The final data type that we will examine is logical data that is often used for decision-making
processes. Since Fortran allows only two possible values (.TRUE. and .FALSE.), we will use
logical data where we need to repeatedly use the result of a logical expression. Without logical
data, we would have to repeat the logical expression as many times as required. But by setting up
a logical variable we only need to perform the logical comparison once. This will help to prevent
inadvertent typographical and logic errors when you create lengthy programs.

EXAMPLE 8.16

We can store the results of a logical comparison and use that result as many times as necessary. In this example, we will write a program both with and without logical data.

Original program without logical data:

```
        PRINT *,'Enter X'
        READ *,X
        IF(X*X < 3.0 .AND. X < 0.0 .OR. COS(X) >= 0.2 ) THEN
           A = 1.0
        ELSE
           A = 2.0
        END IF
        T = X + A
        U = 2 * X
        IF(X*X < 3.0 .AND. X < 0.0 .OR. COS(X) >= 0.2) THEN
           B = 10.0
        ELSE
           B = 0.0
        END IF
        W = T + U + A + B
        PRINT *,'T, U, W=',T, U, W
        END
```

Program utilizing logical variable:

```
        LOGICAL TEST
        PRINT *,'Enter X'
        READ *, X
        !************************************************************
        ! Once the logical variable is declared with the LOGICAL
        ! statement, we can assign a value (true or false) with
        ! an assignment statement, or a logical operator.
        !************************************************************
        TEST = X*X < 3.0 .AND. X < 0.0 .OR. COS(X) >= 0.2
        IF (TEST) THEN
           A = 1.0
        ELSE
           A = 2.0
        END IF
        T = X + A
        U = 2 * X
        IF (TEST) THEN
           B = 10.0
        ELSE
           B = 0.0
        END IF
        W = T + U + A + B
        PRINT *,'T, U, W=', T, U, W
        END
```

The second version has two advantages. The first advantage is that the logical expression (X*X < 3.0 .AND. X < 0.0 .OR. COS(X) > = 0.2) is executed only once, saving a little bit of computer run time. For the above example, the savings would be trivial. But, when writing programs that loop through a section of code thousands of times, such savings can become significant. In real engineering problems, it is not uncommon to have loops that execute millions of times. And if decisions within those loops are based on logical tests such as those above, the use of logical variables improves the overall program speed.

The second advantage is that the conditional expression appears in one place only. If you had to modify the conditional expression in the first program, you would have to make two editing changes. The second program, on the other hand, requires a change in only one expression.

8.9 DEBUGGING TIPS

When you write a program it is always a good idea to program defensively. Try to anticipate errors, and take advantage of as many simplifications as the language allows you to take. Here are a few suggestions along these lines:

- Whenever it's possible to allow the computer to automatically assign properties for you, use that feature. It saves on errors and adds to the versatility of the program. An example is the "(*)" option when declaring a string variable in a subprogram. Another example is the "A" edit descriptor without a specified length (see Example 3.13).
- Consolidate programming segments wherever possible. Use a logical variable so that logical expressions need not be repeated. PARAMETER statements are another example of this philosophy. Consolidation usually speeds up a program's execution and usually makes the software more maintainable.

Even with the best defensive programming, errors are going to happen in spite of your best efforts. As we have seen in other chapters, debugging consists of removing syntax, run-time, and logic errors. Usually, the compiler will give you diagnostic messages about the syntax errors, and these messages can be used to remove the simplest errors. But as with debugging problems with the other data types, errors with character and logical data will still require you to trace the program in order to locate the problem. So once again, tracing becomes an important tool. When debugging programs containing character strings and variables, treat them as one-dimensional arrays and do the following:

- Create a table for each character variable. Each table should have as many columns as there are characters in the variable. For example, if the character string will have 10 characters, make a table with 10 columns. As you read in (or generate) the variable, place each character into its own column within the table. This will make substring manipulation particularly easy.
- Each time the character variable changes, enter a new row in the table. The last row represents the current value of the string variable.

EXAMPLE 8.17

Trace through the following program. Use ' ~ ' to indicate spaces for clarity.

```
CHARACTER (LEN=10) :: STRING
DATA STRING/'SONG.BIRD'/
STRING(1:1) = STRING(4:4)
```

```
STRING(4:4) = STRING(9:9)
STRING = STRING(1:2)//STRING(2:2)//STRING(4:4)
PRINT *, STRING
END
```

Program Trace:

Set up character variable STRING with the characters SONG.BIRD~
Move the 4th character to the first position – STRING becomes GONG.BIRD.
Move the 9th character to the 4th position – STRING becomes GOND.BIRD
Concatenate the first two letters of STRING with the 2nd letter and the 4th letter
      of STRING, resulting in 'GO'//'O'//'D' = 'GOOD'
Print out the contents of STRING

Variables:

STRING	1	2	3	4	5	6	7	8	9	10
	S	O	N	G	.	B	I	R	D	~
	G	O	N	G	.	B	I	R	D	~
	G	O	N	D	.	B	I	R	D	~
	G	O	O	D	~	~	~	~	~	~

Output:

GOOD

Solved Problems

8.1   Indicate which of the following assignment statements are valid or invalid. For the valid examples, determine the value assigned to the variable. Assume that the character variable X has length 20, Y has length 30, and Z has length 40.

   (a) X = 'This is a test"   (b) X = a string
   (c) Y = 'and he said, "this is a test"'   (d) X = 'what''s that?'
   (e) Z = "I don't know!"

   (a) Invalid – mismatched delimiters (both must be ' or ")
   (b) Invalid since data are not contained within apostrophes or quotes
   (c) Valid – The internal apostrophes (' ') are printed: *and he said, 'this is a test'*
   (d) Valid – The double apostrophes ('') appear as a single apostrophe: *what's that?*
   (e) Valid – Quote marks can also be used to mark character constants: *I don't know!*

8.2   Write a program to determine your computer's default character set (ASCII or EBCDIC) by utilizing the difference in the ASCII and EBCDIC collating sequences.

```
!*************************************************************
! In the ASCII character set, the capital letters come before
! the lowercase letters, while the reverse is true for EBCDIC
!*************************************************************
IF ('A' < 'a') THEN
    PRINT *,'ASCII collating sequence used.'
    DO I = 1, 128
        PRINT *, CHAR(I)        ! Prints the ASCII character set
    END DO
ELSE
    PRINT *,'EBCDIC collating sequence used.'
    DO I = 1, 128
        PRINT *, CHAR(I)        ! Prints the EBCDIC character set
    END DO
END IF
END
```

8.3   Determine all of the possible substrings constructed from the following strings.

   (a) 'a'   (b) 'He'
   (c) 'string'   (d) 'a test'

   (a) a, null   (b) H, e, He, null
   (c) s, t, r, i, n, g, st, tr, ri, in, ng, str, tri, rin, ing, stri, trin, ring, string, null
   (d) a, [space], t, e, s, t, a[space], [space]t, te, es, st, a[space]t, [space]te, tes, est, a[space]tes, [space]test, a[space]test, null

8.4   Determine the values of the indicated substrings. Assume that ALPHA has the value 'abcdefghij1234567890' with length 20.

(a) ALPHA(1:1)   (b) ALPHA(3:5)
(c) ALPHA(11:)   (d) ALPHA(:)

(a) 'a'   (b) 'cde'
(c) '1234567890'   (d) 'abcdefghij1234567890'

8.5   For the relational expressions given below, determine the resulting logical value. Use the
ASCII collating sequence.

(a) ('John' < 'Jim')   (b) ('Pat' >= 'Alex')
(c) ('John' < 'jim')   (d) ('Sue' > 'bob')
(e) ('This' < 'That')   (f) ('12' > '2')
(g) ('Helene' <= 'helene')   (h) ('Long string' > 'LONGER STRING')

(a) False – 'o' does not come before 'i'   (b) True – 'P' comes after 'A'
(c) True – 'J' comes before 'j'   (d) False – 'S' does not come after 'b'
(e) False – 'i' does not come before 'a'   (f) False – '1' does not come after '2'
(g) True – 'H' comes before 'h'   (h) True – 'o' comes after 'O'

8.6   Write a program which reads in a list of names (last, first) and phone numbers as a single
string, and returns the list in alphabetical order.

```
CHARACTER (LEN=50) :: LIST(100), LISTMIN, SWAP
PRINT *,'Number of names in the list (100 max.)?'
READ *, N
DO I = 1, N
   PRINT *, 'Enter Last Name, First and phone number'
   READ *, LIST(I)
END DO
!*************************************************************
! Start the sorting operation using the sorting process from
! Example 6.9
!*************************************************************
DO I = 1, N-1
   LISTMIN = LIST(I)
   INDEX = I
   DO J = I+1, N
      IF (LIST(J) < LISTMIN) THEN
         LISTMIN = LIST(J)
         INDEX = J
      END IF
   END DO
   SWAP = LIST(I)
   LIST(I) = LIST(INDEX)
   LIST(INDEX) = SWAP
END DO
!*************************************************************
! After sorting, print out the sorted list
!*************************************************************
DO I = 1, N
   PRINT *, LIST(I)
END DO
END
```

8.7   Write a subprogram that performs the same function as ADJUSTR.

```
!*********************************************************
!   IN = string to be adjusted
!   OUT = string after adjustment
!   NUMCHR - number of characters in the string
!   NBEG = position where blanks begin to appear at the end
!          of the string.
!*********************************************************
SUBROUTINE ADJUSTC(IN,OUT)
   CHARACTER*(*) IN, OUT
!*********************************************************
! First, determine the length of the string IN
!*********************************************************
   NUMCHR=LEN(IN)
!*********************************************************
! Determine where the extra blank spaces begin
!*********************************************************
   I = NUMCHR
   DO WHILE (IN(I:I) == ' ')
     I = I - 1
   END DO
   NBLANK = NUMCHR - I
!*********************************************************
! Move all the characters one space to the right
!*********************************************************
   DO I= NUMCHR, NBLANK, -1
      OUT(I:I) = IN(I-NBLANK:I-NBLANK)
   END DO
   RETURN
END
```

8.8   Write a program that prints a border of "*"s around a text string such as

```
***************
*This is a test*
***************
```

```
!*************************************************************
! Determine the length of the string. Then add one '*' to the
! beginning, and one '*' to the end of the string. Finally,
! print out one line of stars of length LEN(STRING)+2.
!*************************************************************
CHARACTER INPUT*50, NEWIN*52, LINE*52
PRINT *, 'Enter the string'
READ "(A50)", INPUT            ! Use of embedded FORMAT as an
                               ! option to the FORMAT statement.
!*************************************************************
! Determine the length of the string
!*************************************************************
NCHAR = 50
DO WHILE(INPUT(NCHAR:NCHAR) == ' ')
   NCHAR = NCHAR -1
END DO
!*************************************************************
! Add stars to the beginning and end of the string
!*************************************************************
NEWIN = '*'//INPUT(1:NCHAR)//'*'
!*************************************************************
! Now print out the new string preceded and followed by a
```

```
! series of stars of length NCHAR+2
!***********************************************************
DO I = 1, NCHAR + 2
   LINE(I:I) = '*'
END DO
PRINT *, LINE
PRINT *, NEWIN
PRINT *, LINE
END
```

8.9 Modify Example 8.3 so that the beginning and ending regions can be read in at run time. Currently, the program is set to plot from −pi to pi.

```
INTEGER :: COLS, ROWS
PARAMETER(COLS=80, ROWS=20, PI=3.1416)
CHARACTER (LEN=1) :: SCREEN(ROWS, COLS)
DATA SCREEN/1600*' '/
!***********************************************************
! New section to read in XMIN and XMAX
!***********************************************************
PRINT *,'Enter starting and ending X values:'
READ *, XMIN, XMAX
!***********************************************************
! Calculate the star position in the plot. The functions for X
! and Y have been modified to take into account XMIN and XMAX.
!***********************************************************
DO JX = 1, COLS
   X = XMIN + (JX-1)*(XMAX-XMIN)/(COLS-1)*-2
   Y = SIN(X)
   IY = 1 + NINT((Y-1.0)/(-2.0)*(ROWS-1))
   SCREEN(IY,JX) = '*'
END DO
!***********************************************************
! Output section is unchanged
!***********************************************************
DO I = 1, ROWS
   PRINT *, (SCREEN(I,J), J = 1, COLS)
END DO
END
```

8.10 Predict the output of the PRINT statements below if X = '12345678901234567890'. (See Section 3.4 for description of embedded format instructions.)

(a) PRINT *, X   (b) PRINT "(' ', 1A5)", X

(c) PRINT "(' ', 2A) ", X(1:3), X(1:3)   (d) PRINT "(' ', A5) " , X, X

(a) 12345678901234567890   *(Free formatting)*

(b) 12345   *(Truncation after 5 characters)*

(c) 123123   *(Repeat factor with auto length)*

(d) 12345   *(When insufficient number of edit descriptors, the formatting*
12345   *reuses the edit descriptors including the new line)*

8.11 Rewrite the alphabetical sorting (Example 8.10) to utilize the character lexical comparison functions (LLT, LLE, LGT, or LGE). This would effectively force sorting based on the ASCII collating sequence even if your machine uses the EBCDIC collating sequence.

```
CHARACTER (LEN=20) :: LIST(100), LISTMIN, SWAP
PRINT *, 'Number of names in the list (100 max.)?'
READ *, N
DO I = 1, N
   PRINT *,'Enter name', I,' between apostrophes'
   READ *, LIST(I)
END DO
!***********************************************************
! Start the sorting operation
!***********************************************************
DO I = 1, N-1
   LISTMIN = LIST(I)
   INDEX = I
!***********************************************************
! Change the conditional test to use LLT
!***********************************************************
   DO J = I+1, N
      IF (LLT(LIST(J),LISTMIN)) THEN
         LISTMIN = LIST(J)
         INDEX = J
      END IF
   END DO
   SWAP = LIST(I)
   LIST(I) = LIST(INDEX)
   LIST(INDEX) = SWAP
END DO
DO I = 1, N
   PRINT *, LIST(I)
END DO
END
```

8.12 Trace through the following program and predict the output. Assume that the input is 'This is a test' and that the number of times, $n = 1$, which will cause the message to shift for 1 complete cycle.

```
CHARACTER LINE*15, DUMMY*1
PRINT *,'Enter the message string (15 char max.)'
READ "(A)", LINE
PRINT *,'Enter the number of times to run'
READ *, N
DO I = 1, LEN(LINE)*N
   DUMMY=LINE(1:1)
   LINE = LINE(2:)//DUMMY
   PRINT "(A)", LINE
END DO
END
```

<u>Variable Listing:</u>

N:	1
I:	1, 2, 3, 4, 5, 6, 7, 8, 9, 10, 11, 12, 13, 14, 15, 16
DUMMY:	T, h, i, s, ~, i, s, ~, a, ~, t, e, s, t
LINE:	Individual substrings of the variable LINE are shown in the table below:

	1	2	3	4	5	6	7	8	9	10	11	12	13	14	15
I=1	T	h	i	s	~	i	s	~	a	~	t	e	s	t	~
I=2	h	i	s	~	i	s	~	a	~	t	e	s	t	~	T
I=3	i	s	~	i	s	~	a	~	t	e	s	t	~	T	h
I=4	s	~	i	s	~	a	~	t	e	s	t	~	T	h	i
I=5	~	i	s	~	a	~	t	e	s	t	~	T	h	i	s
I=6	i	s	~	a	~	t	e	s	t	~	T	h	i	s	~
I=7	s	~	a	~	t	e	s	t	~	T	h	i	s	~	i
I=8	~	a	~	t	e	s	t	~	T	h	i	s	~	i	s
I=9	a	~	t	e	s	t	~	T	h	i	s	~	i	s	~
I=10	~	t	e	s	t	~	T	h	i	s	~	i	s	~	a
I=11	t	e	s	t	~	T	h	i	s	~	i	s	~	a	~
I=12	e	s	t	~	T	h	i	s	~	i	s	~	a	~	t
I=13	s	t	~	T	h	i	s	~	i	s	~	a	~	t	e
I=14	t	~	T	h	i	s	~	i	s	~	a	~	t	e	s
I=15	~	T	h	i	s	~	i	s	~	a	~	t	e	s	t

Output:

The effect would be to have the message ('This is a test') printed onto the screen 15 times with letters shifted to the left on successive lines. If your computer system responds to carriage control characters such as '+' in a FORMAT statement, however, the program can be modified to always have the output appear on the same line. This gives the appearance of having the message scroll to the left side of the screen.

Supplementary Problems

8.13 Indicate the validity of the following assignment statements. For the valid examples determine the value assigned to the variable, assuming that X is declared as a character variable of length 20, Y of length 30, and Z of length 40.

(a) Y=a_string

(b) X='what's this?'

(c) Y='That''s all.'

(d) Z='he said,"she said, 'they did. . .'"'

8.14 Write a program to print out your computer's character set utilizing the functions outlined in this chapter. Have the program determine if the ASCII or EBCDIC character sets is used. The ASCII character set has 128 characters with the collating number ranging from 0 to 127. The EBCDIC character set has 256 characters (0 to 255). Note that some characters in these sets will not print.

8.15 Determine all of the substrings that are possible from the following strings:

(a) 'z'

(b) 'She'

(c) 'range'

(d) 'values'

8.16 Determine the values of the indicated substrings. Assume that the character variable ALPHA has the value 'abcdefghij1234567890' with length 20.

(a) ALPHA(:1)

(b) ALPHA(5:9)

(c) ALPHA(21:)

(d) ALPHA(4:3)

8.17 For the following relational expressions, determine the resulting logical values. Use the EBCDIC collating sequence.

(a) 'John' < 'Jim'

(b) 'Pat' >= 'Alex'

(c) 'John' < 'jim'

(d) 'Sue' > 'bob'

(e) 'Long' > 'LONGER'

(f) 'This' < 'That'

8.18 Write a program which reads in a TITLE string (30 characters max) and a NAME string (30 characters max). Then print a string of 80 characters with TITLE left justified (starts the string with no preceding blanks) and NAME right justified (ends the string with no trailing blanks). Any intermediate characters should be filled with "."s. (For example: TITLE='Student', NAME='John Jones' results in: Student...................John Jones)

8.19 Modify Example 8.3 so that the beginning and ending domain and range can be read in at run time. Currently the program plots a domain from −pi to pi with a range of values from

−1 to 1. If a value is generated beyond the array index domain, ignore that data point (see also Solved Problem 8.9.)

8.20 Predict the output of the following PRINT statements. X is a character variable of length 20 with the value '12345678901234567890'.

   (a) PRINT "(' ', A)", X   (b) PRINT "(' ', A10)", X(1:5)
   (c) PRINT "(' ', 2A)", X(1:3)//X(1:3)   (d) PRINT "(' ', 'X=', A)", X

8.21 Modify Example 8.15 to code a message by swapping the characters abc. . .ABC. . . with zyx. . .ZYX. . . Verify that the program works by entering a coded message back into the program to see if it is correctly deciphered.

8.22 Trace through the following program and predict its output.

```
CHARACTER LINE*25, DUMMY*4
DATA LINE/'all that is forever keep'/
LINE(5:10) = LINE(5:8)//''''//LINE(11:)
DUMMY=LINE(4:4)//LINE(1:3)
LINE(1:10) = LINE(5:10)//DUMMY
LINE(11:) = LINE(12:)
LINE(14:) = LINE(2:2)//LINE(20:20)//LINE(10:10)
LINE(14:14) = LINE(16:16)
LINE(16:16) = LINE(6:6)
PRINT *,LINE
END
```

Answers to Selected Supplementary Problems

8.13 (a) Invalid since the string is not inside apostrophes or quote marks.
     (b) Invalid since the internal apostrophe (') needs to be entered twice ('')
     (c) Valid
     (d) Invalid since inner set of quote marks (") is illegal

8.14
```
IF ('A' < 'a') THEN
    PRINT *,'ASCII collating sequence used.'
    LIMIT=127
ELSE
    PRINT *,'EBCDIC collating sequence used.'
    LIMIT=255
END IF
DO I = 0, LIMIT
    PRINT *,'Character ',I,' is |',CHAR(I),'|'
END DO
END
```

8.15 (a) z, null

(b) S, h, e, Sh, he, She, null

(c) r, a, n, g, e, ra, an, ng, ge, ran, ang, nge, rang, ange, range, null

(d) v, a, l, u, e, s, va, al, lu, ue, es, val, alu, lue, ues, valu, alue, lues, value, alues, values, null

8.16 (a) 'a'   (b) 'efghi'

(c) Invalid – index out of range   (d) null string

8.17 (a) False – 'o' does not come before 'i'

(b) True – 'P' comes after 'A'

(c) False – 'J' does not come before 'j'

(d) True – 'S' comes after 'b'

(e) False – 'o' comes before 'O'

(f) False – 'i' comes after 'a'

8.18
```
CHARACTER*30 TITLE, NAME
CHARACTER*80 LINE
!************************************************************
! Load decimal points into all positions of LINE
!************************************************************
DO I = 1, 80
   LINE = LINE//'.'
END DO
PRINT *,'Enter the TITLE'
READ '(A)',TITLE
PRINT *,'Enter the NAME'
READ '(A)',NAME
!************************************************************
! Left justify the title with ADJUSTL and right justify the name
! with ADJUSTR functions
!************************************************************
TITLE=ADJUSTL(TITLE)
NAME=ADJUSTR(NAME)
!************************************************************
! Now add periods to any blank spaces in TITLE and NAME
!************************************************************
DO I=30,1,-1
   IF (TITLE(I:I) == ' ') THEN
      TITLE(I:I)='.'
   ELSE
      EXIT
   END IF
END DO
DO I=1,30
   IF (NAME(I:I) == ' ') THEN
      NAME(I:I)='.'
   ELSE
      EXIT              ! Leaves the loop when there is no blank
   END IF
END DO
```

```
!*************************************************************
! Now copy TITLE into the first 30 positions of LINE and NAME
! into the last 30 positions
!*************************************************************
LINE(1:30)=TITLE
LINE(51:80)=NAME
PRINT *,LINE
END
```

8.19
```
INTEGER :: COLS, ROWS, IY, JX
PARAMETER(COLS = 80, ROWS = 20)
REAL :: X, Y
CHARACTER (LEN = 1) :: SCREEN(ROWS, COLS)
SCREEN = ' '
PRINT *,'Enter starting and ending X values:'
READ *, XMIN, XMAX
PRINT *,'Enter minimum and maximum range values:'
READ *, YMIN, YMAX
DO JX = 1, COLS
!*************************************************************
! From column value calculate X. From Y value calculate row
! number.
!*************************************************************
    X=XMIN+(JX-1)*(XMAX-XMIN)/(COLS-1)
    Y=SIN(X)
    IY=ROWS-NINT((Y-YMIN)/(YMAX-YMIN)*(ROWS-1))
    IF (1 <= IY .AND. IY <= ROWS) SCREEN(IY,JX)='*'
END DO
DO I = 1, ROWS
    PRINT *,(SCREEN(I, J), J = 1, COLS)
END DO
END
```

8.20

(a) 12345678901234567890   *(Automatic length assignment)*

(b) 12345   *(Formatted larger than required, which causes padding with blanks)*

(c) 123123   *(The two strings are concatenated together and only one of the A edit descriptor is used)*

(d) X=12345678901234567890   *(Formatting with a constant string in the format statement)*

8.21
```
CHARACTER (LEN=53) :: OUTALPHA, INALPHA
CHARACTER (LEN=50) :: INPUT
!*************************************************************
! Note the inclusion of a blank space at the beginning of INALPHA
! and in the middle of OUTALPHA.
!*************************************************************
INALPHA = ' abcdefghijklmnopqrstuvwxyzABCDEFGHIJKLMNOPQRSTUVWXYZ'
OUTALPHA = 'zyxwvutsrqponmlkjihgfedcba ZYXWVUTSRQPONMLKJIHGFEDCBA'
PRINT *,'Enter a string'
READ *,INPUT
DO K=1, 50
    I=INDEX(INALPHA, INPUT(K:K))
    INPUT(K:K)=OUTALPHA(I:I)
END DO
PRINT *,'Coded message:',INPUT
END
```

8.22 <u>Program Trace:</u>

Assign 'all that is forever keep' to character variable LINE

Concat:	LINE(5 to 10) becomes LINE(5 to 8)//''''//LINE(11 to 25), or
	LINE(5 to 10) becomes 'tha'//''''// ~ forever ~ keep, or
	LINE(5 to 10) becomes 'tha''
Concat:	LINE(1 to 10) becomes LINE(5 to 10)//LINE(4)//LINE(1 to end), or
	LINE(1 to 10) becomes 'that''// ~ //'all ~ ', or
	LINE(1 to 10) becomes 'all ~ that's'
Replace:	LINE(11 to end) becomes LINE(12 to end)
	LINE(11 to end) becomes 'forever ~ keep ~ ~ '
Concat:	LINE(14 to end) becomes LINE(2)//LINE(20)//LINE(10)
	LINE(14) becomes LINE(16)
	LINE(14) becomes 's'
Concat:	LINE(16) becomes LINE(6)
	LINE(1 to end) becomes 'that's ~ '//'all ~ '//'folks ~ ~ ~ ~ ~ ~ ~ ~ ~ ~ '

<u>Variables:</u>

DUMMY: ~ , a, l, l

LINE: Individual substrings of LINE are shown in the following table:

program line ⇓	1	2	3	4	5	6	7	8	9	0	1	2	3	4	5	6	7	8	9	0	1	2	3	4	5
2	a	l	l	~	t	h	a	t	~	i	s	~	f	o	r	e	v	e	r	~	k	e	e	p	~
3	a	l	l	~	t	h	a	t	'	s	s	~	f	o	r	e	v	e	r	~	k	e	e	p	~
5	t	h	a	t	'	s	~	a	l	l	s	~	f	o	r	e	v	e	r	~	k	e	e	p	~
6	t	h	a	t	'	s	~	a	l	s	~	f	o	r	e	v	e	r	~	k	e	e	p	~	~
7	t	h	a	t	'	s	~	a	l	l	~	f	o	h	k	l	~	~	~	~	~	~	~	~	~
8	t	h	a	t	'	s	~	a	l	l	~	f	o	l	k	l	~	~	~	~	~	~	~	~	~
9	t	h	a	t	'	s	~	a	l	l	~	f	o	l	k	s	~	~	~	~	~	~	~	~	~

<u>Output:</u>

that's all folks

Chapter 9

Data Files

9.1 INTRODUCTION

Up to now, you have done all input and output through the keyboard and the terminal screen (CRT). When your program encountered a READ * command, you typed in the data, one item at a time. Similarly, when a PRINT * statement occurred, the computer sent output to the screen. While this is convenient, there is no permanent record of the program results. As soon as the CRT screen is cleared, all output is lost. There are many times, however, when it would be desirable to send data to a file. Once this is done, another program or user could access this information later.

It is sometimes desirable to be able to read data values from a file rather than to enter them from the keyboard. A good example is when you are writing a program that requires a large amount of input data. Let's assume that your program requires 100 data points and that you have set it up without the use of an input file. Whenever you rerun the program, you must re-enter the data by hand. So if you needed to run the program 10 times before you removed all the bugs, you would have entered a total of 1000 data points by hand! If instead, the data had been read from a data file, you would have entered the data only once. An even better scheme has the computer itself generate the data (perhaps through a computer-controlled data acquisition system) and enter it into a file for you. This way, you don't need to enter the data even once!

A data files is really no different from other types of files, such as the one in which you store your program. Such a file may be manipulated with commands from the operating system. For example, you can type the file onto your CRT screen, send the file to the system printer(s), or make duplicate copies of the data on another disk. One of the biggest advantages of data files is that you can access them from within your program. Thus, you can send your output to an alternate output device instead of the CRT. Other options might be a printer, floppy or hard disks, FAX modems, plotters, CD disks, and so forth.

In this chapter, we will focus on the technique for diverting I/O from within a program to a device other than the CRT. To do this, there are three things that you must add to your program:

- Instructions to open a file
- Instructions to communicate with the designated file
- Instructions to close the file when finished

In previous chapters, when we had the simple task of printing directly to the CRT, there was no need to worry about these things. All we had to do was enter the command for I/O to send the data directly to the proper device. Unless told otherwise, the computer will communicate exclusively through the CRT and the keyboard, which are termed the *default I/O devices*.

EXAMPLE 9.1

Here is a simple example of how to write to a data file named EXPER.DAT:

```
OPEN(UNIT=8, FILE='EXPER.DAT', STATUS='NEW')
WRITE(8,*) DIST, TIME, VELOC
CLOSE(8)
```

The first statement, OPEN(...), contains all the information needed to set up a file with the name 'EXPER.DAT'. For simplicity, we will refer to the file by a shorthand notation called the UNIT. This unit number comes in handy since it is easier to type the single number (8) than to use the full file name in every I/O statement. Thus, in subsequent statements when we refer to 8, we are really referring to its equivalent file name 'EXPER.DAT'. The final listing in the OPEN statement shows the *status* of the file. As we will see shortly, it will be either 'NEW', 'OLD', 'SCRATCH', or 'UNKNOWN' indicating whether the file needs to be created, already exists, is only temporary, or unknown, respectively.

The second statement, WRITE(8,*) *list* , is used to direct the output to the desired file. Remember that we have given the file the short name of 8. Thus, the WRITE statement tells the computer to send the output to the UNIT=8 and which has the corresponding file name 'EXPER.DAT'. The final statement of the example, CLOSE(...), simply closes the file after we finish with it.

A similar set of statements can be used to read from a data file. The primary difference from the output statement is that the file must already exist to read from it. Therefore, its STATUS will be 'OLD' or 'UNKNOWN'.

EXAMPLE 9.2

In the following example, we will read data from a file named 'NOBEL.DAT' and assign the data to the variables WEIGHT, MASS, and DENSITY. Notice that the file must already exist in order to read from it.

```
OPEN(UNIT=3, FILE='NOBEL.DAT', STATUS='OLD')
READ(3,*) WEIGHT, MASS, DENSITY
CLOSE(3)
```

Notice that the READ statement goes to unit #3, which is the shorthand notation for the file 'NOBEL.DAT'. Also note that the status of the file is 'OLD' indicating that it is a valid file for reading. If the status had not been 'OLD' or 'UNKNOWN', a syntax error would have resulted.

9.2 TYPES OF FILES

Fortran recognizes two types of files — *sequential* and *direct access*. Some compilers allow other types of files, but these are rarely used and we will not discuss them here. Sequential files are those in which the records within the file are read in sequence. Direct access files, on the other hand, allow you to access any individual record within the file regardless of its position.

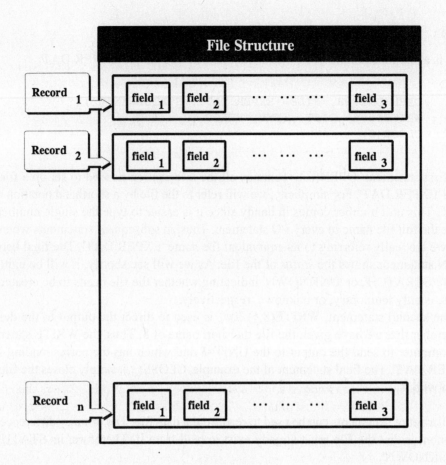

Fig. 9–1

To help you understand the terminology in this chapter, refer to Fig. 9–1. A file is a block of memory that is given a name determined by the user. For permanent storage, a file is placed in nonvolatile memory such as a hard or floppy disk, while for temporary storage, files are placed into the computer's volatile memory. The file consists of a series of *records*. A record is a convenient-sized block of data that you establish to store *fields* of data. Individual data values are stored within the fields, and each type of data has a different field size. Recall that alphanumeric character data can occupy any size field, while numeric data occupy fixed field widths. The computer reads (or writes) one record at a time. Thus it is possible that some of the fields within a record may not be read at all, depending on the structure of the I/O statements. For example, if your READ statement contains only one variable, but the record contains three numbers, the last two numbers in the record will be unread and therefore lost.

Sequential files must read the records in the order that they were written into the file. Direct access files, on the other hand, can move to any record and read (or write) that one only. When data are written to a file, the two types of files behave very differently. When you write to a sequential file, the data values can only be written at the end of the file. If you write the data to any other position, all subsequent entries are erased. Direct access files, on the other hand, allow you to write to any record in the file without disturbing any other records. Engineers and scientists tend to rely almost exclusively on sequential files, so we will focus on them. Direct access files are used less frequently in the sciences, but are used very frequently when dealing with large data files — census data, tax returns, or bank records, for example.

9.3 OPENING A SEQUENTIAL FILE

The OPEN statement contains information about the attributes of the file to be used for I/O. There are a large number of options available with the OPEN statement, only a few of which were shown in the first two examples. In the general form of the OPEN statement shown below, only the first two items in the parentheses are required, while the remaining items are optional:

OPEN ([UNIT=] *integer expression*, [FILE=] *string*,
          [ACCESS=*string*,]
          [ACTION=*string*,]
          [BLANK=*string*,]
          [DELIM=*string*,]
          [ERR=*statement label n*,]
          [FORM=*string*,]
          [IOSTAT=*integer variable*,]
          [PAD=*string*,]
          [POSITION=*string*,]
          [RECL=*integer expression*,]
          [STATUS=*string*,]

Only a few of the options listed above are part of the Fortran standard. However, since almost all commercial compilers have all or most of these options, we present them all here. As an example, the attributes POSITION, ACTION, DELIM, and PAD are not available in the Fortran 77 standard, so be careful when using them since this may make your programs less portable. As stated earlier, only the UNIT and FILENAME attributes are required. But use of the others may make it easier for you to handle many of the problems that occur.

The attribute UNIT is required and specifies the identifying number of the file to be accessed. The statement "UNIT=" may be omitted, but an integer constant or variable must appear.

EXAMPLE 9.3

The following statements are equivalent and open a file that we will refer to as unit #3:

```
OPEN(UNIT=3,...)          or          OPEN(3, ...)
READ (3,*) X, Y                        READ (3,*) X, Y
```

You may also use an integer variable or expression to specify the unit number, but this is rarely used. Be careful when selecting unit numbers, since most systems reserve a few unit numbers for their own use. For example, on many computer systems, UNIT=5 is reserved for the CRT screen. Apart from these few reserved unit numbers (set by the computer administrators), the only other restriction is that the number must be between 1 and 99.

The attribute FILE specifies the name of the file connected to the specified unit number. You may use either a character string or a character variable that can be read in at execution time. The statement FILE= may be omitted if this file name comes second. The allowed name of the file will vary from computer to computer, so be careful to check the file naming conventions on your system.

EXAMPLE 9.4

The following statements are equivalent and indicate that the file to be opened has the name 'VOLTS.DAT':

```
        OPEN(UNIT=3,FILE='VOLTS.DAT',...)
        READ (3,*) X, Y
```
or
```
        OPEN(3,'VOLTS.DAT',...)
        READ (3,*) X, Y
```

EXAMPLE 9.5

You may specify the file name to be a variable that is read in at execution time, provided that you have properly set up the name as a character variable. In the following example, we use the character string stored in NAME to create the desired file entered by the user:

```
        CHARACTER (LEN=10) :: NAME
        PRINT *, 'Enter output file name:'
        READ *, NAME

        OPEN(UNIT=16, FILE=NAME,...)
        WRITE (16,*) X, Y
```

When you declare the character variable, be sure to set up the variable with sufficient characters for the machine that you are using. For example, 10 characters is the customary limit on a file name on desktop computers. But some larger computers allow more characters, typically in the range of 13 to 20. Finally, note in this example that the input of the file name is interactive and is entered at the time that the program is run.

The attribute ACCESS specifies whether the file is *sequential* or *random access*. In a sequential file, all preceding items in the file must be read to get to the one that you are interested in. Direct access files, on the other hand, permit you to go directly to the position of the data item.

EXAMPLE 9.6

This program opens a sequential file 'OUT.DAT' and reads ten data points into the array X:

```
        REAL, DIMENSION(10) :: X
        OPEN(UNIT=9, FILE='OUT.DAT', ACCESS='SEQUENTIAL',...)
        READ (9,*) (X(I), I=1,10)
```

If you omit the ACCESS attribute, then 'SEQUENTIAL' is assumed. Thus, the following is equivalent to the previous three statements.

```
REAL, DIMENSION(10) :: X
OPEN(UNIT=9, FILE='OUT.DAT', ...)
READ (9,*) (X(I), I=1,10)
```

Most applications in engineering and science require sequential access, so this latter form is more common.

EXAMPLE 9.7

Some compilers have an optional ACCESS='APPEND' instruction available for sequential files. When this is included, any new data being written to the file will be written at the end of the file, immediately after the last data point. Previous data will not be disturbed.

```
┌─────────────────────┐
│                     │
│  17.9               │      Data file before new data are appended
│  21.6               │
│  <end of file>      │
│                     │
└─────────────────────┘
```

When the following program executes, the new data values will be added to the end of the file, and the end of the file indication will move down the required number of lines.

```
X=4.1
OPEN(UNIT=9, FILE='OUT.DAT', ACCESS='APPEND', ...)
WRITE (9,*) X
```

```
┌─────────────────────┐
│                     │
│  17.9               │      Data file after new item is appended
│  21.6               │
│  4.1                │
│  <end of file>      │
│                     │
└─────────────────────┘
```

The ACTION attribute allows you to provide a degree of protection for your files. The allowed commands are 'READ', 'WRITE', and 'READ/WRITE', which limit you to read only, write only, or both reading and writing only from the specified file, respectively. Thus, if you specify ACTION='READ', you will not be allowed to write to that file. This prevents you from losing data by accidentally overwriting them.

EXAMPLE 9.8

The following example opens a sequential file 'SALES.DAT' for reading in the data and, at the same time, protects the file from having anything written to it:

```
REAL, DIMENSION(10) :: SALES
OPEN(UNIT=11, FILE='SALES.DAT', ACTION='READ', ...)
READ (11,*) (SALES(I), I=1,10)
```

Once the ACTION='READ' is included as an attribute of the file 'SALES.DAT', that file will be protected against accidental erasure. Some compilers also offer additional options with the ACTION attribute to allow you to safely share files between multiple READ or WRITE statements, so check your manual for further details.

The attribute BLANK has only two values — 'NULL' or 'ZERO' which will determine how blanks at the beginning of a number are to be interpreted. If 'NULL' is used, the computer will ignore blanks, but choosing 'ZERO' will cause the leading blanks to be interpreted as zeros.

EXAMPLE 9.9

Assume that we have the following data file named 'NULLZERO.DAT' (Note: blank=~)

```
~~~~4.2
~~2.3~~
1.7~~~~
<end of file>
```

Data file: 'NULLZERO.DAT'

If we read the file with the following program segment, the leading blank spaces (indicated by ~) are converted to zeros, but the trailing blank spaces are ignored.

```
OPEN(UNIT=10, FILE='NULLZERO.DAT', BLANK='ZERO', ...)
READ (10,*) A, B, C
```

will produce:

```
A=00004.2
B=002.3
C=1.7.
```

The attribute DELIM selects the character that will be used to mark the beginning or end of character strings in a data file. The three possible values are 'APOSTROPHE', 'QUOTE', and 'NONE'. If 'APOSTROPHE' or 'QUOTE' is used, that character will be used to identify the character string, and any internal apostrophe or quote marks will be doubled. If, however, 'NONE' is specified, then any internal apostrophes or quotes will be unaffected.

EXAMPLE 9.10

Assume that we have the following data file named 'DELIM.DAT' that contains a series of character strings:

```
'this is"nt a test'
"this is"nt a test"
<end of file>
```
Data file: 'DELIM.DAT'

If we specify quote marks as the delimiter, the data will be read as follows:

```
CHARACTER (LEN=20) :: TEST1, TEST2
OPEN(UNIT=10, FILE='DELIM.DAT', DELIM='QUOTE', ...)
READ (10,*) TEST1, TEST2
```

This will result in the following assignments:

TEST1 ← this isn't a test　　　　　　　TEST2 ← this is"nt a test

When reading the first line of the data file, the computer treats the internal quotes as a single quote, based upon the leading delimiter ('). But in the second line of the data file, the leading delimiter is the double quote ("), so the internal quote is treated as a double quote.

The ERR command is useful because it allows you to *trap errors*. If an error occurs while attempting to communicate with a file, control transfers to the statement specified by *sl* in the ERR=*sl* statement. This gives you a chance to try again or to undertake another procedure.

EXAMPLE 9.11

Assume that we have the following data file named 'OUT.DAT':

```
9.654
1.256
3.450
<end of file>
```
Data file: 'OUT.DAT'

If we attempt to run the following program segment, an error will occur because we will reach the end of the file (EOF) before we have read in all the specified data:

```
REAL, DIMENSION(5) :: X
OPEN(UNIT=4, FILE='OUT.DAT', ...)
READ (4,*) (X(I), I=1,5)
```

We can use the ERR attribute to handle such errors, as shown below:

```
     REAL, DIMENSION(5) :: X
     OPEN(UNIT=4, FILE='OUT.DAT', ERR=10, ...)
     READ (4,*) (X(I), I=1,5)
        :
10   STOP 'ERROR IN DATA FILE'
```

There is an alternate way to do the same thing, in which we embed the error handling within the READ command. This is done by adding ERR=*sl*1 or END=*sl*2 clauses:

READ(*unit, format*, ERR=*sl*1, END=*sl*2)

If the end of the file is reached before all the data are read, control will transfer to statement label 2 (*sl*2), while any other error will cause control to transfer to statement label 1 (*sl*1).

The FORM attribute has only two possible options, FORMATTED or UNFORMATTED. The formatted option permits the program to read data in a converted form, while the unformatted option will read in data from a file as binary strings. Almost all of your files will be of the formatted type. Some files, however, are stored as binary files because they are smaller and because they can be read and written more quickly than formatted files.

EXAMPLE 9.12

If you wish to store data in a binary file, you can do this simply by adding the statement FORM='UNFORMATTED' to the OPEN statement.

```
REAL, DIMENSION(5) :: X
OPEN(UNIT=4, FILE='TEST.DAT', FORM='UNFORMATTED', . . . .)
WRITE (4) (X(I), I=1,5)
```

This will write all the data in binary form to the indicated file. Once this is done, the only way we can read the data within this file would be to use a corresponding READ statement that was opened with the FORM='UNFORMATTED' statement.

The IOSTAT attribute allows you to receive information from the computer about the type of error that has occurred. This instruction is different from the others in that you are receiving rather than sending data. If no error occurs, the integer variable in the IOSTAT=*integer variable* is set to zero. But if an error does occur, then the variable is set to a nonzero value. You can use this value to do something. Perhaps you want to retry reading the file, or read another file, or print an error message. The point is that you now have some control over handling errors. The exact value of the variable returned is compiler dependent, but the following are typical values:

integer variable	<	0	*(end of file error)*
integer variable	=	0	*(no errors)*
integer variable	>	0	*(other types of errors)*

EXAMPLE 9.13

In the following program segment, a message will be printed whether the file 'IOSTAT.DAT' was read correctly or not:

```
REAL, DIMENSION(5) :: X
OPEN(UNIT=8, FILE='IOSTAT.DAT', IOSTAT=ITEST,...)
READ (8,*) (X(I), I=1,5)
SELECT CASE (ITEST)
   CASE(:-1)
      PRINT *, 'End of file error'
   CASE(0)
      PRINT *, 'No problems'
   CASE(1:)
      PRINT *, 'Other type of error'
END Select
```

After the file is read, an integer value will be assigned by the computer to the variable ITEST. In the case select structure, we examine the value of ITEST. If it is negative, the error message "End of file error" is printed. If ITEST is zero, the message "No problem" is printed, and if ITEST is positive, "Other type of error" is printed.

Once you find what the other error codes are for your compiler, you can add these to an expanded case select block. These error codes will be machine dependent, so it may affect the portability of your program. Therefore, we recommend that you stay with this simple segment.

The PAD option, if selected, will deliberately add extra blank spaces when a list of input variables requires more data than the record (line) in the data file contains. There are only two values allowed, 'YES' and 'NO'.

EXAMPLE 9.14

In the following program segment, data will be read into a character variable DUMMY which requires 20 characters to fill it, but the data file contains a smaller number of characters (8 in this case):

```
CHARACTER (LEN=20) :: DUMMY
OPEN(UNIT=8, FILE='PAD.DAT', PAD='YES',...)
READ (8,*) DUMMY
```

If we use this program to read the following data file:

ABCDEFGH
<end of file>   Data file: 'PAD.DAT'

the value assigned to DUMMY will be padded with an extra 12 blank spaces to fill out the 20 spaces reserved for the variable:

DUMMY='ABCDEFGH~~~~~~~~~~~~'

The PAD clause can only be used with input statements. If you attempt to use it with an output statement, a compiler error will occur. If the instruction is omitted, the compiler assumes a value of 'YES'.

The POSITION option changes the position of a hypothetical pointer within a sequential file. After communicating with a file, this pointer "points" to the next position in the file. The POSITION command will change that position to one of three possibilities — 'ASIS', 'REWIND', or 'APPEND'. The 'ASIS' option leaves the file unaffected, while the 'APPEND' option moves to the end of the file. The 'REWIND' option moves the pointer to the beginning of the file.

EXAMPLE 9.15

In the following program segment, the hypothetical pointer will be reset to the beginning of the file before it reads the first data point:

```
OPEN(UNIT=2, FILE='POINTER.DAT', POSITION='REWIND',...)
READ (2,*) N
```

The STATUS attribute is used to indicate the type of file that is being accessed. The possible values are 'NEW', 'OLD', 'UNKNOWN', or 'SCRATCH'. If the STATUS attribute is omitted, a value of 'UNKNOWN' is assumed. The value of STATUS indicates whether the file has already been created ('OLD'), should be created ('NEW'), is temporary ('SCRATCH'), or has a status of unknown ('UNKNOWN'). The use of STATUS should be intuitive, since you cannot read data from a file that does not exist.

EXAMPLE 9.16

In the following program segment, we will open the file STATUS.DAT and read data from it. We will then create a second file and then send the data (in reverse order) that we have just read to the new file 'TEST.DAT'.

```
OPEN(UNIT=1, FILE='STATUS.DAT', STATUS='OLD')
OPEN(UNIT=2, FILE='TEST.DAT', STATUS='NEW')
READ (1,*) (X(I), I=1,10)
WRITE (2,*) (X(I), I=10, 1, -1)
```

The first OPEN statement tells the computer to go to file 'STATUS.DAT' and associate it with unit 1. The READ statement will then open that file and read the data. Notice that the OPEN statement tells the computer that the file should already exist, hence its STATUS='OLD'. Once the data have been read, they are then sent to the newly created file 'TEST.DAT', which is associated with unit 2 and STATUS='NEW'.

Most of the data file work that you will need to do requires only the UNIT, FILE, and STATUS attributes in the OPEN statement. The additional specifiers are rarely required except for error-trapping purposes. So most OPEN statements that you will see will be of the form:

```
OPEN(UNIT=4, FILE='MINE.DAT', STATUS='OLD')
```

9.4 CLOSING A SEQUENTIAL FILE

You close files in your program with the CLOSE statement whose general form is:

CLOSE ([UNIT=] *integer expression,*
　　　　[ERR=*statement label n,*]
　　　　[IOSTAT=*integer variable,*]
　　　　[STATUS=*string,*])

Any attribute in brackets ([...]) is optional and can be left out. The UNIT= *integer expression* has the same meaning as in the OPEN statement. It is the only attribute that is required with the CLOSE statement. All other attributes (ERR, IOSTAT, STATUS) are optional.

EXAMPLE 9.17

The following program segment opens a file 'TESTCLOSE.DAT', writes a value to that file, and then closes it after the data have been written to the file:

```
OPEN(UNIT=3, FILE='CLOSE.DAT', STATUS='NEW')
WRITE (3,*) X, Y
CLOSE(UNIT=3)
```

Just as with the OPEN statement, the unit number must always be included, but the UNIT= clause is optional. Thus, an equivalent way of writing the program segment is:

```
OPEN(3, 'CLOSE.DAT', STATUS='NEW')
WRITE(3,*) X, Y
CLOSE(3)
```

Actually, the entire CLOSE statement may be omitted since the computer closes all files when the program terminates. But it is not a good idea to leave files open since you may inadvertently write to the file in another part of the program.

The STATUS attribute associated with the CLOSE statement is different from the one used with the OPEN statement. The only allowable values of STATUS are 'KEEP' and 'DELETE'. If 'KEEP' is selected, the file is made permanent for future use, but if 'DELETE' is chosen, the file is deleted immediately. If the file status is not specified, 'KEEP' is assumed.

If the file in the OPEN statement has STATUS='SCRATCH', then the computer will <u>always</u> delete the file after you finish. Even if you use STATUS='KEEP' in the CLOSE statement, the machine will delete the file. Once you declare a file to be a scratch file, you cannot save it.

The two other attributes (IOSTAT and ERR) used in the CLOSE statement are both optional and have the same meaning as that described earlier with the OPEN command. Therefore we will not repeat them here.

9.5 SEQUENTIAL FILE POSITIONING STATEMENTS

There are a few additional commands used with files that you may find useful. These allow you to move around within a file and to mark the end of the file. The first of these commands allows you to rewind the file to the beginning. Its general form is

REWIND ([UNIT=] *integer expression,*
         [IOSTAT=*integer variable,*]
         [ERR=*statement label n,*])

where all of the attributes have the same meaning as before. The only required attribute is the file number with or without the optional clause UNIT=. The error-trapping attributes are optional.

EXAMPLE 9.18

Some computer systems may require you to rewind a file before you attempt to read it. So even though it is not required, it may be a good idea to rewind before reading to improve the portability of your programs. The following program segment rewinds the file 'REWIND.DAT' before attempting to read it:

```
          OPEN(UNIT=3, FILE='REWIND.DAT', STATUS='OLD')
          REWIND (UNIT=3, ERR=10)
          READ (3,*) X, Y
          CLOSE(UNIT=3)

     10   STOP 'FILE REWIND ERROR'
```

In this example, we first opened the file and attempted to rewind it. If an error occurs, control will transfer to the STOP statement and print out the error message. If the rewind is successful, the program proceeds to read the required data and then closes the unit. Notice that you can rewind a file only after it has been opened.

The second positioning statement allows you to backspace one record within the file. Whereas the REWIND command goes to the beginning of the file, the BACKSPACE command moves back only one record. Its general form is

$$BACKSPACE~([UNIT=]~integer~expression,~[IOSTAT=~integer~variable,]$$
$$[ERR=~statement~label~n])$$

All of the attributes have their usual meaning. The only required attribute is the file number with or without the optional UNIT= clause. The error-trapping attributes are optional. This statement is useful when you need to reread data because of a reading error.

EXAMPLE 9.19

In the following program segment, we will read a value of X from a data file. If an error occurs during reading, we will backspace and try again.

```
      OPEN(UNIT=7, FILE='BACK.DAT', STATUS='OLD')
      READ (7,*, ERR=3) X
          :
3     BACKSPACE (7)
      READ (7,*) X
          :
      CLOSE(UNIT=7)
```

We have added an error-trapping option to the READ statement in this example. If a read error occurs, control transfers to statement label 3, where the computer is instructed to backspace one record and reread the data. This is about the only use of the BACKSPACE command.

The third statement is used to place an end-of-file indication into a file. Its general form is:

$$ENDFILE~([UNIT=]~integer~expression,~[IOSTAT=~integer~variable,]$$
$$[ERR=~statement~label~n])$$

All of the attributes have their usual meaning. The only required attribute is the file number with or without the optional UNIT = clause. The error-trapping attributes are optional.

EXAMPLE 9.20

In the following program segment, we read values from a data file until an end-of-file is encountered. At this point, we write a message to the screen. We can then begin to do other work. For example, we could begin computations on the numbers just entered.

```
      REAL, DIMENSION(100) :: X, Y
      OPEN(UNIT=11, FILE='EOF.DAT', STATUS='OLD')
      OPEN(UNIT=12,'FILE='CONTINUE.DAT', STATUS='NEW')
      READ (11,*, END=9) (X(I), I=1, 100)
          :
9     WRITE (12, *) (Y(I), I=1,100)
      ENDFILE (12)
          :
      CLOSE(UNIT=12)
```

Once again, we have added an END option to the I/O statement. When the computer comes to the original EOF mark, control will transfer to statement label 9 where the new data will be written. When finished writing, the program places an EOF mark at the new end.

The EOF command is generally not needed since this is automatically added to the end of a file when it is closed. So the use for this statement is very limited.

9.6 DIRECT ACCESS FILES

The second type of file is the direct access file. Recall that the distinguishing feature of this type of file is that we can communicate with a single record within the file without having to go through all the other records. But in order to do this, we need to specify a *record number* that points to the specific record. We will do this in the READ or WRITE statement. Also, the OPEN statement is slightly different with direct access files. The record length must be the same for all records in the direct access file. This is done with the RECL attribute in the OPEN statement:

```
OPEN ([UNIT=] integer expression, [FILE=] string,
        [ACCESS=string,]
        [ACTION=string,]
        [BLANK=string,]
        [DELIM=string,]
        [ERR=statement label n,]
        [FORM=string,]
        [IOSTAT=integer variable,]
        [PAD=string,]
        [POSITION=string,]
        [RECL=integer expression,]
        [STATUS=string,])
```

The RECL clause indicates the length (in number of columns) of each record within the file. You can determine the length of the record by simply counting the number of columns that the data occupy. In many ways, this is similar to the way that we set up the output fields in formatting. All the other attributes have the same meaning as those discussed previously.

EXAMPLE 9.21

In the following program segment, we will open the direct access file 'RECL.DAT' in which the data within the file have a record length of 23:

```
     OPEN(UNIT=3, FILE='RECL.DAT', ACCESS='DIRECT',&
               FORM='FORMATTED', RECL=23, STATUS='NEW')
     WRITE (3, 5, REC=34) 'Value of N is:', N
  5  FORMAT(A14, I9)
```

We used the ACCESS='DIRECT' clause to create a direct access file. When the file is formatted, the RECL is determined by the number of columns that the data occupy. Thus, in this example, we had 14 characters and 9 digits, for a total of 23. This number appears in the clause RECL=23.

The new clause (REC=34) within the READ statement indicates that the data in the I/O list are to be written to the 34th record. Any previous data in that location will be lost, but no other data will be disturbed.

The attributes UNIT, FILE, and RECL are required with direct access files, while FORM and STATUS are optional. If FORM is omitted, the computer assumes 'FORMATTED' for sequential files and 'UNFORMATTED' for direct access files. So, in the previous example if we had left out the FORM attribute, the file would have been different from the RECL=23 that we used. This is due to the fact that unformatted files are stored in bytes and are machine dependent. In most cases, it is better to stay with formatted files, because the storage method for unformatted files will vary.

9.7 DEBUGGING

There are several problems that you might run into when using data files. The things to watch out for are:

- You attempt to write to a file before it is opened or you try to read from a file after it is closed.
- You attribute the wrong status to a file that results in a conflict with the I/O command that follows.
- You mix attributes designed for sequential and direct files.
- Any attempt to replace a record in a sequential file will result in the remainder of the file being erased.

Once you have diagnosed which type of error has occurred, it is usually a simple matter to correct the problem. Each of these problems is illustrated in the examples below.

EXAMPLE 9.22

If you attempt to access a file before it has been opened (or after it has been closed), you will receive a run-time error.

```
OPEN(UNIT=3, FILE='MINE.DAT', STATUS='NEW')
WRITE(3,*) DIST, TIME, VELOC
CLOSE(3)
READ(3,*)   X , Y , Z
```

Once you close a file, you cannot access it again unless you use another OPEN statement. Thus, in the example above, the third line has closed the file. After that point, you cannot try to read from or print to the file.

EXAMPLE 9.23

If you attempt to read from a file, the proper status attribute in the OPEN statement must be STATUS='OLD'. Otherwise, you will be attempting to read from a file that doesn't exist yet, and you will receive a run-time error.

```
OPEN(UNIT=4, FILE='MINE.DAT', STATUS='NEW')
READ(4,*) DIST, TIME, VELOC
CLOSE(4)
```

The OPEN statement has specified the file 'MINE.DAT' will be created as a new file. Yet, we attempt to read from the file not yet been created. Therefore, a run-time error occurs.

EXAMPLE 9.24

If you mix attributes designed for sequential and direct files, an error will occur.

```
OPEN(UNIT=5, FILE='TEST.DAT', ACCESS='SEQUENTIAL', &
     RECL=32, STATUS='NEW')
WRITE(5,*, REC=14) DIST, TIME, VELOC
CLOSE(5)
```

The file TEST.DAT was declared to be a sequential file, yet a record length was specified, and the WRITE statement included a REC= command. Both of these options are used for direct access files, not sequential files. Therefore, an error message will result.

EXAMPLE 9.25

If you attempt to write to a sequential file at any position other than the end of the file, all the remaining data will be lost. Assume for example that we had the following data file:

12.34
14.57
43.56
13.687
13.56
2.78
−0.45
<end of file>

Data file before reading

If we now read a value, and attempt to replace it with a revised value, then everything after that point will be lost. For example, assume we read the first three values, backspace one position, and then rewrite a new value in the third record of the file:

```
OPEN(UNIT=6, FILE='REPLACE.DAT', STATUS='OLD')
READ(6,*) X, Y, Z
        :
(Compute new value of Z)
        :
BACKSPACE (6)
WRITE(6,*) Z
CLOSE(6)
```

This will result in the following change to the data file:

12.34
14.57
new value of Z
erased
erased
erased
erased
<end of file>

Data file after updating information

The revised file would not have the four blank lines indicated in the file. Instead, the end-of-file record would appear immediately after the new value of Z. We showed the erased records to reinforce the fact that everything after a new entry to a sequential file will be erased. To do what we wanted to do in this example, we would need to use a direct access file.

EXAMPLE 9.26

There is one final area where an unexpected error may occur. This is in the use of carriage control characters with data files. Generally, you only use a carriage control character (CCC) when the output is going to be sent to a printer or a CRT. The CCCs are not needed when the data are being sent to a data file. The problem occurs when you attempt to send the data file to a printer at a later date. In this case, the CCCs would be needed, but they are not included in the file. Therefore, some of the data may be truncated. Consider the following data file:

9.3425
6.234
6.324
<end of file>

Data file

If you now type this file on a printer, the following output will result:

```
.3425
.234
.324
```

If the CCC is omitted, the computer will use the first character in the record to reset the printer. In the case shown, this corresponds to the first digit of each number being lost. In fact, you may not even be aware of the problem, since the loss of a single digit is not obvious. The solution to this problem is to use CCCs when using formatted output to a data file.

Solved Problems

9.1   Locate the syntax and run-time errors in the following program statements:

   (a) `OPEN(UNIT=114, FILE='TEST.DAT')`
   (b) `OPEN(20, 'TEST.DAT', ACCESS=SEQUENTIAL)`
   (c) `CLOSE(UNIT=7, FILE='TEST.DAT', STATUS='SCRATCH')`
   (d) `OPEN(3, 'SCRATCH')`
   (e) `OPEN(9, FILE='IO.DAT', ACCESS='DIRECT')`
        `READ(9,*,RECL=7) X`
   (f) `OPEN(11, FILE='THERMAL.DAT', ACCESS='DIRECT', RECL=14)`
        `WRITE(11,*,REC=13) A, B, C`

   (a) The unit number may not exceed 99 on many computers.
   (b) Sequential should be inside apostrophes ('SEQUENTIAL').
   (c) A CLOSE statement does not use the "FILE=" attribute.
   (d) No errors, but the file name will be 'Scratch'. This does not refer to the status.
   (e) Direct access files require a record length (RECL) attribute in the OPEN statement.
   (f) The variables A, B, and C, will occupy approximately 24 columns (assuming a maximum of 8 columns each). Therefore, the RECL clause is inadequate.

9.2   Write OPEN statements to accomplish the following:

   (a) Create a sequential file called 'WEIGHTS.DAT'
   (b) Connect to a file called 'INPUT' as an old file on unit 6.
   (c) Open a file called 'RESULTS' as a new file on unit 5.
   (d) Open a scratch file on unit 7.
   (e) Open a file 'DATA.DAT' whose status is uncertain on unit 4.

   (a) `OPEN(UNIT=1, FILE='WEIGHTS.DAT', STATUS='NEW')`
   (b) `OPEN(UNIT=6, FILE='INPUT', STATUS='OLD')`
   (c) `OPEN(UNIT=5, FILE='RESULTS', STATUS='NEW')`
   (d) `OPEN(UNIT=7, STATUS='SCRATCH')`
   (e) `OPEN(UNIT=4, FILE='DATA.DAT', STATUS='UNKNOWN')`

9.3   The following exercises are designed so that you can find out the limitations or extensions of your Fortran compiler. Run small programs to find out if the following suggestions work. You may also need to consult the documentation for your system.

(a)   What is the UNIT number for CRT output and keyboard input on your system? If there are two such numbers such as 5 or 6, is there any difference in the way that each behaves?

(b)   What is the set of valid unit numbers on your system? Do any other unit numbers have any special significance, such as tape drives, floppy disks, optical scanners, or plotters? (You need to ask the system administrators to answer these questions.)

(c)   Some compilers will allow the use of * for unit directed I/O. If that's the case, the following are equivalent. Does your system support this feature?

```
PRINT *, X          is equivalent to   WRITE(*,*) X
```

9.4   Assume that we have a file that contains the following data:

```
1, 2, 3
4
5                          Data file 'INPUT'
6, 7
<end of file>
```

What are the values of the variables if the file is read with the following program segments? (Assume the file has the attributes UNIT=7, FILE='INPUT', STATUS='OLD')

(a)   `READ(7,*) A, B, C`
(b)   `READ(7,*) A, B, C, I, J`
(c)   `READ(7,*) A`
      `READ(7,*) B`
      `READ(7,*) C, I`
(d)   `READ(7,*) (X(I), I=1, 7)`

(a)   Each READ statement reads one record. So the first numeric field is assigned to A, the second to B, and the third to C. This results in the assignments: A=1.000000, B=2.000000, and C=3.000000.

(b)   The READ statement requires five numeric values to assign to the variables. But the first record contains only three values, so additional records are read until all the variables have values. The result is A=1.000000, B=2.000000, C=3.000000, I=4, and J=5.

(c)   The first READ statement needs only one value for assignment. Therefore, it uses only the first field within the first record. The second and third values are ignored. The second READ statement then begins input with the second record, and the third READ begins with the third record. The result is: A=1.000000, B=4.000000, C=5.000000, and I=6.

Notice that the values 2 and 3 from the first record are never read.

(d) The single READ statement requires seven values to fill the X array. This can only be achieved by reading beyond the first record until all values are assigned. The result is $X_1=1.000000$, $X_2=2.000000$, $X_3=3.000000$, $X_4=4.000000$, $X_5=5.000000$, $X_6=6.000000$, $X_7=7.000000$.

9.5 In all of the previous examples, we knew in advance what the name of the input or output file would be. But many times we will not have this information. Therefore, it is desirable to enter the desired file name at execution time and proceed to open the desired file. Write a program segment which will accomplish this task.

```
!***************************************************************
! We will declare FILENAME to be a character variable and use
! this to hold the desired file name.
!***************************************************************
CHARACTER (LEN=20) :: FILENAME
PRINT *, 'Enter desired file name:'
READ *, FILENAME
!***************************************************************
! Now that the file name has been entered, use it to create
! the file. Notice that we do not include single quote marks
! around the file name since it is a character variable.
!***************************************************************
OPEN(UNIT=1, FILE=FILENAME, STATUS='NEW')
WRITE(1,*) …
     :

END
```

9.6 Write a program to read a file 'CONCENTR.DAT' whose records contain concentrations of various species, [a], [b], and [c] in a chemical reaction. Assume that the data are written to the file with the format specifier (3F10.6). Read in one record at a time, and for each set of concentrations compute the rate constant defined by

$$k = \frac{[a][b]}{[c]}$$

Print the results ([a], [b], [c], and k) to the screen. If an error occurs during the read operation, print the message "Input Error!" When the end-of-file occurs, terminate the program and print the message "Calculations Complete."

```
!***************************************************************
! Open the file and then read one set of [a], [b], and [c]
! values at a time. Use these to compute k and print the
! results. Include in the READ statement the options ERR=
! and END=. These will detect read errors and end-of-file
! respectively.
!***************************************************************
```

```
        REAL :: K
        OPEN(UNIT=1, FILE='CONCENTR.DAT', STATUS='OLD')
        DO WHILE(.TRUE.)! One way to set up an indefinite loop
          READ(1,10, ERR=20, END=30) A, B, C
10        FORMAT(3F10.6)
          K=A*B/C
          PRINT *, A, B, C, K
        END DO
20      STOP 'Input Error!'
30      STOP 'Calculations Complete'
        END
```

9.7   Assume that data from a bacteria-growth experiment are stored in two files 'GROWTH.DAT' and 'POTENCY.DAT' with the following formats

'GROWTH.DAT'

10/12/93	23:47	1234568
10/13/93	11:47	1458450
10/14/93	06:34	1534389
10/15/93	09:23	1637238
<end of file>		

'POTENCY.DAT'

10/12/93	23:47	147.345
10/13/93	11:47	146.234
10/14/93	06:34	148.346
10/15/93	09:23	147.225
<end of file>		

The first two columns in each file represents the date and time, respectively, at which the data were taken. The third column represents the number of cells (in 'GROWTH.DAT') and their potency (in 'POTENCY.DAT'). Write a program that opens both files and merges them into a new file 'BACTERIA.DAT' with the following format:

10/12/93	23:47	1234568	147.345
10/13/93	11:47	1458450	146.234
10/14/93	06:34	1534389	148.346
10/15/93	09:23	1637238	147.225
<end of file>			

```
!****************************************************************
! Open all three files at the same time, but give each a
! different unit number.
!****************************************************************
      CHARACTER DATE*12, TIME*7
      INTEGER :: NUMCEL
      OPEN(UNIT=1, FILE='GROWTH.DAT', STATUS='OLD')
      OPEN(UNIT=2, FILE='POTENCY.DAT', STATUS='OLD')
      OPEN(UNIT=3, FILE='BACTERIA.DAT', STATUS='NEW')
```

```
!***************************************************************
! Set up a loop to read the data from GROWTH.DAT and POTENCY.DAT
! and merge them. Be sure to remove redundant information before
! writing it to the new file. If an end-of-file specification
! is encountered, stop.
!***************************************************************
      DO WHILE (.TRUE.)
         READ(1,*, END=10) DATE, TIME, NUMCEL
         READ(2,*, END=10) DATE, TIME, POTENC
         WRITE(3,*) DATE, TIME, NUMCEL, POTENC
      END DO
10    STOP 'End of Input Data'
      END
```

9.8   Write a program to read the file 'CIRCUIT.DAT' and count the number of records n in the file. Assume that each record was written with the format (X, 2(F10.2, 2X)). The first field within each record represents the voltage V_j, and the second field represents the current I_j. After reading in the data, compute the power P dissipated by the circuit and the average current I_{avg} given by

$$P = \sum_{i=1}^{i=n} V_j I_j$$

$$I_{avg} = \sum_{i=1}^{i=n} \frac{I_j}{n}$$

```
!***************************************************************
! Open the file and read the data using the same format that
! was used to save it.
!***************************************************************
      REAL V(1000), I(1000), IAVG, ISUM
      OPEN(UNIT=1, FILE='CIRCUIT.DAT', STATUS='OLD')
      N=1
      DO WHILE(.TRUE.)
         READ(1, 10, END=20) V(N), I(N)
10       FORMAT(1X, 2(F10.2, 2X))
         N=N+1
      END DO
20    PRINT *, N, 'Data records read'
!***************************************************************
! Now that all the data have been entered, use N to compute the
! required values of P and IAVG.
!***************************************************************
      P=0.0
      ISUM=0.0
      DO K=1, N
         P=P+V(K)*I(K)
         ISUM=ISUM+I(K)
```

```
      END DO
      IAVG=ISUM/N
      PRINT *, 'Power Dissipated= ', P
      PRINT *, 'Average Current= ', IAVG
      END
```

9.9 Assume that you are hired as a technician to conduct a lengthy series of chemical experiments. The project is set up so that each experiment takes one day to complete. At the end of each day, the data that you have collected are stored in a data file called 'DATA.DAT' in the following format:

Date   Tester's Name Temperature   Humidity   Concentration   Activity

Also, at the top of the file in the first record is the number of experimental entries (N). Write two programs to accomplish the following:

- Enter the data into the file at the end of a day
- Read any specified record within the file when needed to make corrections

```
!********************************************************
! The best way to handle this problem is with a direct access
! file which will allow us to go to a specific record within
! the file without having to read all the data. Also, the
! direct access file will allow us to correct any one of the
! records without losing any of the others.
!       We will store the total number or records to date in the
! first record. This will allow us to interrogate this value at
! the end of each day so that we know where to store the newest
! results. Once we have this number, we will store the daily
! results in N+1. Also, we will have to update the first record.
!********************************************************
      CHARACTER DATE*8, NAME*20
      REAL :: TEMP, HUMID, CONCEN, ACTIV
      PRINT *, 'Enter today''s date (d/m/y):'
      READ *, DATE
      PRINT *, 'Enter your name:'
      READ *, NAME
      PRINT *, 'Enter temperature and humidity:'
      READ *, TEMP, HUMID
      PRINT *, 'Enter concentration and activity:'
      READ *, CONCEN, ACTIV
!********************************************************
! Open the file, extract the first data value, and assign to
! N. The record length will be set at 80, which is larger than
! the sum of the columns that we will need for all the data.
!********************************************************
      OPEN(UNIT=1, FILE='DATA.DAT', ACCESS='DIRECT', RECL=80)
      READ(1, REC=1) N
```

```
!*****************************************************************
! Write the new data to REC=N+1, and update the first record
!*****************************************************************
WRITE(1, REC=N+1) N+1, DATE, NAME, TEMP, HUMID, CONCEN, ACTIV
WRITE(1, REC=1) N+1
CLOSE(1)
END
!*****************************************************************
! Program to correct faulty data. The program asks for the
! record number for the correction. Then the data stored there
! are retrieved and displayed for examination and corrected.
!*****************************************************************
CHARACTER DATE*8, NAME*20
REAL :: TEMP, HUMID, CONCEN, ACTIV
PRINT *, 'Enter record number of faulty entry:'
READ *, NREC
OPEN(UNIT=1, FILE='DATA.DAT',ACCESS='DIRECT',RECL=80)
READ(1, REC=NREC) N, DATE, NAME, TEMP, HUMID, CONCEN, ACTIV
PRINT *, 'Enter correct date (d/m/y):'
READ *, DATE
PRINT *, 'Enter correct name:'
READ *, NAME
PRINT *, 'Enter correct temperature and humidity:'
READ *, TEMP, HUMID
PRINT *, 'Enter correct concentration and activity:'
READ *, CONCEN, ACTIV
!*****************************************************************
! Write the corrected data to REC=NREC.
!*****************************************************************
WRITE(1, REC=NREC) N, DATE, NAME, TEMP, HUMID, CONCEN, ACTIV
CLOSE(1)
END
```

9.10 Write a program that interactively reads in a student's performance in a course and creates a file 'GRADES' in which each record consists of the following data:

ID Number   *Name*   *Midterm Exam*   *Final Exam*   *Homework*   *Quizzes*

Then create a second program to read this file and compute the student's term grade based on a weight of 40% final exam / 30% midterm exam / 15% homework / 15% quizzes. When the final grades have been computed, create a new file 'AVG' in which only the ID number and the term grade appear.

```
!*****************************************************************
! Read in all the data and send them to the file GRADES.
!*****************************************************************
      CHARACTER (LEN=20) :: NAME(1000)
```

```fortran
      REAL, DIMENSION(1000):: MID, FINAL, HOME, QUIZ
      PRINT *, 'How many students?'
      READ *, N
      DO I=1, N
         PRINT *, 'Enter student''s name:'
         READ *, NAME(I)
         PRINT *, 'Midterm, final, homework, quiz scores?'
         READ *, MID(I), FINAL(I), HOME(I), QUIZ(I)
      END DO
!**************************************************************
! Now put the data into a sequential file.
!**************************************************************
      OPEN(UNIT=9, FILE='GRADES', STATUS='NEW')
      DO I=1, N
         WRITE(9,*) NAME(I),MID(I),FINAL(I),HOME(I),QUIZ(I)
      END DO
      CLOSE(9)
      END
!**************************************************************
! This program will open the file and perform the computations.
!**************************************************************
      CHARACTER (LEN=20) :: NAME(1000)
      REAL, DIMENSION(1000) :: MID, FINAL, HOME, QUIZ, AVG
      OPEN(UNIT=9, FILE='GRADES', STATUS='OLD')
      N=1
      DO WHILE (.TRUE.)
         READ(9,*,END=20) NAME(N), MID(N), HOME(N), QUIZ(N)
         N = N + 1
      END DO
!**************************************************************
! We will compute the weighted average of the exam scores and
! store the result for each student in the array AVG.
!**************************************************************
  20  DO I=1, N
         AVG(I)=0.4*FINAL(I)+0.3*MID(I)+0.15*(HOME(I)+QUIZ(I))
      END DO
!**************************************************************
! Create a new file, consisting of the ID number and the
! average.
!**************************************************************
      OPEN(UNIT=4, FILE='AVG', STATUS='NEW')
      DO I=1, n
         WRITE(4,*) I, AVG(I)
      END DO
      CLOSE(4)
      CLOSE(9)
      END
```

Supplementary Problems

9.11   Locate the syntax and run-time errors in the following program statements:

    (a) `OPEN(61, 'TEST.DAT', STATUS=NEW)`

    (b) `OPEN(11)`

    (c) `OPEN(4, FILE='STRESS.DAT')`
        `CLOSE(4, STATUS='SCRATCH')`

    (d) `OPEN(31, 'STRAIN.DAT', STATUS='NEW')`
        `READ(31,*) (STRAIN(I), I=1,100)`
        `CLOSE(31)`

    (e) `OPEN(19, FILE='TEMP.DAT', ACCESS='DIRECT', RECL=40)`
        `WRITE(19,*) X, Y, Z`

    (f) `OPEN(21, FILE='MATERIAL.DAT')`
        `READ(21, *, REC=4) X`

9.12   Write OPEN statements to accomplish the following:

    (a) Open an existing file named 'TEST1' on unit 10

    (b) Open a file that previously did not exist. Name it 'TEST2' and use unit 9.

    (c) Check to see if the file 'TEST3' has already been opened. If not, then open it as a new file.

    (d) Open two files, one named 'BINARY' to store data in binary format and one named 'DATA' to contain the same data in conventional notation.

9.13   The following exercises are designed so that you can find out the limitations or extensions of your Fortran compiler. Run small programs to find out if the following suggestions work. You may also need to consult the documentation for your system.

    (a) Will your system allow you to drop the CLOSE statement? On many compilers, either of the following will work:

```
        OPEN(UNIT=3, FILE='XXXXX', STATUS='NEW')
        WRITE(3,52)
   52   FORMAT(' THIS IS A TEST ')
        CLOSE(3)
        END
```
       or
```
        OPEN(UNIT=3, FILE='XXXXX',STATUS='NEW')
        WRITE(3,52)
   52   FORMAT(' THIS IS A TEST ')
        END
```

    (b) Some compilers will also allow you to drop the OPEN statement and will give the file a name based on the unit number. For example, if you choose UNIT=11, the compiler will name the file 'FOR011.DAT'. Try running this program segment to see if this option is available:

```
WRITE(11, *) 'This is a test'
END
```

(c) What happens on your system if you forget to CLOSE a file? Write a program that reads data from a file, prints the data to the CRT screen, but does not close the file. Now try running the program a second time.

(d) Does your system allow you to close files manually (through the operating system)? You will need to look in your operating system manual to see if you can issue a command like:

```
CLOSE ALL
```

Note that this is <u>not</u> a Fortran command that is inside your program. Instead, this is sent to the operating system.

9.14   Assume that we have a file that contains the following data:

```
11
22
33
44          Data file 'INPUT'
55
66
<end of file>
```

What are the values of the variables if the file is read with the following program segments? (Assume the file has the attributes UNIT=5, FILE='INPUT', STATUS='OLD'.)

(a) `READ(5,*) A, B, C`
(b) `READ(5,*) A, B, C`
     `REWIND(5)`
     `READ(5,*) I, J`
(c) `READ(5,*) A`
     `READ(5,*) B`
     `BACKSPACE(5)`
     `READ(5,*) C, I`

9.15   Run the following program on your computer to find out how your compiler handles carriage control characters (or lack of them) in data files. Will the program correctly read the data if there is no blank space at the beginning of each line? Will the first character of each line be used as the carriage control character? Here is a small program to read the file 'CCC.DAT'.

```
!**************************************************************
! Program to see how your computer handles lack of carriage
! control characters in a data file.(See also Example 9.26.)
!**************************************************************
      OPEN(3, FILE='CCC.DAT', STATUS='OLD')
      READ(3,*) X, Y, Z
      CLOSE(3)
!**************************************************************
! Now that the data have been read, are it printed out exactly
! as entered in the data file?
!**************************************************************
      PRINT *, X, Y, Z
      END
```

Note: The first digit of 123.456 and 789.012 should be in column 1.

Column 1
↓   'CCC.DAT'

```
123.456
789.012          947.012
<end of file>
```

9.16 Write a program that will read in at execution time the unit number and the file name of a file to be opened. Then open that file and read in values and assign them to the array X until all the data have been read. The file has one numeric value per record with an unknown number of records.

9.17 Write a program that reads values of X from a data file 'COUNTS' and computes the average value, the largest and smallest values, and their positions within the list. Write these values into a new data file 'STAT'.

9.18 Assume that there is a file 'ORDERED' in which the real data are organized in ascending order. Write a program that will read in a new value from the keyboard and insert it into the proper position within the file.

9.19 A data file 'HEART' lists personal data of several thousand people taking part in a medical experiment on heart disease. Each record is organized as follows:

ID Number   Name   Date of Birth   Weight   Height   Cholesterol Level

Write a program that will search the file to match a given name. If the name is found have your program display all the information in that record. Then prompt the user to enter corrected data.

9.20   Assume that there is a sequential data file 'STOCK' which lists the following information about each of the items for sale in a large store:

Stock Number   Description   Unit Price   Number on Hand   Number Sold This Year

Write a program that will read in all the items and compute the total value of the inventory plus the amount of sales for the year.

Answers to Selected Supplementary Problems

9.11   (a)   NEW should be inside single quotes (STATUS='NEW').
      (b)   No file name is specified, but some compilers may accept this and give the file a default name such as 'FOR011.DAT'
      (c)   A scratch file is not given a name since it is not saved.
      (d)   Reading from a file before any data have been written to it causes a run-time error.
      (e)   Direct access files require the WRITE command to contain the "REC=" clause.
      (f)   If the ACCESS attribute is not specified, Fortran assumes a sequential file. Therefore, the "REC=" clause inside the READ statement is improper since this is used only with direct access files.

9.12   (a)   `OPEN(UNIT=10, FILE='TEST1', STATUS='OLD')`
      (b)   `OPEN(UNIT=9, FILE='TEST2', STATUS='NEW')`
      (c)   `OPEN(UNIT=2, FILE='TEST3', STATUS='UNKNOWN')`
      (d)   `OPEN(UNIT=1, FILE='BINARY', FORM='UNFORMATTED', STATUS='NEW')`
            `OPEN(UNIT=2, FILE='DATA', STATUS='NEW')`

9.14   (a)   Each READ statement reads one record. So the first numeric field (11) is assigned to A, but there are no more fields in that record. Therefore, the next value will come from the next record and will be assigned to B. Similarly, the third value comes from the third line. This results in the assignments: A=11.00000, B=22.00000, and C=33.00000.
      (b)   The READ statement assigns the first three values to A, B, and C. Then the file is rewound to the beginning. So when the next READ statement is executed, it will begin with the first two values and assign them to I and J. The result is A=11.00000, B=22.00000, C=33.00000, I=11, and J=22.
      (c)   The first READ assigns the first value (11) to A. The second READ assigns the second

value (22) to B. The BACKSPACE command will move the pointer from the third record (the next in line) back one record. The next two values (22 and 33) are then assigned to C and I. The result is: A=11.0000, B=22.0000, C=22.0000, and I=33.

9.16

```
!*******************************************************************
! Read in the unit number and the file name as a character
! string. Then open this file and assign the values to X. We use
! a conditional loop with an END=option in the read statement.
!*******************************************************************
        CHARACTER (LEN=20) :: FILENAME
        REAL, DIMENSION(1000) :: X
        PRINT *, 'Enter file name and unit number:'
        READ *, FILENAME, IUNIT
        OPEN(UNIT=IUNIT, FILE=FILENAME, STATUS='OLD')
        I=1
        DO WHILE(.TRUE.)
           READ(IUNIT,*,END=20) X(I)
           I=I+1
        END DO
   20   PRINT *, I-1,' Records were found'
        END
```

9.17

```
!*******************************************************************
! First, open the file and read the values into the array
! X. Note that we may not know in advance the number of records
! in the file, so we need to look for the end-of-file record.
!*******************************************************************
        REAL X(1000), LARGE
        INTEGER :: POSMAL(1), POLARG(1)
        OPEN(UNIT=1, FILE='COUNTS', STATUS='OLD')
        N=1
        DO WHILE(.TRUE.)
           READ(1,*,END=20) X(N)
           N=N+1
        END DO
   20   N=N-1
        PRINT *, N,' Records were found'
!*******************************************************************
! Now compute the average of the numbers in the list
!*******************************************************************
        AVG=SUM(X)/N
!*******************************************************************
! Now look for the largest and smallest values and their
! positions. The MINLOC and MAXLOC functions require that
! the requested positions of the minimum and maximum values
! respectively be returned to a one-dimensional array. The
! number of elements of this array must match the rank of the
! array being searched. In this case, the array X has a rank
```

```
! of 1. Therefore, the position of the minimum value is sent
! to POSMAL(1).
!*******************************************************************
        SMALL=MINVAL(X(1:N))
        LARGE=MAXVAL(X(1:N))
        POSMAL=MINLOC(X(1:N))
        POLARG=MAXLOC(X(1:N))
!********************************************************************
! Print out the results (LARGE = the largest value, SMALL = the
! smallest value, POSMAL = position of the smallest value,
! POLARG = position of the largest value).
!*******************************************************************
        OPEN(UNIT=2, FILE='STAT', STATUS='NEW')
        WRITE(2,*) 'Largest value and position=', LARGE, POLARG
        WRITE(2,*) 'Smallest value and position=', SMALL, POSMAL
        CLOSE(1)
     CLOSE(2)
     END
```

9.18
```
!*******************************************************************
! Read in the new value from the keyboard.
!*******************************************************************
        REAL, DIMENSION(1000) :: Y, Z
        INTEGER :: POS
        PRINT *, 'Enter new value for storage in the file:'
        READ *, X
!*******************************************************************
! Open the file and read all the values into the array Y. Then
! find the appropriate position to store the new value. We will
! prepare a new array Z that contains the old values of Y and
! the new value of X.
!*******************************************************************
        OPEN(UNIT=1, FILE='ORDERED', STATUS='OLD')
        N=1
        DO WHILE(.TRUE.)
            READ(1, *, END=20) Y(N)
            N=N+1
        END DO
  20    PRINT *, N,'Records found'
!*******************************************************************
! Find the position for the new value.
!*******************************************************************
        DO I=1, N
            IF(Y(I) > X) THEN
                EXIT
            ELSE
                POS=I+1
            ENDIF
        END DO
!*******************************************************************
```

```
! Load Y(1) to Y(POS-1) into Z(1) to Z(POS-1). Load X into
! Z(POS). Finally, load Y(POS) to Y(N) into Z(POS+1) to Z(N+1).
!****************************************************************
        DO I=1, POS-1
            Z(I)=Y(I)
        END DO
        Z(POS)=X
        DO I=POS+1, N+1
            Z(I)=Y(I-1)
        END DO
!****************************************************************
! Now write the array Z into the old file. Notice that when we
! overwrite a file, the old values are destroyed.
!****************************************************************
        REWIND(1)
        DO I=1, N+1
            WRITE(1,*) Z(I)
        END DO
        CLOSE(1)
        END
```

9.19
```
!****************************************************************
! The file must be a direct access file to permit updating. So,
! we will read in the name, open the file, read one record at
! a time, and compare the name to the desired entry. If it
! matches, we stop the search and display the full record. (We
! assume a record length = 80 to make sure that there
! is enough room in the record for the data.)
!****************************************************************
        CHARACTER NAME*20, PERSON*20, BIRTH*8
        PRINT *, 'Enter the Patient''s Name:'
        READ *, PERSON
        OPEN(UNIT=1, FILE='HEART', ACCESS='DIRECT', RECL=80)
        I=1
        DO WHILE(.TRUE.)
            READ(1, REC=I) ID,NAME,BIRTH,WEIGHT,HGT,COL
            I=I+1
            IF(NAME == PERSON) EXIT
        END DO
!****************************************************************
! The patient's record has been found. Print it out.
!****************************************************************
        PRINT *, ID, NAME, BIRTH, WEIGHT, HGT, COL
        PRINT *, 'Enter corrected data:'
        READ *, ID, NAME, BIRTH, WEIGHT, HGT, COL
!****************************************************************
! Now write the corrected data to the file at REC=ID. If the
! requested patient is not found, the program jumps to statement
! label 20, where an error message is printed. This still leaves
! the file open when the program terminates. But the operating
```

```
      ! system will automatically close it.
      !*************************************************************
            WRITE(1, REC=ID) ID, NAME, BIRTH, WEIGHT, HGT, COL
            CLOSE(1)
            STOP 'Changes Made'
        20  STOP 'Patient Entered not in the File'
            END
```

9.20
```
      !*************************************************************
      ! This application works best with a sequential file. Open it
      ! and read each record one at a time. Multiply the unit price
      ! by the number on hand and add it to the running total INVEN.
      ! While we have the record, we will also accumulate the unit
      ! price times the sales this year value and store it in YRSALE.
      !*************************************************************
            CHARACTER (LEN=20) :: DESCRIP
            INTEGER :: SALES
            REAL :: INVEN
            OPEN(UNIT=7, FILE='STOCK', STATUS='OLD')
            INVEN=0.0
            YRSALE=0.0
            DO WHILE(.TRUE.)
               READ(7,*,END=20) ID, DESCRIP, UNIT, NUM, SALES
               INVEN=INVEN+UNIT*NUM
               YRSALE=YRSALE+UNIT*SALES
            END DO
            CLOSE(7)
        20  PRINT *, 'Total Value of Inventory: ', INVEN
            PRINT *, 'Total Number Sold This Year: ', YRSALE
            END
```

Chapter 10

Advanced Features

10.1 OVERVIEW

Fortran 90 represents one of the most extensive revisions of the language. In addition to improving the functionality of existing features, many new capabilities have also been added. Some of these have already been discussed in previous chapters. But there are additional features that do not fit easily into the earlier chapters because of their limited use or advanced nature. Some of the topics have been introduced before very briefly, but they were not explored fully. Therefore, in this chapter, we will reintroduce some of these ideas in much greater detail. Among the topics to be covered are:

- User-defined data types and operators
- Pointers, recursion, lists and tree structures
- Vector processing on supercomputers

The new features of Fortran 90 provide added functionality to tackle problems that would be very difficult otherwise. User-defined data types allow the programmer to manipulate data in a fashion which is more natural to the problem, while user-defined operators allow the programmer to access subprograms in a concise and elegant manner. Also, pointers enable the programmer to tackle problems that deal with lists and tree structures in a much more general fashion.

In the section dealing with supercomputer processing, we will review some of the concepts of computing with parallel processors in Fortran. These ideas allow us to greatly improve our computing speed and capability by relatively simple program modifications.

We should warn you that the last section covers material that is not part of the Fortran 90 standard. Therefore, many of the commands are machine and compiler dependent. But the concepts presented are universal, and only the command syntax will change from one compiler to another.

10.2 STRUCTURES AND DERIVED DATA TYPES

You've already been introduced to the data structure known as the array. Fortran allows you to construct arrays up to seven dimensions. Such arrays can be interpreted as lists (one-dimensional arrays), tables (two-dimensional arrays), and so forth. A restriction placed on the use of arrays is that all of the elements must be of the same type. This means you have an array of integers, or an array of real numbers, or one of the other intrinsic data types. There are applications, however, where it is convenient to have a structure in which different elements may be of different types. For example, consider a database of doctor's patients. Information about each patient might include name, gender, address, phone number, age, and weight. Name, gender, and address would best be stored as character data. Phone number and age could be stored as integers, and weight would be a real number. If we were using only arrays, three types of arrays would be needed as a result of the way that we have set

370

up the data. Therefore, any operation such as adding patients would need to manipulate all of these arrays, which leads to unnecessary duplication. We can get around this problem by creating our own type of data. In this problem, we will call this the PATIENT data type that merges all this data into a single structure, thus making it easier to process and manage all the data at once.

EXAMPLE 10.1

Below is a listing of the structure of the PATIENT data type that we are going to use in the next example. In this new data type, we want to include all of the following:

PATIENT
    NAME: type character
    GENDER: type character
    ADDRESS: type character, one-dimensional array of 4 elements
    ADDRESS(1): contains the street address
    ADDRESS(2): contains the city and state
    ADDRESS(3): contains the ZIP code
    ADDRESS(4): contains the country
    PHONE: type integer
    AGE: type integer
    WEIGHT: type real

Notice that this new data type is formed from several of the intrinsic data types. By setting up data types like this, we no longer have to be bound by the limitations of the six intrinsic types.

Derived Data Types

Data structures allow you to organize your data in a fashion that is suitable for your unique problem since creating a variable of a given structure automatically creates the necessary components. *Derived data types* are how we will implement these user-defined structures. Structures do not necessarily have as many components as the one in Example 10.1. For example, a structure could be as simple as a single one-dimensional array representing a vector. Or, it could have several components of different types as in our example of the PATIENT data type. To set up a user-defined data type, we must declare it in a declaration statement, just as we did with some of the other data types. We set up the derived type with the following format:

      TYPE *data_type_name*
           definitions
      END TYPE *data_type_name*

The data_type_name is the name that we choose to call our personally designed data. For example, we can call it PATIENT_INFO. Between the TYPE and END TYPE statements are a series of other declaration statements that tell the computer how to define the desired new data type.

EXAMPLE 10.2

Example 10.1 lists the information for the desired data type called PATIENT_INFO:

```
TYPE PATIENT_INFO
    CHARACTER(LEN=70) :: NAME
    CHARACTER(LEN=6) :: GENDER
    CHARACTER(LEN=70), DIMENSION (4) :: ADDRESS
    INTEGER :: PHONE, AGE
    REAL :: WEIGHT
END TYPE PATIENT_INFO
```

We have defined the patient's name and gender as character variables of length 70 and 6, respectively. The address is also character, but as a one-dimensional array. Finally, the phone, age, and weight are represented as numerical data.

Once you have defined the new data type, you may declare other variables to possess that particular data type. This is done with the following:

TYPE (*data_type_name*) :: *variable1, variable2, ... , variablen*

where the data type name that you have selected is included inside the parentheses after the keyword TYPE. The list of variables then follows.

EXAMPLE 10.3

Now that we have created the data type PATIENT_INFO, we can declare other desired variables to be of this new type. Assume for example, that we wish the variables STUDENTS and PARENTS to be declared with type PATIENT_INFO. This is how we would do that:

```
TYPE PATIENT_INFO
    CHARACTER(LEN=70) :: NAME
    CHARACTER(LEN=6) :: GENDER
    CHARACTER(LEN=70), DIMENSION (4) :: ADDRESS
    INTEGER :: PHONE, AGE
    REAL :: WEIGHT
END TYPE PATIENT_INFO
TYPE (PATIENT_INFO) :: STUDENTS, PARENTS
```

Notice that the data type specifications come before the declaration of the variables. Once a structure is defined, a function with the data type name is automatically available to assign values. To access the various components of the structure (such as ADDRESS, etc.) we will use the % symbol following the data type name.

EXAMPLE 10.4

Let's add Mary Jones as a new patient and store her information in the variable NEW_PATIENT. This is how we would declare this variable and assign the relevant values:

```
TYPE PATIENT_INFO
    CHARACTER(LEN=70) :: NAME
    CHARACTER(LEN=6) :: GENDER
```

```
      CHARACTER(LEN=70), DIMENSION (4) :: ADDRESS
      INTEGER :: PHONE
      INTEGER :: AGE
      REAL :: WEIGHT
END TYPE PATIENT_INFO
TYPE (PATIENT_INFO) :: NEW_PATIENT
NEW_PATIENT % NAME = 'Mary Jones'
NEW_PATIENT % GENDER = 'Female'
NEW_PATIENT % ADDRESS(1) = '123 Apple Road'
NEW_PATIENT % ADDRESS(2) = 'Somewhere, AnyState'
NEW_PATIENT % ADDRESS(3) = '00000-000'
NEW_PATIENT % ADDRESS(4) = ' '
NEW_PATIENT % PHONE = 1234567890
NEW_PATIENT % AGE = 34
NEW_PATIENT % WEIGHT = 115.5
```

There is another way to perform the assignments, which is more compact:

```
NEW_PATIENT = PATIENT_INFO('Mary Jones', 'Female', &
              (/'123 Apple Road','Somewhere, AnyState', &
              '00000-000', ' '/), 1234567890, 34, 115.5)
```

You will probably find this second method easier to use than the first. The option is yours.

Modules

Sometimes it is necessary to pass large amounts of data between procedures. One method of passing data is through the argument list such as CALL JOE(A, B, C, D, E, F) where the values of A, B, C, D, E, and F are inside the calling statement. However, this method can be inconvenient and prone to errors if there are many values to be transferred.

Modules provide another means of passing data between procedures. Variables that are declared in a module block are shared with any procedure with a USE statement. Each variable in a module is allocated memory only once, and is then shared between the different procedures using this module. Changes in a variable in the main program become accessible in any procedure which uses that module. Likewise, changes in procedures are reflected in other program units accessing the module. In addition to passing variables, modules can also contain procedures and interface blocks. A module is defined using a MODULE block structure:

> MODULE *module_name*
>   *module declaration statements and instructions*
> END MODULE *module_name*

EXAMPLE 10.5

The example below defines a module for sharing variables.

```
MODULE POINT_MODULE
    REAL, DIMENSION(100,3) :: POINTS
    INTEGER :: NUMBER_OF_POINTS
END MODULE POINT_MODULE
```

This module must appear before the main program and the main program must contain the USE
module_name statement to use of the data or definitions inside the module.

EXAMPLE 10.6

Here is an example of a main program and a procedure that share data with a module:

```
!*****************************************************************
! Module from Example 10.5
!*****************************************************************
MODULE POINT_MODULE
    REAL, DIMENSION(100,3) :: POINTS
    INTEGER :: NUMBER_OF_POINTS
END MODULE POINT_MODULE
!*****************************************************************
! The main program reads the number of data points into
! NUMBER_OF_POINTS along with the data set stored in POINTS. These
! are shared with the module POINT_MODULE and the subroutine MAX_X
!*****************************************************************
USE POINT_MODULE
PRINT *, 'Number of Points?'
READ *, NUMBER_OF_POINTS
DO I = 1, NUMBER_OF_POINTS
    PRINT *, 'Enter X,Y,Z for point ', I
    READ *, POINTS(I, :)
END DO
!*****************************************************************
! After data are read in, call the subroutine. Note that data are
! transferred through the module and not the calling statement.
!*****************************************************************
CALL MAX_X(XMAX)
PRINT *, 'Maximum X value was ', XMAX
END
!*****************************************************************
! Subroutine to determine the maximum value of the array POINTS
!*****************************************************************
SUBROUTINE MAX_X(XMAX)
    USE POINT_MODULE
    XMAX=POINTS(1,1)
    DO J = 1, 3
        DO I = 2, NUMBER_OF_POINTS
            IF (POINTS(I, J) > XMAX) XMAX = POINTS(I, J)
        END DO
    END DO
END
```

By using modules, data are passed between the main and external subroutine in a simple and consistent fashion and is consolidated into a single location. Changes can be made more easily, and their effects implemented in as many program units as required.

In some applications, the programmer may find that only specific variables are needed from a module. To limit the number of variables defined by a module, the ONLY option may be added. Also, in some instances you may wish to rename a variable to avoid a variable conflict, or to simplify a name. Renaming is accomplished by using the '=>' option.

EXAMPLE 10.7

To limit the number of variables within the module, you may use the ONLY option:

```
USE POINT_MODULE, ONLY :: NUMBER_OF_POINTS
```

To rename a variable, you may use the "=>' option

```
USE POINT_MODULE, NOP => NUMBER_OF_POINTS
```

The variable NUMBER_OF_POINTS will be called NOP instead. Note that this applies only to the program segment containing the USE statement. Finally, the ONLY and => options can be combined:

```
USE POINT_MODULE, ONLY :: NOP => NUMBER_OF_POINTS
```

Modules can contain declaration statements, TYPE and INTERFACE blocks as we have shown. But modules may also contain procedures such as functions and subroutines. To do this, you must place the word CONTAINS before the first of the procedures inside the module.

User Defined Operators

In addition to defining our own data types, we can also define our own operators. So far, we have used only those operators that deal with mathematical or logical functions such as +, , *, <=, and so forth. Note that these functions are *context sensitive* in the sense that an operation depends on the types of the data submitted to the operator. As an example, we've already seen in the array chapter that with Fortran 90 we can now add two arrays together with a very simple assignment operator.

Existing operators can have their scope enlarged to take into account data types. For example, if a VECTOR data type were established, then addition, subtraction, cross product, and dotproduct could be defined as operators. Addition and subtraction could be accomplished by *extending* the capabilities of the conventional addition and subtraction operators. Cross and dot products can be defined to have their own special operators such as .CROSS. and .DOT. The required steps to create a user-defined operator are:

- Define the necessary data types
- Create an INTERFACE BLOCK to link the operator to the function
- Define a function subprogram to calculate the desired quantity

The INTERFACE BLOCK will contain the instructions on the new operator that we wish to construct. Its format is:

```
INTERFACE (operator)
        interface instructions
END INTERFACE
```

EXAMPLE 10.8

The following example illustrates defining vector addition by extending the + operator.

```
!**********************************************************************
! First, define the data type VECTOR
!**********************************************************************
MODULE VECTORS
   TYPE VECTOR
      REAL, DIMENSION(3) :: VALUE
   END TYPE VECTOR
   !******************************************************************
   ! Now define the interface to the new addition operator
   !******************************************************************
   INTERFACE OPERATOR (+)      ! Extends the + operator to vectors
      MODULE PROCEDURE VECTOR_ADD              ! Access to function
   END INTERFACE                               ! End of INTERFACE BLOCK
CONTAINS
   !******************************************************************
   ! This is where the new operator is defined
   !******************************************************************
   FUNCTION VECTOR_ADD (A, B, A_PLUS_B)
      TYPE(VECTOR) :: A, B, A_PLUS_B
      A_PLUS_B%VALUE = A%VALUE + B%VALUE    ! Array addition
   END FUNCTION VECTOR_ADD
END MODULE VECTORS

   (The main program goes here)

END                                          ! End of main program
```

The INTERFACE BLOCK indicates that the function VECTOR_ADD is to be used when two vectors are connected by the plus (+) operator. But the normal rules of arithmetic will still apply for other uses of the plus sign such as a scalar + a scalar (5+3 for instance).

EXAMPLE 10.9

This example illustrates a main program using the user-defined operator for vector addition.

```
!**********************************************************************
! Copy the module VECTORS from the previous example.
```

```
!*********************************************************************
MODULE VECTORS
   TYPE VECTOR
       REAL, DIMENSION(3) :: VALUE
   END TYPE VECTOR
   INTERFACE OPERATOR (+)          ! Extends the + operator to vectors
       MODULE PROCEDURE VECTOR_ADD           ! Access to function
   END INTERFACE                             ! End of INTERFACE BLOCK
CONTAINS
   FUNCTION VECTOR_ADD (A, B, A_PLUS_B)
       TYPE(VECTOR)   :: A, B, A_PLUS_B
       A_PLUS_B%VALUE = A%VALUE + B%VALUE    ! Array addition
   END FUNCTION VECTOR_ADD
END MODULE VECTORS
TYPE(VECTOR) :: A, B, C                      ! The main program
PRINT *, 'Enter Vector A:'
READ *, A
PRINT *, 'Enter Vector B:'
READ *, B
C = A + B                                    ! Use the new + operator
PRINT *, 'A + B=', C
END
```

The module begins with the TYPE declarations for the vectors, followed by the INTERFACE BLOCK that allows access to the new definition of addition. After the vectors A and B are entered, they are added with the C=A+B statement. In this context, the '+' sign requires the use of the function defined in the INTERFACE BLOCK to add A and B since both are vectors. The appropriate instructions for the vector addition are found in the function subprogram that follows the main program.

In the preceding example, we illustrated how to extend or *overload* one of the standard operators. But it is also possible to construct new operators if they abide by the following rules:

- The user-defined operator must start and end with "."
- The new operator name is no more than 31 letters and follows the usual Fortran naming convention for variables.

There are two types of operators that we can write – *unary* and *binary*. The unary operators work with only a single quantity, while binary operators work with two. Also, when we construct our own operators, we need to establish how these operators will fit into the hierarchy of operators. The convention within Fortran 90 for user-defined operators is as follows:

- Higher priority for binary operators (operating from left to right within the operator)
- Lower priority for unary operators

In addition, all user defined operators have lower priority than any of the intrinsic operators such as +, *, <, .AND., and so forth.

EXAMPLE 10.10

This example illustrates creating a unary operator .XZREFLECT. which takes a vector and reflects it across the xz-plane. This is done by taking the y values and changing their signs.

```
MODULE REFLECT
   TYPE VECTOR
      REAL, DIMENSION(3) :: VALUE
   END TYPE VECTOR
   INTERFACE OPERATOR (.XZREFLECT.)
      MODULE PROCEDURE VECTOR_XZREFLECT
   END INTERFACE
CONTAINS
   !*************************************************************
   ! This is the function that defines the new operator
   !*************************************************************
   FUNCTION VECTOR_XZREFLECT(A) RESULT(REFLECT_A)
      TYPE(VECTOR):: A, REFLECT_A
      REFLECT_A=A
      REFLECT_A%VALUE(2)=-A%VALUE(2)
   END FUNCTION VECTOR_XZREFLECT
END MODULE REFLECT
```

The INTERFACE BLOCK allows us to reference the new operator .XZREFLECT., which is defined in the function that follows. Once this is done, all we need to do in a program is use an assignment statement such as B=.XZREFLECT. A to reflect the vector A and assign the result to the new vector B.

Overloading of existing operators is acceptable as long as the data types are different from operations already assigned. In this fashion it is also possible to have an operator perform on both binary and unary functions. For example, negation (-) is a unary operator that works on real and integers. But, negation can also be used for VECTORS or any other data type that we define.

Generic Operators

It is also possible to create interface blocks to use procedures based on the context of the argument data. Such procedures are referred to as *generic*. Generic procedures are useful when you have a number of structures that are related but not identical. For example, structures could be created for geometrical shapes such as circles and rectangles. It would be convenient if a single subroutine could ask the user for a key dimension for any of those data types. Then, user-defined operators could be used to calculate such values as area.

EXAMPLE 10.11

In the following subroutines, we define data types CIRCLE and RECTANGLE and then determine the area of a circle or a rectangle.

```
MODULE GEOMETRY
   TYPE CIRCLE
       REAL :: RADIUS
   END TYPE CIRCLE
   TYPE RECTANGLE
       REAL :: LENGTH, WIDTH
   END TYPE RECTANGLE
CONTAINS
   !**************************************************************
   ! Subroutine for computing the area of a circle
   !**************************************************************
   SUBROUTINE AREA_CIRCLE(X, AREA)
      TYPE(CIRCLE) :: X
      AREA=3.14159*X%RADIUS**2
   END
   !**************************************************************
   ! Subroutine for computing the area of a rectangle
   !**************************************************************
   SUBROUTINE AREA_RECTANGLE(X, AREA)
      TYPE(RECTANGLE) :: X
      AREA = X%LENGTH*X%WIDTH
   END
END MODULE GEOMETRY
```

Notice that the argument X in the subroutine statement is different in each case. In the first subroutine, X has only one element RADIUS in the TYPE declaration statement. The second subroutine, on the other hand, has X defined as a structure having two elements (LENGTH and WIDTH). Therefore, the INTERFACE BLOCK that we set up will be able to distinguish between the two by looking at the argument X that is being transferred. If X is defined as TYPE(CIRCLE), then the subroutine AREA_CIRCLE will be chosen. But if X is defined as TYPE RECTANGLE, then the subroutine AREA_RECTANGLE will be chosen for the calculation. This is the INTERFACE BLOCK for these operations:

```
INTERFACE AREA_OBJECT
   MODULE PROCEDURE AREA_CIRCLE
   MODULE PROCEDURE AREA_RECTANGLE
END INTERFACE
```

Now, combining all these elements into a single module, we obtain:

```
MODULE GEOMETRY
   TYPE CIRCLE
       REAL :: RADIUS
   END TYPE CIRCLE
```

```
     TYPE RECTANGLE
         REAL :: LENGTH, WIDTH
     END TYPE RECTANGLE
     INTERFACE AREA_OBJECT
         MODULE PROCEDURE AREA_CIRCLE
         MODULE PROCEDURE AREA_RECTANGLE
     END INTERFACE
CONTAINS
     SUBROUTINE AREA_CIRCLE(X, AREA)
         TYPE(CIRCLE) :: X
         AREA=3.14159*X%RADIUS**2
     END
     SUBROUTINE AREA_RECTANGLE(X, AREA)
         TYPE(RECTANGLE) :: X
         AREA = X%LENGTH*X%WIDTH
     END
END MODULE GEOMETRY
```

If we call AREA_OBJECT, either the AREA_CIRCLE or the AREA_RECTANGLE subroutine will be executed depending on the type of argument being used.

Pointers

Pointers represent a new capability for Fortran. A pointer can most easily be thought of as a substitute (*alias*) for a variable (or *memory location*). By assigning a pointer to a variable, that variable can be accessed not only by its name but also by the name of the pointer.

Pointers are declared in the same fashion as any variable. However, the POINTER attribute is required along with the data type such as REAL, INTEGER, and so forth. For variables that will be the target of a point (meaning that they will be given an alias), the TARGET attribute must be present. A pointer is assigned to a variable using the pointer assignment '=>'. Thus, the statement *pointer-name => variable-name* can be read as: pointer-name is an alias for variable-name.

EXAMPLE 10.12

In this example, we create the pointers P1 and P2 along with variables V1 and V2:

```
REAL, POINTER :: P1, P2
REAL, TARGET :: V1, V2
V1=1.23
V2=4.56
!*****************************************************************
! Now, assign the pointer P1 to V1 and P2 to V2
!*****************************************************************
P1 => V1
P2 => V2
!*****************************************************************
! If we assign a value to the pointer, we are also assigning the
! same value to the associated variable. In this case, we give a
```

```
! value to P1, which at the same time, gives the same value to V1.
!*****************************************************************
P1= 2.34
!*****************************************************************
! Pointers can also point to another pointer. In the following
! statement, we make P2 the alias for P1. Since P1 is the alias
! for V1, both P1 and P2 are now pointing to V1.
!*****************************************************************
P2 => P1
```

Pointers must be of the same type, kind, and dimension as the target variables that they are pointing to. Thus, both the pointers and the variables were declared as REAL. Figure 10-1 is a visualization of this process that will help explain this meaning and use of pointers:

**Fig. 10-1
Visualization of
Pointers**

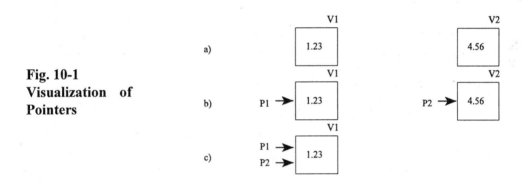

In step (a), V1 and V2 receive numerical values, represented here as boxes holding the assigned values. In step (b), the pointers P1 and P2 are assigned to V1 and V2, respectively. Thus the values of 1.23 can be referenced in two ways – by its variable name V1 or by its pointer P1. In a similar way, V2 and P2 reference the value 4.56. Finally, in step (c), we can have one pointer assigned to another pointer. This was done in the program with the statement P2 => P1. In this case, P2 will point at the same location where P1 is pointing. Note that we did not need to declare P1 with the TARGET attribute in the declaration statement.

Pointers can point to a memory location directly. This is accomplished with the ALLOCATE statement. The general form of the allocate statement is:

ALLOCATE (*pointer-name*)

This command allocates memory based on the pointer's type, kind, and dimension, and then assigns the pointer to that memory location. Consider this memory as an unnamed variable. The use for such a variable will soon become clearer. To deallocate memory, the DEALLOCATE (*pointer-name*) command is used. This will release the pointer from memory (making the pointer undefined, or not pointing to anything) and remove the allocated memory. Once a pointer is undefined, it can no longer be accessed as a variable. It can only appear as the target of a pointer assignment.

Finally, you can make a pointer undefined without deallocating its memory (the pointer may be pointing to a variable that you would wish to keep) by using the command:

NULLIFY (*pointer-name*).

EXAMPLE 10.13

Shown below are examples of the ALLOCATE, DEALLOCATE and NULLIFY commands:

```
REAL, POINTER :: P1,P2    ! Create P1 and P2 as pointers
ALLOCATE (P1)             ! Create a memory location assigned to P1
P1=12.0                   ! Value is assigned to the memory location
P2=>P1                    ! P2 now also points to the same memory as P1
NULLIFY(P2)               ! P2 is now undefined
DEALLOCATE(P1)            ! Memory for P1 has been removed and P1 set
                          ! to undefined.
```

The key actions taking place in this program are shown in Figure 10-2:

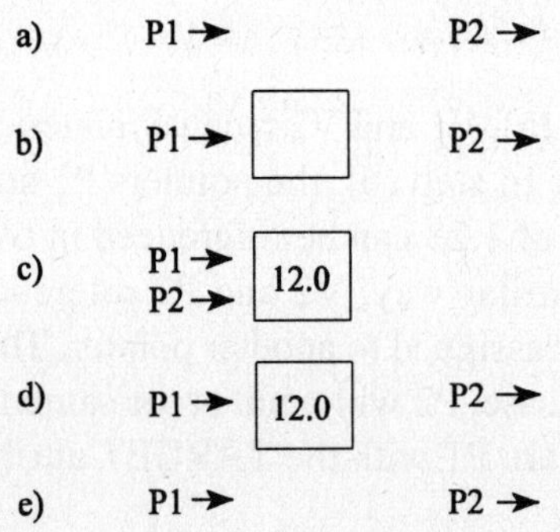

**Fig. 10-2
Use of ALLOCATE,
DEALLOCATE, and
NULLIFY Statements**

a)   P1 →   P2 →

b)   P1 → [   ]   P2 →

c)   P1 →
      P2 → [12.0]

d)   P1 → [12.0]   P2 →

e)   P1 →   P2 →

In step (a), the pointers P1 and P2 are created by the declaration statement and are both unassigned. The ALLOCATE statement reserves a memory space associated with P1, but at this time, the memory location has no numerical value. The assignment statements (P1 = 12.0 and P2 => P1) cause a value of 12.0 to be stored in the memory location and to have both pointers targeted at this location as shown in step (c). The NULLIFY (P2) statement releases the P2 pointer, which is now no longer pointing at anything (step (d)). Finally, the DEALLOCATE (P1) statement removes the memory location that was storing the value of 12.0. This action (step (e)) has two consequences − it erases the numerical value and it releases the pointer P1.

To test whether a pointer is undefined or not, the ASSOCIATED (*pointer-name*) intrinsic function is available. If the specified pointer is defined, a value of .TRUE. is returned. If it is not defined, then the value is .FALSE.. A second optional argument is available for a second pointer. When this option is used, the function returns a .TRUE. value only if both pointers are associated with the same memory location.

EXAMPLE 10.14

The following example will test pointers P1 and P2 for their status.

```
REAL, POINTER :: P1, P2
REAL, TARGET :: V1, V2
V1=1.0
V2=2.0
P1 => V1                            ! P1 points to V1
PRINT *, ASSOCIATED (P1)           ! will print .TRUE.
PRINT *, ASSOCIATED (P2)           ! will print .FALSE.
PRINT *, ASSOCIATED (P1, P2)       ! will print .FALSE.
P2 => V1
PRINT *, ASSOCIATED (P1, P2)       ! will print .TRUE.
NULLIFY (P1)
NULLIFY (P2)
PRINT *, ASSOCIATED (P1, P2)       ! will print .FALSE.
```

Two problems can occur when dealing with pointers: *a dangling pointer* and *an unreferenced storage location*. A dangling pointer occurs when its memory has been deallocated by some indirect action that makes the pointer undefined.

EXAMPLE 10.15

This example illustrates the problem of a dangling pointer.

```
REAL, POINTER :: P1, P2
ASSOCIATED(P1)              ! P1 is allocated memory
P2 => P1                    ! P2 points to the same memory as P1
DEALLOCATE(P2)              ! P2 is deallocated
PRINT *, P1                 ! ERROR: deallocating P2 simultaneously
                            ! deallocated P1: pointer undefined.
```

The dangling pointer is schematically shown in Figure 10-3. In step (a), P1 and P2 are defined but not associated by the program declaration statement. The ASSOCIATED program statement then reserves memory for P1 as shown in step (b). The pointer assignment statement (P2 => P1) causes both pointers to be associated with the reserved memory location in step (c). Finally, in step (d) when P2 is DEALLOCATED, so is P1, since they are associated to each other.

Thus, when we attempt to print out the value of P1, an error will occur since both P1 and P2 are undefined.

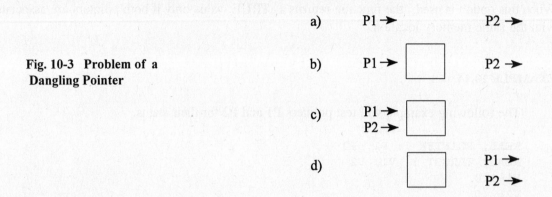

Fig. 10-3   Problem of a
Dangling Pointer

The second type of error is due to *unreferenced storage*. Unreferenced storage occurs when you do not deallocate an allocated pointer before assigning it as a new alias. When this occurs, allocated memory is used but can not be retrieved. This is not a significant concern when dealing with single variables. However if this error occurs with arrays and large data structures, the result can be poor execution performance since a large number of unnecessary memory storage sites may be allocated but not used.

EXAMPLE 10.16

This example illustrates unreferenced storage.

```
REAL, POINTER :: P1
REAL, TARGET :: R1
ASSOCIATE(P1)               ! P1 is assigned memory
P1 = 2.345                  ! Memory for P1 is assigned a value
R1 = 3.21
P1 => R1                    ! P1 is reassigned as the alias to R1. This
                            ! results in an error due to unreferenced
                            ! storage since the value stored in P1's
                            ! original memory can no longer be accessed
```

The problem of unreferenced storage is shown in Figure 10-4. The two declaration statements in the program establish a pointer (P1) and a target (R1) shown as step (a). In step (b) the ASSOCIATED statement creates a vacant storage location pointed to by P1. The two assignment statements assign the values 2.345 to P1 and 3.21 to R1, respectively, as shown in step (c). Finally, when the DEALLOCATE statement disconnects P1 from the memory location holding the value 2.345, an unreferenced storage error occurs. Note in step (d) of Figure 10-4 that P1 is no longer pointing at any memory location and that the previous memory location still has a value stored there. Since there is no way to retrieve the value of 2.345, an error will be reported.

**Fig. 10-4 Problem of
Unreferenced Storage**

a)   P1 ➤   R1

b)   P1 ➤ [ ]   R1 [ ]

c)   P1 ➤ 2.345   R1 3.21

d)   2.345   R1 3.21   P1 ➤

Linked Lists

While pointers bring with them a potential for problems, they provide the mechanism to build dynamic structures. Prior to Fortran 90, a Fortran program required that all memory be allocated at the beginning of the program. With the added capability of allocatable arrays, Fortran 90 programs can be written to utilize only the memory they need for a particular part of a problem. While this is a useful utility, allocatable arrays require that you can calculate the size of the array needed to solve the problem. For some problems, however, you do not know how much memory is needed until the data are entered at execution time. For problems such as these, dynamic structures utilizing pointers are a preferred solution, since dynamic structures can grow and shrink as needed.

This section provides an example of a commonly encountered structure known as a *linked list*. A linked list can be thought of as a list with variable length. Each element in the list (also called a *node*) points to the next entry in the list. Linked lists are useful when you wish to insert entries in the list at arbitrary locations.

It is convenient to represent a linked list by boxes (or *nodes*), each containing a data value and a pointer to the next box in the list. The general form of the node will be:

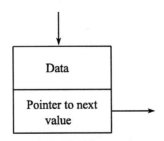

We enter the node from the top, use the data value stored there, and then proceed to the next node indicated by the pointer. For example, if we had a list of numbers such as 19, 6, 14, 20, this is how it might be represented as a linked list:

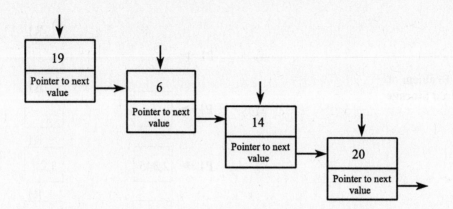

To help us in explaining how a linked list can be implemented in a Fortran program, we will present a more formal graphical representation in Figure 10-5 for variables and pointers that form a linked list.

Fig. 10-5 Graphical Representation of Variables and Pointers.
   a) real variable
   b) real undefined pointer
   c) real pointer pointing
       to a real variable
   d) real allocated pointer

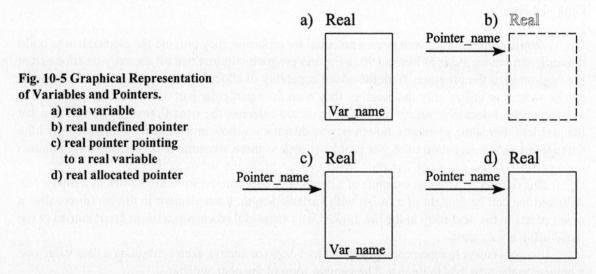

In this figure, we introduce a method for graphically representing variables and pointers. If the memory location, represented by the box, is allocated by a program instruction, we show it as a solid line. If it is not allocated, then the line is dashed. The type of the variable or pointer (REAL in this example) is shown above the upper left corner of the box. If the memory location represents a named variable, then the name appears in the lower left corner, and if a value is present, it is shown inside the box. Pointers will be distinguished from variables by the presence of an arrow with the pointer name above the arrow. This graphical representation contains more information than that shown to demonstrate the concept of a linked list at the beginning of this section. For example, we have added the variable names, the pointer names, the data types, and whether the variables have been assigned data values. We will find this notation helpful when we write the Fortran program.

If the node consists of a more complex structure, such as a user-defined data type, we will represent it by a box with the various components shown inside. This point is illustrated in Example 10.17.

EXAMPLE 10.17

The array is one structure that you are already familiar with. It consists of elements, each with the same characteristics. An example would be the REAL array VECTOR defined in Example 10.5. This array consists of 3 elements, each of type REAL.

```
TYPE VECTOR
    REAL, DIMENSION(3) :: VALUE
END TYPE VECTOR
```

In the following figure, we show how we will represent VECTOR as a node in a linked list. Using our notation, we must indicate the components of the data type, and the variable name. The vector components are represented by the inner box in this figure. When we get to more complex structures, there may be several boxes inside the outer box.

Fig. 10-6 Graphical Representation of a Single Node of the Vector Structure

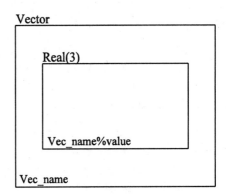

With the graphical tools illustrated in Figures 10-5 and 10-6 we can now begin to investigate linked lists. A linked list is a collection of items or nodes. Each node contains a value and a pointer to the next node in the list. In the following examples we will be constructing a linked list for names, which will be entered in alphabetical order. The routines that we will construct will be:

- Step 1 — Function to create an empty name list
- Step 2 — Function to test for an empty name list
- Step 3 — Subroutine to add a name to the list
- Step 4 — Subroutine to delete a name from the list
- Step 5 — Subroutine to print the list

EXAMPLE 10.18

In this example, we will write a program to search a linked list for a particular name. This list will already be in alphabetical order. Each node in the list will contain a character value and a next node pointer index. The structure of a node is shown in Figure 10-7:

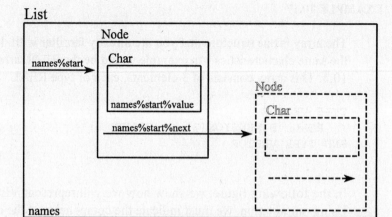

**Fig. 10-7 Node Structure
for Linked List of Names**

Before proceeding, we should take some time to understand this figure. The linked list consists of nodes, each of which contains a name and a pointer to the next node in the list. Inside the outermost box are two smaller boxes, each labeled as a node. The node will be a user-defined data type consisting of a character string for the names and a pointer to the next node. Inside the node, the value stored there will use the variable names%start%value and the pointer will use the variable names%start%next. When we get to the end of the list, the pointer is not allocated. Rather than repeating the entire node structure again in a dotted outline, a dotted arrow is displayed for simplicity.

```
TYPE NODE
    CHARACTER (LEN=20) :: VALUE
    TYPE(NODE), POINTER :: NEXT
END TYPE NODE
```

The list structure will consist of a single NODE pointer.

```
TYPE LIST
    TYPE(NODE), POINTER :: START
END TYPE LIST
```

In order to write the program, we must write the function to create an empty list (step 1).

```
FUNCTION NEWLIST() RESULT(NEW_LIST)
    TYPE(LIST), POINTER :: NEW_LIST
    NULLIFY (NEW_LIST%START)
END FUNCTION NEWLIST
```

Now, to create a new list stored in NAMES, we use the following code in the main program:

```
TYPE(LIST):: NAMES
NAMES=NEWLIST()
```

The process of adding elements to the list is to search through the list until a value greater than the name to be inserted is found. While searching the list, two pointers will be used to keep track of the current node and the previous node. Once a value is found that is greater than the value to be added, the %NEXT pointer of the previous node will be allocated, creating a memory location and automatically linking the previous nodes %NEXT pointer to it. The new name will be assigned to the %VALUE portion of the new node, and the %NEXT pointer of the new node will be assigned to the current node pointer value.

This process works well except for an empty list. Since a previous pointer needs to be assigned, an empty list will be created with a single dummy node at the beginning. To accommodate this change, the NEWLIST function will need to be modified (Step 2).

```
FUNCTION NEWLIST( ) RESULT(NEW_LIST)
   TYPE(LIST), POINTER :: NEW_LIST
   ALLOCATE(NEW_LIST%START)           ! Create dummy node
   NULLIFY (NEW_LIST%START%NEXT)      ! Nullify pointer to next node
END FUNCTION NEWLIST
```

The new empty list is illustrated in Figure 10.8.

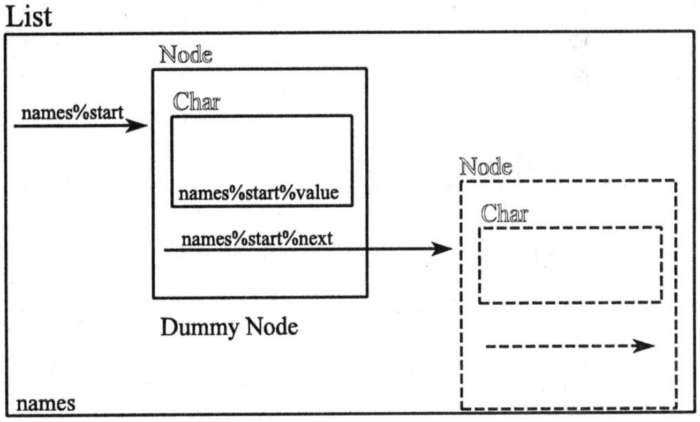

Fig. 10-8 New Empty Name List with Dummy Node

Step 3 is to write the subroutine to add a new name:

```
SUBROUTINE ADDNAME(THE_LIST,THE_NAME)
   CHARACTER (LEN=20) :: THE_NAME
   TYPE(LIST), POINTER :: THE_LIST
   TYPE(NODE), POINTER :: CURRENT_PTR, PREVIOUS_PTR
   PREVIOUS_PTR => THE_LIST%START            ! Assign Previous Pointer
   CURRENT_PTR => THE_LIST%START%NEXT        ! Assign Current Pointer
   DO
      IF(.NOT.ASSOCIATED(CURRENT_PTR))EXIT   ! End of structure reached
      IF(CURRENT_PTR%VALUE>THE_NAME) EXIT    ! Name > input name found
      PREVIOUS_PTR => CURRENT_PTR            ! Update  pointer to current
      CURRENT_PTR => CURRENT_PTR%NEXT        ! Update pointer to next
   END DO
   ALLOCATE(PREVIOUS_PTR%NEXT)               ! A-Make new node linked to
                                             ! previous node
   PREVIOUS_PTR%NEXT%VALUE = THE_NAME        ! B-Assign the new value
   PREVIOUS_PTR%NEXT%NEXT => CURRENT_PTR     ! C-Assign value to pointer
END SUBROUTINE ADDNAME
```

To demonstrate how this subroutine works, we will add two names to a null list. The second name 'Bill' will be inserted before the first 'Martin'.

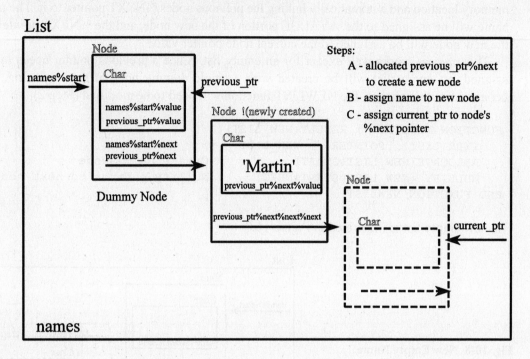

Fig. 10-9 Adding the Name 'Martin' to a Null List

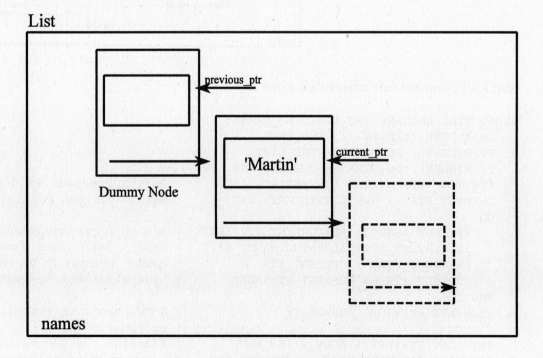

Fig.10-10   Locating the Proper Position to Add the Name 'Bill' to the Existing List

List

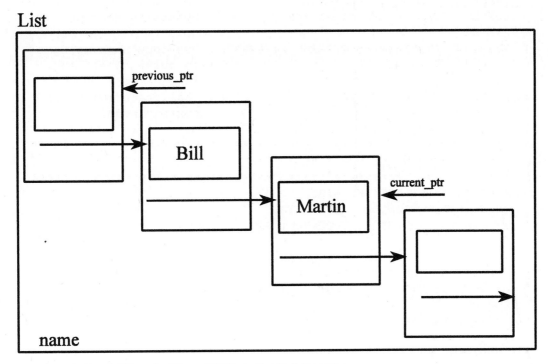

Fig. 10-11   Adding the Name BILL to the Existing List

The process outlined in Figure 10-9 illustrates what happens when a name is entered at the end of the list (triggered by the %next node not being allocated), and Figures 10-10 and 10-11 illustrate how names can be entered anywhere in the list.

The procedures to check for an EMPTY list (step 2), DELETE name (step 4), and PRINT list (step 5) are as follows:

```
FUNCTION EMPTY(THE_LIST) RESULT(THE_RESULT)
   TYPE(LIST), POINTER :: THE_LIST
   LOGICAL :: THE_RESULT
   THE_RESULT = .NOT.ASSOCIATED(THE_LIST%START%NEXT)
END FUNCTION EMPTY
!****************************************************************
! A subroutine to delete a name
!****************************************************************
SUBROUTINE DELETENAME(THE_LIST,THE_NAME)
   TYPE(LIST), POINTER :: THE_LIST
   TYPE(NODE), POINTER :: CURRENT_PTR, PREVIOUS_PTR
   CHARACTER (LEN=20) :: THE_NAME
   PREVIOUS_PTR => THE_LIST%START          ! Initialize previous_ptr
   CURRENT_PTR => THE_LIST%START%NEXT       ! Initialize current_ptr
   DO
   IF(.NOT.ASSOCIATED(CURRENT_PTR))RETURN      ! End of list
```

```
     IF(CURRENT_PTR%VALUE==THE_NAME) EXIT    ! Name found
     PREVIOUS_PTR => CURRENT_PTR             ! Update previous_ptr
     CURRENT_PTR => CURRENT_PTR%NEXT         ! Update current_ptr
     END DO
     PREVIOUS_PTR%NEXT => CURRENT_PTR%NEXT ! Previous%next assigned
                                            ! to current%next and
                                            ! jump name.
     DEALLOCATE(CURRENT_PTR)                 ! Deallocate memory of
                                            ! current node.
END SUBROUTINE DELETENAME
!**************************************************************
! Subroutine to print the list.
!**************************************************************
SUBROUTINE PRINTLIST(THE_LIST)
   TYPE(LIST), POINTER :: THE_LIST
   TYPE(NODE), POINTER :: CURRENT_PTR
   DO
      IF(.NOT. ASSOCIATED (CURRENT_PTR)) EXIT  ! End of list
      PRINT *,CURRENT_PTR%VALUE
      CURRENT_PTR => CURRENT_PTR%NEXT
   END DO
END SUBROUTINE PRINTLIST
```

One instruction that we have used several times in this example deserves special note. This is the program instruction given by IF (.NOT.ASSOCIATED (CURRENT_PTR)) EXIT. The ASSOCIATED function determines whether the current pointer has been assigned. If not, the value returned is *false* which is then inverted to *true* by the .NOT. operator. The pointer will not be associated when the program reaches the end of the list. Thus, the conditional clause given by .NOT. ASSOCIATED (CURRENT_PTR) will become *true* at the end of the list. The loop will then terminate.

Trees

Linked lists provide a means to create dynamic lists that can expand, contract, and allow for arbitrary additions at any location in the list. Notice also that linked lists connect elements in a serial fashion.

Another type of structure that is commonly encountered is the *tree* structure. Trees allow branching in more than one direction — for example, a binary tree branches in two directions. Thus, each node will have two or more pointers pointing to the next node:

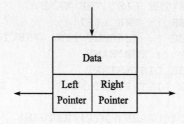

When we add additional nodes to this diagram, we will begin to see the tree pattern beginning to emerge:

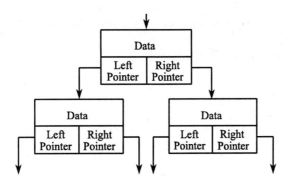

A tree which has two branches such as the one above is called a *binary* tree. Other types of trees are also possible with more branches than the one shown. However, we will not use them here.

In this section we will be looking at an *ordered* binary tree. This tree structure will be used to efficiently sort a list of names. The application is the same as the one presented for the examples of the linked list. However, the ordered binary tree that we show here is a much more efficient means of sorting. The sort time for a linked list containing 1,000 items with the binary tree is approximately 145 times faster than the previous method we showed you. The time savings is even greater for larger lists. For a list with 1,000,000 items for example, the tree approach is almost 73,000 times faster. Thus, it is worthwhile to use the more complicated tree method to benefit from the higher speed.

The node of a binary tree contains a character variable and two pointers representing a left subtree and a right subtree, both of which are binary tree nodes. The left subtree branches to other nodes for values less than the value stored in the current tree, while the right subtree branches to other nodes with values greater than or equal to the value stored in the current tree. This process is similar to the binary search algorithm that we discussed in Chapter 6. Before we show you the program for the sorting process with balanced binary trees, we want to demonstrate the graphical representation of the process, Figure 10-12, using our adopted notation.

Fig. 10-12 Graphical Representation of a Binary Tree Node

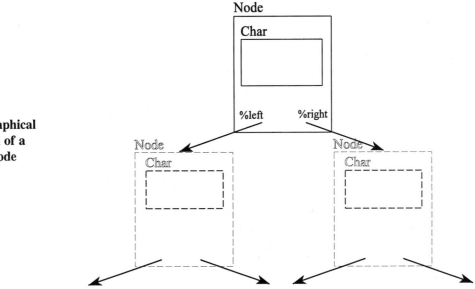

The process we will use for filling in the tree is as follows:

- If the node is empty assign the name to the node's value
- If the node is not empty and the name is less than the node's value, repeat this process on the left branch
- If the node is not empty and the name is greater than or equal to the node's value, repeat this process on the right branch.

This process is a recursive one since the second and third steps are repeated until the condition in step one is satisfied. Thus, recursion is a natural concept to use when processing tree structures. Without recursion, this would be a very difficult task.

EXAMPLE 10.19

This example illustrates the process of filling out an ordered tree using the names 'Martin', 'Peggy', 'Patrick', and 'Alex'.

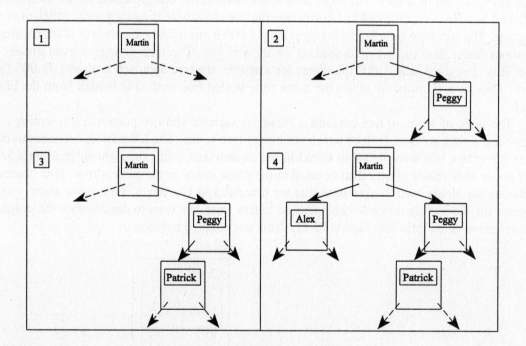

Fig. 10-13   Example of Filling in an Ordered Binary Tree

We will treat this as a four-step problem. In step 1, we read in the first name ('Martin') and create a node for it. In step 2, we read in the next name ('Peggy') and compare it to the name in the first node. Since 'Peggy' comes after 'Martin' in the ASCII collating sequence, we will put this new name into the node to the right of 'Martin'. The next name ('Patrick') is read in (step 3) and we determine where to put it. First, we compare it to node 1 ('Martin') and see that we should go to the right. Then we compare it to the value in that node ('Peggy') and decide that 'Patrick' should go to the left. Finally, we read in the last name ('Alex') and begin with the first node. Since 'Alex' < 'Martin', we go to the left. As we develop this program, we will refer to the steps in this algorithm.

```
MODULE TREES
   TYPE TREE                              ! Define the tree structure
      TYPE(NODE), POINTER :: ROOT
   END TYPE TREE
   TYPE NODE                              ! Define the node structure
      CHARACTER(LEN=20) :: VALUE
      TYPE(NODE), POINTER :: RIGHT, LEFT
   END TYPE NODE
CONTAINS
   FUNCTION NEWTREE () RESULT(THE_TREE)   ! Create a new tree if needed
      TYPE(TREE), POINTER :: THE_TREE
      NULLIFY(THE_TREE)
   END FUNCTION NEWTREE
   !**************************************************************
   ! The subroutine to add a name using the 3 steps. Notice that we
   ! need to use a recursive subroutine to add a value to a node.
   !**************************************************************
   RECURSIVE SUBROUTINE ADDNAME(THE_NODE, THE_NAME)
      TYPE(NODE), POINTER :: THE_NODE
      TYPE(NODE), POINTER :: CURRENT_PTR
      CHARACTER (LEN=20) :: THE_NAME
      IF(.NOT.ASSOCIATED(THE_NODE)) THEN          ! Step 1
         ALLOCATE(THE_NODE)
         NULLIFY(THE_NODE%RIGHT)
         NULLIFY(THE_NODE%LEFT)
         THE_NODE%VALUE=THE_NAME
         RETURN
      END IF
      IF(THE_NAME < THE_NODE%VALUE) THEN
         CALL ADDNAME(THE_NODE%RIGHT, THE_NAME)    ! Step 2
      ELSE
         CALL ADDNAME(THE_NODE%LEFT, THE_NAME)     ! Step 3
      END IF
   END SUBROUTINE ADDNAME
   !**************************************************************
   ! Printing the list in ascending order is accomplished using the
   ! same approach as adding elements. If a node has a value and no
   ! subtrees, print the value. But, if a node has a left subtree,
   ! then that subnode should be printed before printing the node's
   ! value. After printing the node value, if the node has a right
   ! subtree, then it too should be printed.
   !      1) if node has a left subtree, apply this algorithm
   !         to print the left subtree
   !      2) print the node's value
   !      3) if the node has a right subtree, apply this algorithm
   !         to print the right subtree
   !**************************************************************
```

```
            RECURSIVE SUBROUTINE PRINTNAMES(THE_ROOT)
                TYPE(NODE), POINTER :: THE_ROOT
                IF (ASSOCIATED(THE_ROOT)) THEN
                    CALL PRINTNAMES(THE_ROOT%LEFT)
                    PRINT *, THE_ROOT%VALUE
                    CALL PRINTNAMES(THE_ROOT%RIGHT)
                END IF
            END SUBROUTINE PRINTNAMES
        END MODULE TREES
```

10.3 FORTRAN COMPUTING ON SUPERCOMPUTERS

This section serves as an introduction to the concerns of programming on a supercomputer. Supercomputers have the distinction of being extremely fast, but top performance is obtained only if the program has been optimized to take advantage of the unique design of the supercomputer being used. Optimizing a program to run on a conventional computer may result in improving run times by less than a factor of 2 (or 1/2 the time). In contrast, optimization of a supercomputer program can easily reap returns that are measured in orders of magnitude. Therefore, optimizing programs by judicious use of the available structures and good programming style is of utmost importance.

With supercomputers becoming available to more users, the need to understand how they work, and how to make them work best, is of concern. This section is intended to give you a basic understanding of supercomputers.

What Is a Supercomputer?

The definition of a supercomputer is usually understood to represent the fastest computer available at any given time. This definition, of course, is fluid — today's supercomputer is tomorrow's desktop workstation. Therefore, this definition of a supercomputer is not very useful.

Another common definition of a supercomputer is any computer that can perform multiple tasks simultaneously by using multiple processors. For example, some supercomputers are made from 2–4 very past microprocessors, while others are made from hundreds of slower processors. In contrast, conventional computers utilize a single processor to perform their work.

The software on a supercomputer is also different from that found in single processor machines. While software in the operating system of a conventional computer (single processor) manages many users with many tasks, at any given time the computer is actually only working on a single task at any given time. Supercomputers, on the other hand, can utilize multiple processors for a single program (provided the program is written so that this can occur).

There are two basic types of supercomputers: vector and parallel. Some supercomputers are actually a combination of these two types.

Vector Machines

A vector machine is one in which multiple processors are used in a "pipeline" or assembly line fashion to perform multiple operations. By having different processors perform different tasks, the effect is to see data flowing in and out of the pipeline at the speed of the slowest process. In effect, a vector processor keeps all the components of a system busy at the same time. The goal is to minimize the amount of idle time for any part of the system.

A useful analogy for vector processing is an assembly line for building cars. The actual time it takes to build a single car from start to finish is approximately 12 hours. But because there are many cars going through the line at the same time, each at a different stage of assembly, the cars roll off the assembly line at a rate of about 1 per minute. A similar thing occurs in vector processors.

Parallel Machines

Parallel machines use multiple processors in a different way. They execute operations in parallel or concurrently. To demonstrate this concept, consider a DO loop in which two arrays of 100 elements are being added to generate another array.

```
DO I=1,100
    A(I) = B(I) + C(I)
END DO
```

It is possible to assign 100 processors to perform this task of array addition. Each processor would have its own element number to evaluate for the expression. Disregarding the extra time (called overhead) needed to get all the processors to work in synchronization, the resulting execution time should be improved by a factor of 100. For example, we could set up something like this:

```
A(1)=B(1)+C(1)          ! Processor 1
A(2)=B(2)+C(2)          ! Processor 2
        . . .
A(100)=B(100)+C(100)    ! Processor 100
```

Once we understand how parallel processors work, we can begin to look at small changes to our programs that can mean the difference between only being able to access a single processor, or utilizing many. Consider the following examples of coding that perform the same tasks.

EXAMPLE 10.20

The following program segments compute the value of $Z(I) = X(I)*Y(I)+Z(I)$ in two different ways. One will do the computation much faster than the other on a vector processor.

```
! Scalar version              ! Vectorized version
DO I= 1, N                    DO I= 1, N
    XY=X(I)*Y(I)                  Z(I)=X(I)*Y(I)+Z(I)
    Z(I)=XY+Z(I)              END DO
END DO
```

The example program on the left employs the *supplemental* variable XY to store an intermediate result. This is a very common practice when programming a long equation. Because the scalar variable XY is present in the DO block of the program on the left, some machines cannot easily vectorize the process. The example on the right consists entirely of array operations which is more readily vectorized. The result of such a simple change can dramatically affect the execution time for the process on a supercomputer.

Fundamentals

Before discussing how to better utilize supercomputers, it will be necessary to have a basic understanding of resources used in supercomputers and even conventional computers.

Clock cycle time and performance : To synchronize the events inside the computer, a clock is used. The clock can be thought of as the heart beat of the computer. For our purposes nothing happens in a time interval smaller than 1 cycle (clock tick). As a result, the computer's performance is inversely proportional to the clock cycle time. A computer can issue a maximum of 1 instruction per clock cycle. For a computer that has a 100-nanosecond (100×10^{-9}- second) clock cycle, it is possible to calculate the maximum rate of instructions executed per second.

EXAMPLE 10.21

Calculate the maximum instructions per second for a computer with a 100-nanosecond clock speed.

1 instruction per cycle/(100×10^{-9} seconds per cycle) = 10×10^6 instructions/second

The clock speed is sometimes presented in megahertz (MHz), where 1 Hertz = 1 cycle/second. The 100 nanosecond clock speed represents a 10 MHz clock. Because of the large number of instructions per second, the rate is usually given in millions of instructions per second or *Mips*. Thus 10×10^6 instructions/second is equivalent to 10 Mips.

The Mips rating just calculated represents a theoretical maximum. Because many instructions take more than a single clock cycle, and resource conflicts occur, the actual Mips rating is somewhere between 1/10 to 1/2 the theoretical value.

On a conventional computer all instructions are processed through a single processor, so the clock speed and the performance are closely linked. In supercomputers, because multiple processors will be active, it is possible to exceed the theoretical maximum of 1 instruction per clock cycle.

Most scientific and engineering applications involve floating-point arithmetic. Consequently a performance measure known as *megaflops* (millions of floating-point operations) is commonly used when presenting a supercomputer's performance.

Registers: Registers are a form of very fast memory used to hold instructions and data inside the CPU. They are expensive, so there are few of them compared to the computer's main memory. They are capable of delivering their contents to the CPU in a single clock cycle. Usually, three kinds of registers are present:

- *Address registers* which hold addresses of memory locations
- *Operand registers* which hold the data currently being manipulated
- The *instruction stack* which holds the instructions for the program

Functional Units: Originally computers were designed so that one instruction was issued at a time. Each instruction had to go to completion before processing the next. By partitioning the CPU into functional units (hardware in addition to the single CPU) it is possible to allow for independent calculations to take place simultaneously. Consider the equation given by the assignment statement:

```
R=A*B+(C+D)
```

For this equation it is possible to perform the A*B operation (multiplication) and the (C+D) (addition) operations simultaneously.

Such functional units are being utilized in desktop computers. For example, a *math co-processor* is a functional unit that accelerates the performance of a computer when performing intensive numerical calculations such as in CAD (computer-aided design) applications or complex arithmetic calculations.

There are few instructions that take place in a single clock cycle. One way of accelerating the ability to accept data into a functional unit is to divide the data into a number of segments that take a single clock cycle to execute. This is known as a *segmented functional unit*. For example, the addition operation might take 4 cycles. By dividing the addition operation into 4 independent segments it is possible to accept additional data into the functional unit after a single clock cycle.

Memory Banks : With functional units able to deliver data at the rate of one result per clock cycle, it is necessary to utilize memory in a way that can accept data at the same speed. Register memory is fast enough to accept the data. However, register memory is too expensive to be used as the computer's main memory. Typically a CPU may have a few hundred registers compared to the millions of bytes necessary for physical memory.

One way to realize the speed necessary is to use multiple memory banks. This concept is analogous to segmented functional units. By creating multiple memory banks, it is possible to access data from the various banks sequentially. Consider the case where it takes 8 clock cycles to retrieve a value from memory. By having 8 memory banks, it is possible to request a value from bank 1, then in the next clock cycle bank 2, ... up to bank 8. Then bank 1 is ready to process a new request. This can be accomplished as long as the values to be retrieved are distributed across the 8 data banks.

EXAMPLE 10.22

Based on an access time (also known as memory bank cycle time) of 8 clock cycles with 8 memory banks, the following program would run efficiently,

```
DO I = 1, 8
   X(I) = X(I) + 1.0
END DO
```

In the case where the retrieved values are not in consecutive memory banks, conflicts can occur. Consider the following code which performs the same number and kind of calculations:

```
DO I = 1, 57, 8
    X(I) = X(I) + 1.0
END DO
```

The step size of 8 results in all data coming from bank number 1. As a result, 8 clock cycles must pass before the memory bank can be accessed again. Memory conflicts occur when the stride (step size) causes a memory bank to be accessed in less than the bank cycle time.

The Compiler and Programming Examples

With a basic understanding of the resources utilized by a computer, we will now look at the functions performed by the compiler to allocate resources efficiently. This section will be concerned with vector machines. Vector machines have been the most popular in the scientific community and have received the most attention from compiler manufacturers since vector processing lends itself more readily to standard Fortran. Parallel machines typically require special libraries of routines that must be utilized by the programmer. This puts the burden of utilizing a parallel processor machine entirely on the programmer. The process of optimizing vector operations is better understood and as a result, optimizing compilers are commercially available for these machines.

A compiler is a program which takes the source code and converts it into machine code for execution by the computer. A simple compiler converts the program directly into code with no optimization. Optimizing compilers (virtually all modern ones) search the source code for constructs that can be simplified or moved to produce better code, resulting in minimization of the operations needed to perform the same tasks.

Machine-Independent Optimization Techniques : These techniques are independent of the computer on which they are implemented and most compilers will perform these optimizations.

One of the easiest and most productive techniques in programming is to move computations that do not change to outside the body of a loop. We sometimes call this *invariant code relocation*.

EXAMPLE 10.23

The execution speed of a program can be improved if you place any invariant numerical computations outside a loop. This prevents a repetition of a computation whose value has already been computed. There is no need to repeat it.

```
DO I = 1, 100
    X(I) = X(I) + 10.0 + XSHIFT
    Y(I) = Y(I) * YSCALE / XSCALE
END DO
```

The terms 10.0+XSHIFT and YSCALE/XSCALE are invariant terms. Because their values will not change during the execution of the loop, these values should first be calculated outside the loop and stored. The effective loop would look like this:

```
A = 10.0 + XSHIFT
B = YSCALE / XSCALE
DO I = 1, 100
   X(I) = X(I) + A
   Y(I) = Y(I) * B
END DO
```

The first loop presented would execute 400 floating point operations while the second, optimized version would execute only 202. One way you can help yourself is to group the invariant terms together to make it easier for the compiler to locate possible areas of savings.

```
X(I)=10.0+X(I)+XSHIFT   ! May be missed by the compiler: combine
                        ! invariant terms
X(I)=X(I)+10.0+XSHIFT   ! Better visibility of invariant code:
X(I)=X(I)+(10.0+XSHIFT) ! Even better visibility of invariant code:
                        ! use parentheses.
```

Another place where invariant code is encountered is with expressions involving a string of constants. When there are a number of consecutive constants, the invariant value is determined at compilation time and is utilized inside the loop, rather than recomputing it inside the loop each time.

EXAMPLE 10.24

Here is an example of invariant code consisting of constants:

```
DO I = 1, 100
   VOL(I) = 4.0 / 3.0 * 3.1415927 * R(I)**3
END DO
```

The value of 4.0/3.0*3.1415927 is evaluated at compile time, thus eliminating 2 of the 4 floating point operations in the loop. The effective loop implemented is,

```
memoryA = 4.0 / 3.0 * 3.1415927   !(done at compile time)
DO I = 1, 100
   VOL(I) = memoryA * R(I)**3
END DO
```

We have added a new variable memoryA to indicate what is created by the compiler to avoid redundant computations. An optimizing compiler will automatically place this computation before the loop and use the result to compute the 100 array elements VOL(I).

We favor use of constant expressions because it makes the program more readable and is less error prone than direct conversion (replacing 4.0/3.0*3.1415927 by 4.1887903).

Another simple change that you can make in your programs to improve computing efficiency is to recognize common subexpressions used in a number of expressions. By first evaluating these common expressions, duplicate floating point operations can be removed.

EXAMPLE 10.25

If the same calculation is repeated several times within a loop, remove the repetitious subexpression and evaluate it once.

```
DO I = 1, 100
    D(I) = SQRT(X(I)**2 + Y(I)**2)
    H(I) = X(I) / SQRT(X(I)**2 + Y(I)**2)
    V(I) = Y(I) / SQRT(X(I)**2 + Y(I)**2)
END DO
```

In this code, SQRT(X(I)**2 + Y(I)**2) is a common sub-expression. It is better to evaluate this subexpression as a separate variable and then place this variable in the common expressions.

```
DO I = 1, 100
    sub_expression = SQRT(X(I)**2 + Y(I)**2)
    D(I) = sub_expression
    H(I)=X(I)/sub_expression
    V(I)=Y(I)/Sub_expression
END DO
```

Combining common subexpressions is very much like relocating invariant-code outside a loop. However, in this example, the expression had to stay inside the loop because of the changing variables.

Machine-Dependent Optimization Techniques : There are several techniques that depend on the architecture of the computer on which they are being run. These techniques involve effective utilization of resources such as registers, functional units, and memory.

One important technique is known as *instruction scheduling*. We've already investigated processes that allow for overlapping events. For example, segmented functional units allow for data values to be processed before a preceding value has been completely evaluated. This overlap was then extended into memory access by having multiple memory banks. To be able to take advantage of overlapping operations, the compiler will try to schedule resources.

As programmers, we can help the compiler by writing code that does not overload a particular resource (memory access, functional units, etc.) so that optimization can be achieved.

EXAMPLE 10.26

The order in which mathematical operations are executed is important as we demonstrate in this evaluation of a polynomial such as:

```
Y=A+B*X+C*X**2+D*X**3
```

If the computer being used has a single functional unit for addition and a single functional unit for multiplication, the evaluation as written will result in each unit producing a bottleneck and slowing the computation. To improve the processing, we will rearrange the polynomial using Horner's rule and eliminate the exponentiation operation:

```
Y=A+X*(B+X*(C+D*X))
```

The key to the speed improvement is that the expression above alternates fetches (data retrieval such as retrieving the value of A) and operations. This allows for overlaps to take place and eliminates the explicit exponentiation.

Another place where we can improve speed is to *reduce the operator strength*. Reduction is the process of substituting less costly operators that provide the same result. Instead of using exponentiation to produce the square of a number, for example, we could multiply the number by itself. This is a much more effective way of getting the same result. Here are some common areas where you can help the compiler optimize the code:

- When raising a variable to a whole number, use an integer exponent. For example, use X**2 instead of X**2.0. The real exponent invokes the use of logarithms, while integer exponents utilize successive multiplication. Even better is the use of X*X since it eliminates exponentiation altogether.
- When constants are known, declare them as such so the compiler will know.
- Eliminate constant loops (as shown below) by expanding the equations explicitly. This reduces the need to access memory.

EXAMPLE 10.27

In this example, we remove a constant loop (also known as "unrolling") and express the equation explicitly. The original loop calculates a polynomial which will always have a maximum exponent of 3.

```
Y = 0.0
DO I = 0, 3
   Y = Y + X**I * A(I)
END DO
```

Instead of writing the loop this way, we will rewrite it explicitly as:

```
Y = A(0) + A(1)*X + A(2)*X**2 + A(3)*X**3
```

This will save 4 fetches, 4 add operations, and 5 assignments (initializing Y to zero). By applying Horner's rule as shown in the previous example, additional savings would also result.

Vectorization: *Vectorization* is the process by which the code generated is capable of taking advantage of the vector capabilities of the computer. The compiler does this by two means: *explicit* and *implicit vectorization*.

Explicit vectorization occurs when code is unambiguously interpreted as a vector. This permits use of system-dependent procedures or by use of the vector capabilities intrinsic to Fortran 90. *Implicit vectorization*, which is the only method present in older versions of Fortran, occurs when the compiler itself detects the conditions for vectorization.

Code that is a candidate for vectorization includes:

- Code that contains an assignment of at least one array with an index based on a loop variable (vector array).
- Code that contains at least one recognized *reduction function*, which returns a scalar quantity. An example would be: scalar=scalar+vectorizable expression

Finally, code cannot be vectorized in certain cases when *vectorization inhibitors* are present. Examples of vector inhibitors include:

Recursion in any form	Certain nested IF blocks
Subroutine CALLs	GO TO statements that exit the loop
Any input or output	Backward transfer within a loop
References to external functions	

EXAMPLE 10.28

Here are two examples of good and bad candidates for vectorization

a) This program can be vectorized, since the loop control variable I is used to control the elements of the arrays A, B, and C. Also, no vectorization inhibitors are present.

```
DO I = 1, 100
   A(I) = B(I) / C(I)
   AMAX = MAX(AMAX, A(I))
END DO
```

b) The following program can not be easily vectorized, since the call to the subroutine is a vectorization inhibitor.

```
DO I = 1, 100
   A(I) = B(I) / C(I)
   CALL AMAX(THE_MAX, A(I))
END DO
```

Solved Problems

10.1 Create a data structure to store material properties of metals. Properties include common name, density, and yield strength. Examples of the data are as follows:

Material Name	Density (lb/in^3)	Yield Strength (lb/in^2)
304 Stainless Steel	0.282	30,000
SA53 Carbon Steel	0.286	50,000
1040 Carbon Steel	0.283	60,000

```
TYPE MATERIAL
   CHARACTER (LEN=40) :: NAME
   REAL :: DENSITY
   REAL :: YIELD_STRENGTH
END TYPE MATERIAL
```

10.2 Create a data structure that stores the appropriate geometrical properties for (a) a square, (b) a rectangle, and (c) a circle. All objects should include a position property which stores the x,y coordinates of the center of the object.

```
(a) TYPE SQUARE
       REAL, POINTER :: SIDE
       REAL, DIMENSION (2) :: POSITION
    END TYPE SQUARE
(b) TYPE RECTANGLE
       REAL, POINTER :: WIDTH, HEIGHT
       REAL, DIMENSION (2) :: POSITION
    END TYPE RECTANGLE
(c) TYPE CIRCLE
       REAL, POINTER :: RADIUS
       REAL, DIMENSION (2) :: POSITION
    END TYPE CIRCLE
```

10.3 Create functions to calculate the area and perimeter for the shapes stored in the data structures of Problem 10.2.

```
(a) FUNCTION AREA_SQUARE(THE_SQUARE) RESULT(THE_AREA)
       TYPE(SQUARE), POINTER :: THE_SQUARE
       REAL :: THE_AREA
       THE_AREA=THE_SQUARE%SIDE**2
    END FUNCTION AREA_SQUARE
(b) FUNCTION AREA_RECTANGLE(THE_RECTANGLE) RESULT(THE_AREA)
       TYPE(RECTANGLE), POINTER :: THE_RECTANGLE
```

```
        REAL :: THE_AREA
        THE_AREA=THE_RECTANGLE%HEIGHT*THE_RECTANGLE%WIDTH
    END FUNCTION AREA_RECTANGLE
(c) FUNCTION AREA_CIRCLE(THE_CIRCLE) RESULT(THE_AREA)
        TYPE(CIRCLE), POINTER :: THE_CIRCLE
        REAL :: THE_AREA
        THE_AREA=3.1416*THE_CIRCLE%RADIUS**2
    END FUNCTION AREA_CIRCLE
(d) FUNCTION PERIMETER_SQUARE(THE_SQUARE) RESULT(THE_PERIM)
        TYPE(SQUARE), POINTER :: THE_SQUARE
        REAL :: THE_PERIM
        THE_PERIM=THE_SQUARE%SIDE*4
    END FUNCTION PERIMETER_SQUARE
(e) FUNCTION PERIMETER_RECTANGLE(THE_RECTANGLE) RESULT(THE_PERIM)
        TYPE(RECTANGLE), POINTER :: THE_RECTANGLE
        REAL :: THE_PERIM
        THE_PERIM=2*(THE_RECTANGLE%HEIGHT+THE_RECTANGLE%WIDTH)
    END FUNCTION PERIMETER_RECTANGLE
(f) FUNCTION PERIMETER_CIRCLE(THE_CIRCLE) RESULT(THE_PERIM)
        TYPE(CIRCLE), POINTER :: THE_CIRCLE
        REAL :: THE_PERIM
        THE_PERIM=6.2832*THE_CIRCLE%RADIUS
    END FUNCTION PERIMETER_CIRCLE
```

10.4 Modify the material structure of Problem 10.1 so that an array of yield stresses and testing temperatures are included in the data type. The following table summarizes some of the yield stress (YS) and temperature (T) data for two steels.

Yield Strength (lb/in^2) of Steels as a Function of Temperature

	T = -20C	T = 200C	T = 300C	T = 500C	T = 700C
SA-53 Steel	50,120	50,100	50,000	49,040	43,035
SA-178 Steel	58,735	58,550	58,300	57,600	50,360

```
TYPE MATERIAL
    CHARACTER (LEN=40) :: NAME
    REAL :: DENSITY
    REAL, DIMENSION (5) :: YIELD, TEMP
END TYPE MATERIAL
```

10.5 For the data structures and operators created in Problems 10.2 and 10.3, rewrite the programs to take advantage of modules. Also, add the context-sensitive unary operators .AREA. and .PERIMETER. which return the area and perimeter, respectively, for any of the shapes.

```
!*******************************************************************
! The following module combines all the user-defined data type
! declarations and the appropriate functions for the computations
!*******************************************************************
MODULE SHAPES2D
    !***************************************************************
    ! First, we copy the user-defined data types from Problem 10.2
    !***************************************************************
    TYPE SQUARE
       REAL :: SIDE
       REAL, DIMENSION (2) :: POSITION
    END TYPE SQUARE
    TYPE RECTANGLE
       REAL :: WIDTH, HEIGHT
       REAL, DIMENSION (2) :: POSITION
    END TYPE RECTANGLE
    TYPE CIRCLE
       REAL :: RADIUS
       REAL, DIMENSION (2) :: POSITION
    END TYPE CIRCLE
    !***************************************************************
    ! This is the interface operator to compute the area.
    !***************************************************************
    INTERFACE OPERATOR (.AREA.)
       MODULE PROCEDURE AREA_SQUARE
       MODULE PROCEDURE AREA_RECTANGLE
       MODULE PROCEDURE AREA_CIRCLE
    END INTERFACE
    !***************************************************************
    ! This is the interface operator to compute the perimeter.
    !***************************************************************
    INTERFACE OPERATOR (.PERIMETER.)
       MODULE PROCEDURE PERIMETER_SQUARE
       MODULE PROCEDURE PERIMETER_RECTANGLE
       MODULE PROCEDURE PERIMETER_CIRCLE
    END INTERFACE
CONTAINS
    !***************************************************************
    ! Now, we add the functions from Problem 10.3
    !***************************************************************
    FUNCTION AREA_SQUARE(THE_SQUARE) RESULT(THE_AREA)
       TYPE(SQUARE) :: THE_SQUARE
       REAL :: THE_AREA
       THE_AREA=THE_SQUARE%SIDE**2
    END FUNCTION AREA_SQUARE
    FUNCTION AREA_RECTANGLE(THE_RECTANGLE) RESULT(THE_AREA)
       TYPE(RECTANGLE) :: THE_RECTANGLE
       REAL :: THE_AREA
       THE_AREA=THE_RECTANGLE%HEIGHT*THE_RECTANGLE%WIDTH
    END FUNCTION AREA_RECTANGLE
    FUNCTION AREA_CIRCLE(THE_CIRCLE) RESULT(THE_AREA)
```

```
            TYPE(CIRCLE) :: THE_CIRCLE
            REAL :: THE_AREA
            THE_AREA=3.1416*THE_CIRCLE%RADIUS**2
        END FUNCTION AREA_CIRCLE
        FUNCTION PERIMETER_SQUARE(THE_SQUARE) RESULT(THE_PERIM)
            TYPE(SQUARE) :: THE_SQUARE
            REAL :: THE_PERIM
            THE_PERIM=THE_SQUARE%SIDE*4
        END FUNCTION PERIMETER_SQUARE
        FUNCTION PERIMETER_RECTANGLE(THE_RECTANGLE) RESULT(THE_PERIM)
            TYPE(RECTANGLE) :: THE_RECTANGLE
            REAL :: THE_PERIM
            THE_PERIM=2*(THE_RECTANGLE%HEIGHT+THE_RECTANGLE%WIDTH)
        END FUNCTION PERIMETER_RECTANGLE
        FUNCTION PERIMETER_CIRCLE(THE_CIRCLE) RESULT(THE_PERIM)
            TYPE(CIRCLE) :: THE_CIRCLE
            REAL :: THE_PERIM
            THE_PERIM=6.2832*THE_CIRCLE%RADIUS
        END FUNCTION PERIMETER_CIRCLE
    END MODULE SHAPES2D
```

10.6   Write an interpolation function for finding the yield strength of a material based on the structure in Problem 10.4. The user will enter the material and the temperature at execution time, and your program should return the yield strength for that material at that temperature.

```
    FUNCTION GET_YIELD_STRESS(THE_MATL, THE_TEMP) RESULT(STRESS)
        TYPE(MATERIAL) :: THE_MATL
        INTEGER :: UPPER
        !**********************************************************
        ! First, check to see that the temperature is within the range
        ! of the data stored in THE_TEMP(1) and THE_TEMP(5). If it is
        ! outside this range, return a value of 0.0 for the yield stress.
        !**********************************************************
        IF(THE_MATL%TEMP(1)<=THE_TEMP .AND. &
          THE_TEMP<=THE_MATL%TEMP(5)) THEN
            DO I = 2, 10                ! Loop to find the proper intervals
                UPPER = I              ! for the interpolation
                IF(THE_MATL%TEMP(UPPER) >= THE_TEMP) EXIT
            END DO
            !**********************************************************
            ! Now, do the interpolation between points UPPER and UPPER-1
            !**********************************************************
            STRESS=(THE_MATL%YIELD(UPPER)-THE_MATL%YIELD(UPPER-1))/&
                   (THE_MATL%TEMP(UPPER)-THE_MATL%TEMP(UPPER-1))*&
                   (THE_TEMP-THE_MATL%TEMP(UPPER-1))
        ELSE
            STRESS=0.0
        END IF
    END FUNCTION GET_YIELD_STRESS
```

10.7 Write both recursive and nonrecursive iterative procedures to evaluate the following mathematical functions:

(a) Exponentiation based on X**N = X*X*(N−1) with X**0 = 1 by definition.
(b) The Fibonacci sequence F(N) = F(N−1) + F(N−2) for N>2 and F(1) = 1 and F(2)=1.

(a)
```
! For the iterative solution, the exponential is computed by
! multiplying the value of X by itself N times. Note that the
! final value is contained in the variable THE_ANSWER and is
! returned by the argument list that called the function.
!**************************************************************
FUNCTION EXPI(X, N, THE_ANSWER)
   THE_ANSWER=1.0
   DO I = 1, N
      THE_ANSWER=THE_ANSWER*X
   END DO
END FUNCTION EXPI
!**************************************************************
! For the recursive solution, we need a means of returning the
! answer. Thus, we must provide a RESULT clause containing the
! name of the variable storing the result.
!**************************************************************
RECURSIVE FUNCTION EXPAR(X, N)  RESULT(THE_ANSWER)
   IF(N == 0) THEN
      THE_ANSWER=1.0
   ELSE
      THE_ANSWER=X*EXPAR(X, N-1)
   END IF
END FUNCTION EXPAR
```

(b)
```
!**************************************************************
! For the iterative solution, we store the first two values in
! the series (1, 1) in FN_1 and FN_2. Inside the loop, we add these
! two numbers to obtain the next term in the series. Then we drop
! the oldest term and reassign FN_1 and FN_2.
!**************************************************************
FUNCTION FIBIC(N, THE_ANSWER)
   INTEGER :: N, FN_1, FN_2, THE_ANSWER
   FN_1=1
   FN_2=1
   IF(N <= 2) THEN
      THE_ANSWER=1
   ELSE
      DO I = 3, N
         THE_ANSWER=FN_2+FN_1
         FN_2=FN_1
         FN_1=THE_ANSWER
      END DO
   END IF
END FUNCTION FIBIC
```

```
!***************************************************************
! For the recursive solution, the function will call itself N
! times. Each time, the function tries to calculate the factorial
! of (N-1). When N reaches a minimum value of 1, the process
! reverses, since 1! is defined. Then the value of 2! can be
! computed and so forth.
!***************************************************************
RECURSIVE FUNCTION FIBRC(N) RESULT(THE_ANSWER)
   INTEGER :: N, THE_ANSWER
   IF(N < 1) THEN      ! If N is negative, abort the calculation
      THE_ANSWER = 1
      RETURN
   END IF
   IF(N <= 2) THEN
      THE_ANSWER=1
   ELSE
      THE_ANSWER=FIBRC(N-1)+FIBRC(N-2)
   END IF
END FUNCTION FIBRC
```

10.8 For the examples shown below, determine if either dangling pointers or unreferenced storage are present:

(a)
```
REAL, POINTER :: P1, P2
ALLOCATE(P2)
P1=> P2
DEALLOCATE(P1)
PRINT *, P2
```
(Dangling Pointer: Since P1 points to P2, deallocating P1 simultaneously deallocates the memory for P2).

(b)
```
REAL, TARGET :: X, Y
REAL, POINTER :: XP, YP
X=3.45
ALLOCATE(YP)
YP=6.78
Y=YP
DEALLOCATE(YP)
YP=>X
PRINT *, X, Y
```
(No error: YP is deallocated before it is assigned to a new target.)

(c)
```
REAL, POINTER :: P1, P2
REAL, TARGET :: A, B
ALLOCATE(P1)
P1=10.234
B=3.6
P1=> A
A=7.0
```
(Unreferenced Storage: P1 is allocated and then assigned a new target without first deallocating memory.)

10.9 Using a structure similar to the linked list structure, create a *stack* structure. A stack is a list in which the last value entered is the first one retrieved. To do this, create a function NEWSTACK to temporarily store the numbers as they are entered, a subroutine PUSH to put the integer values onto the stack, and a function POP to take values off the stack. Finally, create a function EMPTYSTACK to check if the stack is empty. Package the structures in a module to create an abstract data type. Use the numbers 1, 2, and 3 to test your program.

```
!**************************************************************
! The modules to define the necessary data types
!**************************************************************
MODULE STACK_STUFF
    TYPE NODE
       INTEGER :: VALUE
       TYPE(NODE), POINTER :: NEXT
    END TYPE NODE
    TYPE STACK
        TYPE(NODE), POINTER :: START
    END TYPE STACK
CONTAINS
    FUNCTION NEWSTACK( ) RESULT(THE_STACK)   ! Store numbers
       TYPE(STACK), POINTER :: THE_STACK
       NULLIFY(THE_STACK%START)
    END FUNCTION NEWSTACK
    SUBROUTINE PUSH(THE_VALUE, THE_STACK)    ! Put numbers onto stack
       INTEGER :: THE_VALUE
       TYPE(STACK), POINTER :: THE_STACK
       TYPE(NODE), POINTER :: HOLD
       HOLD=>THE_STACK%START
       ALLOCATE(THE_STACK%START)
       THE_STACK%START%VALUE=THE_VALUE
       THE_STACK%START%NEXT=>HOLD
    END SUBROUTINE PUSH
    FUNCTION POP(THE_STACK) RESULT(THE_VALUE)! Take values off stack
       INTEGER :: THE_VALUE
       TYPE(STACK), POINTER :: THE_STACK
       TYPE(NODE), POINTER :: HOLD
       THE_VALUE=THE_STACK%START%VALUE
       HOLD=>THE_STACK%START%NEXT
       DEALLOCATE(THE_STACK%START)
       THE_STACK%START=>HOLD
    END FUNCTION POP
    FUNCTION EMPTYSTACK(THE_STACK) RESULT(THE_STATE) ! Is stack empty?
       LOGICAL :: THE_STATE
       TYPE(STACK), POINTER :: THE_STACK
       THE_STATE=ASSOCIATED(THE_STACK%START)
    END FUNCTION EMPTYSTACK
END MODULE STACK_STUFF
USE STACK_STUFF                       !The main program
TYPE(STACK) :: ST1
ST1=NEWSTACK()
```

```
CALL PUSH(1, ST1)                 ! put a value of 1 in the stack
CALL PUSH(2, ST1)                 ! put next value (2) on the stack
CALL PUSH(3, ST1)                 ! put third value (3) on the stack
DO
   IF(EMPTYSTACK(ST1)) EXIT
   PRINT *, POP(ST1)              ! take the most recent value off the
END DO                            ! stack and print it
END
```

10.10 Rewrite the ADDNAME subroutine from Example 10.18 to insert names in *descending* order.

```
SUBROUTINE ADDNAME(THE_LIST, THE_NAME)
   CHARACTER (LEN=20) :: THE_NAME
   TYPE(LIST), POINTER :: THE_LIST
   TYPE(NODE), POINTER :: CURRENT_PTR, PREVIOUS_PTR
   PREVIOUS_PTR=>THE_LIST%START              !assign previous pointer
   CURRENT_PTR=>THE_LIST%START%NEXT          !assign current pointer
   DO
      IF(.NOT.ASSOCIATED(CURRENT_PTR))EXIT   !end of structure
      IF(CURRENT_PTR%VALUE<THE_NAME) EXIT    !find position for new name
                                             !The only change needed is
                                             !to change == to <
      PREVIOUS_PTR=>CURRENT_PTR              !update previous pointer
      CURRENT_PTR=>CURRENT_PTR%NEXT          !update current pointer
   END DO
   ALLOCATE(PREVIOUS_PTR%NEXT)              !make a new node
   PREVIOUS_PTR%NEXT%VALUE=THE_NAME         !assign new value
   PREVIOUS_PTR%NEXT=>CURRENT_PTR           !assign new node pointer
END SUBROUTINE ADDNAME
```

10.11 What is the clock cycle time for a computer with a 33 MHz clock? What would be the range of Mips ratings you could expect for a single processor computer operating at this speed?

33 MHz equals 33 Mips. However, due to resource conflicts, this value would be closer to 1/10 to 1/2 of the calculated rating. Thus, the expected range would be 3.3 to 16.5 Mips.

10.12 How would you improve the following code by techniques that are machine independent?

```
(a) DO I = 1, 100
       CONST=(1.0/28.35*1.0/6.0)*(2.54/12.0)**3   !convert to lbs/cu-ft
       WEIGHT(I)=WEIGHT(I)*CONST
    END DO
(b) TEMP=1.0/(TAN(CA*3.1416/180.0)*2)
    DO I = 1, 20
       VOL(I)=2*(TEMP*DIA(I)+CD(I))*3.1416*(DIA(I)/2)**2
    END DO
```

(a) Better: Put the expression for CONST before the loop. However, this requires additional storage and fetches.

Best: The constant term CONST should be moved. By placing it into the expression, the compiler will evaluate it and remove it from the loop. This also causes the compiler to use fast registers. The resulting segment is:

```
DO I = 1, 100
    WEIGHT(I))=WEIGHT(I)*(1.0/28.35*1.0/6.0)*(2.54/12.0)**3
END DO
```

(b) Move TEMP into the loop where the compiler will evaluate it at compilation time and substitute the appropriate constant. This only works with an optimizing compiler. If you do not have a compiler that optimizes code, you are better leaving the code as written.

10.13 How would you modify the following code for better compiler optimization?

```
PROGRAM Connect_the_dots
PRINT *,'How many dots?'
READ *,NDOTS
CALL GRAPH_START(4105,1)
CALL WINDOW(-100.0,100.0,-100.0,100.0)
RADIUS=80.0
DELTA_THETA=2*3.1416/NDOTS
DO I=0, NDOTS-1
   DO J=I+1, NDOTS-1
      CALL POLAR_MOVE(RADIUS,I*DELTA_THETA)
      CALL POLAR_DRAW(RADIUS,J*DELTA_THETA)
   END DO
END DO
CALL GRAPH_STOP
END PROGRAM Connect_the_dots
```

(Move the DELTA_THETA into the loop. Optimization will result in the compiler moving the code out of the loop, but faster memory will be used when accessing the numerical result.)

10.14 Which programs are candidates for vectorization and which are not? Suggest places where explicit vectorization could be utilized.

(a)
```
INTEGER, DIMENSION (256,256) :: IMAGE
ILEVEL=3
DO I = 1, NROWS
   DO J = 1, NCOLS
      IF(ILEVEL<ABS(NINT(SUM(IMAGE(I-1:I+1, J-1:J+1)))/8.0)) CYCLE
   END DO
END DO
```
(b)
```
INTEGER :: COLS, ROWS
REAL :: X, Y
PARAMETER(COLS=80, ROWS=20)
```

```
CHARACTER(LEN=1), DIMENSION(ROWS, COLS) :: SCREEN
SCREEN=' '                        ! initializes the screen to all blanks
PRINT *, 'Enter starting and ending X values:'
READ *, XMIN, XMAX
PRINT *, 'Enter minimum and maximum range values:'
READ *, YMIN, YMAX
DO JX = 1, COLS
   X=XMIN+(JX-1)*(XMAX-XMIN)/(COLS-1)
   Y=SIN(X)
   IY=ROWS-NINT((Y-YMIN)/(YMAX-YMIN)*(ROWS-1))
   IF(1 <= IY .AND. IY <= ROWS) SCREEN(IY, JX)='*'
END DO
DO I = 1, ROWS
   PRINT *, (SCREEN(I, J), J=1, COLS)
END DO
END
```

(a) The array IMAGE is being assigned a value inside a loop, and the expression is of the form IF(Scalar .logical. vectorizable expression). Thus, since there are no vectorization inhibitors, the program is a candidate for vectorization.

(b) The loops assign a value to the array SCREEN and no vectorization inhibitors are present. Therefore, this is a candidate for vectorization.

10.15 Write a recursive function FINDNAME(THE_NAME, THE_TREE) which returns a logical value of .TRUE. if the name is present in the tree structure presented in Example 10.18. How does your function behave if the values that were entered in the tree were already in descending order? What would have been the best order for the data to be entered?

```
RECURSIVE FUNCTION FINDNAME(THE_NODE, THE_NAME) RESULT(THE_STATE)
   LOGICAL :: THE_STATE
   TYPE(NODE), POINTER :: THE_NODE
   CHARACTER(LEN=20) :: THE_NAME
   IF(.NOT. ASSOCIATED(THE_NODE)) THEN      !Find an unallocated node
      THE_STATE=.FALSE.
      RETURN
   END IF
   IF(THE_NODE%NAME == THE_NAME) THEN       !Found the value
      THE_STATE=.TRUE.
      RETURN
   END IF
   IF(THE_NAME < THE_NODE%NAME) THEN
      THE_STATE=FINDNAME(THE_NODE%LEFT, THE_NAME)      !Search left
   ELSE
      THE_STATE=FINDNAME(THE_NODE%RIGHT, THE_NAME)     !Search right
   END IF
END FUNCTION FINDNAME
```

Supplemental Problems

10.16 Create a data structure to store the parameters of a spur gear. Parameters to be stored include:

(a) number of teeth (integer)
(b) material (use definition from Solved Problem 10.1)
(c) pressure angle (real)
(d) diametrical pitch (real)
(e) face width (real)

10.17 Create a data structure that can store the appropriate geometrical properties for a cube, a rectangular box, and a sphere. Your structure should also include a position attribute which indicates the object's x, y, z position.

10.18 Create functions to calculate the surface area and the volume for the shapes stored in the data structures of the previous problem.

10.19 Create a PART data type for each of the shapes in Problem 10.17. Each data type will have a geometric attribute (one of the shapes), a material attribute (with data type NAME of character type), and density (a real number).

10.20 For the data structures created in Problems 10.17 and 10.18, rewrite your program to take advantage of modules. Also, add the context-sensitive unary operators .AREA. and .VOLUME.

10.21 For each of the PART data types developed in Problem 10.19, create a function to calculate their weights. It is recommended to use the volume functions developed in earlier solutions. Finally, create a generic function WEIGHT that will return the weight for any of the parts.

10.22 Write recursive and iterative functions to evaluate exponentiation based on:
$$X**N = (X**floor(N/2))**2*X \text{ for N even and N>0}$$
$$X**N = (X**floor(N/2))**2 \text{ for N odd and N>0}$$
$$X**0 = 1 \text{ by definition}$$
$$floor(I) = \text{the greatest integer less than or equal to I.}$$

10.23 For the examples provided below, determine if any dangling pointers or unreferenced storage are present:

```
(a) REAL, POINTER :: P1, P2
    ALLOCATE (P1)
    P1=> P2
    DEALLOCATE (P1)
    PRINT *, ASSOCIATED (P1)
(b) REAL, TARGET :: A, B
    REAL, POINTER :: AP, BP
    A=1.0
    B=2.0
    AP=> A
    BP => B
    NULLIFY (AP)
    PRINT *, ASSOCIATED (AP, BP)
(c) REAL, POINTER :: PA, PB, PC
    REAL, TARGET :: R1, R2, R3
    ALLOCATE (PC)
    PC=7.3
    PA => PC
    PB => PA
    R1 = 1.0
    PC => R1
    R2=R1
    DEALLOCATE (PB)
```

10.24 The linked list example in the text (Example 10.17) is well suited for finding values that occur at the beginning of the list LIST%START%VALUE. However, this procedure is inefficient, since a search has to be made to find the end of the list. Rewrite the structure so that the last value in the list is the easiest to find. Rewrite all of the procedures related to the linked list structure for this new structure.

10.25 Create a structure called BOOK composed of nodes called PAGES. A page will have a text attribute that uses a character array of 18 rows with 60 characters on each row, a next pointer, a previous pointer, and a page number attribute. Create procedures to perform the following:
(a) Create a new book
(b) Check to see if the book is empty
(c) Create a new page at the end of the book and assign values to the text
(d) Delete the last page in the book
(e) Create a subroutine VIEW that allows you to go through the book in the forward or backward direction.

10.26 What is the clock cycle time for a computer with a 50 MHz clock? What would be the expected range of Mips ratings for a computer made from a single processor of this speed?

10.27 How would you improve the following code by techniques that are machine independent?

(a)
```
DO I = 1, 100
    CIRCUM(I) = 2.0*3.1416*R(I)
    AREA(I) = 3.1416*R(I)**2
    WEIGHT(I)=CIRCUM(I)+10.0*AREA(I)
END DO
```
(b)
```
DO I = 1, 100
    TEMP(I) = SQRT(X(I)**2+Y(I)**2)
    Z1(I) = Z(I)/TEMP(I)
    Z2(I) = TEMP(I) + X(I) + Y(I)
END DO
```

10.28 How would you modify the code from Solved Problem 7.11 for better compiler optimization?

```
REAL A(3,3), X(3), C(3)
DO I = 1, 3
    PRINT *, 'Enter coef and constants for eq.:', I
    READ *, (A(I, J), J= 1, 3), C(I)
END DO
CALL CRAMER(A, X, C)
PRINT *, 'Solution:', X
END
SUBROUTINE CRAMER(A, X, C)
REAL A(3,3), X(3), C(3), A1(3,3), A2(3,3), A3(3,3)
DENO=DET(A)
IF(ABS(DENO) < 0.00001) STOP
DO I = 1, 3
    DO J = 1, 3
        A1(I, J) = A(I, J)
        A2(I, J) = A(I, J)
        A3(I, J) = A(I, J)
    END DO
END DO
DO I = 1, 3
    A1(I, 1) = C(I)
    A2(I, 2) = C(I)
    A3(I, 3) = C(I)
END DO
X(1) = DET(A1)/DENO
X(2) = DET(A2)/DENO
X(3) = DET(A3)/DENO
END
REAL FUNCTION DET(A)
REAL A(3, 3)
DET = A(1,1)*(A(2,2)*A(3,3)-A(2,3)*A(3,2)) -A(1,2)*(A(2,1)*A(3,3)&
    -A(2,3)*A(3,1))+A(1,3)*(A(2,1)*A(3,2)-A(2,2)*A(3,1))
END
```

10.29 Which of the following programs are candidates for vectorization? Suggest places where explicit vectorization could be utilized.

```
(a) FUNCTION FIT(X, XS, YS, NUM) RESULT(SUM)
    INTEGER :: NUM
    REAL, DIMENSION(NUM) :: XS, X
    SUM = 0.0
    DO IY = 1, NUM
       PROD = 1.0
       DO IX = 1, NUM
          IF (IX == IY) CYCLE
          PROD = PROD * (IY - XS(IX)) / (X(IY) - X(IX))
       END DO
       SUM = SUM + PROD * Y(IY)
    END DO
    END FUNCTION FIT
(b) SUBROUTINE LSQ(N, X, Y, M, B, R)
    REAL, DIMENSION(N) :: X, Y
    REAL ::  M
    SUMX = 0.0
    SUMX2 = 0.0
    SUMY = 0.0
    SUMY2 = 0.0
    SUMXY = 0.0
    DO I = 1, N
       SUMX = SUMX + X(I)
       SUMY = SUMY + Y(I)
       SUMX2 = SUMX2 + X(I)**2
       SUMY2 = SUMY2 + Y(I)**2
       SUMXY = SUMXY + X(I)*Y(I)
    END DO
    M = (N*SUMXY-SUMX*SUMY)/(N*SUMX2-SUMX**2)
    B = (SUMY-M*SUMX)/N
    R = (N*SUMXY-SUMX*SUMY)/SQRT(N*SUMX2-SUMX**2)*(N*SUMY2-SUMY**2)
    END SUBROUTINE LSQ
```

10.30 Write a subroutine to "load" a binary search tree such that the values are distributed to minimize unallocated nodes (sometimes called a "bushy", "balanced", or "complete" tree). For example, given the values a, b, c, d, e, f, and g, the resulting tree should look like this:

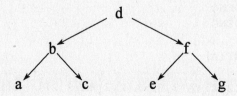

One method to perform this is:
(a) determine the value that is in the middle of the list and put it into the current node
(b) go back to the list and those values to the left of the value just stored will go to the left

    node. Then perform step (a)

(c) go back to the list and those values to the right of the value just stored will go to the right node. Then perform step (a)

(d) stop when the length of the list reaches zero

Answers to Selected Supplemental Problems

10.16
```
TYPE SPUR_GEAR
    INTEGER :: NUM_TEETH
    TYPE(MATERIAL) :: MATL
    REAL :: PRES_ANGLE
    REAL :: DIAM_PITCH
    REAL :: FACE
END TYPE SPUR_GEAR
```

10.17
```
TYPE CUBE
    REAL :: SIDE
    REAL, DIMENSION (3) :: POSITION
END TYPE CUBE
TYPE BOX
    REAL :: DEPTH, WIDTH, HEIGHT
    REAL, DIMENSION (3) :: POSITION
END TYPE BOX
TYPE SPHERE
    REAL ::  RADIUS
    REAL, DIMENSION (3) :: POSITION
END TYPE SPHERE
```

10.18 (a)
```
FUNCTION AREA_CUBE(THE_CUBE) RESULT(THE_AREA)
    TYPE(CUBE) :: THE_CUBE
    REAL :: THE_AREA
    THE_AREA=6*THE_CUBE%SIDE**2    ! area of a cube = 6*(x**2)
END FUNCTION AREA_CUBE
```
  (b)
```
FUNCTION AREA_BOX(THE_BOX) RESULT(THE_AREA)
!*************************************************************
! The area of a box = 2(area side 1) + 2(area side 2) + 2(area
! side 3).
!*************************************************************
    TYPE(BOX) :: THE_BOX
    REAL :: THE_AREA
    THE_AREA=2*THE_BOX%HEIGHT*THE_BOX%WIDTH+2*THE_BOX%HEIGHT*&
             THE_BOX%DEPTH+2*THE_BOX%WIDTH*THE_BOX%DEPTH
END FUNCTION AREA_BOX
```
  (c)
```
FUNCTION AREA_SPHERE(THE_SPHERE) RESULT(THE_AREA)
```

```
      !*************************************************************
      ! The area of a sphere  = 4 * pi * r**2
      !*************************************************************
         TYPE(SPHERE) :: THE_SPHERE
         REAL :: THE_AREA
         THE_AREA=4.0*3.1416*THE_SPHERE%RADIUS**2
      END FUNCTION AREA_SPHERE
  (d) FUNCTION VOLUME_CUBE(THE_CUBE) RESULT(THE_VOLUME)
      !*************************************************************
      ! The volume of a cube = side**3
      !*************************************************************
         TYPE(CUBE) :: THE_CUBE
         REAL :: THE_VOLUME
         THE_VOLUME=THE_CUBE%SIDE**3
      END FUNCTION VOLUME_CUBE
  (e) FUNCTION VOLUME_BOX(THE_BOX) RESULT(THE_VOLUME)
      !*************************************************************
      ! The volume of a box = (height)*(width)*(depth)
      !*************************************************************
         TYPE(BOX) :: THE_BOX
         REAL :: THE_VOLUME
         THE_VOLUME=THE_BOX%HEIGHT*THE_BOX%WIDTH*THE_BOX%DEPTH
      END FUNCTION VOLUME_BOX
  (f) FUNCTION VOLUME_SPHERE(THE_SPHERE) RESULT(THE_VOLUME)
      !*************************************************************
      ! The volume of a sphere = 4/3*pi*R**3
      !*************************************************************
         TYPE(SPHERE) :: THE_SPHERE
         REAL :: THE_VOLUME
         THE_VOLUME=4.0/3.0*3.1416*THE_SPHERE%RADIUS**3
      END FUNCTION VOLUME_SPHERE


10.19 TYPE PART_CUBE
         TYPE(CUBE) :: GEO
         REAL :: DENSITY
         CHARACTER :: NAME*30
      END TYPE PART_CUBE
      TYPE PART_BOX
         TYPE(BOX) :: GEO
         REAL :: DENSITY
         CHARACTER :: NAME*30
      END TYPE PART_BOX
      TYPE PART_SPHERE
         TYPE(SPHERE) :: GEO
         REAL :: DENSITY
         CHARACTER :: NAME*30
      END TYPE PART_SPHERE
```

```
10.20 MODULE SHAPES3D
        TYPE CUBE                                    ! See problem 10.17
          REAL :: SIDE
          REAL, DIMENSION (3) :: POSITION
        END TYPE CUBE
        TYPE BOX                                      ! See problem 10.17
          REAL :: DEPTH, WIDTH, HEIGHT
          REAL, DIMENSION (3) :: POSITION
        END TYPE BOX
        TYPE SPHERE                                   ! See problem 10.17
          REAL ::  RADIUS
          REAL, DIMENSION (3) :: POSITION
        END TYPE SPHERE
      !*************************************************************
      ! DEFINE THE INTERFACE OPERATORS
      !*************************************************************
      INTERFACE OPERATOR(.AREA.)
         MODULE PROCEDURE AREA_CUBE
         MODULE PROCEDURE AREA_BOX
         MODULE PROCEDURE AREA_SPHERE
      END INTERFACE
      INTERFACE OPERATOR(.VOLUME.)
         MODULE PROCEDURE VOLUME_CUBE
         MODULE PROCEDURE VOLUME_BOX
         MODULE PROCEDURE VOLUME_SPHERE
      END INTERFACE
    CONTAINS
      FUNCTION AREA_CUBE(THE_CUBE) RESULT(THE_AREA)    ! See problem 10.18
         TYPE(CUBE) :: THE_CUBE
         REAL :: THE_AREA
         THE_AREA=6*THE_CUBE%SIDE**2                   ! cube area=6*(x**2)
      END FUNCTION AREA_CUBE
      FUNCTION AREA_BOX(THE_BOX) RESULT(THE_AREA)      ! See problem 10.18
         TYPE(BOX) :: THE_BOX
         REAL :: THE_AREA
         THE_AREA=2*THE_BOX%HEIGHT*THE_BOX%WIDTH+2*THE_BOX%HEIGHT*&
                  THE_BOX%DEPTH+2*THE_BOX%WIDTH*THE_BOX%DEPTH
      END FUNCTION AREA_BOX
      FUNCTION AREA_SPHERE(THE_SPHERE) RESULT(THE_AREA) ! See problem 10.18
         TYPE(SPHERE) :: THE_SPHERE
         REAL :: THE_AREA
         THE_AREA=4.0*3.1416*THE_SPHERE%RADIUS**2
      END FUNCTION AREA_SPHERE
      FUNCTION VOLUME_CUBE(THE_CUBE) RESULT(THE_VOLUME) ! See problem 10.18
         TYPE(CUBE) :: THE_CUBE
         REAL :: THE_VOLUME
         THE_VOLUME=THE_CUBE%SIDE**3
      END FUNCTION VOLUME_CUBE
      FUNCTION VOLUME_BOX(THE_BOX) RESULT(THE_VOLUME)  ! See problem 10.18
         TYPE(BOX) :: THE_BOX
         REAL :: THE_VOLUME
```

```
            THE_VOLUME=THE_BOX%HEIGHT*THE_BOX%WIDTH*THE_BOX%DEPTH
        END FUNCTION VOLUME_BOX
        FUNCTION VOLUME_SPHERE(THE_SPHERE) RESULT(THE_VOLUME)
            TYPE(SPHERE) :: THE_SPHERE
            REAL :: THE_VOLUME
            THE_VOLUME=4.0/3.0*3.1416*THE_SPHERE%RADIUS**3
        END FUNCTION VOLUME_SPHERE
    END MODULE SHAPES3D
```

10.21 ```
            ! The weight of the box is the density times the volume. We get
            ! the density from the data value stored in THE_CUBE%DENSITY.
            ! Then, we use the previously defined functions to obtain the
            ! volume of cubes, boxes, and spheres given in Supplementary
            ! Problem 10.20
            !**
            MODULE SHAPES3D
                TYPE CUBE
                    REAL :: SIDE
                    REAL, DIMENSION (3) :: POSITION
                END TYPE CUBE
                TYPE BOX
                    REAL :: DEPTH, WIDTH, HEIGHT
                    REAL, DIMENSION (3) :: POSITION
                END TYPE BOX
                TYPE SPHERE
                    REAL :: RADIUS
                    REAL, DIMENSION (3) :: POSITION
                END TYPE SPHERE
                TYPE PART_CUBE
                    TYPE(CUBE) :: GEO
                    REAL :: DENSITY
                    CHARACTER :: NAME*30
                END TYPE PART_CUBE
                TYPE PART_BOX
                    TYPE(BOX) :: GEO
                    REAL :: DENSITY
                    CHARACTER :: NAME*30
                END TYPE PART_BOX
                TYPE PART_SPHERE
                    TYPE(SPHERE) :: GEO
                    REAL :: DENSITY
                    CHARACTER :: NAME*30
                END TYPE PART_SPHERE
                INTERFACE OPERATOR(.AREA.)
                    MODULE PROCEDURE AREA_CUBE
                    MODULE PROCEDURE AREA_BOX
                    MODULE PROCEDURE AREA_SPHERE
                END INTERFACE
                INTERFACE OPERATOR(.VOLUME.)
                    MODULE PROCEDURE VOLUME_CUBE
                    MODULE PROCEDURE VOLUME_BOX
```
```

```
         MODULE PROCEDURE VOLUME_SPHERE
      END INTERFACE
      INTERFACE OPERATOR(.WEIGHT.)
         MODULE PROCEDURE WEIGHT_CUBE
         MODULE PROCEDURE WEIGHT_BOX
         MODULE PROCEDURE WEIGHT_SPHERE
      END INTERFACE
   CONTAINS
      FUNCTION AREA_CUBE(THE_CUBE) RESULT(THE_AREA)
         TYPE(PART_CUBE), POINTER :: THE_CUBE
         REAL :: THE_AREA
         THE_AREA=6*THE_CUBE%GEO%SIDE**2      ! area of a cube = 6*(x**2)
      END FUNCTION AREA_CUBE
      FUNCTION AREA_BOX(THE_BOX) RESULT(THE_AREA)
         TYPE(PART_BOX), POINTER :: THE_BOX
         REAL :: THE_AREA
         THE_AREA=2*THE_BOX%GEO%HEIGHT*THE_BOX%GEO%WIDTH&
              +2*THE_BOX%GEO%HEIGHT*THE_BOX%GEO%DEPTH&
              +2*THE_BOX%GEO%WIDTH*THE_BOX%GEO%DEPTH
      END FUNCTION AREA_BOX
      FUNCTION AREA_SPHERE(THE_SPHERE) RESULT(THE_AREA)
         TYPE(PART_SPHERE), POINTER :: THE_SPHERE
         REAL :: THE_AREA
         THE_AREA=4.0*3.1416*THE_SPHERE%GEO%RADIUS**2
      END FUNCTION AREA_SPHERE
      FUNCTION VOLUME_CUBE(THE_CUBE) RESULT(THE_VOLUME)
         TYPE(PART_CUBE), POINTER :: THE_CUBE
         REAL :: THE_VOLUME
         THE_VOLUME=THE_CUBE%GEO%SIDE**3
      END FUNCTION VOLUME_CUBE
      FUNCTION VOLUME_BOX(THE_BOX) RESULT(THE_VOLUME)
         TYPE(PART_BOX), POINTER :: THE_BOX
         REAL :: THE_VOLUME
         THE_VOLUME=THE_BOX%GEO%HEIGHT*THE_BOX%GEO%WIDTH&
              *THE_BOX%GEO%DEPTH
      END FUNCTION VOLUME_BOX
      FUNCTION VOLUME_SPHERE(THE_SPHERE) RESULT(THE_VOLUME)
         TYPE(PART_SPHERE), POINTER :: THE_SPHERE
         REAL :: THE_VOLUME
         THE_VOLUME=4.0/3.0*3.1416*THE_SPHERE%GEO%RADIUS**3
      END FUNCTION VOLUME_SPHERE
      FUNCTION WEIGHT_CUBE(THE_CUBE) RESULT(THE_WEIGHT)
         TYPE(PART_CUBE), POINTER :: THE_CUBE
         REAL :: THE_WEIGHT
         THE_WEIGHT=VOLUME_CUBE(THE_CUBE)*THE_CUBE%DENSITY
      END FUNCTION WEIGHT_CUBE
      !*************************************************************
      ! Weight of a box
      !*************************************************************
      FUNCTION WEIGHT_BOX(THE_BOX) RESULT(THE_WEIGHT)
         TYPE(PART_BOX), POINTER :: THE_BOX
```

```
      REAL :: THE_WEIGHT
      THE_WEIGHT=VOLUME_BOX(THE_BOX)*THE_BOX%DENSITY
   END FUNCTION WEIGHT_BOX
   !****************************************************************
   ! Weight of a sphere
   !****************************************************************
      FUNCTION WEIGHT_SPHERE(THE_SPHERE) RESULT(THE_WEIGHT)
      TYPE(PART_SPHERE), POINTER :: THE_SPHERE
      REAL :: THE_WEIGHT
      THE_WEIGHT=VOLUME_SPHERE(THE_SPHERE)*THE_SPHERE%DENSITY
   END FUNCTION WEIGHT_SPHERE
END MODULE SHAPES3D
```

10.22
```
! First, the iterative solution:
! The MOD function returns the remainder of integer division. If
! MOD(N,2) = 0 the number is even. If MOD(N,2) = 1, the number is odd.
!****************************************************************
FUNCTION EXPBI(X, N) RESULT(THE_ANSWER)
   REAL :: X, THE_ANSWER
   THE_ANSWER=1.0
   DO I = 1, N/2                        !note the integer arithmetic
      THE_ANSWER=THE_ANSWER*X
   END DO
   IF(MOD(N, 2) == 1) THEN
      THE_ANSWER=THE_ANSWER*THE_ANSWER*X
   ELSE
      THE_ANSWER=THE_ANSWER*THE_ANSWER
   END IF
END FUNCTION EXPBI
!****************************************************************
! Now, the recursive solution:
!****************************************************************
RECURSIVE FUNCTION EXPBR(X, N) RESULT(THE_ANSWER)
   REAL :: X, THE_ANSWER
   IF(N < 0) THEN
      PRINT*, 'ERROR, N<0'
      RETURN
   END IF
   IF(N == 0) THEN
      THE_ANSWER=1.0
   ELSE IF(MOD(N,2) == 0) THEN
      THE_ANSWER=EXPBR(X, N/2)*EXPBR(X, N/2)
   ELSE
      THE_ANSWER=EXPBR(X, N/2)*EXPBR(X, N/2)*X
   END IF
END FUNCTION EXPBR
```

10.23 (a) A dangling pointer exists since P1 points to P2, and deallocating P1 simultaneously deallocates the memory for P2.

(b) No error since no allocation took place, so dangling pointers or unreferenced storage is not an issue.

(c) A dangling pointer exists since deallocating PB simultaneously deallocated PA. PC is still defined since it is pointing to R1.

10.24

```
MODULE TEST
    TYPE NODE
        CHARACTER (LEN=20) :: VALUE
        TYPE(NODE), POINTER :: PREVIOUS
    END TYPE NODE
    TYPE LIST
        TYPE(NODE), POINTER :: LAST
    END TYPE LIST
CONTAINS
    FUNCTION NEWLIST( ) RESULT(NEW_LIST)
        TYPE(LIST), POINTER :: NEW_LIST
        ALLOCATE(NEW_LIST%LAST)
        NULLIFY(NEW_LIST%LAST%PREVIOUS)    !nullify previous node
    END FUNCTION NEWLIST
    SUBROUTINE ADDNAME(THE_LIST, THE_NAME)
        CHARACTER (LEN=20) :: THE_NAME
        TYPE(LIST), POINTER :: THE_LIST
        TYPE(NODE), POINTER :: CURRENT_PTR, PREVIOUS_PTR
        PREVIOUS_PTR => THE_LIST%LAST%PREVIOUS !assign previous &
        CURRENT_PTR=> THE_LIST%LAST                !current pointers
        DO
            IF(.NOT.ASSOCIATED(CURRENT_PTR))EXIT !structure end
            IF(CURRENT_PTR%VALUE>THE_NAME)EXIT   !name location
            CURRENT_PTR=>PREVIOUS_PTR            !update current and
            PREVIOUS_PTR=>PREVIOUS_PTR%PREVIOUS  !previous pointers
        END DO
        ALLOCATE(PREVIOUS_PTR)                !make new node
        PREVIOUS_PTR%VALUE=THE_NAME           !assign value to node
        PREVIOUS_PTR=>CURRENT_PTR             !assign next pointer
    END SUBROUTINE ADDNAME
    FUNCTION EMPTY(THE_LIST) RESULT(THE_RESULT)
        TYPE(LIST), POINTER ::THE_LIST
        LOGICAL :: THE_RESULT
        THE_RESULT=.NOT.ASSOCIATED(THE_LIST%LAST%PREVIOUS)
    END FUNCTION EMPTY
    SUBROUTINE DELETENAME(THE_LIST, THE_NAME)
        TYPE(LIST), POINTER :: THE_LIST
        TYPE(NODE), POINTER :: CURRENT_PTR, PREVIOUS_PTR
        CHARACTER(LEN=20) :: THE_NAME
        PREVIOUS_PTR=> THE_LIST%LAST%PREVIOUS   !initialize previous
        CURRENT_PTR=> THE_LIST%LAST             ! & current pointers
        DO
            IF(.NOT.ASSOCIATED(CURRENT_PTR))RETURN !end of list
            IF(CURRENT_PTR%VALUE==THE_NAME)EXIT    !name found
            CURRENT_PTR=> PREVIOUS_PTR             !update current &
```

```
                PREVIOUS_PTR=> PREVIOUS_PTR%PREVIOUS !previous pointers
           END DO
           PREVIOUS_PTR%PREVIOUS=>CURRENT_PTR%PREVIOUS
           DEALLOCATE(CURRENT_PTR)
       END SUBROUTINE DELETENAME
       SUBROUTINE PRINTLIST(THE_LIST)
          TYPE(LIST), POINTER :: THE_LIST
          TYPE(NODE), POINTER :: CURRENT_PTR
          CURRENT_PTR=> THE_LIST%LAST
          DO
             IF(.NOT.ASSOCIATED(CURRENT_PTR))EXIT
             PRINT *, CURRENT_PTR%VALUE
             CURRENT_PTR=>CURRENT_PTR%PREVIOUS
          END DO
       END SUBROUTINE PRINTLIST
    END MODULE TEST
```

10.25 MODULE TEST

```
    !****************************************************************
    ! This is a two-way linked list, since we can go in either
    ! direction.
    !****************************************************************
    TYPE PAGE
       CHARACTER(LEN=60), DIMENSION(18)::TEXT        !limited to 18 lines
       INTEGER :: PAGE_NUMBER
       TYPE(PAGE), POINTER :: NEXT, PREVIOUS
    END TYPE PAGE
    TYPE BOOK
       TYPE(PAGE), POINTER :: START
    END TYPE BOOK
CONTAINS
    !****************************************************************
    ! Function that initializes the book by deallocation the pointer.
    !****************************************************************
    FUNCTION NEWBOOK( ) RESULT(THE_BOOK)
       TYPE(BOOK), POINTER :: THE_BOOK
       NULLIFY(THE_BOOK%START)
    END FUNCTION NEWBOOK
    !****************************************************************
    ! If book is empty, THE_STATE is set to a value of true.
    !****************************************************************
    FUNCTION EMPTYBOOK(THE_BOOK) RESULT(THE_STATE)
       TYPE(BOOK), POINTER :: THE_BOOK
       LOGICAL :: THE_STATE
       THE_STATE=.NOT.ASSOCIATED(THE_BOOK%START)
    END FUNCTION EMPTYBOOK
    !****************************************************************
    ! Subroutine to enter the text on a new page.
    !****************************************************************
    SUBROUTINE NEWPAGE(THE_TEXT, THE_BOOK)
       CHARACTER(LEN=60), DIMENSION(18) :: THE_TEXT
```

```
      TYPE(BOOK), POINTER :: THE_BOOK
      TYPE(PAGE), POINTER :: NEXT_PAGE_PTR, CURRENT_PAGE_PTR
      IF(EMPTYBOOK(THE_BOOK)) THEN                    !add first page
         ALLOCATE(THE_BOOK%START)                     !only if the book
         NULLIFY(THE_BOOK%START%NEXT)                 !is empty
         NULLIFY(THE_BOOK%START%PREVIOUS)
         THE_BOOK%START%TEXT=THE_TEXT
         THE_BOOK%START%PAGE_NUMBER=1
         RETURN
      END IF
      CURRENT_PAGE_PTR=> THE_BOOK%START               !sets the pointer
      CURRENT_PAGE_PTR=>CURRENT_PAGE_PTR%NEXT
      DO
         IF(.NOT.ASSOCIATED(NEXT_PAGE_PTR))EXIT
         CURRENT_PAGE_PTR=>NEXT_PAGE_PTR
         NEXT_PAGE_PTR=>NEXT_PAGE_PTR%NEXT
      END DO
      ALLOCATE(NEXT_PAGE_PTR)
      NEXT_PAGE_PTR%TEXT=THE_TEXT                      !enter text onto page
      NEXT_PAGE_PTR%PREVIOUS=>CURRENT_PAGE_PTR         !update the pointer
      NEXT_PAGE_PTR%PAGE_NUMBER=CURRENT_PAGE_PTR%PAGE_NUMBER+1
      NULLIFY(NEXT_PAGE_PTR%NEXT)
END SUBROUTINE NEWPAGE
!********************************************************************
! Subroutine to delete a page
!********************************************************************
SUBROUTINE DELETEPAGE(THE_BOOK)
      TYPE(BOOK), POINTER :: THE_BOOK
      TYPE(PAGE), POINTER :: NEXT_PAGE_PTR, CURRENT_PAGE_PTR
      IF(EMPTYBOOK(THE_BOOK)) THEN                    ! is book empty?
         PRINT*, 'The book is empty!'
         RETURN
      END IF
      CURRENT_PAGE_PTR=>THE_BOOK%START                !if not empty, start
      NEXT_PAGE_PTR=>CURRENT_PAGE_PTR%NEXT            !at first page
      DO                                              !find the last page
         IF(.NOT.ASSOCIATED(NEXT_PAGE_PTR)) EXIT     !exit if at end
         CURRENT_PAGE_PTR=>NEXT_PAGE_PTR             !resets pointer to
         NEXT_PAGE_PTR=>CURRENT_PAGE_PTR%NEXT        !skip a page
      END DO
      DEALLOCATE(CURRENT_PAGE_PTR)                    !deallocate last page
END SUBROUTINE DELETEPAGE
!********************************************************************
! Subroutine to view the book in either direction
!********************************************************************
SUBROUTINE VIEWBOOK(THE_BOOK)
      TYPE(BOOK), POINTER :: THE_BOOK
      TYPE(PAGE), POINTER :: CURRENT_PAGE_PTR, NEXT_PAGE_PTR
      TYPE(PAGE), POINTER :: PREVIOUS_PAGE_PTR
      CHARACTER  :: INPUT
      IF(EMPTYBOOK(THE_BOOK)) THEN                    ! see if book is empty
```

```
              PRINT*, 'The book is empty!'
              RETURN
          END IF
          CURRENT_PAGE_PTR=>THE_BOOK%START              !start on page 1
          NEXT_PAGE_PTR=>CURRENT_PAGE_PTR%NEXT          !and set pointers
          PREVIOUS_PAGE_PTR=>CURRENT_PAGE_PTR%PREVIOUS
          DO
              PRINT "(18(A60, /), /, I3, '<P>revious, <N>ext, or &
                       <Q>uit?')",CURRENT_PAGE_PTR%PAGE_NUMBER,&
                 CURRENT_PAGE_PTR%TEXT
              READ "(A1)", INPUT                        !prints a page
              IF(INPUT=="Q" .OR. INPUT=="q")EXIT        !stops view if needed
              IF(INPUT=="N" .OR. INPUT=="n")THEN        !view next page
                 IF(.NOT.ASSOCIATED(NEXT_PAGE_PTR)) THEN
                    PRINT*, "This is the last page, <return> to continue"
                    READ "(A1)", INPUT
                    CYCLE
                 END IF
                 CURRENT_PAGE_PTR=>NEXT_PAGE_PTR
                 NEXT_PAGE_PTR=>CURRENT_PAGE_PTR%NEXT
                 PREVIOUS_PAGE_PTR=>CURRENT_PAGE_PTR%PREVIOUS
              ELSE                                      !views previous page
                 IF(.NOT.ASSOCIATED(PREVIOUS_PAGE_PTR)) THEN
                    PRINT *, "Page 1, <return> to continue"
                    READ "(A1)", INPUT
                    CYCLE
                 END IF
                 CURRENT_PAGE_PTR=>PREVIOUS_PAGE_PTR
                 NEXT_PAGE_PTR=>CURRENT_PAGE_PTR%NEXT
                 PREVIOUS_PAGE_PTR=>CURRENT_PAGE_PTR%PREVIOUS
              END IF
          END DO
      END SUBROUTINE VIEWBOOK
   END MODULE TEST
```

10.26 50 MHz equals 50 Mips. However, due to resource conflicts, this value reduces to 1/10 to 1/2 of this value. Therefore, the expected range would be 5 to 25 Mips.

10.27 (a) Rewrite the AREA evaluation as 3.1416*R(I)*R(I) to replace the exponentiation by multiplication. Also, this will produce a common term (3.14159*R(I)) for two successive calculations, which the compiler may calculate only once.

(b) Make TEMP a single-valued variable instead of an array. This reduces the storage needs from 100 memory references to only 1.

10.28
```
REAL, DIMENSION (3,3) :: A
REAL, DIMENSION (3) :: X, C
DO I = 1, 3
   PRINT *, 'Enter coef and constants for eq. 1:'
   READ*, (A(I, J), J= 1, 3), C(I)
END DO
```

```
CALL CRAMER(A, X, C)
PRINT*, 'Solution:', X
END
SUBROUTINE CRAMER(A, X, C)
REAL, DIMENSION (3,3) :: A, A1, A2, A3
REAL, DIMENSION (3) :: X, C
IF(ABS(DET(A)) < 0.00001) STOP
!*********************************************************************
! The only substantive changes are the replacement of the array
! processing by array functions and subarrays. On a vectorized
! machine however, this will improve the performance.
!*********************************************************************
A1=A                          ! use array processing instead of loops
A2=A
A3=A
A1(:,1)=C                     ! use subarrays instead of loops
A2(:,2)=C
A3(:,3)=C
X(1) = DET(A1)/DENO
X(2) = DET(A2)/DENO
X(3) = DET(A3)/DENO
END
REAL FUNCTION DET(A)
REAL A(3, 3)
DET = A(1,1)*(A(2,2)*A(3,3)-A(2,3)*A(3,2))-A(1,2)*(A(2,1)*A(3,3) &
      -A(2,3)*A(3,1))+A(1,3)*(A(2,1)*A(3,2)-A(2,2)*A(3,1))
END
```

10.29 (a) The inner loop does not assign a value to an array. However, the scalar*vector reduction function is present. But, a vector inhibitor is present in the form of CYCLE statement. Therefore, this is not a candidate for vectorization.

       (b) This is a candidate for vectorization since there is a scalar+a vectorizable expression. Also, no inhibitors are present. Finally, the summation loops could be written with array constructors to simplify them.

10.30
```
RECURSIVE SUBROUTINE FILLTREE(THE_NODE, THE_LIST, N, LSTART, LSTOP)
      INTEGER :: N, LSTART, LSTOP
      CHARACTER(LEN=20), DIMENSION(N) :: THE_LIST
      TYPE(NODE), POINTER :: THE_NODE
      MIDDLE=(LSTART+LSTOP)/2     !start with middle value - d
      THE_NODE%NAME=THE_LIST(MIDDLE)
      IF(LSTART == LSTOP) RETURN  !if list length is 0, then we are
                                  !finished, so return. Then use the
                                  !function recursively to place the
                                  ! values on the left side
      CALL FILLTREE(THE_NODE%LEFT, THE_LIST, N, LSTART, MIDDLE-1)
                                  !now place the values on the right side
      CALL FILLTREE(THE_NODE%RIGHT, THE_LIST, N, MIDDLE+1, LSTOP)
END SUBROUTINE FILLTREE
```

Index